COLLEGE SPORTS TRADITIONS

Picking Up Butch, Silent Night, and Hundreds of Others

Stan Beck
Jack Wilkinson

THE SCARECROW PRESS, INC.
Lanham • Toronto • Plymouth, UK
2013

Published by Scarecrow Press, Inc.
A wholly owned subsidiary of The Rowman & Littlefield Publishing Group, Inc.
4501 Forbes Boulevard, Suite 200, Lanham, Maryland 20706
www.rowman.com

10 Thornbury Road, Plymouth PL6 7PP, United Kingdom

British Library Cataloguing in Publication Information Available

Library of Congress Cataloging-in-Publication Data
Beck, Stan, 1948–
   College sports traditions : picking up butch, silent night, and hundreds of others /
Stan Beck, Jack Wilkinson.
       pages cm
   Includes bibliographical references and index.
   ISBN 978-0-8108-9120-3 (cloth : alk. paper) — ISBN 978-0-8108-9121-0 (ebook)
   1. College sports—Miscellanea.   I. Title.
   GV705.B38 2013
   796.043—dc23

                                                                            2013019396

Printed in the United States of America.

"The Army–Navy game is one of my favorite events of the year."

—Joe Biden, vice president of the United States

"No million dollar, no-cut contracts. No agents. Just athletes giving it all they have—[Indiana's Little 500 is] the essence of sport."

—Brent Musburger

"My entire life has been one big heart attack watching Cal games. . . . If you win a Big Game, you're an icon at Cal."

—Adam Duritz, Counting Crows front man
and lifelong Golden Bears superfan

"At each home game, during the first time out in the second half, our cheer-leaders (twelve-time national champions) slide around the floor spelling "Kentucky," and a special person from the crowd is asked to come out to make the "Y," something I have done both alone and with my family. . . . I was having the best curtain call of my entire life right there in Rupp Arena, feeling adored by the people who mean so very much to me: The people of Kentucky."

—Ashley Judd, actress

A sign in Notre Dame's locker room says, "Tradition Never Graduates."

Texas A&M: "From the outside looking in, you can't understand it. And from the inside looking out, you can't explain it."

"It's not rare to watch a game and not know the names of the people sitting next to you. Or where they're from. Or what they do. But you know all the same words to all the same cheers. And chants. And songs. You know the same hand signals. Wear the same colors. Remember the same traditions. You are completely different on every level except that one, way down deep, where loyalty resides and nothing else matters—like who you are, where you're from, and what you do."

—The Hyundai Show Your Loyalty campaign

"The Monon Bell Classic [between Wabash & DePauw] is just as passionate and tension ridden as any game you're ever going to play in. It's like playing in the Super Bowl."

—Pete Metzelaars, who played in four Super Bowls
as a member of the Buffalo Bills

"There are no words to accurately describe true loyalty. It runs too deep. Touches places in us that even memory can't reach. Where we are both our strongest and most vulnerable. So, instead, we use examples to describe our loyalty. Analogies. Anecdotes. Stories that, as they're told over and over, by more and more people, become something more indelible than even the truth. They become tradition. To be reenacted and retold by the next generation. Followed by the next. And the next. And the next."

—The Hyundai Show Your Loyalty campaign

"Tradition is what separates us from professional sports."

—Mike Krzyzewski, Duke basketball coach

CONTENTS

PREFACE

I saw my very first college sports tradition over fifty years ago, as a Boy Scout attending an Auburn football game. The sight of the untethered eagle before the kickoff was something that I have never forgotten. Many years later, while attending a home game at West Point, I witnessed the game ball being parachuted into the stadium by some of our country's finest young men and women. When I asked an older gentleman sitting next to me if that happened at every home game, he replied, "Yep. And not just because we have the planes, and the parachutists . . . it's important!" So with those vivid images that never left my mind, I set off on a personal journey to document as many of the wonderful college sports traditions as I could find. This book is only a destination on my ongoing journey.

Your college and university was asked to participate . . . they all were. Each sports information director, athletic director, and university president received a personalized letter from me asking for their unique traditions. They were told that none were too trivial to mention, just to send them to me. And in they poured. From the largest of the big schools to the smallest of the little schools, each was equally proud of their traditions. If your favorite isn't listed, please accept my apology and submit it to me at stan. beck@collegesportstraditions.com or via my website: www.collegesportstraditions.com. I will ensure that it gets into any subsequent edition that might be considered.

TRADITIONS PERSONALLY WITNESSED BY THE AUTHORS

- $2.00 Bills (Football), Clemson University
- The 12th Man (Football), Texas A&M
- A capella national anthem (Basketball), Harding University
- Aggie War Hymn (Football), Texas A&M
- "Air ball" (Basketball), Duke University
- Alma Mater (Various Sports), University of Notre Dame
- Baptist (Southern), Tunes (Various Sports), Wake Forest University
- Battle for the Leather Helmet (Football), Clemson University and Boston College
- Battle of the Blues (Basketball), Duke University and the University of North Carolina
- Between the Hedges (Football), University of Georgia
- Bevo (Football), University of Texas
- Big Red's Birthday Party (Mascots), Western Kentucky University
- Blowing a Conch Shell (Swimming), Rollins College
- Boomer Sooner and Oklahoma! (Football), University of Oklahoma
- Bowden Bowl (Football), Clemson University and Florida State University
- Budweiser Jingle (Football & Basketball), Georgia Tech
- Calling of the Hogs (Football), University of Arkansas
- Cameron Crazies (Basketball), Duke University
- Candy-Striped Warm-Up Pants (Basketball), Indiana University
- Clapping Until Team Scores (Basketball), University of Tennessee
- College Game Day Flag (Football), Washington State University
- Colored-Lights on the UT Tower (Various Sports), University of Texas
- Cowbells (Football), Mississippi State University
- Cutting Down Basketball Nets (Basketball), North Carolina State University
- Drake Relays (Track and Field), Drake University
- Duel in the Desert (Basketball), University of Arizona and Arizona State University
- First-Friday Parade (Football), Clemson University
- Fish Toss (Ice Hockey), University of New Hampshire
- Flyover during National Anthem (Football), Army–Navy
- Frog Horn (Football), TCU
- Gator Chomp (Football), University of Florida
- Governor's Cup (Football), University of Georgia and Georgia Tech
- "Hail to the Victors" (Various Sports), University of Michigan

- "Hang on Sloopy" (Football), The Ohio State University
- Head of the Charles (Crew), Many Schools
- Helmet Stickers (Football), Florida State University
- "Hey, John" (Ice Hockey), University of New Hampshire
- Hook 'em Horns Hand Sign (Football), University of Texas
- How 'Bout Them Dawgs? (Football), University of Georgia
- Howard's Rock (Football), Clemson University
- Ice-skating Cheerleaders (Ice Hockey), University of Minnesota
- Iconic Venues:
  ° Allen Fieldhouse (Basketball), University of Kansas
  ° Assembly Hall (Basketball), Indiana University
  ° Bobby Dodd Stadium at Historic Grant Field (Football), Georgia Tech
  ° Bryant-Denny Stadium (Football), University of Alabama
  ° Cameron Indoor Stadium (Basketball), Duke University
  ° Carrier Dome (Football / Basketball), Syracuse University
  ° Cole Field House (Basketball), University of Maryland
  ° Dean Dome (Basketball), University of North Carolina
  ° Death Valley, (Football), Clemson University
  ° Death Valley, (Football), LSU
  ° Drake Stadium (Track & Field), Drake University
  ° Franklin Field (Various Sports), University of Pennsylvania
  ° Harvard Stadium (Football), Harvard
  ° Hayward Field (Track & Field), University of Oregon
  ° Hinkle Fieldhouse (Basketball), Butler University
  ° Homewood Field (Lacrosse), Johns Hopkins University
  ° Jordan-Hare Stadium (Football), Auburn University
  ° Kyle Field (Football), Texas A&M
  ° Legion Field (Football), University of Alabama–Auburn University
  ° Louisiana Superdome (Football), Various Schools
  ° Madison Square Garden (Basketball), Various Schools
  ° Michie Stadium (Football), Army
  ° Navy-Marine Corps Stadium (Football), Naval Academy
  ° Neyland Stadium (Football), University of Tennessee
  ° Notre Dame Stadium (Football), University of Notre Dame
  ° Original Fiesta Bowl (Football), Sun Devil Stadium, Arizona State University
  ° Original Orange Bowl (Football), University of Miami
  ° Original Spectrum (Basketball), Big 5
  ° Original Sugar Bowl (Football), Tulane University

- ° Pauley Pavilion (Basketball), UCLA
- ° Rose Bowl (Football), Various Schools
- ° Rupp Arena (Basketball), University of Kentucky
- ° Sanford Stadium (Football), University of Georgia
- ° The Palestra (Basketball), Big 5
- ° The Pit (Basketball), University of New Mexico
- ° The Swamp (Football), University of Florida
- ° Memorial Gymnasium (Basketball), Vanderbilt University
- ° Williams-Brice Stadium (Football), University of South Carolina
- Keeper of the Frog Horn (Football), TCU
- "Kernkraft 400" (Basketball), Wake Forest University
- Kiss Your Date (Football), Texas A&M
- Krzyzewskiville (Basketball), Duke University
- March On (Football), Army and Naval Academy
- Martha, the Mop Lady (Basketball), Indiana University
- Midnight Yell Practice (Football), Texas A&M
- Most Played Southern Rivalry (Football), Auburn University–University of Georgia
- Most Played Rivalry (Football), Lehigh University–Lafayette College
- Mutual Respect Rivalry (Football), Army–Navy
- Nova, the War Eagle (Football), Auburn University
- Open the Gate (Football), Wake Forest University
- Orange Balloon Release (Football), Clemson University
- Palmetto Bowl (Football), Clemson University and the University of South Carolina
- Picking Up Butch (Football & Basketball), Middlebury College
- Pink-the-Rink (Ice Hockey), Fredonia State University
- Play Like a Champion Today (Football), University of Notre Dame
- Players Running Through the Block-T (Football), University of Tennessee
- Pregame Video at the Phog (Basketball), University of Kansas
- Presidential Walk from One Sideline to the Other at Halftime (Football), Army–Navy
- Raising Helmets during Alma Mater (Football), University of Notre Dame
- Ralphie's Pregame Run (Football), University of Colorado
- Ramblin' Wreck (Football), Georgia Tech
- Ramblin' Wreck From Georgia Tech (Various Sports), Georgia Tech
- Rammer Jammer Yellowhammer! (Football), University of Alabama
- Red Balloon Release (Football), University of Nebraska

- Red River Rivalry (Football), University of Oklahoma–University of Texas
- Reveille Graves (Football), Texas A&M
- Ringing the Chapel Bell (Football), University of Georgia
- Rivalry Games:
  ○ University of Alabama–University of Tennessee
  ○ Army–Navy
  ○ Auburn University–University of Georgia
  ○ Clemson University–University of South Carolina
  ○ Duke University–University of North Carolina
  ○ University of Georgia–University of Florida
  ○ University of Georgia–Georgia Tech
  ○ Lafayette College–Lehigh University
  ○ University of Michigan–The Ohio State University
  ○ University of Notre Dame–USC
  ○ University of Oklahoma–University of Texas
  ○ Penn State–University of Pittsburgh
  ○ Williams College–Wesleyan University
- Rock Chalk, Jayhawk, KU! (Basketball), University of Kansas
- Rolling-the-Quad (Various Sports), Wake Forest University
- Rolling Toomer's Corner (Football), Auburn University
- Rollout Signs (Basketball), at The Palestra, University of Pennsylvania
- RUF/NEKS Shotguns (Football), University of Oklahoma
- Samaritan's Feet (Basketball), Various Schools
- Script Ohio (Football), The Ohio State University
- "Silent Night" (Basketball), Taylor University
- Sing-Second (Football), Army–Navy
- Smokey the Cannon (Football), University of Texas
- Sod Cemetery (Football), Clemson University
- Sod Cemetery (Football), Florida State University
- Sooner Schooner (Football), University of Oklahoma
- Stanford Band (Football)
- Stanford Tree (Football)
- Storming the Court, a #1 team has been defeated (Basketball) University of Miami over Duke University in 2013
- Tailgating at the Grove (Football), Ole Miss
- Tailgating with the Volunteer Navy on the Tennessee River (Football), University of Tennessee
- Taps (Football), University of Texas
- Texas Bonfire (Football), Texas A&M

- Textile Bowl (Football), Clemson University and North Carolina State University
- The Game (Football), Harvard–Yale
- "The Good Old Song" (Football), University of Virginia
- The Hawk (Basketball), St. Joseph's University
- "The Hokey Pokey" (Football), Virginia Tech
- The Irish Guard (Football), University of Notre Dame
- "The Notre Dame Fight Song" (Football/Basketball), University of Notre Dame
- The Pull (Tug-of-War), Hope College
- The Swarm (Football), Georgia Tech
- The Williams Walk (Football), Williams College
- The World's Largest Outdoor Cocktail Party (Football), University of Georgia–University of Florida
- Tie-Dyed Nation (Basketball), Wake Forest University
- Tiger Pushups (Football), Clemson University
- Tigerama (Football), Clemson University
- Touchdown Jesus (Football), University of Notre Dame
- Traveler (Football), USC
- Ugas' Mausoleum (Football), University of Georgia
- Upside Down Hook 'em Horns Sign (Football), University of Oklahoma
- Wave-the-Wheat (Various Sports), University of Kansas
- War-Chant Arm Motion (Football and Basketball), Florida State University
- We Are . . . Penn State (Football), Penn State
- "We Are the Boys of Old Florida" (Football), University of Florida
- "Welcome to the Jungle" (Football), Wake Forest University
- "William Tell Overture" Timeout (Basketball), Indiana University
- Yell Leaders (Football), Texas A&M

ACKNOWLEDGMENTS

STAN'S ACKNOWLEDGMENTS

My Family:

I'd like to thank my family. My wife, Cary, for her constant encouragement; my daughter, Katie Agress, for her encouragement and help with Facebook and Twitter; my son-in-law, Adam Agress, for website help with www .collegesportstraditions.com; my son, Gill Beck, for his constant encouragement; my daughter-in-law, Nicole Beck, for obtaining the photographs that are included in this book; and, Anne and Jay Cooper for their early encouragement.

Those Providing Advice and Counsel:

Thanks to Jeff Schultz for introducing Jack and me; Anne Devlin, my literary agent; Christen Karniski, a wonderful editor; Tony Barnhart, for his encouragement and advice; and Tim Cortes, whose unique artwork graces the book's cover. I would also like to acknowledge from Hyundai Motor America, Steve Shannon, vice president marketing, Monique Kumpis, senior manager, advertising, and especially Trea Reedy, senior group manager, experiential marketing. Trea's leadership and vision continue to be of great help to me. From Innocean Worldwide, I'd like to acknowledge Ed Miller, executive creative director; Shawn Wood, creative director; Tyson Brown, associate creative director; Joe Reynoso, art director; Casey Nichols, account supervisor; Chrissy Borgatta Liuzzi, senior art producer; Maria Ortega, project manager; Shannon Inouye, Mindi Barber, Molly McLaughlin, Suzanne Cheng, Josh Lieber and especially Bryan Di Biagio, account director. This Innocean team was responsible for *The Hyundai Show Your Loyalty Campaign*, and allowed me to use their magnificent creative work to illustrate some wonderful college traditions.

I'd also like to acknowledge Andrew Giangola with IMG College; Tom Fuller and Bob Hope; Marty Appel, the world's best publicist; and Paco Underhill, for his early encouragement and explanation of the publishing business from a writer's perspective.

Colleagues and Friends

I'd like to acknowledge my new friends at various colleges and universities, and those who hosted me: Dick Quinn, Bill Peterson, Scott Goode, Eric Smith, Jerry Reilly, Jeff Meredith, Paul Just, Brad Nadeau, Debby Jennings, Penny Hite, Helen Smith, T. J. Manastersky, Tom Renner, Rick Morris, Mark Brand, Kelli Sampson, Scott Morse, Phil LaBella, J. D. Campbell, and especially "Butch" Varno, a true inspiration.

Those Who Helped Me with Research, or in Other Ways

I'd like to acknowledge Scott and Stephanie Simpson, who met me only briefly, but responded by sending me books about Texas A&M traditions; Fred West, Breck Weingart, and Mike Barkett, each of whom gave me free tickets to watch their favorite schools; Joe Halverson, Amber Blecker, Mike Hite, Anissa German, and Jenny Stewart, who helped with some research; Karen DePaolo for her research and encouragement; and especially Michelle DePaolo, who did all of my database work. Also, Cody Smith and Mike Olivella for some very special photos that are included; the hundreds of colleges/universities that made me aware of their traditions, and the many that provided photos included in this book; and the local radio stations and newspapers that were excited that I cared about their traditions.

My Friends Who Encouraged Me Early and Often

With apologies to those I have missed: The Gentlemen's Club, who never doubted their "potentate" would do this; Angela Rothen, who submitted my very first tradition; John DeMonica; Dave and Kathy Lindsey; Stan Clymer; Greg Morris; Betty Blank; and especially Ken Weingart.

JACK'S ACKNOWLEDGMENTS

Sports Information Directors

To Middlebury's Brad Nadeau, for all his help on Picking-Up Butch; Georgia Tech's Dean Buchan and Mike Stamus, for all things Tech; Penn's Mike Mahoney, for updates on Dan Harrell and The Palestra; Georgia's Claude Felton, for all things UGA and being the best; Kansas' Chris Theisen, for info on the Phog and KU hoops history; Utah State's Doug Hoffman, for the latest on Wild Bill; Georgia State's Allison George for Samaritan's Feet information; David Housel for his Auburn Tiger Walk 1989 perspective; and Tim Bourret for his Clemson and Notre Dame expertise.

Scribes

Mark Blaudschun, a Jersey guy; Mike Jensen; Rick Cleveland; Steve Hummer; Mark Bradley; Tom Stinson; Bill Rankin; Baylor's Todd Copeland, an esteemed historian; Vahe Gregorian; Rick Reilly; Tim Layden.; Tom O'Toole; Ivan Maisel; Malcolm Moran; Carroll Rogers; Dan Lauck; Patty Rasmussen; Tom Kertscher; and especially Jeff Schultz, who introduced Stan and me.

In Memoriam

Furman Bisher; Beano Cook; again, Paul Hemphill; Edwin Keeble, the architect of Vandy's Memorial Gym and the father-in-law I never got to meet; Tommy; Fitz and Jack; Pegs; Aunt Kay and Aunt Rene, for driving us to all those Army–Navy games in Philly; Rick Majerus; the Wizard of Westwood and Nell Wooden; and the incomparable Al McGuire.

Sporting Friends of Distinction

Tom Merritt; Fran Connors; Rick Sabetta; Paul and Dorothy Shea; the Fowlers, Lynn and Candace; the Petit-Bolster family: Barbara, C. J., and Caroline; Barbara Wilkinson, who knows and lived her hoops; Bill Cook, a true Tech Man; Jim Misudek; Karla Hudecek; Bill Fowler; Ron Lacey; Mike Cingiser; Tom MacDonald; Larry Hausner; Looie, as in Carnesecca; At Manuel's, Brian Maloof and company, especially Bill McCloskey; Pete Van Wieren; Dr. Sparky Reardon of Ole Miss for his perspective on The Grove; and Scott Blusiewicz.

Marty Appel, the ultimate professional.

To Stan "the Man" Beck, for inviting me to join him on this venture, and for putting up with me.

And finally, my family: my wife, Janet Ward, and our daughters Ali and Katharine. The joys of my life, sporting and otherwise. The Stantons of Sayville, L .I., and "Auntie M," as my sister Kathleen calls our beloved Aunt Maureen Dahler.

INTRODUCTION

As Arch Lamb, founder of Texas Tech's *Saddle Tramps* so aptly put it many, many years ago, "A tradition without heart, is only a habit." We could not agree with Arch more, and on the following pages you will find hundreds of truly wonderful traditions with heart.

Rubbing Howard's Rock and *rolling Toomer's Corner*. The clanging of a victory bell. *The Calling of the Hogs*: "Wooooooooo. Pig. Sooie!" One man's *Tomahawk Chop* is another fan's *Gator Chomp*.

They're college sports traditions, and God bless 'em, every one. (Okay, maybe not Speedo Guy at Duke. But his era was, well, brief. But hey, he's long gone now, and fully clothed, and Cameron Indoor Stadium is safe again for small children and foes shooting free throws.)

And for you. You're a college fan. You love what you like, alum and fan alike. It's your school, your team, your customs and colors, songs and cheers. And woe unto those who try to mess with any of it.

You sing the fight songs and alma maters, and watch the mascot do push-ups: the garden-variety, two-handed ones, and the occasional one-armed, Rocky Balboa PATs (that's pushups after touchdowns. One for every point scored).

There's *Touchdown Jesus* on the Notre Dame library and the irreverent *Stanford Band* loose on the field at halftime. The shimmying *Stanford Tree*, too. In Knoxville, where the *Volunteer Navy* is docked on the Tennessee River, a Tennessee Vol *runs onto the field through the Block-T.*

It's *Army–Navy*. Harvard–Yale. Boola Boola. It's college sports traditions.

There are more than a thousand of them out there. Traditions like no other at big-time BCS schools, but also hundreds more on smaller, leafier campuses of academia. Some customs are well into their second century, while others are largely unknown outside their campuses.

At Williams College in Massachusetts, since 1971, the Ephs have triumphantly walked *The Walk* up Spring Street and into Williamstown after a football homecoming win over Amherst or Wesleyan. Time was, as townspeople cheered them, the Ephs—still in their uniforms—would stop at the St. Pierre Barber Shop. Not for a haircut, but rather a celebratory cold beer, or a victory cigar. Or both. Now, the players drop in at that barber shop for a soft drink, a celebratory stogy, or even a shaved head.

Give the Williams Ephs an A. Or perhaps an A+ for their other unique traditions for cross-country and softball. How many different ways can their cross-country mascot be kidnapped by Williams' rivals? Read on.

At John Brown University, an NAIA school in Siloam Springs, Arkansas, the men's basketball home opener has begun thusly for three decades: After the Golden Eagles' first basket, fans break out toilet paper brought along for just this occasion, and then gleefully *hurl hundreds of rolls onto the court*. A flick-and-roll of sorts. We're number one-ply!

Who cares about the annual technical foul? What, we worry? For a few joyous minutes, John Brown's home court lies a-smothered in TP. The crowd's lovin' it. Maybe Mark Twain was right after all. "The less there is to justify a tradition," Twain opined, "the harder it is to get rid of it."

What was it the philosopher George Santayana once said? Curious George didn't know a kicking tee from the Wing-T, but he knew this: "The best men in all ages keep classic traditions alive."

Thus, explaining why every Georgia fan traditionally *barks like a bulldog* on football Saturdays. All together now, all 92,000 of you between the hedges: "Goooooooo DAWGS! Sic 'em! Woof-woof-woof-woof-woof!!!"

Or why students at Taylor University in Upland, Indiana, *wear their pajamas* to a basketball game before final exams each December, remain "silent" until the home team's tenth point, and join arms and sing "Silent Night" as the game winds-down.

Before every opening kickoff at Clemson, the Tigers charge down the hill behind one end zone in Death Valley and *rub Howard's Rock*—as bald and rock-hard as the late, great, stubborn coach Frank Howard's head—for luck. Somewhere, Howard's smiling.

At St. Joseph's University in Philadelphia, the heralded Hawk mascot (on scholarship, mind you) *flaps his wings nonstop* throughout every basketball game—home and away—and runs figure eights on the court during timeouts.

On average, the Hawk flaps nearly 3,500 times during a regulation 40-minute game. How do we know this? Someone from ESPN actually counted once, using a sophisticated, high-tech gizmo: a Flap-o-Meter.

On Hawk Hill they cry, "The Hawk will never die!"

At Virginia Tech, at the end of every third quarter, Hokie fans rise and in unison, sing and put their right feet in, their right feet out, their right feet in, and they shake 'em all about. They do the Hokey Pokey and they turn themselves around. That's what it's all about in Blacksburg.

By definition, traditions are inherently, well, traditional. *Roll Tide*. *War Eagle*. *Hail to the Victors*, valiant and otherwise.

There's Carolina Blue and Duke Blue Devils. Never confuse the two. Never.

There's the Red River Rivalry: Texas–Oklahoma. Or is it Oklahoma–Texas? Depends on which side of the river you come from and call home. Either way, make that sign with your fingers and try to hook 'em, Horns. Or, if you're from Oklahoma, do the "hook 'em, Horns" sign upside down!

Virginia Tech's band leading the crowd in "the Hokey Pokey." *Virginia Tech*

Flecks of 23.9 karat gold from the Golden Dome itself help make Notre Dame's *freshly painted helmets* glisten anew every Saturday. Say what? Did someone say Golden Flake?

For more than a half century, Golden Flake has been the preferred potato chip of Alabama fans. Ever since the early years, then the halcyon days of Bear Bryant's classic Sunday morning coach's show. It was must-see Bear TV. Now remember to wash down those Golden Flakes with a Coca-Cola, mamas and daddies.

And at Ohio State, before the opening kickoff in the Horseshoe, as Ohio Stadium is reverentially known by fans, a senior sousaphone player in the Buckeye marching band gets the honor of *dotting the "i"* in the script Ohio.

As the band moves from its traditional block O, it morphs into what looks to the uneducated eye like an Etch-a-Sketch scribble. Wait. That's no scribble. It's script. A capital script O, now looping into a lowercase "h," and then an "i," and finally a small "o." Yet something's missing. Not for long.

Here he comes. The chosen one. A senior sousaphone player, singled out for the honor of dotting the "i" in the script Ohio. He does so with great fanfare and flare, his exaggerated dot a human exclamation point. A pounce, perhaps, or taking an emphatic knee.

The crowd goes nuts. Always. Hey, it's Ohio. It's also one of the signature moments in college sports. A tuba tradition like no other.

Nice band writing, Buckeyes. Great pageantry. Good try, Columbus. But the most poignant, moving, and meaningful tradition in all of college athletics can be found in, of all places, Vermont. At, of all schools, Middlebury College.

Picking Up Butch. It's about a local man, in his midsixties, named Butch Varno, who's confined to a wheelchair with cerebral palsy, and a fresh batch of freshmen football and basketball players each fall who, for fifty-plus years . . .

Well, read on. You'll see. It's the most mutually uplifting pick-me-up in college sports and the finest tradition. Yet, you never know when another one will pop up, when a Desmond Howard will strike the Heisman pose in the end zone, or a faceless fan will chop or chomp for the first time. But not the last.

"The human soul can always use a new tradition," a one-time Citadel point guard-turned-author wrote in *The Lords of Discipline*.

Sometimes," Pat Conroy realized, "we require them."

TRADITIONS BEFORE THE GAME

Our definition of a tradition is that it must be an action, complete with a start and a finish, and then continued over a period of years. Teams that indicate they have a "winning tradition" need not apply. In sports, there are occasional instant classics. There are rarely instant traditions.

At least, not until the second time.

Fans, students, alums, and townies have ample time before a sporting event to dream up something fun to do, and then to continue it game after game after game.

There are *pregame flyovers*, majestic and loud. The service academies, Army, Navy, and Air Force often *parachute-in game balls*. Army and Navy, as well as many nonmilitary schools, carry their *game balls in relays for hundreds of miles* prior to rivalry showdowns.

Objects are touched by players as they enter a stadium. *Rocks are rubbed* for good luck. *Cannons, statues, and inspirational quotes* on plaques are touched, too.

One large university has more than 20,000 fans *practice their "yells"* (never cheers) in the stadium each Friday night at midnight before home football games. At a much smaller school, the women's basketball players *play cribbage on the team bus* en route to road games. Two very different before-the-game traditions.

The second time Colgate hockey fans *threw Big Red chewing gum* at the Cornell Big Red before the "Star-Spangled Banner" on home ice in

Hamilton, New York, Cornell fans replied in *unkind*. They littered their Lynah Rink with tubes of *Colgate toothpaste* flung at the visiting Red Raiders before the national anthem in Ithaca. Ever since, the puck drops here and there, along with gum and, occasionally, gooey toothpaste.

Speaking of tossing things . . .

There is no more dramatic before the game tradition in college football than *Chief Osceola*'s entrance at Florida State University's (FSU) home games. Since 1978, before every opening kickoff at Doak Campbell Stadium in Tallahassee, a student wearing war paint, dressed in authentic Seminole Indian attire and astride his horse, Renegade, rides to midfield while carrying a flaming spear. There, he *flings and plants the spear* as more than 80,000 'Noles fans go nuts.

While this may strike some as politically incorrect, it has the full cooperation and blessing of the Seminole Tribe of Florida.

But first, a little history: FSU's Osceola is named for the legendary Seminole Indian chief of the 1800s, born in Georgia near the banks of the Tallapoosa River. In 1962, a Florida State sophomore named Bill Durham, a member of the homecoming committee that fall, envisioned a student dressed as Osceola charging onto the gridiron aboard an appaloosa named Renegade and planting a flaming spear at midfield.

Durham got no support for his vision until the autumn of 1977, after Bobby Bowden had become the 'Noles head coach. Durham approached the Seminole Tribe of Florida, explained his idea and sought their approval for a student to portray and honor the great chief. The Seminoles approved. And so, before the 1978 opener against Oklahoma State, the legend of Osceola, and Renegade debuted with the tribe's blessing.

Since then, adorned in authentic regalia designed by the women of the Seminole tribe, Osceola and Renegade have turned each

FSU's Osceola and Renegade.
©Mike Olivella

opening kickoff into a traditional spectacle while paying homage to the original Osceola and the Seminole Tribe. Both rider and Renegade know how to make an entrance.

PREGAME TRADITIONS BY SCHOOL

Agnes Scott College (Basketball): *Links Forming a Chain*

The players and coaches carry around links from a chain (yep, the Ace Hardware type) each day, and on game day they link them all together, in a show of unity.

Air Force (Football): *Flyovers and Parachutes*

Flyovers are announced before the start of each game. Conditions permitting, the *Wings of Blue*, the Air Force Academy *parachute team, jumps* into Falcon Stadium prior to kickoff.

Arkansas State University (Basketball): *Indian Uprising*

The *Indian Uprising* began in the 1980s, where all fans stand for the opening tipoff.

University of Arizona (Football): *Haka*

During pregame warm-ups, the team performs a *haka*. The haka—also performed by Hawaii and a few other schools—is a traditional ancestral war dance believed to have started with the ancient people of New Zealand. Some teams use the dance as a tribute to Samoan team members (past or present). While the performance by New Zealand's rugby teams before their matches have made the haka widely known around the world, college fans first took notice when teams did the chants and dance during nationally televised games.

Bryant University (Various Sports): *Rubbing the Bulldog's Paw*

Bryant has a Bulldog statue at the entrance to their stadium (Bulldog Stadium). The entrance is a gateway to their other facilities as well, with baseball and softball and the track and field turf complex on the other side of the football stadium. Fans, as they enter the stadium, *rub the right paw of the Bulldog statue* on the right side. It's only right to do it.

Bryant University fans are encouraged to rub the right side of the right paw of the Bulldog, before a game. *Bryant University*

Bryant University invites fans of its athletic teams to be part of a new tradition of rubbing the right paw of the bulldog statue on the right side entering into Bulldog Stadium.

Like our alumni and fans the bulldog is dependable, committed, and a source of unwavering strength for the Bryant community.

University of California (Cal) (Football): *California Victory Cannon*

The *California Victory Cannon* was presented to Cal's *Rally Committee* in time for the 1963 *Big Game* with Stanford. It is shot off at the beginning of a game. It was once kept on the sidelines, but now is mounted on *Tightwad Hill*, above the stadium.

Colorado State University (Football): *Jingling Keys*

Prior to the opening kickoff of each game, as well as the kickoff following a Rams' scoring play, fans throughout Hughes Stadium *jingle sets of keys*. Let's hear those car keys jingling, ring-ting-tingling, too. "Jingle Bells," all the way.

University of the Cumberlands (Football): *Touching the Wrought Iron Horse*

On May 20, 1991, the only child of the university president and Mrs. Taylor was killed in an automobile accident. It was the night before young Jim

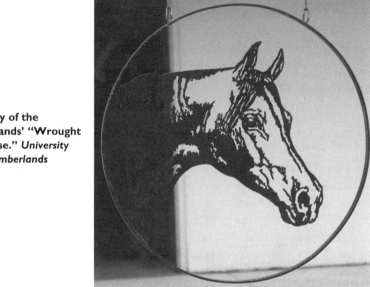

University of the Cumberlands' "Wrought Iron Horse." *University of the Cumberlands*

would have graduated from high school. Due to the generosity and enormous support for the Taylor's during their time of grief, many contributions were made to the college in honor of young Jim. It was this support that made possible the construction of the football, track, and soccer complex. The Board of Trustees voted unanimously to name the complex the *James H. Taylor II Stadium* after president and Mrs. Taylor's son. It seemed fitting since young Jim was the first ball boy when football was reinstated in 1985. In 1994 before the first football game of the season, the stadium was dedicated in honor of young Jim. During the dedication, young Jim's horse, Big 'un, which he adored, was led around the track by his two cousins. It was a riderless horse and his boots were placed backwards in the stirrups to symbolize he would never ride again. It was that same day that the tradition of *touching the wrought iron horse* was born. The wrought iron horse is a symbol of young Jim's love of horses and stands as a blessing to the team. Each game, as the football team emerges from the tunnel, they gently tap the horse for good luck.

Dallas Baptist University (Various Sports): *Regiment Cannon*

The Regiment Cannon is fired to begin athletic events.

East Carolina University (Various Sports): *Ghost on the Wind Poem*

The 2005 poem by Alfred H. Lockamy, titled "The Ghost on the Wind," is read—dramatically—as a welcome message prior to the start of ECU home sporting events.

East Carolina University (Football): *Raising the Jolly Roger Flag*

The Jolly Roger refers to the colors or flag of a pirate ship's captain. Pirate vessels looked like all other merchant ships of that era. Once a pirate was in striking distance of a targeted vessel, they would declare their intentions by showing their true colors. Various pirates had different flags which were well known to those who sailed the sea. Most depictions of the Jolly Roger include skull and crossbones, generally seen on a black field. The Jolly Roger was used to instill fear into one's enemies, and in many cases ships would surrender to a band of Pirates when this fearsome banner was raised. East Carolina hoists the colors (*raising the Jolly Roger*) just before the opening kickoff at home Pirate football games.

Florida Atlantic University (Football): *Kickoff Chant*

Just before every kickoff, the crowd starts to make lots of noise. When the ball is kicked everyone yells, "FAU" and when the ball is caught, "Owls."

University of Georgia (Tennis): *Chant before Match*

> "Who's that comin' down the tracks? (repeat);
> It's the mean machine in red and black (repeat);
> Ain't nothing finer in the land (repeat)
> Than the bond we share between each man (repeat)
> Go Dawgs!" (repeat)

University of Georgia (Football): *Cheers for the Cheap-Seats*

Before the railroad-end of Sanford Stadium was closed off (by adding seats), fans could sit on the railroad tracks and watch the game. UGA's cheerleaders would enter the stadium close by and never failed to lead the railroad-track watchers in a cheer, give them pom-poms, and so forth. On occasion, fans would also occupy the exact opposite end of the stadium (on the bridge) the night before with couches, tables, etc., for all-night parties. The cheerleaders often appeared on the bridge, to lead cheers there as well.

University of Hawaii (Football): *Haka*

The *haka* is an original war dance performed by the University of Hawaii football team. Prior to the 2007 football season, the team used a different dance which they then altered. The dance was introduced to the team by Tala Esera, a player who did the routine on his own high school team back in 2006. Although the dance has come under controversy in the following years, a now politically correct version of the *Maori War Dance* is used before and after home games. It is still considered too intimidating, so the Hawaii players do not face their opponents while doing it.

Illinois State University (Football): *Battle Bird*

Give 'em the bird: *The Battle Bird*, that is. Before each home athletic competition, Illinois State student athletes touch the Battle Bird, a likeness of the Redbird logo. The ceremony signifies a dedication to Illinois State and a common bond to the school's other student athletes, past and present. The sculpture was unveiled in 2000. Each year, a Redbird fan bids for the right to be known for a full year as the *Keeper of the Bird*.

John Brown University (Volleyball): *Candy for Fans*

For over ten years, the JBU volleyball team has *distributed candy* to the fans following the introductions at the beginning of volleyball matches on the JBU campus. Sweet.

University of Kansas (Basketball): *Pregame Pomp*

Pregame traditions includes students *holding up newspapers* during the opponent's player introductions, as well as a *bone-chilling video montage* paying homage to KU's most legendary players, coaches, teams, and moments.

Linfield College (Various Sports): *Lord's Prayer*

Immediately following each traditional pregame national anthem, fans may notice the Wildcats gathered closely together on one knee in a huge circle with heads bowed. While the ritual may look somewhat unusual, the Wildcats are actually just carrying out a tradition of reciting the *Lord's Prayer* as they complete their pregame routine. The Lord's Prayer is also recited by the football team, immediately following every Friday afternoon practice. Speaking of The Lord's Prayer brings to mind former Florida State coach Bill Peterson, a good coach and one of the funniest—if unintentionally so—sportsmen of all time. Once, after gathering his players and giving the 'Noles an inspired pregame pep talk, Peterson, the Master of Malapropos, said, "OK men, let's take a knee and bow our heads and say the Lord's Prayer." Somberly, Peterson began: "Now I lay me down to sleep . . ."

University of Maine (Ice Hockey): *Camp-out for Tickets*

Students often *camp-out all night* for hockey tickets in *IceStation Zebra*–like subzero weather. Brrrrr.

University of Maryland (Basketball): *Newspaper Shaking*

At home basketball games, the students often pretend to read the paper as the visiting team is introduced. Nicknamed *"Newspaper Shaking,"* the students arrive at the arena with newspapers for the opposing player introductions. While reading the newspaper, the students make sure to shake it vigorously which is why the tradition is aptly named Newspaper Shaking.

University of Maryland (Football): *Pet the Terp*

Fans outside of Maryland's stadium *rub the half-ton bronze statue* of Testudo for good luck.

University of Memphis (Football): *March Around*

March Around happens about ten minutes before kickoff. At that point, the spirit squads and band, as well as their live *Bengal Tiger mascot TOM III* (stands for *Tigers of Memphis*) circle the field and get the fans ready for the team to run out of the tunnel before the game.

Monmouth College (Softball): *Prayer Circle & Lineup Announcement*

The Monmouth College softball team forms a *prayer circle* before each game. At the end of the prayer, the lineup is read with the players clapping slowly at the beginning and speeding up as the coach proceeds from the leadoff-hitter to the nine-hitter. By the time the last hitter's name is read, the team erupts in applause.

University of Nebraska (Football): *Touch a Horseshoe and Tunnel Walk*

After leaving the locker room, Nebraska players and coaches *touch a lucky horseshoe* and begin walking a winding path lined with red carpet. The pathway is packed with fans that help cheer the players on before they take the field, exiting through the tunnel. The first *Tunnel Walk* was in 1994 and is set to the song "Sirius" by Alan Parsons Project. Although it is one of the more modern traditions, the Tunnel Walk has garnered a huge amount of fan support.

University of Nebraska (Football): *Pep Rally inside a Local Establishment*

It's an *intimate football pep rally* with the entire Nebraska marching band *crowded into a local lounge*.

University of Nevada-Las Vegas (UNLV) (Basketball): *Explosive Pregame Show*

Twenty-four strobes and sixty pyrotechnic effects deliver the most electrifying two minutes and forty seconds in college hoops.

UNLV's explosive pregame show. *UNLV*

North Dakota State University (Football): *Slap-the-Bison*

Players *slap a picture of a snorting bison* hanging above the dressing room door. The emblem of the bison also travels with the team to road games.

Northern Illinois University (Football): *Jingling Keys*

Northern Illinois fans *shake keys* prior to the kickoff.

Northwest Missouri State University (Football): *Cannon*

At home football games, a *cannon*, located at the Phi Sigma Kappa fraternity house across the street from Bearcat Stadium, is fired before opening kickoffs.

Northwestern University (Football): *Trust-Yourself Board*

Beginning in 1999, players leaving and entering the locker room touch the board and remind themselves of that trust. The *Trust-Yourself Board* usually rests on an N-shaped shrine in the locker room.

Northwestern University (Football): *Jingling Keys*

Began in the late 1970s. Fans either love or hate the tradition of *jingling keys* prior to kickoff. Many students and fans now incorrectly believe this to be an insulting gesture aimed at the opposing fans. However, the origin of the key shake is innocent, and it did not originate with NU—other colleges and even high schools have been doing this for far longer.

Northwestern University (Various Sports): *Camping Out*

The tradition of *pitching tents and camping out for athletic tickets* is a part of modern student life at Northwestern.

University of Notre Dame (Football): *Painting the Gold Helmets*

On Monday evenings, prior to each game, the team's student managers *paint all football helmets gold*, using paint containing real 23.9-karat gold dust. The gold particles that are used on the helmet were collected from the regilding on the Notre Dame dome in 2007.

Notre Dame paints their helmets "gold" before each week's game. *Notre Dame University*

University of Notre Dame (Football): *"Play Like a Champion Today" Sign*

Coming out of the locker room, players *slap the famous "Play Like a Champion Today" sign.*

Notre Dame players touch the "Play Like a Champion Today" sign, as they leave the locker room. *Notre Dame University*

University of Notre Dame (Football): *Lighting Candles /*
Team Mass

Fans *light candles* at Notre Dame's grotto and pray for their team's success. The team also holds *a team mass* at the Basilica before home games.

New York University (NYU) (Women's Basketball): *Taking the*
Subway to Road Games

The Mets and Yankees may host New York City's most popular Subway Series, but the New York University women's basketball team takes the phrase a bit more literally for its intracity rivalry games. NYU not only played a team just a few subway stops away in its first road contest of 2011–2012, but the squad actually *took the subway* to the game at the Polytechnic Institute of NYU. The Violets boarded the F-line at the Broadway-Lafayette station in Manhattan's Greenwich Village and got off at Jay Street–Metrotech in downtown Brooklyn. After a short fifteen-minute trip, the squad made the brief walk from the station to Poly's Jacobs Gymnasium. The subway trip is one of approximately three that NYU make to road games each season. The squad also rides the train to its contests at Baruch and Hunter, each of which is in Manhattan. "These kids choose NYU because

NYU's basketball team
taking the subway to
road games. *NYU Sports
Management Information
Department*

it is in one of the greatest cities in the world, and life in New York revolves around the subway," said Violet coach Stefano Trompeo. "This is just part of the experience of going to school in New York City. That's why we love NYU—you can do things here that you can't do anywhere else."

Oakland University (Basketball): *Team Reads Their Creed in the Locker Room*

Oakland's basketball team *reads their creed* while in the locker room prior to each game.

University of Pittsburgh (Basketball): *Shaking Hands with the Media*

Before every home game, each Pitt starter *shakes hands with every person at the press table*, including long-time radio commentators Dick Groat and Bill Hillgrove.

University of Pittsburgh (Pitt) (Various Sports): *Touching the Millennium Panther*

Players often touch various things prior to a game, but at Pitt—in order to bring good luck to the university's teams prior to athletic contests—students, alumni, and fans get into the act by *rubbing the nose of the Millennium Panther* located outside the William Pitt Union. This tradition was featured in a national television advertisement for the 2012 Hyundai Tucson.

Rollins College (Swimming): *Blowing a Conch Shell*

Rollins swimming team *blows a conch shell* as an announcement of their team cheer. They have been doing this for over twenty years, and as a result, their swimming alumni call themselves the ex-conchs. The school's mascot—the Tars—are tall-ship sailors, so the conch horn fits in well.

Rutgers (Football): *First Game Statue*

Unlike fans at other colleges, Rutgers alums and fans have a singular, touching tradition, much like the Scarlet Knight football players themselves. Before every home football game, the team walks the walk: *the Scarlet Walk* and, for good luck, *touches the First Game Statue*. It commemorates the first college football game ever played between Rutgers and Princeton on November 6, 1869. Amos Alonzo Stagg (ask your father) was six years old then. But nearly a century-and-a-half later, a tradition before every Rutgers home game honors the very first collegiate game. Thanks, Jersey boys.

University of South Carolina (Football): *The Cockaboose Railroad*

The Cockaboose Railroad is like no other tailgating tradition in the country. Twenty-two cabooses line a railroad track just outside Williams-Brice Stadium—but these rail cars don't move, and they certainly aren't something you would see passing by on the end of a train. Running water, cable television, air conditioning and heating, and a living room, highlight each and every Cockaboose.

University of Southern California (USC) (Football): *Kick the Flagpoles*

Fans *kick the flagpoles* for good luck as they walk from USC to its football games in Los Angeles Memorial Coliseum across the street.

The University of South Carolina's unique tailgating location.
South Carolina Athletics

University of Tennessee (Football): *Slapping the Sign*

Football players *slap a sign* saying *"I Will Give My ALL for Tennessee Today"* as they exit the locker room.

University of Tennessee (Swimming/Diving): *Home Water*

A swimming/diving tradition that has proven to be a favorite of Tennessee fans is the ritual that takes place prior to away dual meets and championships meets. Prior to the opening event, a Tennessee swimmer will *pour a bottle of water from their home pool into the opponent's water*. The tradition, started by Coach Ray Bussard, excites both fans and foes alike.

Texas A&M (Football): *Midnight Yell Practice*

At midnight before each home football game at Kyle Field or at a pre-designated location at away games, the fans gather together to practice the yells (never cheers) for the next day's game. Led by the *yell leaders*, and the *Fightin' Texas Aggie Band*, the 12th Man files into the stadium to participate in *Midnight Yell Practice* to practice yells, sing the *War Hymn*, and joke about their opponents. At the conclusion of the yell practice, the stadium lights are extinguished and fans *kiss their dates*. This is also done as practice, because Aggies are expected to mug down, or kiss their dates, every time the football team scores on the field. *Sports Illustrated* named Midnight Yell as one of the 100 Things You Gotta Do Before You Graduate. 20,000-plus fans go to Midnight Yell Practice before home football games. And if you go, be certain to say, "Howdy" to everyone that you see— because they will say it you!

Texas State University (Football): *Bobcat Victory Ball*

Dedicated in 2006, the *Bobcat Victory Ball* is a gigantic football sculpture that sits on a marble base outside the main entrance of Bobcat Stadium. All persons entering the complex are encouraged to rub the ball for luck.

Texas Tech (Football): *Saddle Tramps Wrapping Statue*

Saddle Tramps form a big circle on the field before each football game, ring cowbells, and chant "go-fight-win." Also, before every home football game the Saddle Tramps *wrap a statue* of Will Rodgers and his horse,

Soapsuds, with red crepe paper. Will Rogers and Soapsuds have also been wrapped in black crepe paper to mourn national tragedies.

Virginia Tech (Football): *Touching the Hokie Stone*

Inside the tunnel that the players run through prior to the game is a stone from the university's quarry with the phrase, "For those who have passed, for those to come, reach for excellence." Each player touches the stone en route to the field. Some would argue that the Hokie Stone contributes to—perhaps even serves as a foundation of—Hokie Spirit. The native limestone, mined at the university's own quarry, has defined the campus scene for more than a hundred years. The rocks have become so integral to the aura of Virginia Tech that the Board of Visitors decreed in the mid-1990s that all buildings constructed in the central campus thenceforth must be clad in Hokie Stone.

University of Washington (Football): *Sailgating*

Washington is the home of *Sailgating* on Lake Washington. Rowers shuttle fans from boats to their lakeside stadium prior to football games.

West Virginia University (Football and Basketball): *Rifle Firing*

The *Firing of the Rifle* is a tradition carried out by the Mountaineer Mascot to open several athletic events. The Mountaineer points the gun into the air with one arm and fires a blank shot from a custom rifle, a signal to the crowd to begin cheering at home football and basketball games.

Williams College (Cross-Country): *Tossing T. Bear*

Williams College's school mascot isn't a bear, but their cross-country team has a stuffed bear as their mascot. It all began in a peaceful New England town, on a not-quite-sleepy New England campus, in October of 1978. Williams' freshman Gordon Coates awoke and went to run in the North Adams Fall Foliage Road Race. In the postrace raffle his number was called. While pawing through the offerings on the prize table, the freshman was "encouraged" by his teammates to select a huge stuffed bear royally seated there. They chanted "take the bear, take the bear" . . . Gordon succumbed to peer pressure, grabbed the bear, and ran back to the team. Thus *The Bear* was born. In the next meet, the team decided to throw the

Williams College cross-country team tosses T. Bear in the air prior to every meet. *Williams College*

bear skyward as a pre-race psyche-up. It worked, as they beat Coast Guard and WPI. The bear became a good luck symbol for the team as they upset MIT at the very next meet. MIT decided to get even with the Williams harriers by pulling a little prank the next time they met. They barely snuck the bear away from an unsuspecting Coach Pete Farwell by inviting him for some refreshments, and it took an exchange of pun-filled letters to get the bear returned at the next meeting of the teams. The Techies took the chance to put their own mark upon the good luck mascot by sewing a varsity "T" upon his bare chest. Precedent was set: teams would steal the Williams' bear and return him soon after, leaving some new fashion statement upon the bear. During periods when the bear has been kidnapped, the Williams harriers have been known to wear black armbands or headbands, plant bear trap signs on courses, and often toss "surrogate bears" (shirts, pillows, other teddy bears). The Ephs even won a national championship while bearless.

University of Wisconsin–Green Bay (Basketball): *Cribbage*

Just prior to away games, the women's basketball team engages in a *game of cribbage*.

2

TRADITIONS DURING THE GAME

*F*ish *flung on the ice* after a hockey goal. An Ivy League school that *tosses toast at their cheerleaders* at the start of the fourth quarter. *Fans jumping up and down*, up and down, stomping strong enough to make structural engineers very, very afraid. These are a few of our favorite traditions that take place during the game.

And don't forget the *"William Tell Overture" Timeout* during Indiana University home basketball games. It's enough to make the late Clayton Moore, the Lone Ranger of TV legend, smile.

During the under-eight minutes media timeout in the second half of each Indiana Hoosier home game, the Indiana University (IU) pep band and cheerleading squad performs the "William Tell Overture" and transforms Alumni Hall into one hellacious home court advantage. While the band blares the overture, cheerleaders race around the court carrying eighteen IU flags. The under-eight tradition, which began more than thirty years ago, has often been called the greatest college timeout in the country.

But a favorite in-game tradition of ours is *Silent Night*, as only the crowd at tiny Taylor University in Upland, Indiana, can perform it.

On a weekend in December, just before final exams and for more than twenty years now, Taylor students play *the pajama game*. They wear pajamas to the gym and, at least initially, no one speaks or cheers. Not when the teams warm up, not when the starting lineups are introduced, not even when play begins. Not until Taylor scores its tenth point. Then the gym erupts. Fans stand and roar. Students race up the sideline and across the baseline. It's a sonic boost to the Trojans' ego, and the small gymnasium at the NAIA evangelical Christian school in Upland, Indiana, might as well be Alumni Hall.

"It sounds like an episode of *Oprah*, and she's giving something away," Tony Reali of ESPN's *Pardon the Interruption* once said on an episode of *PTI*.

With about two minutes left to play, and irrespective of the score, while the teams continue to play, the Taylor crowd links arms and sings a heartfelt rendition of "Silent Night"—all three verses. After the game, students gather at the campus student center, where they enjoy Christmas music, baking and eating Christmas cookies, addressing Christmas cards to our troops, making gingerbread houses, and the inevitable Christmas songs with a karaoke machine. The climax of the night is when the university president and his wife read *the Christmas Story* to the students.

A one-time assistant coach conceived the Silent Night game in the late 1980s. A decade later, it was a full-house, full-blown Christmas tradition and wonder.

In its 2010 Christmas issue, *Sports Illustrated* paid tribute to the hoopla of Silent Night, when all isn't calm but all is bright and right in Taylor's little corner of the world.

TRADITIONS DURING THE GAME BY SCHOOL

University of Arizona (Football): *Banner*

At the beginning of the second half, for the duration of the kickoff, a large-*block "A" banner is unfurled* and held up by the center of the *Zona-Zoo* (student section).

University of Arizona (Softball): *Linda Ronstadt Songs*

There is no tradition on the Arizona Wildcats campus more fantastically obscure, lovely, and regionally perfect, than the one at Hillenbrand Stadium that is more than twenty years old. For well over 600 home games since Hillenbrand opened in 1993, players and fans have heard the same two first-inning *Linda Ronstadt songs*. When the Wildcats take the field, the public address system blares "Palomita de los Ojos Negros," a track from the Tucson-born Ronstadt's 1991 album, *Mas Canciones*. The announcer follows with "Juegen pelota"—play ball. In the bottom half of the inning, "La Mariquita," another traditional song from the same album, serenades the opposing team's pitcher as she throws warm-up tosses.

There's also protocol. Each song starts when the first player crosses the baseline, and ends when the warmed-up pitcher steps on the rubber to start the frame. On rare occasions, in tournaments when the University of Arizona (UA) is a visiting team, the songs are swapped so the Wildcats feel at home. In a time where every utterance at UA games seems to come with a sponsor's message, the first inning sails along, unencumbered, while the music plays. Both songs are entirely in Spanish. Most players have no idea what they mean, and opposing teams often have expressions of *what the heck is going on right now?* And this tradition, like many others, was never meant to be tradition. UA media-relations director Tom Duddleston was given *Mas Canciones* by his mom, Betty, after it came out in late 1991. The album featured Ronstadt's brothers Peter and Mike on vocals. At the time, Peter was Tucson's police chief. Duddleston had seen Linda Ronstadt, a Tucson native, play with the Stone Poneys, and was a fan. "We were thinking of things to do to make things festive," Duddleston said. "What's more festive than that?" He stumbled upon "Palomita de los Ojos Negros" first, when the team took the field, and soon added "Mariquita." At first, they were played from a tape recorder, with a microphone propped on a plastic cup with the bottom torn out. Maybe one day Linda will sing these two songs live, during the first inning.

University of California (Football): *Card Stunts*

The University of California (Cal) rooting section is credited with establishing one of the most time-honored traditions in college football—*performing card stunts* at college football games. Cal began this activity for the 1910 "Big Game," a rugby match between California and Stanford. The original stunts performed that afternoon depicted the *Stanford Axe* and a big blue "C" formed on a white background. The tradition is a crowd favorite at Memorial Stadium, as several times each season Cal students perform as many as ten different stunts, using more than 5,000 cards. The painstaking process of plotting the positions of the cards, which once took days to complete, is now aided by computers that add to the precision of the images produced in the card section.

University of California-Irvine (Baseball): *Dugout Captain*

The dugout captain leads the team with various hat-related (and other) movements, (i.e., "deuces" is a series of hat movements when the count is 2:2, with two out.)

University of Connecticut (Basketball): *Prior to the First Points*

Fans stand and clap until the Huskies score.

Cornell University (Ice Hockey): *Fish Thrown on the Ice*

A fish was chosen to be thrown on the ice at the Cornell/Harvard game in 1974 because, well, it was gross. This was done in retaliation for Harvard fans throwing a frozen chicken (since Cornell had an agricultural college) on the ice after a Harvard goal the year prior. It began with Cornell pelting Harvard players with fish before the start of the second period and tying a live chicken to Harvard's net during the schools' next meeting. The intense rivalry and Cornell's fish-throwing tradition persists.

East Carolina University (Football): *No-Quarter Flag*

Following the end of the third quarter, the East Carolina Pirates raise a *No Quarter Flag* to start the fourth quarter of home football games. The flag raising is accompanied by thrilling music and fans are encouraged to join-in the excitement. Students and fans show their opponents that the Pirates will give no quarter by crossing their arms in imitation of the skull and crossbones. They cheer loud, stomp their feet, and show their team that these Pirates will give No Quarter! The Pirates' red No Quarter Flag is flown from the beginning of the fourth quarter throughout the remainder of the game to show that the Pirates will fight on until the end, giving no mercy to their opponents.

Florida Atlantic University (Football): *Fourth Quarter Roar*

At the beginning of the fourth quarter, the band plays Queen's "We Will Rock You," as the students and fans stomp loudly on the metal stands.

University of Houston (Basketball): *Jingling Keys*

During the last minute of a University of Houston basketball contest in Hofheinz Pavilion, the fans begin breaking out their keys (house keys, car keys, locker keys, etc.) and jingling them. This is the fans way of telling the team to bring home the victory and the opposing team's bus driver to go ahead and start the bus.

Houston Baptist University (Various Sports): *Dogs Up*

Their mascot is a Husky and they have a hand sign of a dog's head. At each free throw, set point, or match point, the announcer implores the crowd by saying, "*Dogs up*," at which time all in attendance raise the hand signal of the dog's head, which is held aloft until the free throw is done or the point is over. Typically this is accompanied by their real Husky (mascot) barking.

Manhattan College (Baseball): *7th-Inning Stretch*

In the 1880s, Brother Jasper brought the then little-known sport of baseball to Manhattan College and became the team's first coach. Since Brother Jasper was also the prefect of discipline, he supervised the student fans at Manhattan College baseball games while also directing the team itself. During one particularly warm and humid day when Manhattan was playing against a semipro baseball team, Brother Jasper noticed students were becoming restless and edgy as the team came to bat in the seventh inning of a close game. To relieve the tension, Brother Jasper called time-out and told the students to stand up and stretch for a few minutes until the game resumed. Since the college annually played the New York Giants baseball team in the late 1880s and into the 1890s at the Polo Grounds, the Manhattan College practice of *the 7th-inning stretch* spread into the major leagues, where it subsequently became the time-honored custom we all recognize today.

University of Maryland (Football): *Rattling Keys*

Students jingle their keys, rather than cheer, to keep the noise down on key offensive plays for the Terrapin football team.

University of Maryland (Football): *Move Those Chains*

When the Terps make a first down, fans remind the sideline chain crew of what they need to do, beginning with a long loud "Oh!" followed by three "*Move those chains!*" chants while giving the first down signal.

University of Missouri (Football): *The Missouri Waltz*

At the end of the third quarter, Tiger fans sway in time as the band plays "The Missouri Waltz."

University of Northern Iowa (Basketball): *Interlude Dance*

"Interlude" is a student-penned techno song. When played during a time-out, students go into a sort of freaky flash mob.

Northwestern University (Football): *Put Your Hands Up in the Air!*

Put Your Hands Up in the Air began in 2010 and is similar to the Cubs' seventh-inning stretch. The song of the same name bellows across the stadium at the beginning of the fourth quarter, introduced by a famous alumnus or a local celebrity (the first to take part was *Da Coach* himself, Mike Ditka). The crowd reaction, as prompted by the introduction, is as you would expect.

Palestra Games (Basketball): *Rollout Signs*

Five teams in the Philadelphia area (LaSalle, Penn, St. John's, Temple, and Villanova) often play each other at the Palestra. *Palestra rollouts* are a proud Big 5 tradition that has spanned the decades of the rivalry's history. At Big 5 games, rival opponents often create long (horizontal) banner messages to support their teams and razz their opponent's confidence.

For many years "rollout signs" were used at Big 5 games played at the Palestra. *University of Pennsylvania*

University of Pennsylvania (Football): *Toast Toss*

The *Toast Toss* is between the third and fourth quarters of every home football game. For several decades, the tradition between the third and fourth quarter was for students to sing a song entitled "Drink a Highball." They held their glasses high while singing, and when they reached the final line, "Here's a toast to dear old Penn!" they drank their highballs. Needless to say, the university tried to crack down on this practice and eventually banned alcohol from the stadium. The idea for the Toast Toss came from *The Rocky Horror Picture Show*. As you might know, that movie is very interactive, and includes a part where the audience throws toast at the screen. Members of the Penn Band saw the movie and got the idea to throw toast as they sang the final line of "Drink a Highball." It has been a tradition ever since.

University of Pittsburgh (Basketball): *Coming Out of a Basketball Game*

During a game, when a Pitt player gets subbed out, he will always acknowledge every person on the bench—even the managers and trainers—with either a handshake or a fist pound.

Penn students "Tossing Toast" at the end of the third quarter. *University of Pennsylvania*

Purdue University (Football): *Crowd Sings "Shout"*

Beginning in 2006, between the third and fourth quarters of home football games, the crowd is led in the singing of "Shout" by a local celebrity. Leaders of this classic song have ranged from Neil Armstrong to Drew Brees to Bob Griese to the National Spelling Bee champion.

Southern Miss (Football): *Seymour's Sidekicks Spirit Line*

Seymour's Sidekicks Spirit Line consists of children who are members of Seymour's Sidekicks and their parents, and forms at the start of the second half of a home football game as the Golden Eagles enter the playing field.

Syracuse University (Basketball): *Fans Clapping until Team Scores*

Syracuse fans *stand and clap* their hands at the beginning of each half until the basketball team scores their first points.

University of Tennessee (Basketball): *Fans Clapping until Team Scores*

Tennessee fans *stand and clap* their hands at the beginning of each half until the basketball team scores their first points.

Tennessee Tech (Basketball): *The Blizzard*

The Blizzard is a tradition that started in 1984 when students celebrated the first successful shot made by Tennessee Tech in a basketball game against Middle Tennessee State University (MTSU) by throwing showers of *Tech Squares* (toilet paper) into the air. Since MTSU moved to the Sun Belt Conference, the Blizzard is now performed against Austin Peay State University.

University of Southern California (Football): *Lighting the Cauldron*

The Trojan mascot *lights the Olympic Cauldron* (from the 1932 and 1984 Summer Games) at the end of the third quarter.

University of Utah (Football): *False Start Tally*

Whenever the opposing team receives a false start penalty The MUSS (spirit group) hangs a "5" in front of the student section, indicating the five-yard penalty. There is a running total for the entire season.

Western Kentucky University (Various Sports): *Red Towels*

Western Kentucky fans, at all events, *wave red towels* in honor of one of their former basketball coaches who clutched a red towel through 1,062 games. Towels were initially dyed to differentiate the physical education towels from the athletic towels, but the dyed towels bled terribly. Cannon was approached and indicated that they could manufacture the red towels.

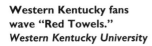

Western Kentucky fans wave "Red Towels."
Western Kentucky University

University of Wisconsin (Football): *Jump Around*

On October 10, 1998, a Wisconsin football tradition was born when this House of Pain song blasted through the stadium speakers and 80,000 people shook the place by *jumping up and down* to the song. After an up-roar over an administration attempt to nix the song, the chancellor reversed the decision and it continues still, between the third and fourth quarters of each home football game. The entire stadium shakes as students and fans jump around. The Rose Bowl has traditionally not allowed schools to engage in many of their own traditions, but in 2012, they made an exception for "Jump Around." They also allowed Oregon's similar tradition of "Shout." In the event that the Rose Bowl had not relented, Wisconsin fans were being urged to download the song onto their phones/MP3 players and play it in unison as they all jumped around. Also as a contingency, the Wisconsin Band learned the piece. This is often called the rowdiest three minutes in college football.

3

TRADITIONS AFTER A SCORE

What is it about flying fish and college hockey that makes them such a perfect pair? Let Detroit Red Wings fans litter the ice with celebratory octopuses. Let other NHL fans anoint a player's third goal of the night by tossing hats on the ice to punctuate a hat trick. In collegiate hockey, the fish is the chosen projectile of choice.

Nowhere, it seems, more than at the University of New Hampshire (UNH) in Durham. For four decades and counting, the New Hampshire *Fish Toss* has driven Wildcat fans, well, wild. Following New Hampshire's first goal of the game, a fish is thrown on the ice. Should the Wildcats somehow go scoreless through three periods, the fish is later thrown on the university president's front porch. Not to worry. It's rare that UNH doesn't score and that the president's porch stinks.

What invariably happens is this: after New Hampshire scores its first goal, heads turn and all eyes in the Towse Rink at the Whittemore Center Arena focus on the opponent's goal. As if on cue, up and over the boards comes a flying fish, now gliding across the ice. The Wildcat crowd erupts. Fish sticks, all around.

The tradition took hold back in the early 1970s. So says Bob Norton, a former New Hampshire assistant coach. "It goes back to when we were playing a Division II team, and our program had gone way past theirs. I remember they (Wildcat fans) threw out this dinky thing and they called it a Division II fish."

University of New
Hampshire fans "Toss
a Fish on the Ice,"
after their team's
first goal. ©2013 Cody
Smith Photography

"I guess," Norton said, "they were trying to tell them they weren't worthy of a first-rate fish."

Nope. This was a guppy or a minnow, not Moby Dick. But the fine art of fish-tossing became a big hit. A local fraternity, Zeta Chi, took it upon themselves to fling the fish after New Hampshire's first goal. It was a symbolic gesture, the opposing goalie fishing the puck out of the net. UNH fans ate it up, and still do.

These days, Wildcat head coach Dick Umile likes to tell this fish story. In the early 1990s, the home team in college hockey received a penalty if fans flung objects on the ice.

"At all these different rinks," Umile said, "people were throwing things—tennis balls, newspapers—and it was really holding up the game. It's the Maine weekend, and the cops won't let the kid in with the fish."

"I'm in the office before the game, and the students come to get me," he continued. "So I go down there, get the fish from the cops, and as we're walking in with the fish in the bag, the kids say, 'But coach, we're going to get a penalty!'

"I say, 'Don't worry about it. We'll kill the penalty. Just throw the fish.'" Sound fishy? Nope.

TRADITIONS AFTER A SCORE BY SCHOOL

University of Alaska Anchorage (Ice Hockey): *Fish Toss*

A *fish is tossed* on the ice after the first home team goal.

University of Arizona (Football): *Push-ups*

In a similar tradition to other schools' mascots, after every Arizona score, Wilbur the Wildcat does as many *pushups* as the Wildcats have points while the crowd counts his push-ups. However, unlike other mascots, Wilbur does his push-ups one-handed.

Arizona State University (Football): *Fireworks*

During a football game after the Sun Devils score, *fireworks* are shot in celebration of the scoring.

Bowling Green State University (Ice Hockey): *Students Respond after Hockey Goals*

When the Falcons score a goal the student section *holds up the number of goals scored on their fingers* until the announcer says the goal and who scored it over the PA system. Then everybody *waves their fingers* yelling and then *counts in unison* the number of goals followed by "we want more" (4x) and "go" (6x) and singing "Ay Ziggy Zoomba" (unofficial fight song) as many times as there are goals.

Cal (Football): *California Victory Cannon*

The California Victory Cannon is shot off after each score. Only once, against Pacific in 1991, did the Bears score too many times, racking up twelve touchdowns before the cannon ran out of ammunition.

University of California, Santa Barbara (Soccer): *Tortilla Tossing*

Since 2004, fans have showered the Gauchos with tortillas after a goal is scored. This same practice was previously in effect during basketball games, but was banned in 1997.

Clemson University (Football): *Push-ups*

In 1978, the Clemson Tiger began doing *push-ups* after touchdowns. This is such a sacred tradition that the sports information director for Clemson actually tracks the number of push-ups in a game, in a season, and so forth. The record for one game is 465, while the season record is 1,549. In 2012, the university president dressed in the Tiger mascot outfit and did the push-ups for one game. He then unmasked himself, much to the fans' delight!

Colorado State University (Football): *The Cannon*

No sound is sweeter to Ram fans or more disheartening to opponents than the boom of the *Colorado State University Army ROTC cannon* at Hughes Stadium. The ROTC has been firing the cannon for every point scored by the home team at football games since 1954.

University of Delaware (Football): *Victory Bell*

Academy Bell, *College Bell*, and *Victory Bell*—the University of Delaware bell has had many names over the years. Purchased in the autumn of 1834, the bell was initially rung to wake students and summon them to class. Housed in its own framework on the college grounds, the bell was the subject of many student pranks. Stories range from students tying the bell's clapper to its rim to inverting the bell so it could be filled with water on freezing winter nights to hiding the rope that was used to ring it. Maybe to prevent access by students or perhaps to fulfill a reference in the original college building's plans, a cupola was erected in 1852 atop the college's first building (now Old College). College administrators thought the limited-access belfry would cut down on the number of student pranks, but from 1852 to 1881, the shenanigans continued. Rumor has it that students had a perennial quest to get a cow into the belfry. The design of the stairway and ladder leading up to the cupola prevented it from happening, but students did manage to get a bull to the top of the building's front steps in June 1854. In 1917, the original college building underwent a major facelift that resulted in the removal of the cupola. Now homeless, the bell was moved to the basement of the Agricultural Experiment Station (today's Recitation Hall) and was forgotten. It was not until 1934 that the College Bell was rediscovered during planning for the college centenary. The bell, once retrieved, was moved to Memorial Library, where it again remained silent for

The Delaware Bell is rung after each score in football. *University of Delaware*

many years. In 1952, the University of Delaware called the bell to service once again, this time as the Victory Bell in the new Delaware Stadium. It is here that the tradition of *ringing the bell* after a touchdown began.

East Carolina University (Football): *Cannon*

It is unclear exactly when East Carolina University (ECU) began using a cannon to hype up the crowd and intimidate its opponents at home football games, but one thing is certain, it has become a staple in the Pirate tradition. The use of the cannon goes back to at least 1967, when East Carolina officially gained university status. Around 1974, an accident involving one of the football players put the use of the cannon on hold. After the player scored a touchdown, he inadvertently ran in front of the cannon, which was placed just beyond the end zone, and when fired it knocked him to the ground. This set off a frenzy of questions about the safety of the cannon by administrators and fans. And from 1974 to the early 1990s, ECU was without its cannon. The cannon is now fired at the end of the national anthem, when the team runs onto the field, after each time the Pirates score, and at the conclusion of all games.

Florida Atlantic University (Football): *Cannon and Pushups*

After each score, Florida Atlantic University's ROTC *shoots a cannon* and then *does push-ups* (along with their mascot, Roary) matching the number of points scored.

Illinois State University (Football): *Redbird Victory Bell*

Since the 1966 Illinois State University (ISU) football season, the *Redbird Victory Bell* has been on the sidelines at Hancock Stadium for ISU game days. The Victory Bell, which is now operated by various student groups throughout the season, leads the team onto the field prior to kickoff. During the game, the Victory Bell is rung after each Illinois State touchdown and is used to signal a win of the Redbird football team for all to hear. It is also a mainstay in the annual homecoming parade. Initially called Bone's Victory Bell, in honor of Illinois State University's ninth president, Dr. Robert Bone, the Victory Bell was also used for the *March-on-Wesleyan*, when Illinois State and Illinois Wesleyan once played each other in a football cross-town rivalry.

John Brown University (Soccer): *Cannon Fired*

During men's soccer games on campus, for each goal the John Brown University team scores, a *cannon is fired* from behind the goal.

Lake Superior State University (Ice Hockey): *The Horn*

It's a feast for the ears for hockey fans in Sault Sainte Marie, Michigan, when the Lakers are winning. The region's nautical tradition is honored every time the Lakers score a goal, as an authentic Great Lakes ship's *foghorn*, (strategically placed above the goal manned by the visitors in the first and third periods), is blasted in the rink.

University of Maine (Ice Hockey): *Naked Five*

During the game, each time Maine scores a goal the *Naked Five* (members of a fraternity), run around the rink carrying a cowbell. They have no shirts and their chests are painted. One has M, the next A, I, N, E.

University of Maryland (Football): *Cannon Fired*

During home games, a small *cannon is fired* each time the football team scores.

Monmouth College (Football): *Cannon Fired*

Monmouth's *Civil War era cannon*, a gift from the class of 1903, is fired after each Fighting Scots' touchdown at the college's homecoming game.

Murray State University (Football): *Horse Circles Track*

Racer 1 circles the track (touchdown lap) around the football field after each score.

University of Nebraska (Football): *Releasing Helium Balloons*

A global helium shortage, of the second most abundant element in the universe, has affected a long-standing tradition after the Cornhuskers score their first touchdown. Rather than releasing 5,000 balloons, they now release 2,000.

New Mexico State University (Football): *Bell Ringing*

New Mexico State *rings a large bell* when the football team scores.

University of North Texas (Football): *Boomer-the-Cannon*

The Talons, a spirit organization, began this tradition in the 1970 football season as they introduced their newest spirit project: a muzzleloader cannon. The cannon was fired by the Talons cannon crew to signal University of North Texas (UNT) touchdowns, kick off, halftime, and the end of home football games, as well as for special occasions such as University Day. *Boomer* is a Civil War replica, about two-thirds to scale of a six-pound cannon. It was modeled after cannons originally used as light horse battery by the Confederate cavalry. Talons worked for more than three years to gild the cannon, receiving donations from many campus organizations to help complete the project. The carriage was built on a trailer and equipped for highway travel so the Talons could take it on road trips. Although Boomer did go to some away games, many stadiums will not allow it because it fires gunpowder rather than blank cartridges. Boomer was originally fired using wadded newspapers. Because the paper occasionally started small fires, the cannon was not allowed on the Fouts Field's artificial turf. Talons cannon crew members now have an option of three firing methods. After the black powder charge is loaded and pierced, the battery unit, a firing squad of the cannon crew can fire electronically, with a live flame, or with the most frequently used brass cap and trigger hammer. A spark is created causing the black powder to explode and results in Boomer's famous boom. Boomer was also featured in Paramount's 1991 film, *Necessary Roughness*. After the film crew saw and heard Boomer fire, they wrote an extra part in the film just for Boomer's appearance. In the fall of 1996, a safety inspector deemed Boomer unsafe due to the deterioration of the combustion chamber. The Talons acted quickly and purchased a new 250-pound, 43-inch, steel-lined barrel. Years later, UNT's president remarked that Boomer would look even more authentic with a limber. After hearing this, the Talons knew Boomer was still not complete and in the fall of 2007 the limber was introduced. Handcrafted of solid oak, the limber now carries all essentials for firing Boomer and also serves as a seat in parades. Other cannons have come to UNT and been removed due to safety concerns. Boomer is the only remaining cannon allowed on campus.

Northwest Missouri State University (Football): *Push-ups*

Bobby the Bearcat does *push-ups* each time the team scores. The most Bobby has ever done was on September 29, 2007, when Northwest defeated Southwest Baptist 86–13. The total number of push-ups was 677.

Northwest Missouri State University (football): *Cannon*

At home football games a *cannon*, located at the Phi Sigma Kappa Fraternity house across the street from Bearcat Stadium, is fired when the Bearcat football team scores a touchdown.

University of Oklahoma (Football): *Shotguns*

The caretakers of the Sooner Schooner wagon are the spirit group called the RUF/NEKS, who *shoot-off modified shotguns* in celebration of scores by the home team.

University of Oklahoma (Football): *Sooner Schooner*

Since 1964, Oklahoma's two white ponies (*Boomer and Sooner*) have pulled a covered wagon called the *Sooner Schooner* around the field after each score.

SUNY Oswego (Ice Hockey): *Bagels Thrown on Ice*

In 1990, the Plattsburgh Hockey Boosters Club began a tradition of fans throwing hundreds of tennis balls onto the ice after the first SUNY Plattsburgh goal was scored against the visiting Lakers from SUNY Oswego. In 1998, Oswego shutout the Cardinals in Plattsburgh, denying fans the opportunity to throw any tennis balls. This accomplishment led to an Oswego countertradition of *throwing hundreds of bagels* (representing a zero) on their home ice following the first goal scored against the Cardinals in Oswego. This tradition of throwing bagels lasted for eighteen years but was finally ended by school administrators in 2008.

SUNY Plattsburgh (Ice Hockey): *Tennis Balls Thrown on Ice*

In 1990, the Plattsburgh Hockey Boosters Club began a tradition of fans *throwing hundreds of tennis balls* on to the ice after the first SUNY Plattsburgh goal was scored against the visiting Lakers from SUNY Oswego. It is believed that tennis balls were chosen because the head coach for Oswego's hockey team was also the school's tennis coach, and because tennis balls matched the bright yellow color of the Lakers' jerseys. This tradition of throwing tennis balls lasted for 18 years but was finally ended by school administrators in 2008.

University of Southern California (Football): *"Conquest" and Traveler*

Since 1961, whenever USC scores, the band plays "Conquest" and Traveler *gallops around the Coliseum.*

St. Lawrence University (Ice Hockey): *Fire Truck Horn*

For men's and women's ice hockey teams *a siren from an old fire truck is sounded* following each St. Lawrence goal.

Stephen F. Austin State University (Football): *Ole Cotton Cannon*

At every home football game, the Stephen F. Austin State (SFA) ROTC cadets man a 75-mm cannon dubbed *Ole Cotton*. From its station beyond

the south end zone at Homer Bryce Stadium, the big gun puts an exclamation point on every SFA scoring strike, as the cadets fire off a round to rally
the Lumberjacks and their fans.

University of Tennessee (Football): *Smokey Howling*

After each Tennessee touchdown, *Smokey howls*. Bluetick coonhounds
are bred to howl when finding what they are hunting (typically raccoons).
But Tennessee's Smokey's howl is triggered by a combination of applause
and a signal from one of his handlers.

University of Texas (Football): *Smokey the Cannon*

Smokey the Cannon, fires two blank ten-gauge shotgun shells after
each Texas football score, and at the end of the game—after a victory.
The cannon is operated by the *Texas Cowboys*, a men's campus service
organization.

University of Texas (Football): *Taps*

"Taps" is played following touchdowns and extra points at Texas football
games, as well as on thousands of other occasions.

Texas A&M (Football): *Kiss-Your-Date*

After the football team scores a TD or field goal, the *students kiss their
date* (in lean years, the students kissed after each 1st down).

Texas State University (Volleyball): *Point Bobcat and Ace-Your-Face*

After every point scored by the Bobcat volleyball team, the entire crowd
chants the words *"Point Bobcat"* immediately following the announcer's
statement of the sentence. If the Bobcats score an ace, an *Ace-Your-Face*
shirt is thrown into the crowd.

Texas Tech (Football): *Big Bertha*

After each touchdown, the *Saddle Tramps ring Big Bertha* (a large bell
in the end zone).

Union College/Hamilton College/Rensselaer Polytechnic Institute (Ice Hockey): *Oranges Thrown on the Ice*

The tradition of Union fans throwing oranges onto the ice following the first goal of the game scored by the Dutchmen against their rival—Hamilton—started in the late 1980s during the team's Division III days. When the Dutchmen moved up to Division I in 1991, Rensselaer Polytechnic Institute (RPI) became the target of the oranges. Union College's cafeteria would stop serving oranges three days before the game, as students began to accumulate them. The juice from the oranges actually turned the frozen ice the color orange. Also, the home team can be assessed a two-minute delay of game penalty if objects are thrown on the ice after a goal. That happened in a 1997 game between RPI and Union, and caused Union to lose momentum, with the game resulting in a tie. In 2002, Union's coach asked fans to refrain from this tradition. Now fans who throw anything onto the ice are ejected from the building.

West Virginia University (Football): *Musket Firing*

The Mountaineer mascot *shoots his musket* when the team scores.

4

TRADITIONS AFTER THE 00:00'S

For many fans and teams, the fun's just begun as the scoreboard clock winds down to zero. *Postgame traditions* are part of the DNA of college sports.

The props may vary. One school's *Victory Bell* is another's *roll of toilet paper*. Linking arms in Gainesville, Florida, as Gator fans sway and sing in unison "We Are the Boys of Old Florida" is nationally renowned. And since 1967, Eastern Kentucky University's (EKU) victorious football team has rocked the locker room with its rendition of "Cabin on the Hill," a country tune popularized by Lester Flatt and Earl Scruggs. Don't tell the Colonels their victory anthem doesn't resonate, especially when led by team chaplain Howard Miller, an EKU defensive tackle from 1972–1975.

It was once a hallowed and time-honored tradition in college football to *tear down the goalposts* when the home team unexpectedly won a game or snapped a long losing streak. But sadly—or happily if you are a college administrator or the NCAA—jubilant fans seldom sacrifice the goalposts anymore. In fact, many stadiums have electronic goalposts that automatically lower after the game ends. But without someone triggering the lowering of the goalposts, how can you prevent students like those at Georgia Tech in 1990, who after watching their team on TV upset then #1 ranked Virginia, raced to a dark Grant Field and tore down the goalposts there?

While tearing down goalposts is seldom seen, *rushing the court* in basketball is seen very often. Or as Jim Larranaga, head basketball coach at the University of Miami, told the *Sun Sentinel* in 2013 after their upset of then

#1 Duke, "Do you remember when you were in college? How much stress you felt about earning good grades and trying to pass a class? So to come out here and enjoy an athletic event and storm the court with your friends, those are memories. Those are things you remember for a lifetime."

And then there's *The Williams Walk*.

Williams College is an academic powerhouse, if not a BCS contender. The prestigious private school in Williamstown, Massachusetts, in the scenic heart of the Berkshires, is home to what *Sports Illustrated* called "The Best Postgame Tradition in America" in August of 1992.

The history of The Walk following a homecoming victory over arch rivals Amherst or Wesleyan dates back to 1971, Bob Odell's first season as the Ephs' head coach. Odell neither initiated The Walk nor encouraged it. It just happened, as many great college sports traditions do.

That November 13, Williams broke a three-game losing streak to Amherst with a 31–14 win at Weston Field. The field looks more like a high school gridiron: no large stadium, and family, friends, and classmates standing and watching from the sidelines. No tickets necessary. Anyone's allowed to watch for free. It is low-key but high-quality football.

In 1971, in the traditional finale of Williams' eight-game schedule, the Ephs—who'd been outscored 115–49 by Amherst in the three previous meetings—finally turned the corner.

"We were just so darn happy to have beaten Amherst, it did not surprise me to see our team go out the main gate and head up towards Spring Street," Odell said. "I just thought, well, isn't that nice, the boys look like they are having a little fun."

Odell walked over to his car, hopped in and drove back to Cole Field House. Back on the field, a tradition was born.

Many an Eph, still in uniform, has marched up Spring Street toward town after a big homecoming win over Amherst or Wesleyan. But that November day was the first time the team made The Walk en masse. As one.

Sixteen years later, St. Pierre's Barber Shop became the destination of choice for good. David Williams, an Eph star and Williamstown resident, told Roger St. Pierre that if the Ephs won and ended a four-year Walk drought, the boys would be dropping in to celebrate. This came after St. Pierre had told Williams tales of earlier Walks, and wondered if the custom could be revived.

"It was such a great tradition that he wished the players still did it," said Mike McLaughlin, class of 1989 and a senior on that team. "The week before homecoming, Dave told Roger that when we won, we'd be making The Walk. Roger and his long-time assistant Vern said they'd be ready for us.

"There were only about ten of us and we were all underclassmen," McLaughlin continued, "but we made The Walk. When we got to the barbershop, Roger and Vern were ready inside with beer and some hearty congratulations."

There were victory cigars, too, and well-aged stogies for a triumph well earned. "The crowds walking up Spring Street all took notice, and they seemed to get a kick out of it," McLaughlin said. Even Montgomery's twin brother, Gordon, who played for Amherst, stopped by—showered and dressed in a sport coat and tie by then, happy for his brother if not the day's outcome.

"You can't really get 75 to 100 football players into St. Pierre's," David Montgomery said. "But you can if you win the homecoming game."

Dick Farley, the Ephs' new head coach that season, coached until 2003 and is now in the College Football Hall of Fame. He was 16–0–1 in homecoming games, the lone blemish a 0–0 tie with Amherst on a quagmire on Weston Field in 1995.

"It's something the kids started and they got excited about it," Farley said of The Walk. "They don't want to be the team that doesn't walk, I know that much. But I've never seen it and I've no idea what goes on inside [the barbershop], except I've seen a few of the haircuts days later."

At times, a photographer has been admitted to the barbershop shenanigans. A videographer, too, and the occasional celebrity. But mainly it is Roger and the Ephs, celebrating with cigars. Sodas and water are the beverages of choice now. The barbershop rocks to the rhythm of the Williams fight song and the cheers of victory. Eph fans gather outside the shop to cheer and await the victors.

In 2007, ESPN's *Game Day* was on hand for the 122nd game versus Amherst. *Game Day* host Chris Fowler popped in St. Pierre's briefly to congratulate the Ephs and thank them for allowing ESPN access to homecoming and The Walk after their 20–0 victory over Amherst.

These days, the Williamstown Police Department closes Spring Street to traffic and hundreds of fans gather along the street and storefronts, some watching from second-floor apartments. Many more gather outside St. Pierre's to see who, and what, will emerge from the barbershop. Some Ephs have their hair, uh, styled, others shaved or shorn. Hey, the hair grows back and The Walk remains in memory.

"Beating Amherst is always a wonderful thing because they're such worthy opponents," said ex-Eph Ernie Smith. "At the time, there was nothing better. My days at Williams and that day in particular will always remain as a highlight in my life."

"There is no other tradition in college football today that means more to the student-athletes than The Walk," said former Williams coach Mike Whalen, who won his first five homecoming games. "Our players understand that in order to take The Walk up Spring Street, they must prepare as hard as they possibly can during the week before the game. If they're successful and earn the victory, then they're rewarded with The Walk with their teammates, supported by our fans, student body and families."

On November 14, 2009, the morning of homecoming, a group of Williams' football alums gathered to honor one of their own. Dave Shawan was the guy who led the Ephs up Spring Street on their initial Walk in 1971. Thirty-eight years later, that reunion of football alumni also included Shawan's sister, Diane.

Shawan died in 2008, succumbing after a long illness. He was memorialized that morning in St. Pierre's Barber Shop. There, a plaque was unveiled commemorating the birth of The Walk on November 13, 1971. The day Dave Shawan first led Williams up Spring Street. Ever since, no one in college football walks The Walk like the Ephs (as of 2012, the Ephs are 33–8–1 in homecoming games since The Walk started in 1971).

"The Williams Walk" through town after a homecoming victory.
Williams College / Kris Dufour

TRADITIONS AFTER THE 00:00'S BY SCHOOL

University of Arizona (Basketball): *Alma Mater*

At the end of every home game (and each Arizona athletics event where the band is present) the band plays Arizona's alma mater, "All Hail, Arizona!" Students and fans link arms and sway as they sing, and jump up and down while singing the last part of the song.

University of Arizona (Football): *Postgame Concert*

After every home game, fans and the band march to the administration building where the band performs a concert for the gathered fans. At the conclusion of the concert, the bell in the student union clock tower (one of the bells recovered from the *USS Arizona*, sunk at Pearl Harbor) is rung, and everyone responds by yelling "Bear Down!"

Assumption College (Football): *The Victory Bell*

Prior to the start of the 1996 Eagle football season, a large cast-iron bell was donated to the university anonymously. After some discussion, the bell was mounted on a pole and placed near the north end zone at Community Stadium. Following an incident with players from Westminster College during the 1998 season, the bell was moved to the south end zone area where it remains today. Following each Eagle home victory, it is tradition that *senior players take turns ringing the bell while the team sings the fight song.*

Auburn University (Various Sports): *Toomer's Corner*

Toomer's Corner is in the center of town, where the Auburn University campus meets the city of Auburn, and has long been the gathering place for Auburn athletic celebrations. Since 1963, after any football win and significant victories in other sports, Auburn students and citizens alike join forces to roll the trees (and anything else that doesn't move) at Toomer's Corner with toilet tissue. Celebrations after significant football victories can go on for hours and leave the heart of town looking like a blizzard passed through. Due to the well-publicized poisoning of the trees, Auburn announced in 2013 that the iconic trees would have to be removed. The university hosted one last block party at Toomer's Corner on April 20, 2013, to allow fans a final opportunity to gather near the landmarks.

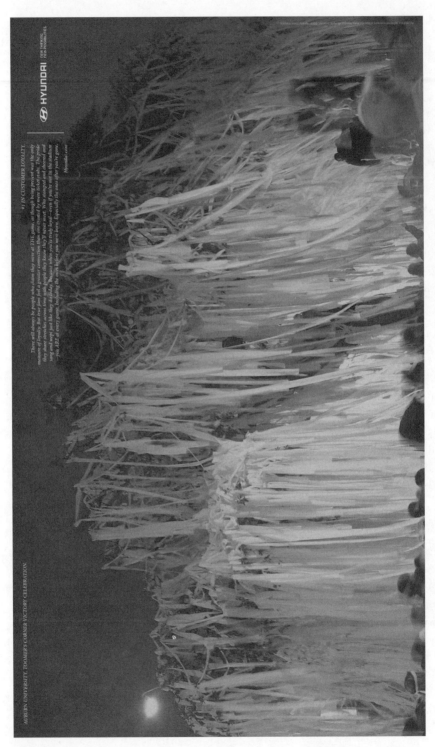

Auburn's "Rolling of Toomer's Corner" after a victory. Claire Harbison; ©CG Harbison Photography

Baylor University (Football): *Helmets Raised*

After a game, Baylor's school song, "That Good Old Baylor Line" is played. Football players traditionally *hold up their helmets* during the playing of the school song.

Bethany College (Kansas) (Various Sports): *Bell Ringing*

When a Swedes' athletic team wins their conference championship, they gather in front of Hahn Gymnasium to *ring the bell* and spread the news to the rest of the campus, regardless of what time of day—or night—it may be. The old bell tower was located southwest of Old Main, but was moved to its present tower outside the gym in the late 1960s.

Bowling Green State University (Football): *Singing "Forward Falcons"*

The team sings "Forward Falcons" after each victory.

Brigham Young University–Hawaii (Basketball): *Free Ice Cream*

At every home basketball game (men's or women's), if Brigham Young University–Hawaii scores 100 points or more and wins, their food services provides *free ice cream* following the game to everyone who attends (and is willing to wait in line for their ice cream). This tradition has led to some interesting twists to their games, including chants from the fans of "Ice Cream!" anytime the team appears on their way to 100 points. Sometimes the chant is, "We want, we want ice cream!" to the tune of "We Will Rock You" by Queen. They have had opposing coaches go into a stalling tactic to prevent them from reaching 100 and they have had their own coach booed when he told the team to dribble out the clock when they were a basket away from hitting 100. They have also had players (usually reserves) feel extraordinary pressure at the free throw line with just seconds remaining in the game and a chance for them to put their team to the century mark with made free throws (they usually fail under the pressure and the chants). The player who puts the team into triple digits is revered as a hero for the night and into the following week.

Dakota Wesleyan University (Football): *Seniors Sing the Fight Song*

When their football team wins at home, the seniors all stand up on the sideline benches and *sing the Dakota Wesleyan University fight song*.

Dakota Wesleyan University (Women's Soccer): *Team Sings after a Victory*

When their women's soccer team wins at home, they get in a circle at midfield after the game and sing "Climbing-Up Sunshine Mountain."

Dallas Baptist University (Basketball): *Victory Bell*

A *bell is rung* after each victory.

Florida Atlantic University (Various Sports): *Alma Mater*

After an athletic contest, the team *sings the alma mater*.

Florida State University (Football): *Sod Cemetery*

FSU has a *sod cemetery*, with grave markers signifying big wins. For nearly six decades, sod games and the Florida State University sod cemetery have been a rich part of the Seminoles' college football history, commemorating many of the greatest victories. In 1962, as the Seminoles completed their Thursday practice in preparation of facing Georgia at Sanford Stadium, Dean Coyle Moore—a long-time professor and member of FSU's athletic board—issued a challenge: "Bring back some sod from between the hedges at Georgia." On Saturday, October 20, the Seminoles scored an 18–0 victory over the favored Bulldogs. Team captain Gene McDowell pulled a small piece of grass from the field, which was presented to Moore at the next football practice. Moore and FSU coach Bill Peterson had the sod buried on the practice field as a symbol of victory. A monument was placed to commemorate the triumph and the tradition of the sod game was born. Since then, before leaving for all road games in which Florida State is the underdog, all road games at the University of Florida and all ACC championship and bowl games, Seminole captains gather their teammates to explain the significance of the tradition. Victorious captains return with a piece of the opponent's turf to be buried in the sod cemetery outside the gates of the practice field. Away from home and against the odds, Florida State sod games represent the most difficult battles on the football field. The sod cemetery stands as a tribute to those triumphs, to be enjoyed by the Seminole faithful.

FSU's "Sod Cemetery" celebrating key victories. Dave Spataro; ©Dave Spataro Photography

Fordham University (Football): *Ringing the Victory Bell*

A *graduating senior rings a bell* after each football victory. The bell was taken off the Japanese ship *Junyo* and was given to the university by Admiral Chester W. Nimitz as a memorial to the dear young dead of World War II.

University of Georgia (Football): *Ringing the Chapel Bell*

The *ringing of the chapel bell* after a Georgia victory is a tradition that continues even though freshmen are no longer ordered to do the chore. In the 1890s, the playing field was located only yards from the chapel, and first year students were compelled to ring the bell until midnight in celebration of a Bulldog victory. Today, students, alumni, and townspeople still rush to the chapel to ring the bell after a gridiron victory.

Lake Superior State University (Ice Hockey): *Gauntlet and Bell Ringing*

After each home ice hockey win, the Lakers, still wearing their hockey gear, change into their tennis shoes, put on tuques (stocking caps), and line up in an order determined by the team (sometimes the leader wears a hard

Lake Superior State's hockey players "Ringing a Bell" after an ice hockey victory. *Lake Superior State University*

hat, a relatively new twist). They *run through a gauntlet of fans* and head outside to ring the *Hololik/Husband Victory Bell*. The impressively large victory bell was acquired from a New York church in 1992. Incidentally, the Lakers won one of their three NCAA titles that year.

University of Nebraska Omaha (Ice Hockey): *Team Sings the Fight Song*

The hockey team convenes in the lobby of their arena and sings their fight song after a win.

University of North Carolina (Basketball): *Fire Jumping*

Students celebrate big basketball victories by *hopping over open flames*.

North Carolina State University (Basketball): *Cutting Down Basketball Nets*

North Carolina State coach Everett Case did not realize he was starting a trend in 1947. He just wanted a souvenir. *USA Today*'s Michael Gluskin wrote a terrific piece on the origins of college hoops' net-cutting tradition in 2005. According to Gluskin, Coach Case was so delighted with the Wolfpack's Southern Conference title win that he decided to cut down the nets as souvenirs. Of course, being a pioneer can be tough. Since Case was the first coach to cut down the nets, arena workers did not have a ladder at the ready for his big moment. Instead, his players had to hoist their coach onto their shoulders as he did his snipping. Case might not have been the true inventor of the *net-cutting tradition*, though. While he deservedly gets credit for being the college coach who popularized the net-cutting ritual, some sources—including Tim Peeler's *Legends of NC State Basketball*—claim Case actually brought the tradition with him from Indiana, where he'd been a hugely successful high school coach before coming to Raleigh to coach the Wolfpack. Either way, cutting down the nets may have remained an obscure Hoosier State tradition had Case not brought the practice to the national stage. And today, even the ladders that are used at the national championship games (and maybe even the regional championships) are sponsored. Only Werner Ladders are used by the winning teams in the postgame net-cutting ceremonies for Divisions I, II, and III men's and women's basketball championships.

University of North Texas (Various Sports): *Tower Lights*

When North Texas played Southern Methodist University (SMU) in the fall of 1974, North Texas lost 7–6. After the game, the administration doors were found painted red and blue. This eventually led to the idea of the current tower lights. Talons (a spirit group) installed the spotlights on McConnell Tower on November 10, 1977. The Talons *turn on the lights* after all North Texas varsity team victories. After evening home football games, Talons lead the victory march from Fouts Field to the tower. Standing atop the administration building steps, the Talons lead the crowd in singing the alma mater and the UNT fight song. The lights are also turned on for special occasions.

Northwestern University (Football): *Singing of "Go U"*

Players rush to the student section to join in singing *"Go U"* after a win. Northwestern premiered "Go U" during the November 23, 1912, game with Illinois. The band played it twice in a row due to the wild crowd reaction. It has become the basis for many other college and high school fight songs.

Northwestern University (Various Sports): *Purple Clock*

This began in 1995 when Northwestern decided to have a little fun by lighting the (normally white) clock face of the *Rebecca Crown Clock Tower* a brilliant purple. The university decided to keep the clock face purple until the team lost a game, and a tradition was born. If the clock face is white and the team wins, the purple returns. One part of the tradition came to an end in 2006 when the team won the last game of the season, the clock stayed purple during the entire off-season. Now during the football off-season, the university uses the purple clock face to denote wins in other Northwestern sports.

Northwestern University (Football): *Trust-Yourself Board*

Beginning in 2008 a new tradition was instituted: placing the helmet sticker of the opposing team on the top of their *Trust-Yourself Board* (in the locker room) after a win.

University of Notre Dame (Football): *Raising Helmets*

Many teams raise their helmets after a win, but Notre Dame *raising their helmets* to the student section after a win or loss is arguably the best example of this.

University of Notre Dame (Various Sports): *Alma Mater*

At the conclusion of every home game, the band plays the *alma mater*, "Notre Dame, Our Mother." Those who stay link arms and sing the lyrics.

Occidental College: *Victory Flag*

A huge orange flag with a block "O" was given to the College in 1934 by *the O-Club*, an organization of varsity lettermen. Designated the *Victory Flag*, it was hung between Johnson and Fowler Halls to celebrate an Occidental victory, whether a debate contest, or athletic event, with some irregularity over the years but for certain after a football victory over rival Pomona College. The flag disappeared from public display sometime in the last half of the 1950s. We wonder where is it now?

The Ohio State University (Football): *Victory Bell*

The *Victory Bell* is rung after every Ohio State football victory by members of Alpha Phi Omega, a tradition that began after the Buckeyes beat California on October 2, 1954. Reputedly the ringing can be heard five miles away on a calm day.

Oklahoma State University (Football): *Lewis Field Leap*

The *Lewis Field Leap* is often done at the conclusion of the singing of the alma mater—and especially after a win by the home team. The Leap, whose name is derived from the original name of Boone Pickens Stadium, started as an impromptu celebration by Cowboy football players who would jump into the Oklahoma State student section. The Leap quickly grew in popularity, and now it is not uncommon to see many players scale the Boone Pickens Stadium walls and join their fellow students in celebrating a Cowboy victory.

St. Joseph's University (Basketball): *Double-Dip/Ultimate Double-Dip*

When St. Joseph's wins a basketball game, a single dip of ice cream is often ordered after a game. If Villanova loses on the same night, it calls for a second color of ice cream, and is known as a *Double Dip*. A cherished tradition by many of the die-hard Hawk fans, the Double Dip is a victory that is twice as sweet. The *Ultimate Double Dip* occurs every time the Hawks beat the Cats.

St. Lawrence University (Ice Hockey): *Fire Truck Horn*

A *siren from an old fire truck is sounded* after each St. Lawrence University win, for both men's ice hockey (since 1977) and women's ice hockey (since 1980).

St. Lawrence University (Various Sports): *Ringing the Victory Bell*

A majority of the St. Lawrence University Division III athletic teams (men and women) ring the *Victory Bell* located in the center of the athletic quad following home victories.

Seton Hall University (Basketball): *Alma Mater*

After a home victory, their men's basketball team links arms and *sings the alma mater*.

Stephen F. Austin State University (Various Sports): *Purple Light*

After every Stephen F. Austin State University victory in any sport, at home or on the road, the university *turns on a large purple light* that sits atop the *Garner Tower*, the tallest building on campus. The building's roof remains illuminated all night to let all who see it know that their Lumberjacks or Ladyjacks were victorious.

University of Texas (Various Sports): *Colored Lights on the UT Tower*

The twenty-seven-story main building—the *UT Tower*—is bathed in orange-colored lights that stands as a beacon to the Longhorns' success.

Orange lights first flooded the tower in 1937. In 1947, guidelines were created for using the orange lights. A Number "1" on all sides highlighted by orange lights signals that the university won a national championship. The full tower glowing orange alone represents a victory over Texas A&M, commencement, and other occasions the president deems appropriate. The tower top bathed in orange symbolizes other victories or a conference title in any intercollegiate sport.

Tower Entirely White
Standard tower lighting

Tower with White Top and Orange Shaft
Academic and staff achievements
> Faculty academic achievements (Academic Convocation)
> Student academic achievements (Honors Day)
> Staff achievements (Staff Recognition Day)
> Academic team achievements with #1 displayed
> Other events at the president's discretion

Tower with Orange Top and White Shaft
Athletic achievements
> Football regular season victories, except Texas A&M
> Non–Bowl Championship Series (BCS) victories
> Other events at the president's discretion

Tower Entirely Orange
Significant Athletic Victories
> Football victories
> Texas A&M
> Big 12 South
> Big 12 championship game
> Big 12 regular season team championship
> Big 12 tournament championships
> Student organization sports club national championships

Tower Entirely Orange with #1 Displayed
Athletic championships
> Football Bowl Championship Series (BCS) #1 vs. #2 win
> NCAA championships for all other sports

Tower Entirely Orange
Campus-wide accolades
   University of Texas' Birthday—September 15
   Commencement
   Texas Independence Day—March 2
   Other campus-wide events at the president's discretion

Darkened Tower with White Cap and Observation Deck
Solemn occasions
   Configuration: All other levels dark, including windows
   UT Remembers (annual memorial service)
   Tower Garden dedication
   Significant solemn occasions, (e.g., Texas A&M bonfire tragedy)
   Other occasions at the president's discretion

Tower Top Split Orange and White with Orange Shaft
Symbolic campus events
   Gone to Texas—welcoming new students to campus
   Other events at the president's discretion

Tower with Special Effects or Numbering
Special effects

The complete list of UT Tower policies can be found in *On Campus*, published by the Office of Public Affairs for The University of Texas at Austin community. Publication is monthly during the academic year, except holiday periods.

Texas Tech (Various Sports): *Victory Bells*

In 1936, *victory bells* were given to Texas Tech as a class gift. The bells rang for the first time at the 1936 class's graduation. It is said that after the win over Texas Christian University, the following year the bells rang throughout the night, keeping Lubbock residents up all night. Thereafter, the bell ringing was limited to thirty minutes. *Saddle Tramps* ring the bells after Texas Tech victories and during special occasions. The Victory Bells— one large and one small, which combine to weigh 1,200 pounds—hang in the east tower of the administration building.

Utah State University (Basketball): *End of Game Chant*

The home crowd makes sure everyone knows who won the game. The creative *winning team/losing team* chant rings out across the arena.

Vanderbilt University (Football): *Players Sing the Fight Song*

Before James Franklin arrived at Vanderbilt (as their head coach), the players did not know the words to "Dynamite," the university's fight song. Now freshmen are forced to learn it, and all players sing it in the locker room after a game. Players also sing the alma mater with fans on the field after games.

Wake Forest University (Various Sports): *Rolling the Quad*

Students cover the quad with toilet paper after big wins. This tradition started in 1961, after a campus move robbed students of a bell to ring in celebration. *Toilet-papering the quad* has become the victory dance of choice for everything from football wins to presidential elections.

West Virginia University (Various Sports): *Singing "Country Roads"*

"Country Roads" is the unofficial song of the university. In 1980, John Denver performed his hit song "Take Me Home, Country Roads" at the dedication of Mountaineer Field, and it has since become tradition for fans to remain in the stands following every Mountaineer victory and sing the song with the players. Although the tradition originated during football games, it is now recognized throughout the university, with the song being performed at various athletic events and ceremonies. *Sports Illustrated* named the singing of "Country Roads" as one of their must-see college traditions.

5

ANNUAL TRADITIONS

Like Christmas, *OOzeball* comes but once a year to UConn. And like Christmas morning, OOzeball's worth its twelve-month wait.

In Hanover, New Hampshire, there's the folly and the ivy of Dartmouth's century-old *Winter Carnival*. In Philadelphia, the *Penn Relays* are a tradition as rich as Philadelphia Brand Cream Cheese, as hometown as Yuengling Lager, as tasty as Tasty Kakes and cheesesteaks. And, if you dare, scrapple.

In Des Moines, the *Drake Relays* rule when outdoor track and field springs to life each spring. Ever seen indoor pole vaulting in a mall? You can here.

And if track and field's your choice of sporting fare, by all means drop by the recently reborn *Beloit Relays* in Wisconsin. Like many sporting perennials—the *Aggie A* at Colorado State, *Midnight Madness* at Maryland, and almost every college—thank you, Lefty Driesell—a fresh coat of war paint on the *Tecumseh Statue* at the United States Naval Academy and hundreds of other annual college traditions, the Beloit Relays long had their own lore, too.

Including, of course, Beloit's *Olde English Country Classic*, which sounds like a Wisconsin craft beer, but is one fine footrace, where cross-country runners jump over bales of hay, water hazards, and who knows what else.

In 1937, when Lou Means was the athletic director at Beloit College, a small liberal arts college in Wisconsin, he established a track event for

The Beloit Relays.
Beloit College

Beloit College
hosts a classic Ole
English cross-country
race each year.
Beloit College

small, liberal arts colleges like Beloit—much like the heralded Drake Relays for larger institutions. The initial Beloit Relays were won by Coe College of Iowa, with Beloit finishing second. Some 146 athletes from 12 colleges took part. That number would grow considerably.

The Beloit Relays were held from 1937–1979, although there were no relays from 1943–1945 during World War II and again from 1973–1974. In those earlier years, more than 300 athletes took part and crowds of more than 3,000 jammed the stadium.

When the legendary Herb Hodges became the track and field head coach in 1947, he led the Buccaneers to team wins in the Relays from 1949–1951 before leaving for the University of Alabama.

The Bucs didn't stop there. When Hodges returned to Beloit in 1954, the team recorded another Relays victory. Down through the years, Beloit had fifty-six individual victories in the Relays, second only to Wheaton College's seventy.

But after a change in the college administration, along with changes in curriculum and scheduling difficulties, the Beloit Relays lay dormant for more than three decades. In the spring of 2013, however, after a thirty-four-year absence, the Beloit Relays were back in the running, conducted on the new Karris Track and Field complex at Strong Stadium. It's wonderful when a beloved annual tradition, long dormant, is reborn again.

For the last half century, however, Beloit's Olde English Country Classic has flourished. A cross-country race that debuted in 1961 has become one of the most popular in the Midwest, and one of the few remaining English-style cross-country competitions. On homecoming weekend, up to forty of the region's top men's and women's teams converge on Beloit's Leeson Park for the women's 5K and men's 8K races. It also attracts a large contingent of cross-country and track and field alumni, who typically run as open competitors.

The open event, which starts with a bugle call and pistol shot, features the competition for the *Shoehorn Trophy*. In 2010, Beloit faculty and staff—along with spouses and partners—outran teams from Ripon College and Lawrence University to take home the Shoehorn. The trophy's comprised of antique running spikes from Beloit's athletic department, and an antique bugle donated by a Beloit faculty member.

The annual *Winter Carnival* at Dartmouth began in 1911, and continues to this day. Its beginnings were modest: snowshoeing and cross-country skiing. It now includes extravagant musical and dramatic productions, the crowning of a Snow Queen, bonfires, toboggan races, snow-sculpting competitions, fireworks, and parades.

Recent carnivals have included a human dogsled race, a polar bear swim, and, in costume, the *Carnival Classic Cross-Country Ski Race.*

In a word? Brrrrrrr. Big Green of Dartmouth wouldn't have it any other way.

Here's mud in your eye: *OOzeball.* A fabulous, if filthy, tradition, that originated at the University of Connecticut, it's been thrice-heralded by *Sports Illustrated* as:

Best Mud Volleyball in the Country.

33rd on the Top 100 Things You Gotta Do Before You Graduate: No Matter the Cost.

Best Use of Dirt (*SI On Campus*)

OOzeball, now a very popular tradition at many colleges, is volleyball played in eight inches of mud on each of twelve courts. It is usually staged as a charity fundraiser. It is always as the headline from a Manchester, Connecticut, Patch.com story said, "There Will Be Mud."

"Forget Sparta," Beren Jones wrote. "This. Is. *OOZEBALL!*"

"The most epic day of the year," UConn student Amy McDavitt said. Coed Carolina Rogi said she didn't play for money, rather "Pride, and lots of mud ... in strange places."

OOzeball, not surprisingly, is held in the spring semester. The mud forces players to adapt to a different style of play than in volleyball. More leaning and lunging than running in the mud. On the UConn campus in Storrs, more than 1,000 players and spectators turn out to watch the mud, sweat, and tears of laughter.

On another OOzeball video, a UConn coed looked into the camera and explained, "This is OOzeball. It's a mess. It's dirty. It's a lot of mud." She paused. "Yes, foosball's fun. But, OOzeball? It's awesome," she said. "You should do it."

In 2013, UConn OOzeball celebrated its thirtieth year. It's the longest-running event of its kind in the country.

As they say in Storrs, "Win or lose, we still OOze."

What began back in 1898 as a *tug-of-war* between high school sophomores and incoming freshmen has become an annual, autumnal tradition at Hope College in Holland, Michigan. One that pulls at the heartstrings as well as the hamstrings, and almost every other muscle in the human body.

The Pull: Tug-of-war, taken to the max.

"To the realm of art," Michael Finkel wrote about it in a 1996 *Sports Illustrated* article. "Or lowers it to the theater of the absurd."

"The Pull" at Hope College. *Hope College*

Picture this: Since 1898, across the cold Black River, 150 feet wide at this particular point, Hope freshmen are on one shore, sophomores on the other. A rope spans the Black River, but to call this line a rope hardly does it justice. Just as, Finkel wrote, "Referring to The Pull as a tug-of-war is like calling Buckingham Palace a nice house."

This particular rope, the Moby Dick of ropes, was made of three-strand Manila hemp—the best use of hemp since Woodstock?—two-inches thick, a 600-foot-long monster that weighed in at 648 pounds.

On one side were eighteen freshmen pullers and eighteen sophomore pullers on the far bank. Pullers pull, yet far more than their own weight. Tryouts for The Pull are open to any Hope freshmen or sophomores. An advisory: Practice can be—no, make that, *are*—brutal. Pull wannabes may have to pull on trees. Trucks. On hefty Pull alums, too.

Eventually, eighteen pullers are selected for each side, with two alternates per team. The chosen ones will obey the *Constitution of the Hope College Freshmen–Sophomore Pull*, a code of conduct of sorts with a preamble, five articles, and twenty-seven bylaws. Or else.

Pullers are educated in the fine art of pulling by several types of coaches: regular coaches, an anchor coach for—what else?—the anchor or last puller of the rope, a moraler for each puller, and others. Moralers are The Pull's equivalent of individual cheerleaders. And upperclassmen coach each team. All told, teams can have as many as ten coaches or more. Hope juniors coaching freshmen, and seniors coaching sophomores. The entire university is involved, so in reality, it is the even years struggling against the odd years.

As a personal touch, pullers get Pull nicknames. No, not Flounder as in *Animal House*. More like Assassin. Earthquake. Lunatic. You know, Harley handles.

Then comes not Zen, but the fine art of The Pull pit. Digging your own personal Pull pit, a foxhole about the size of a two-foot cube. This is where each puller will do most of his or her work and agonizing.

In the early years of The Pull, teams were prone for the first fifteen minutes or so, then stood up simultaneously and pulled from an upright position 'til the bitter—or glorious—end. Nowadays, pullers dig their own pits—two-feet deep, two-feet wide—spacing them about eighteen inches apart, one behind the other. Each pit is reinforced with plywood at the foot, or the end closer to the Black River.

As Zach "Lunatic" Johnson explained to Finkel in 1996, "We dig our own graves."

The puller lies on his side in the hole, bracing his feet against the ply-wood, two hands on the rope between his legs. The Pull's version of a flak jacket is a large vest worn by each puller, cushioned with rolls of toilet pa-per, perhaps, or shag carpet remnants? Hey, whatever works.

This is all synchronized, too. Like wrestlers, pullers have moves that must be coordinated: Heaves. Strains. Counter rocks. Lock-downs. All of these are orchestrated by the head Pull coach, "Playing the part of the coxswain," as Finkel wrote. All of this done while standing on a table in front of the first pit and signaling moves. The moralers, in turn, call the signals to the pull-ers, since they are often too focused to pay attention to the head Pull coach.

With the rope already sprayed with fluorescent orange paint in front of each team's first pit, a whistle is blown. The Pull has just begun. And the crowd that often approaches several thousand, goes crazy!

Moralers—pronounced "morale-ers"—relay their signal caller's instruc-tions, chanting. Finkel recorded it all for *Sports Illustrated*: "Inch and up. Inch and up. Look and look. Heave! Heeeeeeeeeave! Lock and in. Lock and in. Strain! Straaaaaaaaain!" Moralers are also each pullers individual cheering section, often whispering words of encouragement into their puller's ear for three hours, or more.

The pullers and moralers have long become as one. Each boy picks a girl to be his moraler, on occasion renting a tux, getting down on one knee, with a rose in his hand, and asking "Will you please be my moraler?"

She says "yes," and, who knows? It's more than urban legend that many pullers and moralers eventually get married due to the true intimacy of the combined effort for The Pull.

Believe this: not every puller is a guy. In 1995, Keri Law—the Sally Ride of the Pull—became the first woman chosen as a puller. Law, class of 1999, would have competed in that 1995 Pull but injured her knee in practice. She competed as a puller in the 1996 Pull.

You go, Keri.

Some Fun Pull Facts

2012 was the 115th Pull.

The four years when The Pull was not held were 1918, 1943, and 1944 (war years), and 1957 (a flu epidemic on the Hope campus prompted its cancellation).

The Longest Pull: 1977 was three hours, fifty-one minutes. It was called a draw, one of four ties in Pull history (along with 1916, 1926, and 1952). It also prompted a rule change in 1978: The Pull was limited to a maximum of three hours. At the end of three hours, judges may declare a winner by measuring the rope again.

The shortest Pull was in 1956: two minutes, forty seconds.

The shortest Pull after new rules were implemented in 1978: sixty-seven minutes.

Shortest winning margin: In 1995, the sophomore class of 1998 won by two feet, ten inches.

Pull-on, Hope.

ANNUAL TRADITIONS BY SCHOOL

Angelo State University (Rodeo): San Angelo Stock Show

Angelo State is heavily involved in this annual event that has been held for over eighty years, attracting top ropers from across the nation.

Boston College (Football): The Drive

Students look forward to *driving fifteen hours to South Bend*, Indiana, when Boston College plays Notre Dame in football.

BYU-Hawaii (Basketball): *Asia–Pacific Basketball Tournament*

For a number of years, BYU has *hosted the Asia–Pacific Basketball Tournament* every November. This tournament brings teams from the Pacific Rim to Laie, Hawaii, for exhibition games and friendship. Both the men's and women's teams serve as hosts and the games constitute their preseason exhibitions each year. The visiting teams are given chances to play other schools as well (Hawaii Pacific, Chaminade), tour the island, and attend a banquet at the Polynesian Cultural Center for all of the teams. Recently, a women's team came from China, and men's teams from China, Tahiti, and New Zealand also came. Because BYU-Hawaii is an international school (over 50 percent of their student body is international, more than any other school in the United States) their students always give the visiting teams a built-in cheering section, waving their national flags and cheering wildly for the visiting teams. Coincidently, if BYU scores 100 points against an international team, all fans in attendance *get free ice cream.*

Cal State Fullerton (Baseball): *Slapping/Kissing a Sign*

After twenty-one years of traveling to NCAA Regionals, attempting to earn berths into the College World Series, the Titans finally qualified to host a tournament in 2000, and the next year they hosted, and won, a Regional and a Super Regional to qualify for another trip to Omaha— before the home fans for the first time. Spontaneously, after a 9-3 win over Mississippi State, the players ran as a group to right-centerfield and *slapped*, and even *kissed*, *an outfield fence advertising sign* paid for by a player's parent's business with copy that included how many miles (1,544) it was to Omaha. Each subsequent time Cal State-Fullerton has qualified for Omaha (2003, 2004, 2006, 2007 and 2009), the practice has been repeated.

Case Western Reserve University: *The Hudson Relays*

The Hudson Relays is an annual tradition at Case Western Reserve University that occurs on the last weekend before finals every spring semester. It is a relay race between teams drawn from each class year. The race is a distance of 26 miles (42 km). Originally, the race was run from Hudson, Ohio, the original site of Western Reserve University, to the present location of the school in University Circle. Since the mid-1980s, the race has been run entirely in the University Circle area. University tradition is that if a class wins the relay for each of its four years, the team will be rewarded with a champagne and steak dinner with the president of the university. The winning class for each year is carved on a boulder located behind Adelbert Hall.

Clemson University (Football): *First-Friday Parade*

The Clemson football season kicks off each year with the annual *First Friday Parade*. The once-a-year event takes place on the Friday afternoon prior to the first home football game. Floats from various fraternities and sororities and other campus organizations are represented in the parade that rolls down Main Street in Clemson. The parade culminates at the Amphitheater in the middle of campus where the first pep rally of the year takes place. The Grand Marshall of the parade is featured at the Pep Rally. Recent Grand Marshall's have ranged from PGA professional Dillard Pruitt, to College Football Hall of Fame legends Jess Neely and Frank Howard, to noted television announcers Brent Musburger and Ara Parseghian.

Clemson University (Football): *Tigerama*

The Friday evening prior to the homecoming game, *Tigerama* is held in Death Valley, an event that often attracts over 35,000 fans. The homecoming queen and her court are presented in addition to homecoming skits, a pep rally, and a large and loud fireworks display.

Colorado State University (Various Sports): *Aggie A*

The *Aggie A* is a whitewashed rock formation 450' tall by 210' wide that was created by students in 1923. Whitewashing the "A" is done yearly by freshmen students/athletes. During this annual tradition, students have the opportunity to hike to the "A." Before the hike begins, students are given a small white pebble to carry with them. The half-mile hike takes students on a scenic trek leading them to the tip of the "A" where they are met by members of the Student Alumni Connection and learn about the significance of the "A." As students prepare to make their descent back down the hill, they are encouraged to reflect upon the mark they will leave at CSU, and are asked to each leave their pebble as a symbol of that mark.

Colorado State freshmen contribute white stones to the "the Aggie-A" each year. *Colorado State University Athletics*

Colorado State University (Various Sports): *I Love CSU Day*

In 2001, Student Alumni Connection members established *I Love CSU Day*, a day dedicated to demonstrating pride for Colorado State University. On I Love CSU Day, the entire campus community is encouraged to show its green and gold spirit, and the day is marked as a celebration, complete with giveaways, promotions, and entertainment. In recent years, the governor of the State of Colorado has taken notice of this day and has declared April 18 as *Colorado State University Day*. Each year, the governor acknowledges this day by signing a proclamation.

Dartmouth College (Various Sports): *Dartmouth Night*

Dartmouth Night starts the college's traditional homecoming weekend with an evening of speeches, a parade, and a bonfire. Traditionally, the freshman class builds the bonfire and then runs around it a set number of times to match their class year i.e., (the class of 2009 performed 109 circuits, the class of 1999 performed 99, etc.).

Division II Schools: *Harlan Hill Trophy*

This trophy, named for a North Alabama All-American, is given to the best Division II player each year.

Drake University (Track & Field): *Drake Relays*

As part of the *Drake Relays*, a *Beautiful Bulldog* contest is held. The annual winner becomes the mascot of that year's Drake Relays.

East Carolina University (Various Sports): *Spring Festival*

East Carolina has the annual *Great Pirate Purple/Gold Pigskin Party*, a spring festival of baseball, golf, tennis, and their spring football game.

Elmira College (Volleyball): *Halloween Tournament*

Elmira College Women's Volleyball has a doubles tournament tradition. The catch is the tournament is held around Halloween and teams must dress up and play in costume. Each teams' costume has a theme. After the tournament everyone gets a prize and award. The tournament acts as a great buffer between the regular season and post season.

Fredonia State University (Ice Hockey): *Dad's Weekend*

Hockey players and their dads spend a weekend together. One of the highlights is a slide-show showing the players when they were much younger.

Hanover College: *Annual Snowball Fight*

On the night of the first significant snowfall students head to the Quad for the Annual *Snowball Fight*.

Harvard (Swimming): *Iron Man Meet*

Many coaches like to use a swim-the-meet set the day after a big meet. In this workout, swimmers go through and swim the entire meet schedule as a way to stretch themselves out and focus on their swims from the day before. The Harvard men's swim team, however, takes this concept to a physical and mental extreme at their annual *Iron Man* meet. Because, you see, every year, a freshman is voted by his teammates to swim the entire meet schedule … in a meet. Depending on the meet format that is used in any given year, that comes out to roughly 4,200 yards of race-pace swimming in just under 2 hours. Think about that for a second, and try not to cringe. Most swimmers would see such a torturous schedule as a punishment. But to a special group of masochistic freshmen, there is no bigger honor than to be elected as Harvard's Iron Man. This is because it is a sign of respect and acceptance by the rest of the team, which is always a huge hurdle for any freshman to overcome. In the words of Harvard assistant coach Kevin Tyrrell, "the tradition means a great deal, as the freshman who is chosen has earned the respect of the upperclassmen." As a sign of this respect, after the meet the Iron Man is paraded around the pool-deck on a stretcher while Black Sabbath's "Iron Man" blasts from the natatorium's sound system. As far as anyone can specifically remember, the tradition dates back to at least 1996. The list of previous recipients of the honor include the open water World Champion Alex Meyer, and several of the biggest names in the history of Harvard swimming. There is also a diver, Henry Winslow, on the list, which means he must have made a serious impression on his teammates. Former Harvard swimmer Rassan Grant joked once that "there is even speculation that [former President and Crimson swimmer John F. Kennedy] was an Iron Man in the past," though there's no indication that he actually was.

John Brown University (Volleyball): *Rugby Team/Women's Dresses*

At the first home volleyball game, the rugby team *dresses in women's dresses* and parades into the arena just about the time the first game is to begin. They sit/stand behind the bench and cheer on the team (loudly) during the entire match.

Kansas State University (Football): *Harley Day Game*

Harleys circle the stadium before the annual *Harley Day* football game. During Harley Day, Willie (the mascot) wears a leather vest or jacket with leather chaps on top of his usual football jersey and pants and rides into Bill Snyder Family Stadium on a Harley-Davidson motorcycle, followed by 50 other K-State fans on motorcycles.

Longwood University (Soccer): *G.A.M.E.*

G.A.M.E stands for *Greatest Athletic March Ever* and in 2013 (for the 4th year) was held before the first women's soccer match of the season at Longwood University. The march through the town of Farmville, Virginia, features 2,000 students, faculty, staff, alumni, and community members. It starts with a tailgate buffet, then covers an uphill course—over 2 miles—and ends at the soccer stadium with a pep rally. Girls wear custom-designed scarves during the march, and their scarves even have their own Facebook page.

McMurry University (Football): *Homecoming*

McMurry focuses their homecoming on their Indian heritage. Social Clubs build a Tipi Village, a reconstruction of authentic Indian dwellings.

University of Minnesota Duluth (Ice Hockey): *Freshmen Introductions*

Before one of the school's first home football games each fall, the hockey team's upperclassmen tell the freshman hockey players to wear a suit and tie on Saturday, so that at halftime the newcomers can be introduced to the thousands of Bulldog fans at Malosky Stadium. Each year the nattily attired freshmen march to the 50-yard line and wait for their name to be called. And they keep waiting, and waiting, gradually realizing (too late) that the joke is on them. Finally, after a few minutes, the public address announcer usually booms, "Hey, you kids, GET OFF THE FIELD!"

Minnesota State University, Mankato (Ice Hockey): *Hawaiian Night*

This is modeled after Southwestern Minnesota State University's *Hawaiian Night* for basketball. It began in 2012.

University of Missouri/University of Oklahoma (Football): *Peace Pipe*

Starting in 1929, at halftime of the Missouri–Oklahoma game, the *Tiger–Sooner Peace Pipe* was smoked between groups from each school. Sadly, recent conference realignment has affected this long-standing tradition.

University of Missouri (Football): *Homecoming*

Although it's a now-popular tradition at all colleges, *homecoming* is often said to have originated at Missouri. Beginning in 1911, Missouri's director of athletics wanted to spice up the already fierce rivalry between his school and Kansas. In order to do so, he invited all alumni to come home for the game. Several other schools also claim the first homecoming.

University of Missouri (Football): *Seniors After Last Game*

Seniors playing their last game help themselves to one of the white stones making up a vast *Rock M* above the north end zone.

Northwestern University (Various Sports): *Painting the Rock*

The Rock itself, a purple and white chunk of quartzite, was installed by the class of 1902 and briefly served as a water fountain (until the pipes froze and burst). By 1957 students had started slapping coats of paint onto the boulder, often associated with athletic events. The Rock was initially installed a few feet north of Harris Hall. NU moved it to its present location (about 20 yards east) in 1989. The Rock might not be the very first such landmark, but it was among the earliest, and many colleges and high schools have since adopted the paint-your-landmark tradition.

Northwestern University (Various Sports): *Waa-Mu Show*

The Waa-Mu Show began as a joint effort of the University's Women's Athletic Association (WAA) and Men's Union (MU) during the 1928–29 academic year. It soon garnered a reputation as one of the greatest college shows in America and has been an important launching pad for many talented and respected performers (e.g., Cloris Leachman, Paul Lynde, Tony Randall, Warren Beatty, Ann-Margret, et al.). Approximately 50 Northwestern students work to compose music, write lyrics, create a book, and orchestrate the more than 30 original songs that often feature sports themes.

NYU (Various Sports): *The Torch*

NYU has as their athletic emblem, a torch. The school torch is handed down from the oldest faculty member to the youngest graduate each year during graduation ceremonies.

The Ohio State University (Football): *Senior Tackle*

Begun in 1913 by head coach John Wilce, seniors on the team are recognized at the last practice of the season, either before the Michigan game or before departing Columbus to play in a bowl game, by hitting the blocking sled a final time.

The Ohio State University (Football): *Captain's Breakfast*

1934 saw the first *gathering of former team captains for breakfast* on the Sunday following the homecoming game. The event began when local businessman Walter Jeffrey invited twenty former captains to the Scioto Country Club to honor them, and continues today to welcome new captains and award them mugs bearing their names and season.

Penn State (Football): *Senior Speeches*

In a new tradition, during their last practice day, Penn State *seniors each tell the team what Penn State has meant to them.*

Rensselaer Polytechnic Institute (Ice Hockey): *Big Red Freakout*

There's very little love in the air on one night around Valentine's Day each winter when Rensselaer students come to the rink clad head-to-toe in red, and determined to make so much noise that on more than one occasion they've been threatened with a penalty for disrupting play. Students usually get a small freebie (like a red hat or T-shirt) upon entering the rink. The red plastic horns given to students in 1987 produced such a cacophony that the NCAA issued what's now known as the RPI Rule, which bans artificial noisemakers from college hockey rinks. Thirty-three years and counting for the annual *Big Red Freakout.*

St. Lawrence University (Hiking): *Peak Weekend*

This St. Lawrence tradition began in 1982, with the first attempt to *have at least one St. Lawrence student on each summit of all 46 high peaks in the Adirondack Park.* A high peak is a mountain above 4,000 feet in vertical elevation and offers spectacular views of the park. The peaks provide opportunities for all skill levels of hikers to experience the great outdoors. President Willie Janeway initiated this event, first named 46er Day, in the spring of 1982. They were not successful until the second attempt in the fall of '82. Since then, it has been an annual outing club tradition and an extremely popular ritual among the student body. Turnouts often exceed several hundred people for this fun weekend getaway. It usually takes place in October, when conditions in the park are prime and fall foliage is in full swing. Over a three-day window, students coordinate their efforts to summit all 46 peaks.

USC (Football): *Protecting Tommy Trojan*

Tampering with another school's campus landmark is a common practice, but wrapping your own statue? In the week leading up to the football matchup with UCLA, USC students now *wrap their Tommy Trojan statue* in duct tape and stand guard to protect it from being painted by Bruins.

Southern Miss (Football): *Paintings on Walks*

The Legacy of Southern Miss Series: the *Painting of the Eagle Walk* and *Painting the Little Rock*. *The Eagle Walk*, located under the east side of The Rock (M.M. Roberts Stadium) on Eagle Walk Drive, displays the memories of Southern Miss' past and the promise of its future. It is a living monument that recognizes the greatness of all those who, on Saturdays during the fall, have had the privilege of going to battle for the Black and Gold. The Little Rock plays an important role during football season. Before each home game, The Rock is given a fresh coat of gold paint and bears a spirited phrase about that week's opponent.

Southwestern Minnesota State University (Basketball): *Hawaiian Night*

Since the mid-1980s, this event has been played at the culmination of Winter Meltdown (formerly known as *Winter Sux Week*). Fans and students dress in tropical attire, and students once smuggled in a keg of beer in a baby carriage.

Springfield College (Gymnastics): *Exhibition*

What do extreme sports, circus entertainment, dance shows, and popular fitness routines have in common? They're all based in gymnastics, as the recent *101st annual Springfield College Gymnastics Exhibition Show*,

"Gymnastics 101: Basics Taken to the Extreme," made evident, in Blake Arena, on the campus. The college's champion and All-American gymnasts, along with other members of the men's and women's gymnastics teams, student dancers, and others perform a full range of gymnastic feats to ingenious choreography, dramatic special effects, and music from throughout recent decades. "The influence of gymnastics has permeated other sports as well as forms of entertainment throughout our culture," said Springfield College women's gymnastics head coach Cheryl Raymond. "We see it in extreme sports such as freestyle snowboarding, skateboarding, BMX bicycling, X-Games, and more. Popular entertainment such as Cirque du Soleil, Dancing with the Stars, and many popular fitness routines take their inspiration from this century-old sport." Springfield College Men's Gymnastics Head Coach Steve Posner added, "The phenomenal evolution that has arisen from gymnastics leads us to project that the sport will have even greater applications to athletics, fitness and entertainment in the future." Upholding a Springfield College tradition, the dramatic finale of the show contained *a tableaux*: living statuaries by gymnasts in metallic body paint. Themes of recent shows have been aspiration, balance, flexibility, a tribute to the YMCA, an unfolding flower in tribute to the conclusion of the college's 125th anniversary, and a sports theme in tribute to members of the college's athletics hall of fame.

Stanford University (Football): *Bearial*

Before the rivalry game against UC-Berkeley, Stanford holds a mock-somber *Bearial* of UC's mascot *Oski the Bear*. At the end of the procession, an effigy of the bear is impaled on top of White Memorial Fountain, or Claw Fountain as it is more appropriately called.

Stephen F. Austin State University (Football): *Homecoming*

The night before the game, the SFA Band and spirit squads lead a *torchlight parade* through campus and out to the intramural fields, where the torch is used to light SFA's annual homecoming bonfire.

Sul Ross State University (Rodeo): *Rodeo Festivals*

In 1949, Sul Ross State held its first annual (invitational) rodeo, with 12 colleges throughout Texas, New Mexico, Oklahoma, and Colorado attending. This event was instrumental in rodeo subsequently being named a competition sport. Sul Ross has won the national title eight times, placed in the top 10 at the College National Finals Rodeo thirty-three times, and have had six all-around cowboys and cowgirls. The Rodeo Club, of approximately 40 members, holds fundraisers such as *The Cowboy Christmas Ball* (December), *Team Roping's* (summer and occasionally Wednesday nights), *Barrel Racings*, and dances. Events are often held in conjunction with the *Sul Ross Rodeo Exes Reunion* and rodeo (July) and the *Big Bend Ranch Rodeo* (August).

Swarthmore College/Ursinus College (Rugby): *Prom Dress Rugby*

Swarthmore and Ursinus play an annual match of *Prom Dress Rugby*.

University of Texas (Football): *Thanksgiving Day Game*

Texas has played on Thanksgiving 75 times dating to 1895, including 64 games with Texas A&M. Due to conference realignment, these two schools no longer play each other, although annually the Texas State Legislature attempts to rectify this.

Texas A&M (Football): *Bonfire before Texas Game*

Almost every year since 1909, A&M students have built a large bonfire to celebrate their burning desire to beat the hell outta the University of Texas. *Aggie Bonfire* was traditionally lit around Thanksgiving in conjunction with the festivities surrounding the annual college football game between the schools. Though it began as a trash pile, Aggie Bonfire evolved into a massive six-tiered structure, the world record being held at 109 feet. After the collapse of the 1999 structure, causing the death of 11 students and one former student, the university suspended the bonfire indefinitely, but the tradition continues off-campus without direct university involvement, sanction, or participation.

Texas A&M (Various Sports): *Fish Camp*

Many schools have various forms of freshman orientation, but few do it quite like Texas A&M. Sessions are held over four days at an offsite camp, where over 1,000 upperclassmen volunteer in some way to help the incoming freshman. A huge part of this experience is learning the unique Texas

A&M traditions and yells. In fact this camp is also known as *A Freshman's First Tradition*.

Texas Tech (Football): *Kalf Fry*

Kalf Fry is an annual food and music festival that unites Texas Tech and visiting fans the night before one big football game each year. Everyone enjoys (?) Kalf Fries, i.e., fried bull testicles.

Various Schools (Basketball): *Players Singing on the Jumbotron*

When holiday season approaches, several schools (i.e., Maryland, Marquette, Notre Dame) have their players don Santa hats, or reindeer sweaters, and sing their favorite Christmas carols—often butchering them. The videos then are shown on the school's Jumbotron during December games.

Various Schools (Women's Basketball): *Maggie Dixon Classic*

This event is a double-header played in Madison Square Garden each year, for the past seven years. The games are played in honor of Maggie Dixon, the former Army women's coach who died in April 2006 of arrhythmia, probably caused by an enlarged heart. Her death came three weeks after her first season as head coach.

Various Schools (Rowing): *Head of the Charles Regatta*

On a weekend, each October, up to 8,000 rowers from numerous colleges/universities compete while 30,000+ spectators line the Charles River.

Virginia Tech: *Cadet vs. Civilian Snowball Fight*

On the first major snowfall of the year, the students stockpile their ammunition of snowballs and prepare for battle, cadets vs. civilians, in Blacksburg, Virginia.

Western Kentucky University: *Birthday Party for Costumed Mascot*

For 37+ years, each year on December 1st, Western Kentucky students celebrate *Big Red's Birthday* with laser tag, bands, birthday cake, etc. Thousands of students attend the party from about midnight until 2 a.m.

Western Kentucky's Big Red mascot has a birthday party each year. *Western Kentucky University, photograph by Clinton Lewis*

University of Wisconsin–Madison (Football): *Cane Tossing*

Believed to have been tradition for nearly 100 years, third-year law students at the University of Wisconsin run onto the field before the homecoming game wearing bowler hats and *throw a cane through the goalposts.* Legend has it that if they catch the cane on the other side, they'll win their first case.

University of Wisconsin–Platteville (Volleyball): *Yell Night*

This is a weeknight volleyball match that residence hall and student organizations are invited to attend and *yell* throughout the entire contest in support of the UW-Platteville volleyball team. What originally was a pep rally during homecoming has turned into this event. In 2011, a school record 1,252 people attended the game and their student broadcast crew televised the game.

"Cane-Tossing" at halftime of the homecoming game at the University of Wisconsin. *University of Wisconsin Athletic Communications*

Wofford College (Football): *Last Lap*

The Last Lap is a Wofford football tradition initiated by head coach Mike Ayers when he arrived on campus in 1988. Following the final practice of the season, the returning players line up in the end zone at Gibbs Stadium and watch as their senior teammates make a final lap around the game field.

Xavier University (Basketball): *Crosstown Campout*

Before the Xavier and University of Cincinnati basketball game, any student who wants to attend the annual *Crosstown Shootout* between Xavier and UC must participate in this event. Group registration is required and a webpage covers all rules and regulations, as well as the tent registration forms.

6

TRADITIONS INVOLVING BANDS/MUSIC

Call it CST. No, not Central Standard Time, and not just college sports traditions either. It's the *collegiate soundtrack of sports*, and it's more than merely music. More than half notes at halftime. More than full-throated, stadium-sized, uh, choirs chiming in on everything from "We Are the Boys of Old Florida" to the "Budweiser Jingle." From the "1812 Overture" to "Hang on Sloopy."

It's timing and tradition, too. Costumes and customs. *Bagpipes, band days*, and *Boomer Sooner*. And drums, big-ass drums that rock the house and rouse cheers. It's also *a cappella renditions of the "Star-Spangled Banner"* and *"Silent Night"* that will move you to tears.

It's not just the big boys and girls of college sports who have their musical mainstays. At Coastal Carolina in Myrtle Beach, South Carolina, *Myrtle Beach Days* by the Fantastic Shakers, a beach music band back in the day, is played over the PA system after each baseball and softball game. Win or lose, it's good to shag.

In Gainesville, young, middle-aged, and old guys and gals of Florida link arms and sway and sing "We Are the Boys of Old Florida" at the end of each third quarter.

At the Georgia Institute of Technology, which arguably has one of the greatest fight songs in all of college sports—"I'm a Ramblin' Wreck from Georgia Tech"—a bobbing mob of fans punctuates the end of every football third quarter and each second-to-last TV timeout during basketball games. This, while the full marching band or pep band belts out the "Bud-weiser Jingle." They bob up and down randomly, bending their knees and mimicking the enormous heads of the legendary Clydesdales who pull the Budweiser wagon.

Neither Tech's band, nor the institute itself, receives any money from Anheuser-Busch. The band might get a couple of complementary kegs early in the season, but that's it. Then again, as the Yellow Jackets Band and fans know and sing, "When you say Buuuuuud-weiser, you've said it all!"

At Lehigh, one half of the longest continuous rivalry in college sports, the *Marching 97 Band* weaves its way throughout campus buildings, dining halls, and classrooms the week of the Lafayette game. The schools' rivalry is now approaching 150 years and counting.

At Ohio State, hang time doesn't just mean punting. Since 1965, "Hang on Sloopy" is played before each fourth quarter, with Buckeye fans chanting "*O-H-I-O*" between refrains.

In stormin' Norman, Oklahoma, where the woodwinds come sweeping down the plains, the band plays "Boomer Sooner," a variation of Yale's classic "Boola Boola!" A small Conestoga wagon, pulled by ponies, charges

Lehigh's band visits classrooms the week of the Lafayette–Lehigh game.
Lehigh University

onto the field after every Okie touchdown. For true Sooners and Broadway aficionados, the band belts out Rodgers and Hammerstein's "Oklahoma" after extra points.

Has a university's fight song ever been at the top of the Pop Charts? Yep. Read on.

The *Stanford band*, of course, is in a category, and class, of its own. More on that to come, later in these pages. Irreverence, thy name is the Stanford Band.

All of this, and much, much more constitutes the CST. The collegiate soundtrack of sports, which can make you stand and shout and be glad you're alive. It can even wake the living dead, or summon your inner zombie.

For that, you can thank *Splank*.

That's the name Florian Senfter, a German artist from Munich, performs under. He's the guy who wrote, recorded, and popularized "Kernkraft 400" by Zombie Nation. It's the technopop, nonstop ditty that college basketball crowds—and many football fanatics, too—have been hopping up and down to for a decade during timeouts when the home team's rollin' and the house is a'rockin'.

According to Tom O'Toole of *USA Today*, "Kernkraft 400" first surfaced at Marquette University basketball home games in 2002. Later that season, Todd Scheel, whose Milwaukee company FX in Motion introduced "Kernkraft 400" at Marquette games, brought it south to Wake Forest for a big TV game against Duke on February 13, 2003. It was the day before Valentine's Day. When Wake Forest, led by Chris Paul, won in double overtime, Wake Forest fans fell in love with the song, and America saw the Wake students' reaction to it. A tradition was born.

Soon, college basketball, indeed much of college sports, followed suit.

"I think one of the reasons it was successful [for Wake Forest]," Dan Hauser, then the marketing director at Wake, told O'Toole, "is that we played it for a conference game, we won, and it was a team with Chris Paul."

A mania was born. "Hot timeouts" anyone?

As O'Toole explained, "That's when the home team has gone on a run to catch up or pull ahead usually forcing the other team to call a timeout."

"That's the worst time to bring out a promotion or to do something with a sponsor," Hauser told O'Toole. "In a hot timeout we're going with something like Zombie Nation or the fight song."

"If you catch the crowd as they are ramping up to its peak or at its peak and you have a song like that," Hauser said to O'Toole, "the entire arena claps to it and you can sustain that through the whole timeout."

This is not always a good thing.

In 2006, according to a story in *The Daily Collegian*, the student newspaper at Penn State, the university began judiciously using the song at football games in Beaver Stadium, capacity, over 100,000. With the student section jumping up and down to "Kernkraft 400," there were concerns about possible structural damage to the stadium itself. All this thanks to Splank. As Senfter explained to O'Toole in an e-mail, he was into heavy metal music as a teenager and later became a DJ. "I wanted to play my own stuff," he emailed. "That's what got me into producing music."

Growing up, Senfter played "soccer from time to time," he told O'Toole. He is also well aware of his song's popularity at American sports events and its impact on the games people play themselves.

"A quirky electro song," Splank characterized his little ditty-turned-anthem. "Boola-Boola," it ain't. It's much bigger than that.

"It's still a phenomenon to me," Senfter told O'Toole. "The fans have their own mind; you can't plan something like that."

He's heard his song played during the Olympic Games, and knows a Belgian soccer team that plays it after a goal is scored.

What enthralled sports fans, American college kids, and folks worldwide? A "remixed version," he told O'Toole, "with people chanting made it popular at sporting events."

After all the song's popularity, after it's become a hot-button, hot time-outs phenomenon at sporting events, there is one musical mulligan Splank wished he'd taken.

The title.

"Kernkraft 400?" That, he told O'Toole, translates to "Atomic Energy 400." Had Senfter known it would become such a sporting phenomenon, particularly on college campuses, "I would have chosen a friendlier name."

A kinder, gentler Senfter title. But still a rockin' college sports tradition, one that rocks-on to this day. Like the title of Splank's fourth album, which came out on March 9, 2009, just in time for that year's NCAA tournament, it's simply *Zombielicious*.

TRADITIONS INVOLVING BANDS/MUSIC BY SCHOOL

University of Arizona (Basketball): *Responsive Yells*

Before every game, the Pride of Arizona Pep Band splits into four sections in the four sides of McKale Center. They play "Bear Down Arizona" in sequence before the band runs back to the student section in the north stands and plays all of "Bear Down." The band also yells, "Hi fans!" to the fans, who respond by yelling, "Hi band!" and "Hi Sean!" to head coach Sean Miller, who responds by waving to the band. The band also yells "Hi Niya!" to Arizona women's basketball coach Niya Butts.

Bowling Green State University (Various Sports): *Zulu War Chant*

Bowling Green State University's unofficial fight song ("Ay Ziggy Zoomba") is credited to Gilbert Fox, a WWII Army Air Corps bombardier who served in Italy. In 1946, Fox brought back to the university his interpretation based upon a Zulu war chant. It is traditionally sung after every Falcon football victory. It was incorporated into the motion picture *Paper Lion*, the movie based upon George Plimpton's 1966 book of the same name, when Falcon Football Hall of Fame member Mike Weger, playing for the Detroit Lions, sang his own college victory chant in the film.

Carnegie Mellon University (Football): *The Kiltie Band*

Carnegie Mellon's *Kiltie Band*, dressed in full Scottish regalia, including kilts and knee socks, performs during every home football game.

George Washington University: *Carillon Chimes*

As you walk around campus, you will hear the carillon chimes ring out the *George Washington fight song* twice a day at 12:15 p.m. and 6 p.m. The chimes are recorded, but who cares? It's still great.

Harding University (Basketball): *A Capella National Anthem*

Many fans, at many stadiums, join in as the national anthem is performed by a band or singers. But at Harding University, they have taken the crowd's singing to a whole new level. For basketball games, the crowd *sings the national anthem* without benefit of music or a leader. While a pep band is present—and Harding has many accomplished music students and professors—this tradition continues unaltered. It began several years ago when a shy music professor was scheduled to sing, and she asked the crowd to help her out. They did, and the athletic director, who was in attendance, said to the sports information director, "We're doing that again!" Now the PA announcer begins the anthem, and then turns his microphone off while the crowd movingly sings the song.

University of Houston (Various Sports): *The Olympic Trumpet Fanfare*

During the Phi Slama Jama's 1982–1983 season, Greg Talford directed the Cougar Brass to play the "Olympic Trumpet Fanfare" to signify a Cougar victory. In 1984, Robert Mayes directed the "Olympic Trumpet Fanfare" at the Los Angeles Summer Games (which served as the coronation of Houston's very own track and field alumnus, Carl Lewis). Now, this is considered to be the de facto *Houston victory song*, and is played after each victory by the Cougars (at least, when the band or brass is present).

University of Maine: *Fight Song = Pop Hit*

The University of Maine fight song, also known as the "Stein Song," is the only college fight song to make it to the top of the pop charts. It was recorded by Rudy Vallee in 1930 and rose to the top of the charts!

Miami University of Ohio: *The Marching Machine*

In 1971, the *Miami Marching Machine* came into existence. The Marching Machine was built by Kappa Kappa Psi and Tau Beta Sigma and was a gift to the marching band. The Marching Machine was a tank-like structure placed over the tuba instructor's VW bug, and it became the mascot of the band. It was always at the head of all the parades and even made an appearance at a Bengals game. The Marching Machine remained an integral part of the marching band until 1979. Reprise this, Miami!

Northwestern University (Football): *Band Day*

This annual event started in 1956, and Northwestern is believed to have been the first university to do this. High school bands from around the area are invited to participate on the field with Northwestern's marching band during halftime at one game per year. At its peak, *Band Day* featured up to 10,000 high school musicians from nearly 100 local schools, performing at the same time.

Northwestern University: *Purple Haze*

In 1972, the student body voted to change Northwestern's nickname from *Wildcats* to *Purple Haze*. According to some alumni, the band followed suit for a little while by playing the Hendrix tune (the university administration quietly swept the nickname vote under the rug). While it's unclear if the band actually played "Purple Haze" at games in the 1970s, it certainly did in 2008, when the practice was briefly revived.

University of Notre Dame (Football): "1812 Overture"

Between the third and fourth quarters of home games, the Notre Dame marching band plays the finale to the "1812 Overture" as the crowd reacts with synchronized waving of arms, with their fingers in the shape of a "K" for Kelly. ("W" for both Weis and Willingham and "L" for Lou Holtz.)

University of Notre Dame (Football): *The Irish Guard*

A group of ten students dressed in a traditional Scottish kilt and Notre Dame Tartan lead the school's marching band onto the field during home games. Formed in 1949, *the Irish Guard* is an elite group at Notre Dame, and each participant makes the squad only through tryouts each year. Guards must be at least six-foot-two and uphold certain public standards while assisting the marching band in its halftime routine and other performances.

Notre Dame's Irish Guard. *Notre Dame University*

The Ohio State University (Football): *Script Ohio*

To the untrained eye high above the field, it might appear at first that the members of the Ohio State University Marching Band are imitating a snake. In fact, they are executing a highly choreographed, more than seventy-five-year old tradition that brings chills to the fans—and the fans to a roar—at every Buckeyes home game and bowl game. Beginning from a block-O formation, band members loop and strut in unison while playing the four-minute military march "Le Régiment de Sambre et Meuse." By song's end, they've spelled out "Ohio," climaxing when a senior sousaphone player (or other celebrity) performs the honor of *dotting the "i."*

University of Oklahoma (Football): *Opposing Team's Fight Song*

At home games, the band often plays that visiting team's *fight song* while facing their fans.

Purdue University (Football): *World's Largest Drum*

A staple of the school's pregame routine, the World's Largest Drum is wheeled out by a number of honorary pushers, and two other band members who actually beat the drum on either side. The drum cost $911 to make back in 1921 and although its actual measurements are a closely guarded secret, the World's Largest Drum has been synonymous with Purdue University for decades.

Rice University (Football): *The MOB*

Rice's *Marching Owl Band* (the *MOB*), puts on quirky, tongue-in-cheek halftime shows, second only to Stanford's Band. As an example, they once formed a fire hydrant while playing "Oh Where, Oh Where Has My Little Dog Gone?" to mock Texas A&M's mascot, Reveille. Texas A&M students were not amused.

St. Joseph (Basketball): *Banging the Drum*

The drum's hallowed tradition and history are second only to that of the Hawk. Old timers reminiscing about any Hawk game are compelled to make reference to the constantly booming drum. It is believed the drum played a significant role in many an important win. Today this tradition lives on with a new generation of drummers.

St. Olaf College: *Broken Bat Trophy*

Every year since 1974, at 6:30 a.m., twice a week in the spring, the band plays softball against the orchestra for the right to carve their name into a wooden bat.

University of Southern California (USC): *"Fight On"*

Legend has it that during World War II in the Pacific, an American task force attacked an island held by the Japanese. As the Americans stormed the beach, "Fight On" blared from the deck of one of the transports. The American men let out a tremendous roar and eventually won the island.

USC (Football): *Sword Planted at Midfield*

During the band's pregame show, whether at home, or on the road, the USC drum major majestically (or is that tauntingly?) *plants a sword in the middle of the field.* In 2012, UCLA asked that this not take place (since their logo was being stabbed), and USC agreed. Notre Dame allows the gesture when USC visits them, but Notre Dame's logo isn't at midfield being stabbed, either.

USC (Football): *Songs Played with Regularity*

"Tribute to Troy," the incessant stanza of pounding drums and blaring horns, is played after every defensive stop. "Fanfare" is the introduction to "Tribute To Troy" and is played when the band takes the field. "All Right Now" is played after USC gets a turnover. "Another One Bites the Dust" is played after USC gets a sack. "The William Tell Overture" is played at the start of the fourth quarter. "The Emperor's Theme" from *Star Wars* is played when USC is flagged for a major penalty.

University of South Florida (Football): *Stampede Entrance*

USF's marching band, the *Herd of Thunder (HOT)*, first took to the field at the football season home opener against Southwest Texas State on September 11, 1999. Their unique entrance to the field began as a running *stampede* that day and the tradition has continued ever since.

Southern Methodist University (SMU) (Football): *Postgame Concert*

The tradition of *playing a concert from the stands* at the end of a football game dates back to at least 1960 when the band went to Ohio State and played a forty-five minute jazz concert after the game. The Mustang Band always concludes with the SMU alma mater.

SMU (Football and Basketball): *Beanies*

Today the privilege of *the beanie* is afforded only to members of the Mustang Band. As a sign of their commitment to school spirit, the band members wear their beanies during rehearsals, the fourth quarter of SMU football games, and the last five minutes of every SMU basketball game.

SMU (Football): *Best-Dressed Band*

The SMU Mustang Band earned its reputation as *the best-dressed band in the land* because of its multiple uniforms with a style that mimics a swing band, more than a typical marching band. It has thirty-two different uniforms made up of varying combinations of pants, shirts, coats, and ties. Band members wear one uniform for the pregame performance and change to another just before halftime at all SMU football games where the band plays. The uniform style reinforces the music style of a jazz band. They also wear flannel nightgowns and caps, for late night public appearances.

SMU: *Fight Song*

In its early years, the all-male band would drift off to visit with the coeds during the game. The band director came up with the idea of having the remaining trumpets make a buzzing sound to alert the wayward band members to get back to their seats. That buzz—a flutter tongue on a concert F—was incorporated into the start of "Peruna," the official SMU fight song.

Southern Miss (Various Sports): *Southern Miss to the Top*

"Southern Miss to the Top!" is the university fight song and is used on many occasions including after the football team scores.

Southern Miss (Football): *"Are You from Dixie?"*

"Are You from Dixie?" is played after the extra point following a Southern Miss touchdown.

Southern Miss (Football): *"Amazing Grace"*

"Amazing Grace" is played by The Pride of Mississippi Band at halftime of the final home game of each football season.

Southern Miss (Football): *Fifth Quarter Concert*

The *Fifth Quarter Concert* takes place immediately following a Southern Miss home football game when The Pride of Mississippi Band performs a miniconcert from the stadium while fans congregate on the field.

Stanford University (Football): *Controversial Band Routines*

Always controversial, the *Stanford Band*, is perhaps best known for entering the field during "The Play" against Cal. However, the band has been arranging risky and humorous halftime shows for more than thirty years. Some of the band's most controversial routines were a 1990 skit where a drum major conducted the band against Notre Dame dressed as a nun while waving a wooden cross. The band also performed a polygamy skit in 2004 when they played Brigham Young University, which drew national attention. Although the athletic department preapproves all band routines, some occasionally slip by, requiring both the athletic director, as well as the band to issue formal apologies.

The Sudler Trophy: *The Heisman Trophy for Bands*

The Sudler Trophy is an award bestowed on one university marching band every other year, and was an annual award from 1982–2007. Described by a *Los Angeles Times* reporter as the *Heisman Trophy of the collegiate band world*, the award does not represent the winner of any championship, but rather a band surrounded by great tradition that has become respected nationally. No school may be honored with the award twice. According to the official description of the trophy:

> The purpose of the Sudler Trophy is to identify and recognize collegiate marching bands of particular excellence that have made outstanding contributions

to the American way of life. The Sudler Trophy is awarded annually to a college or university marching band which has demonstrated the highest musical standards and innovative marching routines and ideas, and which has made important contributions to the advancement of the performance standards of college marching bands over a period of years.

The trophy measures exactly 22.5 inches from base to the tip of the drum major's mace; precisely the size of a standard eight to five step in marching. Table 6.1 shows the recipients of the Sudler Trophy since its inception in 1982:

Table 6.1. The Sudler Trophy–The Heisman Trophy for collegiate bands (awarded annually from 1982 to 2007, and then began to be awarded every two years)

Year	Recipient	Year	Recipient
1982	University of Michigan	1996	University of Nebraska-Lincoln
1983	University of Illinois at Urbana-Champaign	1997	West Virginia University
1984	The Ohio State University	1998	University of Massachusetts
1985	Florida A&M University	1999	Texas Tech University
1986	University of Texas at Austin	2000	University of Georgia
1987	University of Oklahoma	2001	Texas A&M University
1988	Michigan State University	2002	Louisiana State University
1989	University of Kansas	2003	University of Alabama
1990	University of Iowa	2004	Auburn University
1991	Arizona State University	2005	The Pennsylvania State University
1992	Northwestern University	2006	University of Arkansas
1993	University of California, Los Angeles (UCLA)	2007	Indiana University
1994	James Madison University	2009	Western Carolina University
1995	Purdue University	2011	University of Notre Dame

University of Texas: *Big Bertha*

Texas' band's drum is called *Big Bertha* and is the world's largest bass drum. It weighs 500 pounds and is handled by four drum wranglers.

University of Texas (Various Sports): *"Taps"*

"The Eyes of Texas" is frequently followed by another traditional song, "Texas Fight," better known as "Taps." "Taps" is the official fight song of the University of Texas.

University of Texas: *Thanks for the Memories*

Texas played Texas A&M in football for the 118th (and possibly last time in 2011, due to conference realignments). At halftime the Longhorn Band spelled out "Thanks A&M" while playing "Thanks for the Memories."

Texas A&M (Football): *"Aggie War Hymn"*

More than 80,000 fans sway together, and sing the "Aggie War Hymn," after the third quarter of every home football game, and at any other time the band thinks appropriate.

University of Tennessee (Various Sports): *"Rocky Top"*

"Rocky Top" was written in ten minutes in 1967, and since 1972 has become one of college sports most recognizable anthems. It has five basic chords, and the title is repeated nineteen times.

Wake Forest University: *"Welcome to the Jungle"*

Guns N' Roses' "Welcome to the Jungle" has become a fan favorite at Wake Forest athletic events because of a clever Wake Forest reference.

Wake Forest University: *Baptist (Southern) Tunes*

"When the Quad is Rolled Up Yonder, I'll Be There" is a take on an old Southern hymn. The marching band plays the song during the football pregame and after winning a big game. "Demon Deacon Joy" is also a take on a Southern hymn. Songs frequently present many opportunities to shout *Go Deacs!*

University of Washington (Basketball): *Crowd Singing*

While waiting for basketball games to tip off, Washington fans are known to spontaneously break out into rousing renditions of Queen's "Bohemian Rhapsody" or Bonnie Tyler's "Total Eclipse of the Heart."

University of Wisconsin (Football): *Fifth Quarter*

Many bands stage a miniconcert after games. Wisconsin's marching band takes the field, after a win or a loss, and rocks-out for about twenty minutes. This tradition was started by Wisconsin's band director after a stretch of ten losing seasons and continues today, although Wisconsin now seldom has a losing season.

University of Wisconsin (Ice Hockey): *"Varsity"*

The University of Wisconsin pep band plays "Varsity" (accompanied by 15,000 or so red-clad fans singing and swaying along) prior to the start of the third period at the Kohl Center.

Wright State University (Basketball): *The Spark*

The Spark is a three-minute long dance that the student government encourages students to perform during media timeouts at home games. Some critics call it a three-minute group seizure. It began in 2011–2012.

University of Wyoming (Football): *Beer Song*

Trombone players in this school's band make their way around the stadium during the third quarter of football games, leading the crowd in choruses of the song "In Heaven There Is No Beer." However, tradition dictates that students have to call out requests for the song before it is played.

7

ENTRANCE TRADITIONS

Some teams merely take the field. Others make a nice first impression. And then there are those purists, traditionalists who flat out know how to make an entrance.

In Boulder, what's it all about? *Ralphie*. Colorado buffs roar whenever their football Buffs take the field following *Run Ralphie Run!* Since 1967, home games at Folsom Field start after Ralphie the buffalo snorts and storms madly around the gridiron. Student handlers try to hold on tight to their ropes attached to 1,300 pounds of hell-on-hooves. And to think that Ralphie's traditionally a she. A she who was even elected as homecoming queen in 1971.

In Knoxville, the Vols enter Neyland Stadium by running through the *Block-T*. At Virginia Tech, the Hokies charge into Lane Stadium once their fans are amped by a Metallica anthem. And you thought only Mariano Rivera, baseball's greatest closer, played "Enter Sandman" as his soundtrack.

In Ann Arbor, Michigan makes a grand entrance. The Wolverines charge onto the field as the band plays "Hail to the Victors!" and players jump up to touch that banner: *"Go Blue: M Club Supports You."* Over 105,000 fans go Big Blue bonkers.

Classical music mavens know the melody as "Also Sprach Zarathustra" by Strauss. You know it as the movie theme from *2001: A Space Odyssey*. Since 1983, South Carolina fans know it's their cue to cry "Go Cocks!" before opening kickoff.

And at Georgia Tech, in Bobby Dodd Stadium at Historic Grant Field, the Yellow Jackets take the field in style. They run out behind the *Rambling Wreck*, a restored 1930 Ford Model A sport coupe. With a student behind the wheel, the classic is driven onto the field with pompom-shaking cheerleaders aboard and also *Buzz*, the wise-ass mascot. All while the marching band plays Tech's legendary fight song, "I'm a Ramblin' Wreck from Georgia Tech and a Hell of an Engineer!"

GA Tech's "Rambling Wreck." *GA Tech*

Yet nothing tops the *most exciting twenty-five seconds in college football*. That's Clemson's entrance before every home game in Memorial Stadium, long known as Death Valley. It involves *Howard's Rock*, mass transit, an orange carpet, some of the most fervent fans in college football and a tradition born out of necessity.

In 1942, the first 20,000 seats in Clemson Memorial Stadium were built and ready for the season opener. The shortest entry into the stadium was a walk down Williamson Road from the Fike Field House dressing room to a gate atop the hill behind the east end zone. There were no dressing facilities in the west end zone, just a large clock whose hands turned, and a hand-operated scoreboard.

HOWARD'S
ROCK

FROM
DEATH VALLEY, CA
TO
DEATH VALLEY
CLEMSON, SC
PRESENTED TO
COACH FRANK HOWARD
AND THE
CLEMSON FOOTBALL TEAM
BY
S.C. JONES '19
SEPTEMBER 1966

Clemson's "Howard Rock." *Clemson University*

The Tigers would don their uniforms in Fike, walk down Williamson, enter a gate and jog—not charge—down the hill to warm up.

There was no Memorial mania: No cannons booming, no huge tiger paw flag, no "Tiger Rag" played by the marching band, much less over the PA system. It remained modestly so until the mid-1960s.

By then, Frank Howard had become a legend and iconic coach. He was a great coach, and a gruff yet hilarious character. As Clemson's athletic director, he once denied a student request to fund a crew program. When told what crew was, Howard growled, "What kinda sport is that, where you sit on yo' ass and go backwards?"

In 1965, S. C. Jones, Clemson class of 1919, took a trip to California. It included a stop in notorious Death Valley, where Jones picked up a 2.5 pound rock of white flint. He gave it to Howard as a gift from Death Valley, California, to Death Valley, South Carolina. Howard was duly unimpressed.

The rock sat on the floor in Howard's office for more than a year, serving as a doorstop. Finally, he told Gene Willimon, the executive secretary of *IPTAY*, Clemson's athletic fundraising organization, "Take this rock and throw it over the fence, or out in the ditch. Do something with it, but get it out of my office."

Willimon saved the rock, and it was mounted on a pedestal atop the hill inside Death Valley and above the west end zone. It was unveiled on September 24, 1966, when Clemson hosted Virginia. Down eighteen points with seventeen minutes left, the Tigers won 40–35 on a late sixty-five-yard touchdown pass from Jimmy Addison to Jacky Jackson.

Players began rubbing the rock for luck on September 23, 1967, before Clemson beat Wake Forest 23–6.

Before the Tigers ran down the hill that afternoon, Howard told them, "If you're going to give me 110 percent, you can rub that rock. If you're not, keep your filthy hands off it."

Under Howard and his successor, Hootie Ingram, then under Danny Ford, Tommy Bowden, and now Dabo Swinney, Clemson continues the tradition. After the Tigers finish warming up, they go back into their dressing room under the west end zone stands for final instructions. About ten minutes before kickoff, it's time for mass transit. Or massive transit, given the girth of Clemson's linemen. The Tigers hop aboard two buses, ride behind the north stands to the east end zone and disembark on the hill. Then it's show time.

The band forms two lines, a gauntlet for the players to run through, but not before rubbing Howard's Rock and hurtling down the hill on an orange carpet. Let the cannon boom. Strike up the "Tiger Rag." And the best entrance in all of college football commences once more.

Somewhere, Frank Howard is smiling.

ENTRANCE TRADITIONS BY SCHOOL

Arizona State University (Football): *Tillman Tunnel*

The Sun Devil football team enters every game running through commemorative *Tillman Tunnel* in honor of Pat Tillman, an ASU linebacker from 1994–1997.

Arizona State University (Football): *Pregame Show*

After the pregame show, the band performs "Go Go Devils," also known as "The Al Davis Fight Song," while forming a *pitchfork* at the south end zone for the Sun Devil players to go through during the football team's introduction.

Arkansas State University (Basketball): *Entrance Theme*

Beginning in 1987, players enter to the theme of *2001: A Space Odyssey*.

University of Colorado (Football): *Running of Ralphie*

The *Ralphie Run* at Colorado is one of the most dramatic moments in college sports, as the Buffaloes players run out of their locker room tunnel behind a real, live 1,300-pound animal. Live Buffaloes first appeared on campus in 1934, three weeks after a contest to select an official school nickname was completed. But a live buffalo run as we know it today didn't start until October 28, 1967, for Colorado's homecoming game against Oklahoma State. While Ralphie has five trained student handlers trying to control her with ropes, you just never know. And that's why even opposing players know that Ralphie's run is one of the most notable moments in college sports. You can't afford to ignore it.

University of Florida (Football): *Jumbotron*

A short video showing alligators moving in on their prey, with the theme music from the movie *Jaws* playing in the background, is displayed on Florida Field's *Jumbotron* video screen during every football game before the players come out of the tunnel. ESPN's *College Game Day* analyst, Lee Corso, called it one of the most thrilling moments in college football.

University of Florida (Football): *Touching the Gator*

Before any Florida Gator can trot out onto the field for the kickoff inside Ben Hill Griffin Stadium, he must *tap the sacred gator head* that sits between the locker room and the playing field. It is a tradition that is near and dear to the heart of every Gators football player, coach, and staff member. Players have reported getting chills and goose bumps, not from the crazed 90,000 plus fans roaring just beyond the south end zone entrance, but because of the honor they feel when touching the gator head that stares fearlessly at them as they approach. Some players even claim to gain more energy, internal strength, and confidence after touching the artificial beast that looms just before the most intimidating swamp around.

Georgia Tech (Football): *The Ramblin' Wreck*

The Yellow Jackets have a unique ride leading them into the game: a restored 1930 Model A Ford Sport Coupe—a real classic. This tradition began on September 30, 1961, versus Rice. Many of the former drivers of the *Wreck* have established an endowment to maintain the car. For over fifty years the Wreck has led the team onto the field for every home game, enduring defacement, and even an attempted car jacking on its way home from a game with rival University of Georgia.

Indiana University (Basketball): *Martha, the Mop Lady*

A commercial featuring a beloved mop lady cleaning Assembly Hall, while singing the IU fight song? It's often been said that history repeats itself. For fans of Hoosiers' basketball and *Martha*, that is a very good thing as Indiana Athletics announced in 2010, after a twenty-plus year absence, the original commercial spot would make its return. The commercial (by one of IU's principal basketball sponsors) is shown after the national anthem, and right before tip-off—just as it did in the 1970s and 1980s to get fans into the spirit prior to the game. Martha's obvious passion for IU basketball was (and is) infectious and led to her personal following that was like none other.

Indiana University (Basketball): *Candy-Striped Pants*

Indiana players wear *warm-up pants that are striped red and white* like the stripes of a candy cane. They were first worn by the team in the 1970s under head coach Bob Knight. At the time they were in keeping with the fashion trends of the 1970s, but despite changing styles they have since become an iconic part of playing for Indiana. The pants were originally available only for basketball team members, but are now often worn by teams other than basketball. Also, recent changes in licensing agreements now permit the general public to buy them as well. They have since become a staple at games and other Indiana events, and the basketball recruiting staff has even been known to wear them on high school recruiting visits.

University of Iowa (Football): *The Swarm*

AC/DC is an Australian rock band whose members might have a hard time locating Iowa on a map. But the band's classic hit, "Back in Black," has become a staple at every Iowa Hawkeyes home game. Before the team hits the field, the Kinnick Stadium video board shows the players walking down the tunnel from their locker room—in their black jersey tops, naturally—while the monster guitar riffs stoke the crowd. Instead of racing onto the field, though, the players jog out with hands intertwined, captains at the front of the crowd. It's called *The Swarm*, which Hayden Fry introduced in 1979 as a sign of unity. We assume AC/DC approves.

Ithaca College (Football): *Touching the Rock*

When the football stadium was renamed Butterfield Stadium in honor of former coach Jim Butterfield, a large rock was placed in the end zone closest to the entrance; the plaque dedicating the stadium is embedded in the rock. Players enter past *the Rock* and touch it as they *go onto the field* at the beginning of each game.

Louisiana State University (Football): *Touching the WIN! Crossbar*

Louisiana State University's (LSU) Tigers walk through the locker room and out onto the field—but not before reaching above the doorway to touch a reclaimed section of old crossbar with *"Win!"* painted on it.

University of Miami (Football): *Smoke Show*

Perhaps nothing sums up the mystique of the Miami dynasty in the 1980s and 1990s better than *the Smoke*. Players run through the tunnel onto the field as white smoke engulfs them, the sound of a hurricane blaring through

The University of Miami's "Smoke-Entrance." *University of Miami*

the speakers. There is no more intimidating sight than seeing the 'Canes literally emerging from thin air, like ninjas ready for a fight. But did you know the tradition was started in the 1950s as a way to increase fan interest? University of Miami transportation director Bob Nalette decided fire extinguishers would be used to create the smoke. Today, the smoke and the sound of a hurricane are all that is really needed to get everybody in Miami juiced-up for a game.

University of Michigan (Football): *Touch the Banner*

It's an iconic entrance at an iconic stadium to the tune of an iconic fight song. If you haven't seen Michigan touch the banner at Michigan Stadium, you haven't been paying attention. Before every game, Wolverines players charge out of the tunnel and *leap to touch* the "*Go Blue: M Club Supports You*" banner as the band plays "Hail to the Victors." The tradition began in 1962 as coach Bump Elliott, looking for a way to inspire his 1–5 team, had boosters hold a banner in the tunnel for players to touch on their way to the field. The banner moved to midfield the next year. Players cherish the banner tradition and abide by two rules: Don't miss and don't trip.

Monmouth College (Football): *Bagpipe Band*

Founded by Scottish Presbyterians in 1853, Monmouth College has embraced its heritage. Known as the Fighting Scots, their football team is led

Monmouth College's "Bagpipe Band." *Monmouth College*

into battle as the Scottish warriors were centuries ago, with their *Bagpipe Band leading the football team* onto the field prior to home football games.

The Ohio State University (Football): *Tunnel of Pride*

The *Tunnel of Pride* began with the 1994 Michigan game when all former players who were in attendance formed a tunnel through which the team ran to take the field, and Ohio State beat its rival that day, 22–6. Rex Kern, quarterback of the 1968 national championship team, and then director of athletics Andy Geiger together used the concept as a means of connecting current Buckeyes with those who played before them. The Tunnel of Pride was next formed for the 1995 Notre Dame game, which the Buckeyes also won. In each home game against Michigan since then, the tradition has been repeated.

University of Oklahoma: *Sooner Schooner*

The mascot present at all football games is the *Sooner Schooner*, a Conestoga wagon, pulled by two cream white ponies, *Boomer and Sooner*. In time for the 2005 football season, two new costumed mascots were introduced, based on the ponies who pull the Schooner, named appropriately, Boomer and Sooner. The costumed mascots are identical to each other except for their eye color. Before, the Boomer and Sooner costume mascots, OU was also represented by *Top Dawg*. Top Dawg did some appearances at football games, but was primarily used at wrestling and basketball events. The Sooner Schooner leads the football team's entrance to the field.

Oklahoma State University (Football): *Exiting the Corral*

Oklahoma State's Cowboys are known for riding horses, but OSU's pregame tradition keeps with that theme while switching up the role. The Cowboys make a grand entrance every game day when the team gathers in the tunnel and the door of the corral is shut. The smoke gets going, fills the tunnel until *the ranch hands swing open the corral door*, and the fans go nuts. The players sprint onto the field when the corral opens and lets the Cowboys out, and you know it's on.

University of Oregon (Football): *Duck on a Harley*

Before football games, the team is led into Autzen Stadium by their *Duck mascot riding on the back of a Harley-Davidson motorcycle*.

Purdue University (Football): *Boilermaker X-tra Special*

Since 1979, football players are led onto the football field by *the Boilermaker X-tra Special*, a scale version of a Victorian-era locomotive.

Roanoke College (Lacrosse): *Touching the Bust of John Pirro*

The Roanoke College men's lacrosse team walks past a bust of John Pirro before every home game and ceremoniously *touches his head*. Pirro played and coached at Roanoke, and showed grace in his response to personal adversity (Huntington's Disease).

St. Lawrence University (Ice Hockey): *Fire Truck Horn*

Men's and women's ice hockey teams are greeted upon arrival on the ice to start each period by a *siren from an old fire truck*. Men's hockey first used the siren in 1977. Women followed with the establishment of that program in 1980.

University of South Carolina (Various Sports): *Theme from 2001: A Space Odyssey*

The theme from *2001* corresponds with the university's bicentennial. The theme song from *2001: A Space Odyssey* is played at nearly all Gamecocks athletics events and is most widely recognized for its use with the Carolina football team's pregame entrance, which is regarded as one of the most unique and electrifying in all of college football.

University of Tennessee (Football): *Running Through the Block-T*

At the climax of the Tennessee band's pregame show, the musicians form in a wide-open "T" formation for the players to run through as they exit the tunnel. The tradition began in 1964 when then-head coach Doug Dickey introduced the "T" on the player's helmets. The pregame routine followed shortly after and has become a permanent home game staple for the band, and for the team. The "T" has occasionally been formed for road games, most notably at Liberty Bowl Memorial Stadium in Memphis, at Vanderbilt Stadium in Nashville, and at various other major bowl games.

University of Texas (Football): *Touching the Horns*

You don't step on the field at Darrell K. Royal–Texas Memorial Stadium wearing the burnt orange without taking care of a little business first. Do it however you must, but every player and coach *touches a mounted set of horns* below a sign that reads, "Don't Mess with Texas." A couple of steps later, the roar of the crowd grows, and it's game time. Thousands of players have run their hands across the horns in a variety of ways hundreds of thousands of times. The horns are worn with that kind of traffic, and it's easy to remember the stars like Colt McCoy and Vince Young, who helped age them by running their hands across them before plenty of historic wins.

University of Texas-Pan American (Basketball): *Public Locker Room and Faux Fight Song*

After the coach's pregame instructions, the Broncs funnel into a larger public locker room, where they often encounter the opposing team, refs, and a handful of naked professors that have just finished swimming in the adjoining pool. Following that awkwardness, they continue down a narrow corridor to the court, as the pep band plays what everyone assumes is their fight song, but actually it is "La Adelita," a folk/love song from the Mexican Revolution.

Texas Tech (Football): *Masked Rider*

Originally the *Masked Rider* started as a dare in 1936 and was then called the *Ghost Rider*, because no one knew the rider's identity. These Ghost Riders circled the field at home football games and then disappeared. The Masked Rider did not become an official mascot until 1954, when Joe Kirk Fulton led the team onto the field at the Gator Bowl. Fulton, wearing Levis, a red shirt, a black cape, and mounted on a black horse awed the crowd as the team made one of the most sensational entrances ever. Today, the Masked Rider, with his or her guns up, leads the team onto the field for each home game. The Masked Rider is one of the most visible figures at Tech.

Virginia Tech (Football): *"Enter Sandman"*

The Hokies have taken the field to this Metallica tune since 2000.

Wake Forest University (Football): *Open the Gate*

During home football games there is a famous alum, or other special guest, who *opens the gate* and leads the Demon Deacons onto the field. This person usually rides onto the field with the Demon Deacon on his motorcycle.

West Virginia University (Basketball): *Roll Out the Carpet*

Beginning in 1955, an elaborate gold and blue carpet has been rolled out for the Mountaineers to use as they enter for pregame warm-ups. In addition, in the past, Mountaineer players warmed up with a special gold and blue painted basketball. West Virginia University continued this tradition during the George King era until it was interrupted in the late 1960s. Former Mountaineer player Gale Catlett reintroduced the carpet when he returned to West Virginia in 1978, and it has since become the highlight of pregame introductions at the WVU Coliseum.

The College of Wooster (Football): *Scotland the Brave/ Bagpipe Band*

The College of Wooster runs down a hill as their bagpipe band plays "Scotland the Brave."

8

TRADITIONS REFLECTING THE CULTURE OF THE UNIVERSITY

Traditions are essential to the culture of colleges across the country. They're often the essence of campus life, creating memories that can last a lifetime. Especially in the Lone Star state.

At the University of Texas (UT), there are *guidelines for the lighting configurations of the fabled tower* on the Austin campus. Lighting patterns vary, distinguishing between academic and staff achievements and athletic victories. Traditional orange works to celebrate campus-wide events. A darkened tower ("UT remembers") is used only on solemn occasions.

A committee appointed by the UT president in 2001 revised those lighting configurations and recommended two new ones: white top, orange shaft; and top split orange and white, with orange shaft.

And you thought the Wishbone offense was complex when it debuted at UT.

At Stephen F. Austin (SFA), the *Burn Shirt* tradition lives on. That initiative, begun by the Student Activities Association to increase school spirit, encouraged students to dispose of apparel branded with the names and logos of other universities. Students can trade those schools' merchandise for an SFA T-shirt.

Initially, the discarded rivals' apparel was burned in a bonfire at a spirit rally. In 2007, however, students found a more productive way to dispose of the clothing: donating it to local shelters and charitable organizations. The original intent is intact, though. The Burn Shirts now read: "Lumberjack Spirit Burns in My Soul!"

Texas A&M, of course, has a vast variety of traditions. Beginning, naturally, with its famed *12th man*. But one that I particularly love is their tradition of *Yes Sir*. When visiting a game recently, I noticed a student wearing a t-shirt with the words "Yes Sir" and nothing else printed on it. With A&M's military heritage, I assumed that connection, but when I asked the student, I was told that when a football player is offered a scholarship at Texas A&M, he is to reply in one of several ways (in person, phone, email, fax, etc.), but with only two-words: "Yes, sir." If this tradition still continues, can there be a better example of a tradition reflecting the culture of that university? I think not.

But we also love the tradition at Texas A&M of saying, "*Howdy.*" When I attended a *Midnight Yell Practice*, and the following day's game in 2012, I personally confirmed that every person (students, fans, and stadium work-ers) looked forward to greeting you with the phrase, "Howdy." There can-not be a more friendly campus, anywhere, than Texas A&M.

And then there is Baylor and the *Immortal Ten*, and what is considered to be the first college sports tragedy. In 1995, Chase Palmer was senior class president for Baylor's 1995–1996 school year. The student body president asked him to find a good senior class project to organize. Palmer and two friends "were thinking about things on Baylor's campus, and one thing that

Baylor's "Immortal Ten" Memorial. *Baylor University*

came to mind was the Immortal Ten," he told Tim Woods of the *Waco Tribune-Herald* in 2007. "We talked about it a lot, but didn't have anything to memorialize it."

On January 22, 1927, a wintry, misty, foggy Friday, ten men were killed when a bus carrying the Baylor men's basketball team to a game in Austin against Texas was hit by a train in Round Rock. Twelve others aboard the bus survived. The ten casualties were immortalized.

Their story is told annually by twilight at Baylor's Freshman Mass Meeting on the Wednesday of homecoming week of how first-year coach Ralph Wolf was taking his Baylor team, which had lost to Texas 22–15 earlier that month, to Austin for a Southwest Conference game. How Wolf, whose wife was pregnant and nearly due, considered not travelling with the Bears. But with Baylor on a four-game losing streak, including three conference defeats, Wolf accompanied his team. Tragedy struck, but Wolf survived.

Nearly seventy years later, Palmer, his friends Brett Moyer and Mark Rylander, and many others began raising funds for a memorial to the Immortal Ten. It would eventually become a statuary memorial, consisting of four individual statues of players killed in the wreck, and a bas-relief panel of the six other victims.

"We thought it'd take a couple of years," Palmer said of the fundraising for the project. Instead, it took more than a decade.

"When I started," Palmer told Woods in 2007, "I was in college, single, and had a full head of hair. Now I'm married with three kids, and I'm bald."

A noted western painter and sculptor, Bruce Greene, was commissioned to design and create the memorial. The estimated cost: more than $280,000. This, for statues or sculptures of men who'd died in the 1920s.

"It was tough because all of the people from that time are gone," Palmer told Woods in 2007. "It's not easy to convince people to give money for something that happened so long ago."

Palmer and his friends persisted, raising nearly $178,000 from alumni, various organizations, and student groups. Yet they were still nearly $100,000 shy.

"We just didn't have anywhere else to turn," said Palmer. With help from the Baylor Alumni Association and Student Life Program, nearly $100,000 was raised, and Greene began work on the bronze statues.

He worked on the project for more than three years, so determined was he to sculpt likenesses of the ten as they looked in 1927—players and a yell leader in their uniforms; a writer and scorekeeper aboard the bus, dressed in street clothes; a team manager, also wearing street clothes and carrying a uniform.

However, there were few photographs of the ten from that era. So Greene relied on family photos that were donated and pictures from the Baylor University archives. Yet there were no records of players' heights and weights in 1927.

"We never did find any pictures of the 1927 uniforms," Greene told Woods.

So, Greene recalled, "I did the best I could with what resources we had, and those resources were very limited."

Greene sculpted what Woods described as "a powerful and intricate monument to memorialize the victims of the 1927 crash." The work, consisting of those four individual sculptures and a bas-relief panel of the other six men, was placed in the center of the Baylor campus, near a fountain.

"I feel very good about it," Greene said upon completion of the memorial. "I did the best job I could, so there's some satisfaction in that. The reaction from people who have seen it has been wonderful."

Greene felt a burden, a pressure to commemorate the Immortal Ten and to honor their memories and the tradition they represent. "It was an honor to be asked and a big responsibility," he said. "I've been to the candlelight ceremony with my wife, and I felt that responsibility."

Todd Copeland understands. The director of communications for the Baylor Alumni Association and editor of *The Baylor Line*, a quarterly publication, Copeland told Woods he felt "an onus to be factually accurate" while writing a book: *The Immortal Ten: The Definitive Account of the 1927 Tragedy and its Legacy at Baylor University*.

Copeland returned to the scene of the wreck and re-created the tragedy. Joe Potter, nineteen, a freshman halfback on the football team, was driving the basketball team bus to help pay his tuition. On that fateful January 22, as Copeland discovered and wrote, Potter tried to keep the bus windshield clean of mud and rain, operating the wipers by hand while driving country roads with twenty-one passengers aboard.

They included Coach Wolf, the players, a yell leader, a team manager, an editor from *The Daily Lariat* (the Baylor student newspaper), and a scorekeeper. And, eventually, Ivey Foster, a freshman who'd hitchhiked to Temple, Texas, before flagging down the bus and climbing aboard.

The trip took 3.5 hours, the bus traveling just twenty-two miles per hour on unfamiliar country roads and in increasingly bad weather.

As Copeland wrote, setting the scene:

> The bus motors down a muddy hill as it approaches a railroad crossing in Round Rock, not far from its destination. Near the crossing, the visibility is diminished not only by the muddy windshield but by several buildings to the west.

Although the train sounds its whistle, nobody on the team bus hears it. Potter doesn't see the train, traveling about 60 MPH, till Coach Wolf notices it at the last moment and shouts, "Look out!" Potter is forced to make a split-second decision to try to stop on the wet, muddy embankment or speed up to beat the train hurtling down the tracks. He chooses the latter option.

The *Sunshine Special*, a passenger train from the International and Great Northern Railroad Company, was churning toward the level-grade railroad crossing as the bus came within 100 feet of the tracks.

"The speeding train strikes the rear half of the bus, obliterating it and spewing debris more than 40 yards," Copeland wrote. "Twelve men are spared, either by jumping from the bus before impact or being hurled from it in the chaotic aftermath."

Not so lucky were those destined to be known to subsequent generations as the Immortal Ten.

Potter's passengers began scrambling to the front door and windows, trying to escape. One player, Weir Washam of Waco, dived out of a window, helped by a push from his best friend and teammate, Clyde "Abe" Kelley.

For others, it was too late. The bus slid diagonally across the train's path, leaving the back corner of the vehicle in front of the train engine. The collision, it was said, could be heard for miles. Six men were killed on impact, including two whose bodies were found entwined on the train's cowcatcher. Four more died either en route to, or in, hospitals. There were ten casualties: Kelley Foster, William Winchester, W. E. Murray, Merle Dudley, Sam Dillow, Jack Castellaw, Bob Hailey, R. L. Hannah, Clyde "Abe" Kelly, and James Walker.

"The train swept through the bus just as you would sweep through the room," Louis Slade, a player who survived, told reporters later that day. "Had we just had time to think, many of the boys would have jumped. In the short time we had, though, we could not get the doors opened and those who escaped were simply luckily knocked out of the bus."

Dave Cheavens, managing editor of the *Baylor Lariat*, was on the bus and had sent a telegram to the Associated Press shortly after the accident occurred.

"The heart of Baylor University is torn to shreds at this moment. . . . Nothing like this has ever happened before," said Baylor President Samuel Parker Brooks, who traveled with his athletic director and business manager to Taylor, where the dead and injured were taken in the train's baggage car. The three men visited the morgue and hospital, and met some of the students' families when they arrived at a hotel.

Back in Waco, the small Baylor campus (only about 1,600 students in 1927) was consumed with grief. More than 3,000 mourners attended a memorial service in the auditorium of Baylor's chapel building, which also served as the basketball team's court. Flowers and green and gold streamers were everywhere.

The rest of the 1927 basketball season was cancelled.

The next day, in a eulogy published in the January 23, 1927, edition of the *Tribune-Herald*, Jack Hawkins wrote, "Though Death's icy fingers have written *Finis* across the life of each of The Immortal Ten who are today mourned, their memory will never perish."

Abe Kelley, who'd heroically saved Washam, was the captain-elect of the 1927 football team. That fall, he was honored when the team chose not to replace Kelley as the Bears' captain.

The accident would lead to railroad-crossing safety reform, Todd Copeland reported, though years would pass before such reforms were fully implemented.

The first highway overpass in Texas was eventually built in Round Rock, and the catastrophe, Copeland wrote, "Also led to a longstanding tradition of remembrance at Baylor."

"The story of The Immortal Ten is deeply woven into the fabric of our history and it binds generations of Baylor alumni," former Baylor president John Lilley told the *Tribune-Herald* in 2007. "For 80 years, the memory of the young men who lost their lives, as well as those who escaped the tragedy, have reminded us of the abiding value of faith, community, loyalty, perseverance and hope."

At the 1927 memorial service for the Immortal Ten, Henry Trantham, the head of Baylor's athletic council, spoke these words: "Their lives are lived but not in vain. God's purpose is accomplished in them. The things they stood for are part of the rich heritage of Baylor; their unconquerable spirit will hover around us in the years to come."

REFLECTIONS OF CULTURE BY SCHOOL

Baylor University (Football): *Bobby Jones Award*

During the week preceding each year's homecoming, Baylor presents the *Bobby Jones Award*. This award is given to an outstanding senior player from the previous year for leadership on and off the field. The Baylor coaching staff chooses the recipient. The award serves as a memorial for Jones, the Baylor quarterback who led the Bears to defeat the University of Tennessee in the 1957 Sugar Bowl. His widow, Rosemary Jones, established the award after he died in 1965 in an automobile-train wreck while a member of the Tennessee coaching staff.

Illinois State University: *Torch-Lit Tour of Campus*

New athletes get a *torch-lit sports-history tour* of campus. Around the turn of the twenty-first century, a group of Illinois State student-athletes and administrators began to formulate an event that would welcome new student-athletes into the Redbird family and educate them about the rich history of the athletics department. Together, they created the *annual Walk of Champions*. In August 2001, all new Redbird student-athletes were led on a torch-guided tour by Redbird upperclassmen of historic locations around campus. The event was such a success, that the athletics department made it an annual occurrence. In mid-August, the day before the beginning of classes, Redbird student-athletes, new and old, gather for the Walk of Champions. The culmination of the evening happens outside of Redbird Arena, where each new student-athlete is introduced and given half of a medallion. The other half will be presented to them the night of their senior banquet. One side of the medallion features the Redbird logo, while the other has an inscription of a phrase from the ISU fight song, "To this emblem we'll be true."

Southern Miss: *President's Proclamation*

In 2007, the University of Southern Mississippi issued a *formal procla-mation*—signed jointly by the university president and the head of their alumni association—that ensured the preservation of the traditions of Southern Miss as they were originally intended. In addition to listing each tradition in great detail, the proclamation names the Alumni Association Traditions Committee as the clearinghouse for all proposed changes or alterations to existing traditions. Think they take their traditions serious at Southern Miss? We do.

Stephen F. Austin State University: *Mentor Ring/Big Dip*

One of the newest traditions on campus helps Lumberjacks identify one another long after they graduate and leave Nacogdoches behind. The SFA *Mentor Ring* is a specially designed ring that has been adopted as the uni-versity's official class ring. More than just a piece of jewelry, the Mentor Ring comes with an SFA mentor for each student. These mentors ensure that the students' last months at SFA are on the right track to graduation and beyond. Students receive their Mentor Rings in a ceremony called the *Big Dip*. At this ceremony, held in the middle of campus, students—many of whom are athletes—have their hands dipped in purple dye before being presented with their rings.

University of Texas: *Tower Lighting Guidelines*

On February 2, 2001, President Larry R. Faulkner appointed a committee to recommend a revised set of tower-lighting guidelines:

- Should the tower be lit for individual achievements, as well as "group" achievements?
- What should be the level of recognition?
- What should the lighting pattern be for each level of recognition?
- Should the tower be lit for nonuniversity events?

The committee recommended, and the president approved, the following lighting configurations. A summary of the philosophy on which the committee based its recommendations also is listed.

- Committee philosophy.
- Lighting patterns should distinguish between academic and staff achievements and athletic victories.
- Traditional Orange should be displayed for celebration of campus-wide events.
- Darkened tower ("UT remembers") should be used only for solemn occasions.
- Committee recommends two new lighting configurations: (1) white top, orange shaft; (2) top split orange and white with orange shaft.
- Other lighting options are available.

9

FAN-RELATED/NICKNAME TRADITIONS

They're Johnny Spirit and Mr. Two-Bits. Crazy Lady and Vandy Lance. And there's the clearly caffeinated Mr. Coffee, who only recently stopped perking after personally attending the last 780 Alabama football games.

But to borrow from Grantland Rice, "These are only aliases."

These are fans. Ardent college sports fans. And they are not alone.

There's The IZZone at Michigan State, perhaps the roughest bump on the Big Ten basketball road. There is the Zoo at Pitt, the eRUPPtion zone at Rupp Arena, and the Rowdy Reptiles of Florida basketball.

Wild Bill has rooted for Utah State since, well, ever. Or so it seems. Purdue's Paint Crew crows for hoops coach Matt Painter. From Wake's Screamin' Demons to Wisconsin's Grateful Red, from Washington's Dawg Pack to the Orange Krush at Illinois. Did someone say The Barnyard at Minnesota? The Kennel at Gonzaga? Notre Dame's Leprechaun Legion? Five overtimes, anyone?

These are college kids and grownups, too. Fans all enthralled by the home team.

If you're an undergrad at Vanderbilt University (VU), you're likely one of the Memorial Maniacs! That's the strident student section at Commodores' basketball games, men's and women's. The umbrella spirit organization for all Vandy sports is called Open Dores. Nice. But things get most spirited and most maniacal at men's games in Memorial Gym, often the scene of Memorial Magic.

Memorial Gym, the Fenway Park of southern college basketball, opened in 1952. It was designed by the late, noted Nashville architect Edwin Keeble. Its distinctive design includes team benches behind each baseline, a raised playing floor and balconies that give the place an opera house aura.

"The Balconies that Clyde Lee Built" they're called, in honor of the Vandy hoops great that elevated the basketball program and the need for more seats.

Vandy Lance, as Lance Smith is known, knows his way around. He never attended Vanderbilt but became an ardent VU fan in 1969, when he saw the Commodores beat Bear Bryant's Alabama Crimson Tide. After that, Vandy Lance showed up at most every sporting event.

Johnny Spirit is actually John Sheldon. As a Michigan State student, he, too, began attending almost every athletic function in 1993, painted in Spartans green from head to toe. While Nick Saban was the head coach at Michigan State, he once issued this statement: "Johnny Spirit fits the definition of a super fan."

So did George Edmondson, Mr. Two-Bits to Florida fans, ever since he first led Gator fans in a "Two-Bits" cheer during a 1949 Florida-Citadel football game. George wasn't an alumnus, but became an institution—even upon retiring after 2008.

Terri Jackson? That's the real name and person behind Crazy Lady at Utah. An alumna from more than thirty years ago, Terri does her wild dance before the start of each and every Utes' fourth quarter. Students chant—what else?—"CRA-ZY LA-DY!"

Robert Lipson, a rabid Kansas State fan, once slept in his car overnight in minus-seventeen-degree weather to catch a Wildcats-Iowa State game in Ames. In a word: *brrrrrrr*.

Alas, Ohio State lost Neutron Man when Orlas King, an animated, big-time Buckeye fan, died in 2004.

Those two Washington State University (WSU) flags—one ol' crimson, one ol' white—that you see in the background of every *ESPN Game Day* telecast? You can thank Tom Pounds, the Washington State alum who's waved the flags a time or two but, more importantly, has coordinated the flag relay of Cougars fans since October, 2003. More than 100 WSU fans have participated and kept their flags flying.

When Cecil Samara, the legendary Oklahoma fan, died in 1994, he was buried wearing a red jacket, an OU tie, and a Sooners belt buckle. Despite his wishes, Cecil's family declined his request to have his index finger raised in the "We're Number 1" pose in the casket.

Then there's the remarkable Mr. Coffee. Dick Coffee saw—as in attended—every Alabama football game since 1946. After watching the 2013 BCS championship game, Coffee's streak stood at 780. He died in the summer of 2013, so the last Alabama game that he witnessed was a National Championship. How fitting.

They're super fans, all. But so is at least one celebrated—and celebrity—Kentucky basketball fan: Ashley Judd, whose bluegrass passion for UK hoops is well known and, well, read on.

Ashley Judd's Essay on UK Basketball, from her website, in 2004:

I really have far too many wonderful memories to even begin sharing, so I'll leave you with my most recent. It's also my most emotional. I went to Rupp for Senior Day, cast, sinusitis, bronchitis and all (84–62, UK). Each home game, during the first time out in the second half, our cheerleaders (12 time National Champions) slide around the floor spelling 'Kentucky' and a special person from the crowd is asked to come out to make the "Y," something I have done both alone and with my family. (Some actually say the way I fired up the crowd with my hyperactive Y in 2002 when we were down to Tennessee helped us come back to win! Mr. Wildcat was looking at me, mouth gaping and amusement on his face, even some of the players in the huddle couldn't help but stare. But it ended up right, 64–61, UK). Anyhow, that day, cheerleader Jason Keough hoisted me onto his brave shoulder to carry me and my UK blue cast out to half court, and before the PA had even had a chance to introduce me, I saw that the entire gym (that's 23,000 + people! Have you ever seen a picture of that place?) was giving me a standing ovation. It was the most extraordinary feeling, something you can readily see in my face in the photograph of me with my arms opened wide and eyes closed, soaking up and reciprocating the love and esteem my kindred were giving me. They knew I hadn't been to Rupp all season. They know how much it all means to me, how much it meant to my Papaw Judd and Uncle Brian and all those others about whom I have told you. Back at the Music Box Theatre, at that very moment my play was closing without me, but I was having the best curtain call of my entire life right there in Rupp Arena, feeling adored by the people who mean so very much to me: The people of Kentucky.

FAN-RELATED TRADITIONS BY SCHOOL

Baylor University (Football): *The Line*

The Baylor Line is a longstanding Baylor tradition: a spirit organization composed of only freshmen. The Line wears gold jerseys, each member sporting a unique nickname on the back of the jersey. Before each home football game, the Line gathers on the ramp of the south end zone on the student side at Floyd Casey Stadium. There, the students begin the cheers and help energize the game-day crowd. Led by specially selected students carrying flags leading the freshmen, the Line runs around the field prior to kickoff, then forms an extension to the players' tunnel as the Baylor football team explodes onto the field. The Baylor Line then returns to a reserved section of seats directly behind the opposing team's bench. These are the best seats to cheer on the Bears, heckle the opponents, and help the team to victory.

Boston College (Ice Hockey/Basketball): *Super-Fan Rewards Program*

The *Super-Fan Rewards Program* was initiated to enhance the attendance of student season ticket holders for men's ice hockey and men's basketball. As an effort to try to boost the support for these programs, Boston College athletics in conjunction with student government created a reward's based system given to those students who attend a high percentage of their games. When a student picks up their season ticket package, every ticket that they have is tied to their name. Over the course of the season, students accumulate points for every game they attend. Points depend on the strength of the opponent and the day of the week the game falls on. The more points students receive the greater their chances become of winning great prizes. Not only does their attendance affect their chance of winning rewards, it also affects their chances of receiving season tickets the following year.

Bowling Green State University (Various Sports): *SICSIC*

Since 1946, BGSU's official spirit crew has been an ultrasecretive group called *SICSIC*. New members are chosen during the end of their freshman year in order to replace that year's graduating seniors. Membership in SICSIC is limited to two members in each of the three upper classes. The new members are tapped at the end of their freshman year and pledged at the beginning of their sophomore year. Members are chosen by the active members of the group and every student is eligible. SICSIC members are always masked and their identities are not revealed until the Honors Day Ceremony of their senior year. Their adviser is a member of the faculty or administration, and they also remain anonymous during their period of advisement. If the identity of a SICSIC member is discovered and revealed to the campus, the member gives up their right to membership and a new member is immediately pledged to take their place. All meetings, banquets, and initiations are always held with a high level of secrecy. Correspondence to the group is directed to the office of the president of the university or to an alumni member. One of my personal friends was a SICSIC member, and views it as a unique part of his college experience.

University of California (Football): *Tightwad Hill*

In 1924, college kids (without a lot of money) at Berkeley found a way to watch Cal football games without paying for tickets. By climbing the hills next to the stadium they got a clear, free view of the field. Prior to the recent renovation of Cal's stadium, which now includes aluminum benches, many fans mailed the football coach and athletic director envelopes containing splinters from the broken bench seats. Even after the renovation, some students still forgo the stadium for the open air and views of *Tightwad Hill*.

Colorado State University (Various Sports): *Green Out*

Green Outs were created to encourage Ram fans to wear green on game days and on the Fridays before athletic events. Green Outs have established a tradition of students wearing green shirts to the games, and to make the crowd a unified and intimidating factor in all home games.

Duke University (Basketball): *Cameron Crazies*

Cameron Indoor Stadium is not exactly modern and holds just 9,300 fans, but it is one of the most intimidating places in the country to play. The *Cameron Crazies*, one of the most boisterous and creative student sections anywhere, make sure of that. The Crazies brave the elements (often for months in a tent city known as *Krzyzewskiville*) to get their seats. Face painting is almost part of the game day required attire. The Blue Devils student section has been credited with coming up with the chant of

Duke's "Cameron Crazies." *Duke University*

"air ball!" when an opponent misses everything on a shot. They also once taunted one super-sized opposing player by tying a McDonald's Happy Meal to the end of a fishing pole and dragging it across the front of the bench before a security guard put an end to it.

East Carolina University: *Pirate Attire*

Fans often dress as pirates.

Florida State University (Baseball): *Animals of Section B*

For no apparent reason, this group sings "O'Canada" during baseball games.

University of Georgia (Football): *Spike Squad*

The *Spike Squad* is a dedicated group of UGA fans who cover themselves in body paint and don spiked shoulder pads to cheers the Dawgs to victory.

Georgia Tech: *The Swarm*

The Swarm is a spirit group consisting of approximately 900 Georgia Tech students found seated along the north end zone during home football games and beside the court during basketball games. The Swarm was started by Suzanne ("Suzy Swarm") Robinson of the Ramblin' Wreck Club in 1996 to increase the amount of student participation in the stands. The Swarm was only 250 members when it began in 1996. The group increased to 650 members by 2001 and is currently approximately 900 members strong. All Swarm members donate to the Alexander-Tharpe fund and are given gold t-shirts before every football and basketball season. One of the more popular traditions amongst Swarm members is the *Running of the Swarm*. Because all Swarm seating is general admission, there are no reserved seats. The Swarm members must run once the gate is opened to get the best seats.

Harding University (Basketball): *Rhodes Rowdies*

Harding University recently beat out nine other worthy contenders through a two-week Facebook voting competition and won the "Best Road Trip Destination in College Basketball," presented by Enterprise Rent-A-Car. The entire Harding community, led by the *Rhodes Rowdies*—the moniker of the Bison fan base—came out in full force to push their team to the top, earning the Division II school an in-depth feature on what makes the Rhodes Field House, the Harding University campus and the town of Searcy, Arkansas, a special place for any college basketball fan to visit.

Harvard (Football): *Little Red Flag*

The Little Red Flag is a small silk flag attached to a walking stick, which is carried by the Harvard football team's most loyal supporter and passed on to each following generation. The Little Red Flag was said to have been created by Frederick Plummer in 1888. He made it to fifty-nine consecutive Harvard vs. Yale games and carried the banner with him to each one. The flag was then given to the Harvard man (or woman) in attendance at the game that had seen the most Harvard vs. Yale games in their lifetime.

University of Hawaii: *Palm Fronds*

Fans wave palm fronds for luck.

Hope College (Basketball): *Dew Crew*

Hope College would say, "If passion were a color, it would be orange. If passion were a person, it would be Dutch. If passion were a place it would be Hope. With each bite of passion comes the lingering taste of tradition." Since its founding in 1996, the *Dew Crew* has become contagious. Each graduating class is replaced by a freshman body of eager fanatics. Many have grown up around Hope basketball. Many have grown up with a habit of watching the Dew Crew more than watching the game, and yet some are experiencing the heartbeat of Hope for the first time. But no matter what background Hope students come from, everyone's chest shares the same racing rhythm. Visiting teams put the Dew Crew in their scouting reports. The Dew Crew dominates attendance records and decibel levels while creating a home court atmosphere of passion. For those who play the game, all they need to do is look into a sea of their peers to find motivation. The painted chests of their classmates, the hoarse throats of their resident advisers, professors, and their entire student population in the stands, all combines to unify both athlete and school under an orange and blue flag of passion.

University of Kansas: *No Name for the Student Group*

Unlike almost every other school with a catchy name (often alliterative) for their student section, Kansas is one of the big-name programs that seems not to need a catchy-title. They have *no name for their student section*. But this did not prevent them from winning an inaugural award for student fan-groups last year. KU's 4,000-seat student section has many unique traditions, which include a student-run "camping for seats" system (many days in advance), filling the seats adjacent to James Naismith Court two hours before tip-off, throwing newspaper confetti during player introductions, standing the entire game, and leading the famous Rock Chalk Chant. "We have the best students and fans in the country, and we are thrilled to now have national confirmation of what we have always known," said head coach Bill Self, who has led the Jayhawks into the tournament in each of his nine seasons at Kansas. "Our student section starts prepping for games days before tip-off; they stand by our team the entire game, giving us an unbelievable home-court advantage. We thank the Naismith Awards organization and the Collegiate Licensing Company for establishing this unique award and selecting our Kansas students."

Miami University of Ohio: *Hard Hats*

Student fans often wear red-and-white hard hats.

Michigan State University (Basketball): *IZZone*

At Michigan State, students are clad all in white to support Coach Tom Izzo. A sidenote, Coach Izzo recently asked students not to text or talk on their phones during games!

University of Minnesota (Basketball): *The Barnyard*

Their gym is called the *Barn* due to its unique shape. Therefore the students refer to themselves as the *Barnyard*. Students can often be found in costumes (many barnyard animals) cheering the team on.

Mississippi State University (Baseball): *Left Field Lounge*

Fans sit in the back of their pickup trucks and eat Cajun food; students sometimes give the left fielders hotdogs during the game. It is rumored that this is one of author John Grisham's very favorite places to visit.

Monmouth College (Various Sports): *Students' Company*

In keeping with the college's Civil War history, the college formed their own company known as the *Students' Company*.

University of North Carolina at Charlotte (Basketball): *Basketballs on Heads*

Fans have been known to put partial-basketballs on their heads while others paint their faces green.

Northwestern University (Football): *Spirit Team*

Starting in the 1960s, students have worn unique hats (originally made from hemp). The spirit leader is elected, by the band, and is responsible for leading the band and surrounding fans in cheers. The Spirit Leader wears a black aviator-style cloth helmet that has been passed down from the beginning, and is believed to have belonged to a UN football player who had served in WWII.

University of Notre Dame: *Local Hotel Duplicates Traditions*

In each hotel room in a local South Bend hotel, there is a large framed picture of *Touchdown Jesus*. And in the hotel's lobby is a sign that says "Play like a Champion Today." Business people slap it on their way off to work.

Oakland University (Basketball): *Grizz Gang*

Oakland's student section is known as the *Grizz Gang* and prides themselves in the winning-team/losing-team chant towards the end of winning games.

University of Oklahoma: *RUF/NEKS*

The caretakers of the *Sooner Schooner* wagon are the spirit group called the *RUF/NEKS*. The group was launched in 1915 when an elderly female spectator at an Oklahoma University–Oklahoma A&M basketball game chided the group for raising hell: "Sit down and be quiet, you roughnecks!"

Ole Miss (Football): *Tailgating at the Grove*

Tailgating is an integral part of the college football experience, but while fans of every team tailgate, Ole Miss fans do it with style and more than a little class. *The Grove* is a shaded ten-acre patch of grass in Oxford, Mississippi, that on game days is filled with red and white and blue tents. More than a few candelabras can be seen, and food eaten by Southern belles and men in coats and ties is often served on the best china. Don't forget a stop at the *Hot Toddy Potty* (seriously) after you've sipped your share.

University of Oregon (Basketball): *Pit Crew*

Each year, Oregon basketball and their student section, the *Pit Crew*, gain national recognition. And when March Madness concludes at the end of the college basketball season, that doesn't stop the Pit Crew. Every year in the spring the Pit Crew hosts a three-on-three basketball tournament for students. Nike recently took the Pit Crew under its wing, issuing a specially designed shoe for the Pit Crew. I'm just guessing here, but I bet the Pit Crew may be the only student-fan-group with their own line of shoes. "We're treating them like another team down there," said Tinker Hatfield, Nike vice president of innovation design and special projects. But

Oregon's Student Section: "The Pit Crew." *Lars Topelmann; Lars Topelmann Photography*

not every Pit Crew member received a pair of the shoes, in part because the initial run for the 2011–2012 academic year totaled 500, and there were approximately 1,000 Pit Crew members. As a result, Pit Crew members had to earn them by adhering to standards, attending a certain number of games, and agreeing to a code of conduct. But in a very cool move, ten pairs of the shoes were up for grabs in a raffle during Oregon's version of *Midnight Madness*.

Southern Methodist University (Football): *Mustangs Eleven*

Mustangs Eleven are students within each class year who promote spirit and traditions like Red and Blue Fridays and wearing red shirts at sports events.

University of Tennessee (Football): *Volunteer Navy*

In 1962, former Volunteers broadcaster George Mooney found a quicker and more exciting way to get to Neyland Stadium other than by fighting the notorious Knoxville traffic. Mooney navigated his little runabout down the Tennessee River to the stadium and spawned what would later become known as the *Volunteer Navy*. Today, approximately 200 boats of all shapes and sizes make up this giant floating tailgate party. Tennessee and the University of Washington are among the most prominent institutions with stadiums adjacent to bodies of water.

Texas A&M (Football): *The 12th Man*

Students stand for the entire game, and have attained the name "12th Man." The tradition began on January 2, 1922, at the Dixie Classic where A&M played Centre College. A&M had so many injuries in the first half of the game that Coach Dana X. Bible feared he wouldn't have enough men to finish the game. He called into the stands for E. King Gill, a reserve who had left football after the regular season to play basketball. Although he did not actually play, his readiness symbolized the willingness of all Aggies to support their team to the point of actually entering the game. A&M won 22–14, but E. King Gill was the only man left standing on the sidelines for the Aggies. In recent decades, the 12th Man is represented on the field by a walk-on player who wears the number 12 jersey and participates in kickoffs. In 2012, Texas A&M contacted the Seattle Seahawks about infringement on the "12th man" term, as the term is trademarked.

Texas A&M (Baseball): *RAggies and Aggie Alley*

The *RAggies* are a rowdy student section of approximately 4,000 who position themselves above the opponent's dugout. The RAggies name comes from chants (rags) to torment opposing teams. *Aggie Alley* is a parking lot beyond left field, but students enter a lottery and pay $50 for the right to assemble there and heckle the opposing team's left fielder.

Texas Tech (Football): *Saddle Tramps*

Texas Tech has a spirit organization known as the *Saddle Tramps*. Formed by Tech student Arch Lamb in 1936, this all-male (still!) booster organization supports men's athletics at Texas Tech. The name Saddle Tramp came from the stories of traveling men who would come to a farm for a brief time, fix up some things, and move on. Lamb said he decided that he could fix up some things himself before moving on, and the Saddle Tramps were born. Since that time the Saddle Tramps believe if something was for the betterment of Texas Tech then they would work at it. These Midnight Raiders *paint the campus red* with crepe paper before big home games, form the legendary *Bell Circle* moments before kickoff, ring *Bangin' Bertha*, participate in parades and other campus events (including the *Carol of Lights*), and ring the *victory bells* after Red Raider victories.

Texas Tech (Baseball): *Tech Hecklers*

They even have a *Ten Commandments of Heckling* (i.e., Thou Shall Not Insult the Mother), that has been effect since 1996.

Utica College (Ice Hockey): *Pioneer Posse*

Utica fans utilize unique chants and cheers versus the opposing team (especially for goalkeepers and those in the penalty box).

Wake Forest University (Basketball): *Tie-Dyed Nation*

During home basketball games at Lawrence Joel Veteran's Memorial Coliseum, the stands are filled with fans dressed in yellow and black tie-dye. The *Tie-Dye Nation* gives the Demon Deacons a distinct home-court advantage.

10

INTRAMURALS/CLUB SPORTS TRADITIONS

To paraphrase the Bard, "To play's the thing." Not everyone can play college varsity football, basketball, or lacrosse. But most anyone can play intramural flag football, or in Notre Dame's *Bookstore Basketball* tournament, or pedal a bike like mad. Just join a college club team and you can fish for bass, toss a Frisbee, or hit the ice for . . . *team synchronized skating?* Yes.

College students do all those things and countless other club and intramural sports. Guys and girls just wanna have fun and play games. Cricket anyone? In Cincinnati?. The home of the Reds, Skyline Chili, and the University of Cincinnati Cricket Club? Yes. These guys are serious about their wickets.

Intramurals and club sports are essentials of college life everywhere. You can't study all the time. You've gotta cut class and cut loose once in a while.

For decades, the most venerable sports tradition at Walla Walla College in Washington was the basketball rivalry between dormitory and village students. After World War II, it was reclassified as a vets/civvies rivalry once veterans came home from the service and enrolled in what is now Walla Walla University. The series started informally in the 1920s. In 1957, the rivalry game was renamed in memory of Dr. Henry Louis Sonnenberg, a former teacher and academic dean at Walla Walla. The first *Henry L. Sonnenberg Memorial Trophy* was presented to the 1957 Village team, which squeaked out a 45–44 win.

It later developed into a best-of-three series. At the Seventh Day Adventist school, a women's basketball series was added, later an *Onion Bowl flag football* game, and volleyball, softball, and hockey games, too. But the basketball rivalry waned and was discontinued a few years ago.

Officially, it's known as the *All-Campus Bookstore Basketball Tournament*. But it's better and more widely known as simply Bookstore Basketball. That's the annual outdoor basketball tournament held on the Notre Dame campus each spring semester. It's also the largest five-on-five basketball tournament in the world.

A little history: In 1972, two Notre Dame guys decided the school needed a third sports season to follow football and basketball. And Bookstore Basketball—so named because the tournament finals were originally held on an asphalt court behind the Notre Dame bookstore—was born.

Almost anyone was eligible to play: Notre Dame students, faculty, staff, employees, even priests. Especially Monk; Rev. Edward A. "Monk" Malloy, a tall, lanky, ardent hoopster who later became Notre Dame's sixteenth university president, serving from 1987–2005.

Early on, the idea was to stack your team with athletes, since varsity athletes were eligible to play. In the spring of 1978, thirteen of the fourteen players on Notre Dame's varsity basketball team that reached the 1978 Final Four entered Bookstore Basketball. So did sixty members of Notre Dame's 1977 national championship football team. Now, there's only one varsity basketball player allowed per team. Also, female students and staff from nearby Saint Mary's College and Holy Cross College are welcome as well. So are Notre Dame coeds, who play with gusto.

Early Bookstore Basketball team names included Dolly Parton and the Bosom Buddies; Twice Down the Court and I Wish I Could Breathe; Leon Spinks and the Tooth Fairies; and Forfeit and Bye. Countless others were rejected for being too obscene.

In 2012, Hoops We Did It Again, one of nearly 700 teams participating, rallied to nip SWAG 22–20. The championship game was played outdoors in pouring rain. No one minded. They couldn't wait for Bookstore Basketball 2013 to arrive.

"No million dollar, no-cut contracts. No agents, just athletes giving it all they have. The essence of sports," so said sportscaster Brent Musberger about *The Little 500*, the largest collegiate bike race in the country and the biggest intramural event on the Indiana University campus. Modeled after the Indianapolis 500, riders compete in four-person teams in separate races for men and women around a quarter-mile cinder track at Bill Armstrong Stadium in Bloomington.

The men's race is 200 laps, 50 miles. The women's is 100 laps, 25 miles. Thirty-three teams qualify to compete—just like the number of cars in the Indianapolis 500 at the Brickyard.

The Little 500 began in 1951, established as a way to raise scholarship money for students working their way through college. Since then, the Indiana University Student Foundation (IUSF) has awarded more than $1 million to deserving undergrads. More than 25,000 spectators attend the race every year. You, too, can go online to the IUSF store and buy a Little 500 tumbler for only $20.

The Little 500 also inspired *Breaking Away*, the 1979 Academy Award–winning coming-of-age comedy-drama about four male teenagers who recently graduated from high school. Four working-class kids named Mike (played by Dennis Quaid), Moocher (Jackie Earle Haley), Cyril (Daniel Stern), and Dave Stohler (Dennis Christopher).

They competed as The Cutters, the townies who somehow beat the frat boys. Steve Tesich, who wrote the screenplay, won the Oscar for best original screenplay.

To this day, *Breaking Away* still inspires kids and students on bicycles. To them, "To pedal's the thing."

INTRAMURAL/CLUB SPORTS TRADITIONS BY SCHOOL

Alabama A&M: *Dairy Team*

Alabama A&M has a top-notch *dairy team*, one that's earned multiple gold and silver honors in the National North American Intercollegiate Dairy Challenge. You could look it up. We did.

Ball State University: *Bed Races*

Want to lie down on the job? For more than three decades, Ball State's homecoming has included *bed races* on the Friday of homecoming weekend. There are five-person teams, four pushers and one student riding in a single bed on wheels and holding on for dear life. They compete against the clock, two teams at a time, down a hundred-yard course. There are seven divisions: frat, sorority, independents, residence halls, and so forth. There's a five-second penalty if you go outside the boundaries designated for the race. No sleeping on the job, either.

Boston University: *Unique Club Sports*

At Boston University, there are thirty-two club sports, including snow-boarding, kung fu, and ultimate frisbee. There's even . . . synchronized skating? "Think Rockettes," said Melissa Hampton, a past president of the Terrierettes, who are part of the United States Figure Skating Association and compete competitively against other club teams.

University of California (Club Gymnastics): *Halloween Gymnastics*

Gymnasts dress in Halloween costumes and perform.

California Baptist University: *Fortuna Bowl*

California Baptist has its *Fortuna Bowl*. The intramural flag football season, with both men's and women's teams, culminates in the two championships games in November on the campus front lawn. *Buona fortuna*.

University of California, Davis: *Cycling*

At UC Davis, cycling is a way of life. The Aggies' *coed cycling team* is a multiple-time national champion. Cycling's integrated into the campus and is home to the U.S. Bicycling Hall of Fame and the nonprofit Davis Bike Club. At UC Davis, they put their mettle to the pedal.

University of California, Santa Cruz: *Halloween Gymnastics*

At the UC Santa Cruz, home of the Banana Slugs, another club sport was established in 2007 and heralded thusly: "Slug Gymnasts Make Their Debut." At Halloween, gymnasts perform while dressed in costumes.

Carleton College: *Rotblatt*

Softball anyone? Make that *marathon softball*. At Carleton College in Minnesota, *Rotblatt* is said to be the world's longest—in terms of elapsed time played—intramural sport. Or so they claim. Played once in the spring, this marathon softball game starts at sunrise. It lasts one inning for each year of Carleton's existence. The college was founded in 1866. You do the math. Rotblatt tradition demands that players both bat and play the field with their beverage of choice in one hand. Again, you do the math.

Coker College: *Canoe Race*

At Coker College in Hartsville, South Carolina, each spring brings the *Canoe Race*, a tradition that dates back to 1919. Teams made up of sister classes race across Prestwood Lake in canoes that are stored in the Hazel Keith Sory Clubhouse and Boathouse.

Concordia University (Nebraska): *Synchronized Swimming*

Students at Nebraska's Concordia University perform *choreographed synchronized swimming* programs in child-sized pools. Call these thinkers deep people in the shallow end. Somewhere, Martin Short is smiling.

George Washington University: *Strong Man Contest*

At George Washington University, the annual *strong man contest* includes such events as pulling a pickup truck, the Gold's Gym deadlift, the Zip Car truck pull, the tire flip, the keg toss, and fire hydrant carry medley. And, of course, there is also a *strong woman contest*.

Louisiana Tech: *Powerlifting*

Behold the power of lifting. *Power lifting*, that is, at Louisiana Tech. Since 1974, the Irondawgs power lifting club has been a multitime national champion—both the men's and women's teams.

Mansfield University: *Boxing*

At Mansfield University, the Pennsylvania campus has some 100 clubs and organizations, including *boxing*. It participates in competitions nationally and hosts annual boxing events at Decker Gymnasium. Fight club, indeed.

Naval Academy/St. John's College: *Croquet Between Annapolis Schools*

These crosstown schools have played croquet each spring since 1982.

National Campus Championship Series: *Extramurals Among Colleges*

As part of the *National Campus Championship Series*, schools compete against each other in classic non–varsity sports, such as flag football.

New Mexico State University: *Miniature X-Games*

They love their intramurals at New Mexico State, where about twenty sports are played each semester, including a miniature *X-Games*.

University of Notre Dame: *Full-Contact Tackle Football*

Notre Dame dorms often compete in full-contact tackle football.

Purdue University-Calumet College: *Home Run Derby*

At Purdue-Calumet, intramurals include an annual *home run derby*. You know, like the home run derby at Major League Baseball's All-Star Game, except with softballs . . . and without Chris Berman.

University of South Florida: *Average Joe Olympics*

If you're an athletically average Joe, the University of South Florida's (USF) the place for you, since they have an *Average Joe Olympics*. "Play Like There's No Tomorrow" is the motto at USF, where intramural sports teams and leagues abound.

Southern Illinois University (Regatta): *Cardboard Boat Regatta*

This popular event originated in 1974 at Southern Illinois University. Now regattas are enjoyed by more than 1,500 participants and more than 100,000 spectators across the United States each summer, and more communities join the circuit each year. Colleges known to participate are Notre Dame, Central Michigan, and of course, Southern Illinois.

St. Peter's University: *Unusual Intramural Sports*

At St. Peter's University in Jersey City, New Jersey, the home of the Peacocks and Peahens, as the men's and women's varsity teams are known, it's also home to a vibrant intramural program that includes *badminton*, *bowling, racquetball*, and more.

"The Cardboard Boat Regatta" at Southern Illinois University. *Southern Illinois University*

Stephen F. Austin State University: *Bass Fishing*

At Stephen F. Austin State University in Texas, that's good bass. *Bass fishing*, by the school's acclaimed bass fishing club. They are regularly national championship contenders. Other intramural sports include *dodge ball, wiffleball*, and *three-on-three basketball*. There's also *beep baseball, skateboarding, water boarding* (no, not that kind), and *inline hockey*.

Swarthmore College: *Prom Dress Rugby*

Prom Dress Rugby is one of the highlights of the rugby season at Swarthmore.

University of Tulsa: *Swimming Pool and Bass Fishing*

While it appears to no longer be the case, Tulsa is said to have once filled their school's swimming pool with bass for intramural fishing. Or as Jeff Schultz, my favorite sportswriter told me, "Can you imagine an SEC swimming coach allowing this?"

Utah State University/Weber State University: *Rodeo*

Rodeo, anyone? Utah State and Weber State both have top *rodeo clubs*.

Western Kentucky University: *Ugly Pants Golf Tournament*

Western Kentucky intramurals holds an *Ugly Pants Golf Tournament*. Think Rodney Dangerfield. Think Bill Murray. Think plaid. Bad plaid.

Winthrop University: *Disc Golf*

Winthrop University, in Rock Hill, South Carolina, is home to arguably the nation's best *Frisbee golf* course, or *disc golf*, as the sport is now widely known. Winthrop has two courses: The Lake Course (the shorter of the two), an eighteen-hole walk around beautiful Lake Winthrop, and the Gold Course is one of the toughest anywhere. Some of the best disc golfers from around the world come to play this course and participate in the annual *U.S. Disc Golf Championships*, hosted by Winthrop.

University of Wyoming: *Pushing a Car Up a Ramp*

At Wyoming, student groups compete by pushing a car up a stadium ramp. What could possibly go wrong?

TRADITIONS FOR A GOOD CAUSE

Play well. Do good.

That's not only grammatically correct, it's also what every college strives to do.

Play well on the field, on the court, and in the pool. Do good on campus and in the community, in the lives, especially, of those in need. Make the game-winning shot, yes, but also the gesture. Lend a hand. Donate your time and money. Make the effort. Make a difference.

They're called *traditions for a good cause* with, well, good cause. And they are legion. From *Al's Run* in Milwaukee to *Pink-the-Rink* in Fredonia, New York, to *Samaritan's Feet* on whatever continent and in whichever country Ron Hunter decides to go barefoot this time.

In 1978, the year after Al McGuire and his Marquette Warriors won the 1977 NCAA Championship in his final game as a basketball coach, McGuire launched Al's Run to benefit Children's Hospital of Wisconsin, and also to thank Milwaukee and the southeast Wisconsin community for their support.

A native of Rockaway Beach, New York, Al was one of the most quotable, hilarious, charismatic, and distinctive coaches ever. He was spectacularly successful, too, going 295–80 at Marquette and winning 404 games overall. He was just as successful as a TV broadcast partner with Dick Enberg and Billy Packer. Together, on NBC college basketball broadcasts, they ran the greatest three-man weave in TV sports broadcast history.

McGuire was also one helluva humanitarian. By 1981, Al's Run—an eight kilometer/five-mile run—had raised more than $4.8 million for Children's Hospital of Wisconsin. Since he died of leukemia in 2001 at the age of seventy-two, that total has now surpassed $14 million. That is due to the collegial bond established between McGuire, Marquette, and Milwaukee, a bond—and traditional fundraiser—that exists to this day.

"I don't go to funerals because I bought you a drink while you were alive," McGuire once said. "Anyway, the crowd at a funeral is governed by the weather."

On a cold and rainy January night in Milwaukee, more than 1,000 mourners attended Al McGuire's funeral.

Among the countless college traditions for a good cause are several high-profile ones involving cancer. The V Foundation for Cancer Research was founded in 1993 in honor of Jim Valvano—Jimmy V—the late North Carolina State (NC State) basketball coach whose Wolfpack won the 1983 NCAA championship. The V Foundation has raised millions of dollars in memory of Valvano, who died of cancer in 1993 at the age of forty-seven.

His acceptance speech at the 1993 ESPY's, presented by ESPN, is now the stuff of legend and the foundation's rallying cry, "Don't give up . . . don't ever give up!" said Valvano, who died shortly thereafter. His memory, and foundation, lives on: In November, 2012, ESPN donated another $1 million to the V Foundation.

In men's college basketball, Coaches vs. Cancer unites the American Cancer Society and the National Association of Basketball Coaches (NABC). In women's basketball, the WBCA—Women's Basketball Coaches Association—began a Pink Zone initiative in 2007 in its fight against cancer. The late Kay Yow, the legendary Hall of Fame coach at NC State, served as the catalyst for the Pink Zone after her third recurrence of breast cancer in 2006.

Pink Zone games abound now, and not just at women's basketball games. At Fredonia State, part of the State University of New York system, Pink-the-Rink is all about two things: hockey and fighting cancer.

In late January of 2012, according to the Chautauqua Star newspaper, Fredonia coach Jeff Meredith called his team together after practice and told defenseman Ken Nosky—who wore jersey number 5—"Friday night, you'll be skating for your team, your teammates and Relay for Life."

A campus group, Colleges Against Cancer, had bought the jersey with a donation, to honor the survivors, remember the taken, and encourage people to never give up hope.

Fredonia State's "Pink-the-Rink." *Fredonia State University*

As the week progressed, Meredith informed other players about the pink jerseys those Blue Devils would wear in Friday's game against Morrisville State: Mat Hehr's number 4, for former Fredonia State student Jessa Weber, who died in 2010. Jessa's mother, Barbara, bought the jersey and wrote Meredith about her daughter. Jessa dedicated herself to her academics and Sigma Kappa sorority, so the coach said, "Some of her sorority sisters will probably be in the stands Friday. What a great thing to be able to honor her."

Wendy Rzepkowski. A former resident of Dunkirk, New York, she'd lived four years after being diagnosed with cancer before passing away at age forty-six. "We miss her smile," a friend wrote, "and her sense of humor." A freshman forward, Brian Doust, wore number 23. Not Michael Jordan's 23, but Wendy Rzepkowski's 23, for that smile and humor.

On Thursday, the focus was on Jeremy Richardson, once a star in the Alberta Junior League, a forward whom several major American college programs had recruited. Instead, he signed as a heralded recruit with Division II Findlay in Ohio.

Craig Barnett, then Findlay's coach, recalled a phone call from a friend coaching at Boston College. "He wanted to know how we landed a kid like that."

But en route from Alberta to Ohio, Richardson began feeling sick. Upon arrival at the Fredonia State campus, he was sent to doctors for tests. Diagnosis, skin cancer. Richardson went home and began his cancer treatments, returning to Findlay when classes resumed in January. Although his health improved briefly, the cancer returned, then spread. He died in 2005, two years after being diagnosed.

"Our moms are long-time friends," Alex Perkins, then a sophomore forward at Fredonia, told the *Chautauqua Star*. His family "purchased" the number 11 jersey Perkins wore in memory of Richardson. "It'll be an honor to represent him and his family," Perkins said.

Craig Bennett, by then the former Findlay coach, was in the stands that night. "It would have been great to see Richardson on the back of a jersey playing for me at Findlay," he said. "We had bigger things planned for him."

In 2012, I sponsored a jersey for my good friend, Suzanne Hurt. Attending this game, and accepting the jersey on Suzanne's behalf, was very special to me.

On January 24, 2008, Ron Hunter put his best bare foot forward for the first time. That was the day Hunter, then the head basketball coach at Indiana University-Purdue University Indianapolis, took off his size 13.5 shoes and coached in his bare feet; stomping in anger, getting a player's attention, doing it all for the very best of intentions: For *Samaritan's Feet*, the Charlotte, North Carolina–based humanitarian organization that convinced Hunter to help aid its mission to accumulate and distribute millions of pairs of shoes to poor children in the United States and around the world.

Many other college basketball coaches around the country worked the sidelines in their bare feet that day, and have continued to do so annually ever since. Thousands upon thousands of shoes were donated that day to Samaritan's Feet.

But the need is never ending. especially overseas.

In the summer of 2008, Hunter took his IUPUI team to Peru to play a series of exhibition games but also to distribute shoes. He gave away thousands of pairs after he, players, and volunteers from the organization loaded up an old bus in the capital city of Lima with shoes. Then, Hunter told us, "We drove out to the middle of nowhere."

He remembers in particular one little girl who was living in a home for abused children. "She was crying," said Hunter. He first washed the girl's feet, then slipped on socks and shoes. "She was scared of the process. She'd never had socks before and now I was washing her feet."

He also gave the girl a lollipop to help calm her. She put it in her mouth, then in Hunter's. The big coach and the little girl both beamed.

But when the volunteers ran out of shoes that day, "People started shaking the bus," Hunter remembered. "But we just didn't have enough. There's a long line of children and there's never enough shoes."

Yet he keeps going back. To Africa—first in South Africa—then Nigeria in 2011 with aid workers from Samaritan's Feet. In the summer of 2012, after compiling a 21–12 record in his first season as head coach at Georgia State University, Hunter returned to South Africa, this time with his team.

"I always wonder whatever happened to that little girl," Hunter said of the girl in Peru. "I had people calling me up, wanting to adopt her."

In the mountains of Peru, in Africa, wherever Hunter goes for Samaritan's Feet, there is one constant: "There are just so many kids. We never have enough shoes. Never," he told us. And he shook his head again.

But still, he goes. Still, he coaches, whether in brogans or, once a year, in his bare feet.

"What we were giving them was hope," Hunter said of that very first trip to Peru. "The first time you see the look in a child's eye when you give them shoes and a pair of socks, it's incredible."

It's hope.

Postscript: On Wednesday evening, January 16, 2013, a season-high crowd of more than 2,300 turned out for the *Barefoot for Bare Feet Game* at the Georgia State Sports Arena. On a night to raise awareness and seek donations for Samaritan's Feet, the Panthers made twenty-three of twenty-five free throws, committed just one turnover in the second half, and rallied for a 74–58 win over William & Mary in a Colonial Athletic Association game.

"This," Ron Hunter told the *Atlanta Journal-Constitution*, "is the best team win I've had since I've been at Georgia State."

In more ways than one.

TRADITIONS FOR A GOOD CAUSE BY SCHOOL

Albion College (Cross-Country/Track): *Ugly Sweaters*

Members of the cross-country and track teams wear *ugly sweaters* on Mondays to raise awareness for people in need of warm clothing. They sell the ugly sweaters as a fundraiser, and student-athletes meet each Monday to decide which service projects need their help.

Arizona State University: *Pat's Run*

Arizona State holds a 4.2 mile run that ends at the 42-yard line at Sun Devil Stadium; the *Pat Tillman Foundation's* signature fundraiser generally has between 25,000–30,000 participants (42 was Pat Tillman's jersey number).

Belmont University (Various Sports): *Student-Athlete Talent Show*

Belmont's student athletes hold a talent show to raise money for the Nashville Special Olympics. The talent show stems from their *Bruins Supporting Bruins* program, which allows Belmont teams to earn points throughout the school year by demonstrating support of their fellow athletes.

Bowdoin College: *Common Good Day*

For over a decade, *Common Good Day* has served as an opportunity for Bowdoin College students, faculty, staff, and alumni to join with community members to learn about local organizations through service. This event has consistently served not only as a way to get important work done for individual nonprofit organizations, but also to introduce students to the community in which they live.

Bowdoin College: *Girls and Women in Sports Day*

An annual event where female student athletes from Bowdoin introduce local elementary, middle, and high school girls to a wide variety of sports. The event takes place at Farley Field House on the Bowdoin College campus. Annually, the event attracts over 150 participants from the Midcoast area.

Bowdoin College (Soccer): *Lose-the-Shoes Soccer Tournament*

Each May, Polar Bear student athletes spearhead the *Lose-the-Shoes 3-on-3 Soccer Tournament* at Bowdoin. Lose-the-Shoes is a growing fundraising campaign by *Grassroots Soccer* to raise funds to fight HIV and AIDS in Africa. The tournament also has connected with the *Frannie Peabody Center* in Maine to focus on, and raise money for, HIV and AIDS efforts in Maine.

Bowdoin College: *Relay for Life*

Each spring, Bowdoin hosts a *Relay for Life* event that raises money for the American Cancer Society. Relay for Life is an all-night walk-a-thon where the Bowdoin community comes together to celebrate those surviving, remember those lost, and fight back against cancer. In recent years, participants have raised over $50,000 for this cause.

Bowdoin College (Men's and Women's Ice Hockey): *Skate with a Polar Bear*

An annual event to sponsor a food drive at Watson Arena. Admission to the event is one nonperishable food item for the local food bank, given at its time of greatest need: during the holiday season.

Bowdoin College (Men's Basketball): *Big Brothers/Big Sisters*

Student-athletes are given ample opportunity to serve through local organizations, such as *Big Brothers/Big Sisters* and *Special Olympics* of Maine. Recently, the men's basketball team volunteered at the *Maine Special Olympics Festival*.

Bowdoin College (Women's Ice Hockey): *Breast Health Center*

In an example of team-initiated service, the Bowdoin women's ice hockey team recently raised funds for the *Breast Health Center* at Mid Coast Hospital by accepting donations for pink ribbons at home games. The team presented a check for $1,175 to the hospital.

Castleton State College (Various Sports): *Marathon Dodgeball*

Castleton student athletes recently broke a world record for playing dodgeball for forty-one hours, three minutes, and seventeen seconds. The recipient of this fundraiser was *Right to Play*, an international humanitarian and developmental organization that uses sport and play as tools to effect behavior and social change.

Catholic University (Field Hockey): *Armed Forces Retirement Home*

Each year the CUA field hockey team continues their tradition of volunteering at the *Armed Forces Retirement Home, America's Home of Heroes*

(AFRH), near CUA's campus in Washington, D.C. While there, the student athletes put up Christmas trees, wreaths, and other holiday decorations, as well as chat with the residents. The players enjoy lending their time and artistic flair to make the AFRH campus more festive, and the residents are very grateful for the shared holiday spirit. The AFRH provides a premier retirement community for United States military veterans through a residential quality care and supportive services environment.

Catholic University (Soccer): *Special Olympics*

The CUA women's soccer team recently volunteered their time to help out with the D.C. *Special Olympics* timed trials. The women's soccer team helped by measuring and recording events like the softball throw and the long jump. They also timed and organized the walking and running events on the track. The girls were full of spirit, encouraging and cheering-on all the athletes during their events.

Catholic University (Football): *MLK Day*

Annually on *Martin Luther King Jr. Day*, the CUA football team spends the day giving back to the community by participating in various community services events. Recently it was helping with the renovation of the local Theodore Roosevelt Senior High School. The football team, along with more than five hundred volunteers, teamed up with *City Year*, a national service program dedicated to changing the world. The day was filled with hard work and much needed improvements as volunteers covered graffiti and rebuilt benches. The football team was also able to use their artistic skills by painting several murals in the hallways.

Catholic University (Lacrosse): *Kids on Campus*

Each fall, the women's lacrosse team participates in *Kids on Campus Day* sponsored by Alpha Phi Omega.

Catholic University (Cross-Country): *First Generation College Bound*

The women's cross-country team, along with some members of the men's squad, recently helped make one of *First Generation College Bound's* fundraisers a success. This nonprofit organization, established by women's cross-country head coach Joe Fisher, seeks to help students get into college who would be the first member of their family to do so.

Catholic University (Lacrosse): *Hero's Lacrosse Tournament*

The CUA men's lacrosse team volunteers at the *Hero's Lacrosse Tournament*, held in honor of Army Specialist Thomas "TJ" Barbieri II. SPC Barbieri lost his life during a firefight in Iraq while courageously saving his fellow soldiers. The goal of last year's tournament was to endow a hand-crank racing bike to be used by the *Achilles Track Club Freedom Team*. The bike benefits wounded veterans at Walter Reed Army Hospital.

Catholic University (Tennis): *Stop Child Abuse 10K*

The women's tennis team participates in the *Stop Child Abuse 10K* run at Potomac Park. *Stop the Silence* is a nonprofit organization dedicated to the awareness about and funds to prevent, as well as treat, child sexual abuse. Member of the women's tennis team contribute towards the Stop the Silence campaign, and also complete the race as well.

Catholic University (Cross-Country): *Ronald McDonald House*

The CUA men's cross-country team volunteers at the *Ronald McDonald House* on Quincy Street in Brookland to do household chores.

Colorado State University (Men's Lacrosse): *Mustache Madness*

Collegiate lacrosse teams, including the CSU Rams, are growing out their facial hair across the country. "This is an opportunity to give back to our community," head coach Alex Smith said. "We're a family, we have fun together with events like *Mustache Madness*, but most importantly, we show our support for the greater lacrosse community." The CSU men's lacrosse team competes against more than sixty other teams across the United States to raise money for the *HEADstrong Foundation*, a nonprofit dedicated to funding cancer research and supporting families and survivors of leukemia.

Cornell University: *FACES*

The organization *FACES* stands for Facts, Advocacy, and Control of Epileptic Seizures, and was started a few years ago by two Cornell athletes

(Kristen Hardy, gymnast and Dan Nicholls, ice hockey—each of whom had epilepsy). It is now a fifty-person volunteer nonprofit that is sprouting chapters at colleges all around America.

Creighton University (Volleyball): *All-Night Volleyball*

Creighton has an annual all-night volleyball event for charity.

Franklin & Marshall College (Baseball/Lacrosse): *Start! Heart Walk*

The Franklin & Marshall baseball and women's lacrosse teams recently volunteered at the Lancaster *Start! Heart Walk* as the players and coaches gave up their Saturday morning to help with the event. Players worked in many capacities, including serving as crossing guards throughout Lancaster City, and helping to set-up and break down the event. The Heart Walk is the signature fundraising event for the American Heart Association. The Start! Heart Walk promotes physical activity and heart-healthy living in a fun family environment. It's also the cornerstone event for The Start! physical activity initiative—a hometown celebration for those who have worked hard to embrace healthier lifestyles. The Start! Heart Walk creates hope, inspires change, and celebrates success for all participants who commit to fighting cardiovascular disease and stroke in their own lives.

George Washington University (Basketball): *Pink Zone*

Each year, Colonials women's basketball joins the *Kay Yow/WBCA Cancer Fund* in raising money and awareness to stop breast cancer. Fans purchase and wear Pink gear to the Charles E. Smith Center. *The Pink Zone* is part of a larger women's athletics effort to stop breast cancer each year.

Georgia Tech: *Rainwater Collected*

At Georgia Tech, rainwater is collected from athletic facilities, stored in cisterns, and then used when watering grass across campus. With more than 40 cisterns and 2 million gallons of capacity, Georgia Tech is extending its dual mission of integrating economic development with higher education.

Harvard (Various Sports): *Recent Community Service*

Five Crimson football players were lauded for Summer Youth Enrichment Work

Student-Athlete Advisory Committee organized a successful food and
toy drive
Skating with the Crimson: Harvard hosted the Allston-Brighton Youth
Clinic
Men's lacrosse reached out to Cambridge community
Women's volleyball held a clinic for Big Sisters of Boston
Student-Athlete Advisory Committee collected 250 pairs in the Reuse-
A-Shoe Campaign
Football team hosted an annual bone marrow drive
Harvard soccer hosted America Scores
Harvard athletes raised money for Susan G. Komen for the Cure
Foundation

The Ohio State University: *Zero Waste Program*

In 2013, Ohio State initiated the *Zero Waste Program,* seeking to divert
at least 90 percent of game-day materials from local landfills. The Buckeyes
saw a 61 percent total reduction from the 2010 season and achieved an 82
percent diversion during one game last year.

University of Oregon: *Heimlich Maneuver*

Many athletes, and other students, are taught the *Heimlich Maneuver,* as
part of basic first-aid training. In 2011, during a Rose Bowl pregame meal-
tradition, Mark Asper, an Oregon offensive lineman sprang into action and
saved the life of an Oregon parent.

University of Idaho: *Found-Money Fund*

In 1981, the University of Idaho realized the power of change (as in
coins) and began their *Found Money Fund of Idaho* (FMFI). Students,
faculty, alumni, visitors, or whoever wants to can mail to the fund spare
change or money they have literally found. Some people may think that
the money gained from such an activity would be negligible, but try telling
that to the University of Idaho. Their FMFI, which has already surpassed
$200,000, is projected to be worth more than a billion dollars by 2089, when
it is expected to be used by the university. They publish five-levels-of skill
for finding lost money, and Idaho has a wonderful time with this tongue-
in-cheek tradition.

New Mexico State University/UTEP (Football): *United Blood Services Plaque*

A *United Blood Services Plaque* is presented at halftime to the school with the largest blood drive results.

North Carolina State University (Running): *Krispy Kreme Challenge*

The *Krispy Kreme Challenge* is an annual charity event in which participants run 2.5 miles, eat one dozen doughnuts (totaling 2,400 calories and 144 grams of fat), and run back to the finish line, all in under one hour. The Challenge is held at a few different schools (e.g., Kansas, Kentucky, Florida State) but is most notable at North Carolina State University.

NC State's "Krispy Kreme Challenge." *NC State*

Northwestern University (Dance): *Dance Marathon*

This event began in 1975 and takes in over a half million dollars per year. The *dance marathon* has become one of the country's biggest college philanthropies.

University of Southern California (Swimming): *Swim with Mike Foundation*

This is an annual event held for more than thirty-two years, to help raise money for the *USC Swim with Mike Foundation*. The gorgeous *USC Song Girls* also perform a few dance routines before getting wet for a good cause.

Taft College (Volleyball): *Breast Cancer Awareness*

The Taft College volleyball team has sponsored *breast cancer awareness* on their campus since 1998.

Utica College (Ice Hockey): *New York Sash Teddy Bear Toss*

Teddy bears are tossed on the ice after the first score of the night. The accumulated Teddy Bears are subsequently distributed to *Catholic Charities*, et al. This event has gone on for more than six years, and generally has about 4,000 fans attending this Division III hockey game. If you bring a Teddy bear, you get in free.

Utica College's "Teddy Bear Toss." *Utica College / Jamie Callari*

Various Schools: *Students Donating Blood*

As part of rivalry week, with their main opponent, many colleges/universities have a contest to see which school can donate the most blood. Winning schools often receive a trophy, and related bragging rights, and, often, a donor is randomly chosen for an additional prize.

Various Schools (Basketball): *Coaching Barefooted*

Many coaches support *Samaritan's Feet*, a charity that raises money to provide shoes for children around the world. Opposing coaches often both coach barefooted, in an effort to raise awareness, and funds.

Villanova University (Various Sports): *Help with Sudan and South Sudan*

Many events are planned yearly, including a basketball game with Seton Hall, to focus university-wide efforts on the plight of Sudan and South Sudan.

Wake Forest University: *Brian Piccolo Fundraisers*

Established by students in 1980 in memory of a great Wake Forest athlete/alumnus and Chicago Bears football star that died of cancer. Each year, through a variety of creative events, including *Hit the Bricks* and *Pump up for Piccolo*, students mobilize the campus community in raising awareness of, and monies for, cancer research and treatment at the *WFU Comprehensive Cancer Center*.

Washington College (Basketball and Lacrosse): *Kent County Food Pantry*

For one team, it was the day after a big Centennial Conference victory. For the other, it was the day before the final day of classes, right in the middle of their off-season between the end of fall practice and the beginning of the season. For both teams, it was a chance to give back. The Washington College men's basketball and men's lacrosse teams recently joined together to volunteer at the *Kent County Food Pantry*. The Shoremen helped unload and stock food at the pantry.

⑫

MASCOT TRADITIONS

You know *Bevo* and *Jumbo* and *Traveler* and *Sparty*. *Smokey* and *Big Al*, who know how to party. But do you recall the most famous mascot of all? At least the most recognizable mallard back in the day, circa 1947? That's when the one, the only, *Donald Duck* became the literal cartoon-faced, quack-me-up mascot of the University of Oregon Ducks.

What's a team without a mascot? Who knows? Doesn't everyone have one? Nope. We know of only one college with no mascot. How strange is that?

But in Georgia, the authors are doubly blessed to live in a state that's home to arguably one of the best animal and costumed human mascots in all of college sports. We're talking *Uga*, folks, the University of Georgia's royal line of blue-blooded English bulldogs. He would be Uga IX, previously known as plain ole' Russ, the canine equivalent of a scout team player-turned-SEC star when his predecessor, Uga VIII, suddenly barked his last in 2011. Uga VIII was buried, as are all Ugas, in Sanford Stadium, in a pedigree pooch mausoleum. How 'bout them Dawgs? You betcha.

And what's that buzz? It's *Buzz*, the city slicker Yellow Jacket mascot of Georgia Tech. An Atlanta wise guy—or gal—a student in high-top Cons, bringing lots of good-natured 'tude while wearing an oversized cartoon head of a winged bug.

They're our good fortune, folks. A double shot of magnificent mascots.

The University of Georgia's mascots are buried at Sanford Stadium.
University of Georgia

Eat your hearts out, *Herbie Husker*, the *Syracuse Orange*, the *Yale Bulldog* known as *Handsome Dan*, and all creatures great and small among America's mascots.

So let us now praise famous freshmen. Upperclassmen and women, too, who've donned those hot, stinky costumes that reek of blood, sweat, and cheers. Mascots who make us stand and deliver, cheer in unison, laugh as one, bark if not bite and sing the fight song, the alma mater or the "Budweiser Jingle."

It's a far cry from 1947, when Oregon's first athletic director, Leo Harris, had a flash of athletic director genius. This was long before Phil Knight turned an athletic shoe company into a corporate colossus. More than a half century before the Nike grand poobah outfitted his alma mater's football team in those wonderful unies the Ducks now don.

Back in 1947, the Oregon Ducks were just the Ducks, if not just any ducks. Disney Ducks. Specifically, Donald Ducks.

Or as author Ray Franks wrote in his 1982 book *What's in a Nickname?—Exploring the Jungle of College Athletic Mascots*, "Donald Duck and the Oregon Duck . . . one and the same!"

According to Franks, "Until the 1920s, the University of Oregon had no athletic mascot. But during that decade, the local media began referring to the UO teams as the *Webfooters*, eventually shortened to *Webfoots*. The name became official in 1926 when a student body election was held to designate a mascot. Webfoots won another election, this one in 1932, to again be named the mascot of the UO teams."

Shortly after that, Franks found, "the name Ducks began being substituted for Webfoots, usually in newspaper headlines. Ducks now generally is used as the name for Oregon teams."

In 1947, Leo Harris reached a handshake agreement with Walt Disney: Donald Duck's likeness could serve as the Oregon mascot, as long as it was done, and used, in good taste. The deal, unique at the time, stood for twenty years. Walt Disney Productions provided several versions of Donald for Oregon's use, which continued until the cartoon genius Disney died in 1966.

Upon his death, both parties realized no formal contract had ever been signed granting the University of Oregon the rights to Donald Duck's image. As evidence, Harris could only offer a photograph taken two decades earlier showing the late Disney wearing an Oregon letterman's jacket with the Oregon Duck clearly visible on the front of the jacket.

Not to worry.

In 1973, Disney representatives agreed to negotiate the first written contract for Oregon's athletic department to continue using Donald's image. There were no hitches; it was easy, like water off a duck's back. This was no Mickey Mouse operation or agreement. This was Donald Duck, a beloved worldwide, web-footed cartoon icon who was universally adored. The Oregon Ducks, dressed in their uniforms of emerald green and yellow, looked just ducky. At least until Knight and his designers went all twenty-first-century Technicolor on the uniforms. Oh, the irony of it all. From Disney to Nike. From Donald Duck to "What the duck is *that* they're wearing?!"

Alas, even when Disney gave Oregon the OK to use the Donald's cartoon image, there were problems. Jerry Frei, the Ducks' head football coach for five seasons from 1967–1971, wanted Donald to sport teeth in his orange grill. The better to portray his team's *Fighting Ducks* image. *Mighty Ducks* works, at least in cinema-turned-hockey name circles, but Fighting Ducks? What, no "Molting Ducks?" What was Frei thinking? A daffy Duck's name if there ever was one.

Far worse was the moniker new Oregon men's basketball coach Dick Harter concocted upon arriving in Eugene in 1971. Harter, a hard-nosed, hard-headed, defensive-minded authoritarian refused to even acknowledge the Ducks nickname, much less allow the image of Donald Duck to be used in connection with men's basketball. The *Kamikaze Kids*. That's what

Harter called his players, insisting that any publicity materials from the university athletic media relations department refer to his team as just that. The Kamikaze Kids.

Somewhere, Walt Disney wasn't smiling.

MASCOT TRADITIONS BY SCHOOL

Air Force (Football and Basketball): *Mach-1, the Falcon*

Mach-1 is the official name of Air Force's mascot, although each individual bird also has its own name as well. It takes twelve cadet falconers to care for the total of 12–15 falcons. Since 1965, demonstrations have taken place before football and basketball games. "Falconers often take 2–3 falcons to away games aboard commercial flights, carrying the falcons on their gloves in the main cabin. Airlines often receive complaints about the falcons not being house-broken" (Enderson). Under special permits issued by the United States Fish and Wildlife Service and the Colorado Division of Wildlife, the Academy is permitted to propagate captive falcons. While Auburn may disagree, Air Force is convinced that their mascot is the only performing mascot in the NCAA, since it does much more than just land on

Air Force's Falcon: "Mach-1." *The Air Force Academy*

a falconer's glove. And in case you are wondering, a small battery-powered transmitter is attached to one leg and a bell to the other leg, so that, should the bird not come to the lure as it has been trained, the cadet falconers will be able to follow and safely recover the wayward bird.

Agnes Scott College: *Mascots Vary by Class*

Although *Scotties* is the official mascot, each incoming class is assigned a class color—red, yellow, blue, or green—and votes on a class mascot that correlates with that color. The colors and mascots are intended to establish class pride, particularly during one week of activities called *Black Cat*. If there is dissatisfaction with a class mascot, the class is given the option to revote and choose a different mascot their second year.

University of Arizona: *Married Mascots*

The university's mascots are a pair of anthropomorphized wildcats named *Wilbur* and *Wilma*. The identities of Wilbur and Wilma are kept secret through the year as the mascots appear only in costume. In 1986, Wilbur married his longtime wildcat girlfriend, Wilma.

University of Arkansas (Football): *Tusk*

Tusk IV is a tuskless Russian boar that weighs 250 pounds, can outrun all the football players, and is also capable of giving a kiss on demand.

Auburn University (Football): *Nova, the War Eagle*

Sports Illustrated said in 2011, "Jordan-Hare Stadium gets loud for big hits and TDs but rarely louder than when *Nova* the golden eagle soars overhead and lands near the 50-yard line as almost 90,000 fans scream, 'W-a-a-a-r Eagle!'"

Auburn University (Various Sports): *No Multiple Mascots*

There is only one . . . *Tigers*. There is no such thing as an Auburn War Eagle, an Auburn Plainsman or Plainsmen, or an Auburn Lady Tiger. It is simply Tigers. "War Eagle" is a battle cry and *The Plainsman* is the name of Auburn's student newspaper.

Baylor University: *Periodic Bears*

Baylor gets a new *live bear* as their mascot approximately every two years.

Bowdoin College: *Polar Bear*

Bowdoin's mascot is named in honor of one of their alumni. The tradition of the *polar bear* as a symbol for Bowdoin College can be traced to the discovery of the North Pole on April 6, 1909, by Admiral Robert E. Peary of the Bowdoin Class of 1877.

Butler University: *Blue II, the Bulldog*

NCAA rules prevent "live" mascots from being present during NCAA tournament games, but when Butler made an unexpected run to the 2010 Final Four in Indianapolis (where Butler is located), the school's mascot, *Blue II*, was granted a special exemption and allowed to attend the festivities. Blue II also attended the next year when Butler advanced to the 2011 Final Four in Houston.

Baylor University's Bears.
Baylor University

University of California: *Oski*

California's mascot, *Oski*, became the responsibility of a special spirit committee in 1946. Members of the committee, as well as the mascot, are kept secret from the student body and fans.

Capital One Mascot of the Year: *Mascot of the Year*

Capital One sponsors the annual Mascot of the Year contest. Fans are invited to vote for their favorite college mascot. Each year, several mascots from various Division I FBS/FCS schools are nominated to play a simulated ten-week season. The mascot with the best record is declared the winner and is honored at halftime on a nationally televised game. The winning school is awarded $20,000 toward their mascot program. (see Table 12.1)

University of Colorado: *Ralphie*

Colorado's *Ralphie*, the Buffalo, debuted in 1967, and was even elected homecoming queen in 1971. Many schools have live mascots, but most of them just watch the game passively from the sidelines. Not so with Ralphie, Colorado's 1,300-pound buffalo. Ralphie and her team of six handlers take a lap around the playing field at Folsom Field in Boulder, Colorado, often sending opposing players jumping out of the way.

Table 12.1   Capital One Mascots of the Year

Year	Winning Mascot
2002	Monte the Grizzly from University of Montana
2003	Cocky from University of South Carolina
2004	Monte the Grizzly from University of Montana
2005	Herbie Husker from University of Nebraska-Lincoln
2006	Butch T. Cougar from Washington State University
2007	Zippy the Kangaroo from University of Akron
2008	Cy the Cardinal from Iowa State University
2009	The Bearcat from University of Cincinnati
2010	Big Blue from Old Dominion University
2011	Wolfie Jr. from University of Nevada
2012	Raider Red from Texas Tech University

Colorado's "Running of Ralphie." *University of Colorado Athletics*

Colorado State University: *CAM the Ram*

CAM *the Ram* is the official mascot of Colorado State University. His name reflects CSU history in that the letters of his name stand for Colorado Agricultural and Mechanical College, the university's former name. The Livestock Club once proposed to butcher Cam the Ram V and raffle off his head, after he had presided over six straight losing seasons.

University of Connecticut: *Admiral Byrd's Huskie*

UConn's *Husky (Jonathan III)* went with Admiral Byrd to the Antarctic in 1946–1947.

Duke University: *Mascot's Head atop Rival's Bookstore*

The *USA Today* recently reported that "if students at North Carolina can't get inside the heads of rival Duke, they can at least say they got inside the head of the Blue Devils' mascot." Before a game between these two schools in 2013, Duke's mascot's head was stolen and posted above the University of North Carolina (UNC) bookstore. UNC campus police recovered the head and returned it to Duke's campus police—where a joint investigation is ongoing!

Ferris State University: *Identity of Mascot*

Like many schools, Ferris State keeps the identity of their *Bulldog* mascot a secret.

Goldey-Beacom College: *Legacy as a Mascot*

Freshman Daniel Brennan was selected a few years ago to be the *Lighting Bolt* mascot. Brennan also served three years as his high school's mascot (a Wildcat) at the Howard High School of Technology. Lightning fans overlooked the fact that he was once the same mascot (a Wildcat) as Goldey-Beacom College's crosstown rival, Wilmington University.

Hollins University: *No Mascot*

Is Hollins the only college/university without a mascot? Yep, we think so. And this was even the answer to a *Jeopardy* question once!

University of Illinois: *Chief Illiniwek*

Illinois former mascot, *Chief Illiniwek*, once did a very dramatic war dance.

University of Illinois-Chicago: *Mascot Named After the Fire*

Teams are called the *Flames* for the city's famous fire. A torch is lit before home games.

Kansas State University: *Identity of Mascot*

In the ever-changing lifespan of *Willie the Wildcat*, one thing—at least for the last sixty-five years—has remained constant: the identity of Willie the Wildcat is kept completely secret from students. Since 1947, Willie has remained a secret to his or her peers. The Wildcat is selected only after being elected by a panel appointed by the school's head cheerleading coach.

University of Memphis: *Tiger's Home*

Memphis' tiger mascot lives on campus.

University of Minnesota (Ice Hockey): *Ice Skating Cheerleaders*

They're actually a cross between cheerleaders and a dance-team . . . but whatever you call them, when they do their thing during player introductions, it is very cool!

Murray State University: *Racers and Thoroughbreds*

Originally, Murray State athletic teams were known as the *Thoroughbreds*. Over time, sports writers and editors found the name Thoroughbreds to be too cumbersome for headlines, so they often shortened it to names such as *T-Breds*, *Breds*, *Race Horses*, and *Racers*. Racers began to grow in popularity through the late 1950s, and it was adopted as the official nickname in 1961. At the time the new nickname was adopted, the baseball team had just purchased new uniforms and equipment bags with the Thoroughbreds logo on it, so the team requested and received a one-year extension before adopting the new nickname. Alumni and fans admired the team for keeping the original nickname, so the baseball team remains known as the Thoroughbreds to this day, while all other teams at Murray State are known as the Racers.

Northwestern University: *Defending Hannibal*

Since 1998, Northwestern has been *defending Hannibal*. NU installed a large bronze wildcat statue near the south end zone of Ryan Field just before the 1998 season. Nicknamed Hannibal by the team, the statue was the site of an unspeakable insult at the end of the 1998 Illinois game, when the Illini—victors in a close and sloppy game—planted one of their pumpkin helmets on the wildcat in triumph. Vowing revenge, NU waited until Illinois' return in 2000 and destroyed the Illini 61–23 (while securing the Big Ten title). As the clock struck zero, Wildcat players raced to the statue to fit it with an NU helmet. Hannibal must be protected from anything orange at all costs.

Northwestern University (Football): *Fighting Methodists*

In the 1880s and 1890s, Northwestern was called the *Fighting Methodists*. Sure, this was never officially the football team's nickname, but who cares? It's a great piece of team lore, and it's certainly unique to NU. Or is it?

University of Pittsburgh: *Panthers Around Campus*

Over twenty representations of *panthers* can be found in and around Pitt's campus and athletic facilities.

Purdue University: *Boilermaker Special and X-tra Special*

Purdue's mascot is the *Boilermaker Special*, a wonderful 1800s-era scale locomotive, and they also use a somewhat smaller version called the *Boiler-maker X-tra Special*. We think that Purdue's mascot may be the only known mascot to have been involved in accidents with two different police vehicles over the years.

Purdue University: *Prior Mascots*

Most every college team has a history of various mascot names that didn't make the cut over time, but one of our favorites is Purdue. Purdue has been called the Grangers, Pumpkin-Shuckers, Railsplitters, Cornfield Sailors, Blacksmiths, Foundry Hands, and finally Boilermakers.

Rhode Island School of Design (Various Sports): *Scrotie*

Scrotie is perhaps the most ridiculous mascot ever embraced by a student body. The giant walking penis is awaited by spectators at every university sporting event, and the costume makes sense considering that the teams at the school are also crudely named after male genitalia. The basketball team is known as the *Balls* and the hockey team goes by the name the *Nads*. The names passed through university administration and have become a part of school tradition. The basketball cheerleaders even go by the name the *Jockstraps*, since they support the Balls.

St. Joseph's University (Basketball): *The Hawk*

St Joseph's (Philadelphia) *Hawk* has been flapping its wings for almost sixty years. The Hawk, which celebrated its golden anniversary in 2005–2006, is best known for staying in constant motion, flying in figure-eights, and by flapping its wings throughout every basketball game. The Hawk is unique because it is one of the few mascots in the nation that travels to every game, and the student who holds the position gains a full scholarship. The student, who is selected through an interview process during the previous spring semester, also serves as a team manager for the men's basketball team and travels with the squad. Among the most decorated mascots in the country, the Hawk has garnered numerous accolades in its sixty-year history. *The Sporting News, Sports Illustrated, Sports Illustrated for Kids, Street & Smith's Basketball Yearbook*, and *ESPN College Basketball* magazine have each selected it as the nation's top mascot.

SEC (Football): *Most Live Mascots*

The SEC has four dogs, a hog, a tiger, a rooster, and an eagle. No other conference in college football features more live mascots than the SEC.

University of Southern California (Football): *Tommy the Trojan Statue*

The tradition of *Tommy Trojan* being painted blue and gold by UCLA pranksters was first recorded in October of 1941. Since then, Tommy has been hit often, but now USC maintenance crews cover him with plastic and canvas for protection during the week of the annual UCLA–USC football game. And Tommy's sword has been stolen so often that now, instead of replacing it each time with an expensive brass one, he is given a wooden one.

Southern Methodist University: *Peruna, the Shetland Pony*

SMU's official mascot was named after an early-twentieth-century patent medicine, Peruna Tonic, which was popular for its kick. *Peruna* is a black stallion Shetland pony that attends all home football games. Peruna once kicked the Fordham mascot (a ram) in the head and killed it.

Stanford University: *Tree*

After the school's team was dubbed *Cardinal* (like the color, not the bird) in 1981, the Stanford Band thought the name was lame and decided to create its own mascot. The result is the ridiculously wonderful *Stanford Tree*, a guy in a forty-pound Christmas tree costume, complete with giant goofy grin and top hat. A distinguished committee (athletic director, et al.)

helps choose the student to be the mascot. In one example a very bright student (aren't they all?) wrote an extremely long whitepaper regarding how he planned to self-ignite himself (as the tree), but that it wouldn't be dangerous.

Tennessee Tech: *Eagles*

Beginning in 1952, Tennessee Tech students began to steal an *eagle statue* from a hotel in Monteagle, Tennessee. After being retrieved by the owner of the hotel many different times, the hotel owner later donated the statue to the university. The governor was a friend of the hotel owner, so he brokered the gift, and officially pardoned the students involved.

University of Texas: *Bevo*

While *Bevo* began in 1916, the Texas Longhorn, has actually been a fixture at UT games since 1966. The Longhorn mascot epitomizes the pride and tradition of Texas football, and it's one of the best known stories on the UT campus: During a late night visit to Austin, a group of Aggie pranksters branded the University's first longhorn mascot "13–0," the score of a football game won by Texas A&M. In order to save face, UT students altered the brand to read "Bevo" by changing the "13" to a "B," the "–" to an "E," and inserting a "V" between the dash and the "0." For years, Aggies have proudly touted the stunt as the reason the steer acquired his name. But was the brand really changed? And is that why he's called Bevo? A&M says yes, while Texas says no.

Texas A&I: *Javelina*

Texas A&I's mascot for years was a live *javelina* (which is related to swine). In 1929 the university president was bitten by the mascot. The javelina was found to be rabid and the president underwent treatment for rabies.

Texas A&M: *Reveille*

To the freshmen in the A&M corps of cadets, she's "Miss Reveille, ma'am," and her rank is higher than any other student's in the corps of cadets. She is *never* crated, *never* ungroomed, and *never* left alone. *Reveille* attends classes with her handler, and based on tradition, if she

The University of Texas' "Bevo." The University of Texas Athletic Department

barks in class, class is immediately dismissed. Former-Reveilles are laid to rest outside the stadium, where a scoreboard is mounted on the stadium's wall, so that the revered mascots can keep up with the game. Also before each home game, flowers are placed on the Reveille graves. In 1989, twenty-thousand mourners attended Reveille IV's funeral—a burial with full military honors.

University of Texas-Pan American: *Broncs, not Broncos*

Texas-Pan American believes that when a competing team calls them the Broncos instead of their real name of the *Broncs*, that Texas-Pan American wins. This happened memorably when they upset the University of Indiana basketball team in 1981. Indiana went on to win the national championship that year.

University of Toledo: *Rockets*

Toledo has an actual *rocket* (their mascot) in front of their stadium. It was acquired in 1961.

Tufts University: *Jumbo*

Tufts initial mascot was a stuffed elephant from PT Barnum. When the elephant was destroyed in a 1975 university fire, a small amount of his ashes were saved in a 14 ounce Peter Pan Crunchy peanut butter jar. The jar of ashes is passed from athletic director to athletic director in a formal ceremony. Football players often touch the jar for good luck. Before the fire, students put pennies and other items in the elephant's trunk for good luck during exams. The real *Jumbo* died while saving a baby elephant from a runaway locomotive. The stuffed school mascot arrived on the Hill in 1889, and the name and image have been etched upon Tufts' sports teams, clubs, psyche, school spirit, periodicals, yearbooks, songs, offices, artifacts, campus structures, tchotchkes, and the graduating student body ever since.

Universal Cheerleaders Association: *Mascot of the Year*

See Table 12.2 for a list of Universal Cheerleaders Association Mascots of the Year from 1990–2010.

Table 12.2   Universal Cheerleaders Association Mascots of the Year

Year	Winning Mascot
1990	University of Missouri—*Truman*
1991	Auburn University—*Aubie*
1993	GA Tech—*Buzz*
1994	University of South Carolina—*Cocky*
1995	Auburn University—*Aubie*
1996	Auburn University—*Aubie*
1997	Univ of Utah—*Swoop*
1998	University of Alabama—*Big Al*
1999	Auburn University—*Aubie*
2000	University of Tennessee—*Smokey*
2001	University of Tennessee—*Smokey*
2002	University of Delaware—*YouDee*
2003	Auburn University—*Aubie*
2004	Michigan State—*Sparty*
2005	Michigan State—*Sparty*
2006	Auburn University—*Aubie*
2007	Michigan State—*Sparty*
2008	University of Tennessee—*Smokey*
2009	University of Delaware—*YouDee*
	University of Colorado—*Chip*
2010	University of South Alabama—*SouthPaw*
	University of Colorado—*Chip*

West Virginia University (Various Sports): *Mountaineer*

West Virginia's *Mountaineer* mascot carries a musket that can fire real ammunition, as well as only gunpowder (at WVU events). In 2012, the West Virginia mascot was cited with a $20 hunting fine when he—legally—killed a black bear while hunting. Seems he wasn't wearing the obligatory orange vest.

Williams College: *The Purple Cow*

Williams' unique mascot has been featured on an *ESPN Game Day* commercial, as well as named by *Reader's Digest* in 2011, as "The Most Lovable College Mascot."

University of Wyoming (Football): *Cowboy Joe (pony)*

Cowboy Joe IV, a fourth generation Wyoming mascot, trots around War Memorial Stadium after each Cowboy touchdown, a tradition which started in 1950 when the Farthing family of Cheyenne made a generous donation of a young pony to become Wyoming's mascot. Cowboy Joe also represents UW in parades around the region, appears in Tailgate Park on football game days, and leads the band and team in the pregame *Cowboy Walk*. This beautiful little pony is very popular with Wyoming fans of all ages. Cowboy Joe's handlers are students in UW's College of Agriculture.

University of Wyoming's "Cowboy Joe." *University of Wyoming Photo Service*

Yale University: *Handsome Dan*

Said to be the first live mascot ever, *Handsome Dan* is the official bulldog of Yale University. The school has gone through sixteen Handsome Dan's since the first in 1889. Originally, the dog lived in the Yale Boathouse, but since 1952, Handsome Dan has been cared for by members of the Yale community.

⑬

MISCELLANEOUS TRADITIONS

Most athletic traditions are hallowed, familiar sights and sounds on campuses large and small, throughout the fall. *Homecoming*. The football rivalry game. The season opener. *Parents weekend. The season finale.* Come second semester, there are rites of spring, too.

At Agnes Scott, a prestigious private liberal arts college for women in Decatur, Georgia, there's a literal *write-of-fall*.

On the day of the *Senior Game*, the Division III Scotties' last home soccer match of the season, coach Joe Bergin reads them aloud: The letters he's composed specifically for each of his seniors. In the locker room, before the Scotties head outside to warm up, Bergin begins to talk, and tears start to flow. Personal points are made. Goals are later scored. Always, it's emotional.

In 2012, the Senior Game was a keeper. Agnes Scott won the Great South Atlantic Conference title, defeating Salem College (North Carolina) 5-4 on penalty kicks. Anna Hernandez scored the game-winner. The Scotties, whose mascot is—what else?—a Scottish Terrier named *Victory*, advanced to the NCAA Division III tournament. And every senior had a keepsake of her own, a personalized letter from her coach.

Homecoming? Both Baylor and Missouri, among others, claim to have originated that tradition in 1907. Nearly every college has since staged a homecoming.

Let's see, if Ohio State can have *honorary football captains* at every home game, why can't Ashland College in Ohio? The Eagles invite two football alumni back for every home game to act as honorary captains. They address the team on game day, and take the field for the coin toss. Heads they win, and tails you can't lose, by making an alum an honorary captain for a day. Most schools now do it.

The *Wreck Tech Pajama Parade* at Auburn originated in 1896 before a home football game against Georgia Tech. It's since disappeared due to conference realignments. Alas, Tech and Auburn rarely play these days, so the Auburn tradition of greasing the railroad tracks so that the team train couldn't stop for about five miles (requiring the GA Tech team to walk the five miles), is no more.

At Belmont University in Nashville, the guys in Pembroke Hall are gaga over volleyball. Watching it, that is, and cheering on the women's team.

The century-old, all-male building has housed incoming freshmen since 1913. In more recent times, the Belmont boys of Pembroke have become the volleyball team's staunchest supporters.

"This dorm has camaraderie and it gives me a chance to make friends and participate in community activities," said Chandler Thornhill, a communications major from Alpharetta, Georgia. "If it didn't have these traditions, we wouldn't have this brotherhood."

"My favorite is supporting the volleyball team," said Joel Graham, who is studying marketing and entrepreneurship, and minoring in volleyball fandom. "It's so neat to get all the guys together, get dressed up with our different themes and support the greater Belmont."

The men attend every volleyball match in the fall, wearing costumes or body paint and cheering on their Bruins. Some themes: *Super Hero Night* (come dressed as your favorite super hero); *War Party Night* (a rowdy, if politically incorrect evening, when the guys go Native American and wear headdresses and face paint); and a *Black Tie Affair* (think suits and ties, even a few top hats).

But the Boys in the Hall always turn out for the Belmont–Lipscomb match. That's David Lipscomb, Belmont's Nashville neighbor and archrival. And that's the night the first war party broke out.

Think Florida State fans. Think some Atlanta Braves and Cleveland Indians fans. Think political incorrectness. But that night, with Lipscomb #1 in the conference and the Bison riding a forty-four–match conference winning streak, the Pembroke Bruins brought it on. Before the match and the first spike, they performed a war dance, more Native American-meets-Nashville line dancing than resembling the University of Hawaii's *haka* before its football games. Or the Warriors' newest haka, and their *Hawaiian Ha'a War Chant*. The Pembroke boys faced the Lipscomb side of the net while the entire crowd watched them perform and set the tone for the evening. It not only energized the crowd but also the Bruins, who won the match in four sets and ended Lipscomb's winning streak.

Not surprisingly, after that volleyball match, Belmont president Bob Fisher presented the *Spirit Award Trophy* to Pembroke Hall for showing the most school spirit. Texas A&M has its legendary *12th Man*. Belmont volleyball has Pembroke Hall. And it starts anew each fall when the women's volleyball team helps the new freshmen men move into their dorm. Brilliant planning on the women's part. And even when volleyball season's over, there's always . . . the *Pembroke Masters*, a miniature golf course that wends its way through the dorm's hallways.

History was made recently made. For the first time, a freshman—Texas A&M quarterback Johnny Manziel—won the 2012 *Heisman Trophy* as the best player in college football. The Heisman is the most esteemed individual award in all of American college sports. But what about the *William V. Campbell Trophy*? Or the *Academic Heisman* as it's known?

The Campbell Trophy is awarded by the National Football Foundation and given to the college football player who best combines academics, community service, and his performance on the gridiron. Hence, the Academic Heisman. Unlike other major college football awards that are ostensibly open to players competing at all levels, only players at the Division I level have won the Heisman Trophy. The Campbell Trophy, however, has been won by a player at a lower level. Brandon Roberts, who played at Washington University in St. Louis, an NCAA Division III school, won the Campbell Trophy in 2002.

Otherwise, the list of honorees since 1990—when the *Vincent D. Draddy Trophy* was renamed the *Campbell Trophy*—includes players from familiar big-name institutions: Air Force, Colorado, Virginia, Nebraska, Ohio State, Tennessee, Georgia, Marshall, Miami, Louisiana State, Rutgers, Texas, California, Army, and, for 2012, Alabama center Barrett Jones. Already a three-time Academic All-American (and now a fourth), Jones maintained a perfect 4.0 grade point average in accounting and earned a master's degree as well. During his career, he's started at three different positions on the offensive line for his coach, Nick Saban, who calls Jones "one of the finest human beings that I have ever had the opportunity to coach."

As grand a tradition as Alabama football has, the Crimson Tide never had a Heisman Trophy winner until 2009, when junior running back Mark Ingram Jr. won the award. Now the Tide has an Academic Heisman winner as well.

As a Campbell Trophy recipient, Jones is in esteemed company. Florida's three winners include Brad Culpepper (1991), a sensational defensive lineman, and two other guys you might have heard of: Danny Wuerffel, the 1996 Heisman Trophy winner who led the Gators to their first national championship, and Tim Tebow, the Heisman winner in 2009 who took the Gators to the 2009 national title.

There's another Academic Heisman winner who many still insist should have won the actual Heisman Trophy: Tennessee's Peyton Manning (1997).

Want more traditions? From the *New York Times*, January 3, 2012: "As far as ridiculous college football traditions go, stamping a $2 bill with an orange Clemson tiger paw is pretty benign." Ahem. Well now. These paper Tigers take this tradition seriously.

Before a big road game and especially for a bowl appearance, Clemson students and alumni buy up $2 *bills* from local banks and stamp them with a tiger paw. An orange Clemson Tiger paw. Before Clemson's 2012 Orange Bowl in Miami versus West Virginia, thousands and thousands of Clemson fans brought not only sunscreen but wads of $2 bills.

"By spending stamped $2 bills with abandon," the *Times* reported, "the fans down in Florida believe they make a statement about Tiger pride."

The store clerks and cabbies, of course, have to deal with a denomination that accounts for less than 1 percent of all bills in circulation. But this is Clemson, in South Carolina, a school and a state which revere tradition.

This particular one began in 1977, when long-time rival Georgia Tech wanted to change the date of its annual game with Clemson. The leader of Clemson's IPTAY booster club thought stamping $2 bills and spending them in Atlanta would showcase the financial impact and importance of the rivalry game. A $2 tradition was born. And coincidentally, I was there that day with my wad of $2 bills!

"It's a Clemson calling card," said Wil Brasington, class of 2000 and senior director of alumni relations. "The idea is we'll bring an economic boost to any community the Clemson Tigers are playing in."

"It's just our way of leaving Clemson paw prints all around whatever bowl city we're visiting," said Kirby Player, fifty, then a doctoral student at the university.

Since Player couldn't attend the recent Orange Bowl, he gave some stamped $2 bills to his niece to spend in Florida and spread the wealth and Clemson brand. Player also gave some $2 bills as Christmas gifts, as many true Clemson fans do. His total estimate: fifty $2 bills. That's $100 and fifty Florida exposures for Clemson.

Back home in South Carolina, local bankers are prepared for the $2 holiday crunch. They order extra $2 bills and often provide stamps and ink pads for customers to customize their $2 Tiger bills.

Before that 2012 Orange Bowl, Carlene Woodring, the head teller at First Citizens Bank and Trust on Tiger Avenue in Clemson, told the *New York Times* that nearly $600 in $2 bills had been given out in the two weeks before the bowl. All, of course, stamped with a Tiger paw.

Now, defacing money is technically illegal. As far as Clemson fans and football go, however, it's no biggie. The Secret Service, with jurisdiction over that crime, referred the *Times*, and the practice of printing those $2 bills to the Department of Justice (DOJ). The DOJ declined comment to the *Times*, unless someone brought charges.

No one ever has.

Of course, with plastic all the rage these days and younger Clemson fans paying online and with debit or credit cards, is the customized $2 Tiger bill on the wane?

"You have to go to the bank," Kyle Player, twenty-seven, a Clemson alumna and Kyle Player's niece, told the *Times*. "You have to get the stamp and the ink."

Such an inconvenience.

Clemson coach, Dabo Swinney, sharing a $2.00 bill with a bowl representative.
Clemson University

"If your parents or grandparents haven't told you about the tradition," she said, "younger fans might not even know about the $2 bills."

But other, older, truer Tiger fans do. So, pay it forward: "Hey, buddy. You got change for a $2 with a Tiger Paw on it?"

"Freddie's Dead," the late, great Curtis Mayfield sang on his soundtrack for the 1972 film *Super Fly*. While that fictional Freddie's dead and gone, *Dead Fred* lives on at Centre College in Danville, Kentucky. Although he died in 1953, Fred M. Vinson, Centre Class of 1909, Law 1911 and a former Chief Justice of the United States Supreme Court, is an ever-present presence at his alma mater.

Especially at football games and in presidential election years.

Dead Fred was there for the 2000 vice presidential debate between Senators Joe Lieberman and Dick Cheney. He was there a dozen years later, for the 2012 vice presidential debate between Vice President Joe Biden and Eddie Munster—uh, Representative Paul Ryan. And Dead Fred is always there for every Colonels home football game.

For this, he—and we—can thank the good brothers of the Kentucky Alpha-Delta chapter of Phi Delta Theta. The very fraternity Fred Vinson was a member of while studying law at Centre when he wasn't playing on the baseball, basketball, and football teams.

Since his death in 1953, frat members have taken the oil portrait of Vinson that hangs in the hallway of the chapter house to every home football game and many other big events on campus.

"It's just like he's another one of the guys in the fraternity," senior Oakley Watkins told NBC's John Yang before the 2012 vice presidential debate. "He's another fraternity brother of ours."

"It's one of the quirky little things that makes us different," said sophomore Steve Sims.

"He's not the loudest one, but we know he's there," Watkins told NBC. "So he has his way of being loud."

At the 2000 vice presidential debate, Dead Fred was propped up on a wing chair in the audience. In 2012, however, he was perched on a ledge high above the hall. His frat brothers confessed to Yang that Fred wasn't pleased with the seating arrangements.

"I didn't hear him say anything," Sims said, dead-panned. "But he just had a look on his face. You could tell."

During an illustrious career, Vinson served in all three branches of the federal government. He was elected to three terms in the House of Representatives. He served as treasury secretary under President Harry Truman, who nominated Vinson to the Supreme Court—the last Chief Justice named by a Democrat.

So, NBC's Yang assumed, "You'd think he'd backed President Obama and Vice-President Biden for reelection, right?"

Yang paused. "He's not talking."

But as Phi Delta Theta president Beau Sauley said, "Dead Fred's pretty cool."

And that's no malarkey, my friends.

MISCELLEANEOUS TRADITIONS BY SCHOOL

University of Alabama: *Team Colors Are Important*

Executives at PNC Financial Services Group anticipated that expanding into the Southeast market, with their credit/debit cards, would bring challenges. But they didn't expect the color of their debit cards to be an issue. Soon after PNC started issuing their normal orange-and-blue debit cards, fans at the University of Alabama started to complain. Seems the colors on the cards reminded them of Auburn. "Orange just doesn't sell in Tuscaloosa," said Lou Cestello, PNC's regional president for the Southeast. As a result the PNC cards no longer have colors, but now feature an American flag instead.

The William V. Campbell Trophy: *Academic Heisman*

See Table 13.1 for a list of Academic Heisman winners.

Cedar Crest College: *Free Road Trips*

Free road trips to college sporting events are often offered to Cedar Crest College students.

Clemson University (Football): *Seniors Last Practice*

The Tiger seniors are *carried off the practice field* after their last practice, and a few even take a dip in a local body of water.

Clemson University (Football): *Cocky's Funeral*

During rivalry week with South Carolina, Clemson's campus holds a mock funeral of *Cocky*, the South Carolina mascot. A eulogy is delivered, followed by a cremation.

Table 13.1   The Campbell Trophy–the Academic Heisman

Year	Player	School
1990	Chris Howard	Air Force
1991	Brad Culpepper	Florida
1992	Jim Hansen	Colorado
1993	Thomas D. Burns	Virginia
1994	Robert B. Zatechka	Nebraska
1995	Bobby Hoying	Ohio State
1996	Danny Wuerffel	Florida
1997	Peyton Manning	Tennessee
1998	Matt Stinchcomb	Georgia
1999	Chad Pennington	Marshall
2000	Kyle Vanden Bosch	Nebraska
2001	Joaquin Gonzalez	Miami
2002	Brandon Roberts	Washington University
2003	Craig Krenzel	Ohio State
2004	Michael Muñoz	Tennessee
2005	Rudy Niswanger	LSU
2006	Brian Leonard	Rutgers
2007	Dallas Griffin	Texas
2008	Alex Mack	California
2009	Tim Tebow	Florida
2010	Sam Acho	Texas
2011	Andrew Rodriguez	Army
2012	Barrett Jones	Alabama

College Colors Day (Football): *Sponsored by The Collegiate Licensing Company*

College Colors Day is an annual celebration dedicated to promoting the traditions and spirit that make the college experience great by encouraging people across America to wear apparel of their favorite college or university throughout the day. Additionally, College Colors Day, typically in September, coincides with back to school and the kick-off of intercollegiate athletics, and strives to advocate higher education through increased public awareness, and celebrates the achievements of colleges and universities, acknowledging their fundamental importance. Since its inception in 2005, College Colors Day has grown rapidly across the country. Thousands of organizations and millions of individuals participate annually by donning their team colors and sharing in the college spirit with friends and colleagues. Fans are now encouraged to pledge allegiance to their school through an online voting effort.

Cornell University (Men's Lacrosse): *Hard Hat*

The tradition of the *Hard Hat* began in the fall of 1999. The Hard Hat is a symbol of what Cornell lacrosse players want to represent in every practice and game, so it's with the team every day. Midway through the fall season, a freshman is selected to carry the Hard Hat for the year. The recipient is someone that the coaches feel demonstrates a blue-collar approach to the game of lacrosse: he is driven and selfless, maybe not the most talented player on the field, but consistently the hardest worker. He puts the team first, and embodies how the coaches want Cornell players to act and respond, on or off the field. During the 2004 season, the Hard Hat took on a new significance. On March 17, George Boiardi class of 2004 was struck in the chest with a ball shot by a Binghamton player and died on Schoellkopf Field. Boiardi had carried the Hard Hat his freshman year. "After he passed away it became symbolic of just George," said senior David Mitchell, who was in charge of the Hard Hat that season. "It came to represent a person as opposed to just some ideas. Even for teammates that never met Boiardi in person, they hear his name each week when the coaches talk about playing as hard as George and getting *Boiardi stats*—hustle plays that don't show up in a box score but are integral to the team's success. While one player is selected to carry the Hard Hat, it is symbolic of what each and every member of the program strives for on a daily basis.

Fairleigh Dickinson University: *Relationship with NFL*

Fairleigh Dickinson has a *Giants Back to School* program that started in 1985, when fifteen members of the 1991 Super Bowl Champs enrolled.

Florida Southern College (Baseball): *The Black Swan*

A *black swan* may have been responsible for the FSC baseball team's twenty-eight-game win streak in 1981. The team took a bus to the ballpark and would pass nearby Lake Morton. Every time the bus passed one particular swan, it would bob his head and the Mocs would win, bob and win, bob and win, twenty-eight times. On the twenty-ninth trip, the swan refused to acknowledge the bus despite repeated laps around the lake, and the team lost and the streak came to an end.

Florida State University (Football): *Helmet Stickers*

Many teams award *helmet stickers* for game-day heroics, but what many fans don't know is that Florida State players can lose tomahawk decals as well as earn them. Poor performance on the field, or in the classroom, can cause a player to be stripped of the coveted decals.

University of Georgia (Women's Basketball): *Signing the Statue*

There are many ceramic Bulldog statues around Athens, Georgia that are decorated in unique ways. The Georgia Ladydogs basketball team has one of their own in their coach's office that players get to autograph when they graduate.

University of Georgia (Football): *Football Players Off the High Dive*

During preseason grueling practices, the team is annually surprised: instead of a planned two-hour physical practice, it's off to the university's swimming pool for some team building. *All* of the freshmen, and many of the oversized (300 pounds plus) lineman plunge into the pool from the ten-meter diving platform. Some players can't even swim, but wear a life jacket and are rescued by 4–5 players that drag them out of the pool.

Georgia Southern University (Football): *Magical Water from Beautiful Eagle Creek*

When Georgia Southern resurrected football in 1981, it lacked tradition. A drainage ditch that the team had to cross several times a day during football practice came to be called *Beautiful Eagle Creek* by legendary head football coach Erk Russell. When the Eagles traveled to Northern Iowa during the 1985 playoffs, Coach Russell brought along a jug of Eagle Creek water to sprinkle on the field. The Eagles were victorious and went on to win many national championships with the help of that magical water. Today, the jug is on display at Georgia Southern University and signs have been erected along the creek.

Goldey-Beacom College (Various Sports): *Never Played Each Other*

For over thirty years, prior to merging, the schools of Goldey and Beacom had identical sports teams—including basketball, baseball, tennis, swimming, and golf. They used the same facilities—usually the YMCA and TWCA. They used the same playing courts, and competed against the same area teams— but never once faced off against each other. Never in the history of these neighboring schools did the scoreboard show *Goldey vs. Beacom*.

University of Hawaii (Various Sports): *Rainbow Over Campus*

Starting in 1923 (with the Oregon State game), the school is said to have never lost a contest while a *rainbow* is over the campus.

Hope College (Cross-Country): *Academic All-Americans*

The Hope women's cross-country program has distinguished itself by placing student-athletes on the *All-Academic Team* every year since the honors program was initiated in 1990. No other Division III women's cross-country program has achieved that distinction.

Indiana University East (Various Sports): *Wolfmobile*

IU East teams began using their *Wolfmobile* in 2009. The bus received an award in an international design contest in its very first year. The volleyball team traveled in the Wolfmobile to Lexington, Kentucky, in 2009 on the same weekend as an Alabama at Kentucky football game. Alabama fans staying at IU East's hotel were impressed by their bus. It was a proud

Indiana University-East's Wolfmobile. *Indiana University East*

moment for their athletes to ride in a vehicle that impressed the fans of the team that would go on to win the BCS national championship that year.

University of Iowa (Football): *Pink Locker Room*

For decades, everything in the visitor's locker room at Kinnick Stadium has been *painted completely pink*. From the walls and lockers all the way to the urinals, everything is coated pink. Former Iowa head coach Hayden Fry started the tradition years ago. After majoring in psychology at Baylor, Fry believed that the color pink dampens aggressive and excited behavior, therefore giving his teams a mental edge. As part of a massive renovation of Kinnick Stadium in 2004, things got even pinker and that upset some Iowa law professors and students, who in 2005 protested the locker room on the grounds that it reinforced stereotypes of women and members of the LGBT community as weak. The protests caused a stir for a while, but public opinion seemed strongly in favor of the tradition. As *Washington Post* columnist Sally Jenkins wrote that year, "I'm sure I should be more upset about the pink decor in the visitor's dressing room at Iowa. But as it happens, my violent knee-jerk reaction is that it's merely funny. If the armies of feminism want to change my thinking on that, they're going to have to slap electrodes to my pretty little forehead and zap me until I stop giggling."

Linfield College (Football): *End Zone Couches*

When the weather is warm and dry, perhaps the most comfortable seats at historic Maxwell Field can be found just outside of the south end zone. Students from nearby dormitories and fraternities figure if they can't bring the Linfield game to their living rooms, they'll simply bring their living rooms to the football field. A tradition that began in the late 1960s, the practice of *bringing upholstered furniture* to the football field is one that remains unique among Northwest small colleges.

Louisiana State University (Football): *Growls = Touchdowns*

It is believed that for every growl by *Mike the Tiger* before a football game, the Tigers will score a touchdown that night. And, as every true football fan knows, the Tigers biggest advantage is sunset.

Loyola Marymount University (Basketball): *Ghost of Hank Gathers*

The *ghost of Hank Gathers* is said to haunt Gersten Pavilion.

"End Zone Couches" at Linfield College. *Linfield College*

McDaniel College (Football): *Drive-in Tailgating*

For as long as there have been cars, there have been cars overlooking the gridiron at McDaniel College. It's just sort of how they do football at McDaniel. From Model T's to SUV's, McDaniel College has long provided one of college football's most unique game-day venues. It is not uncommon to see pickup trucks, beds down-to-the-wheels under the weight of grills, sofas and students, backed right up to the edge of the hill that encircles the field. In a 2011 special, The Weather Channel named McDaniel the number 6 Top Tailgating School in the Nation.

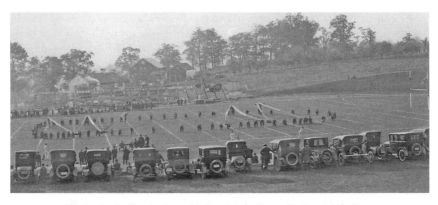

"Drive-in Tailgating" at McDaniel College. *McDaniel College*

Murray State University (Basketball): *Morale Booster* for Injured Players

Local four-year-olds often draw pictures and send them to the injured players.

North Texas University: *Motorized Bell—The Tug*

After the *Spirit Bell* was retired in 1982, many small bells were used by Talons at games but it was just never quite the same. Replacing a 1,600-pound bell would prove to be no easy task. The search for a new bell actually began in 1978 after Talons discovered cracks in the original bell. Over time the cracks grew and warped the sound the bell made until it wouldn't ring at all. Of course no everyday vehicle can carry a 1,600-pound bell, so students discovered a military airport tug on eBay. *The Tug* was a USATS model tug originally designed for the United States Army as a utility aircraft tractor with a 60x90 deck supporting loads up to 2,000 pounds, a perfect match. The USATS is claimed to be the most flexible and reliable aircraft tractor on the market built to meet the demands of today's military, airline, or industrial applications. In order to make the Tug usable and street legal, a great deal of weight needed to be removed. A welder removed as much as possible, welded a carriage onto the deck and mounted the bell. In the fall of 2002 the Tug debuted as the first motorized bell used in collegiate sports. Driven by the Talons cannon crew motor pool, the Tug proudly showcases the bell. In the fall of 2008 wider tires and a new driver carriage were added along with a fresh paint job. Though relatively young by many traditions' standards, the Tug has already become a North Texas tradition.

The Ohio State University (Football): *Buckeye Grove*

Begun in 1934, each player who wins first-team All-American honors is recognized with the planting of a buckeye tree and the installation of a plaque in *Buckeye Grove*, now located near the southwestern corner of Ohio Stadium next to Morrill Tower. Trees are planted in ceremonies held prior to the Spring Game. All 126 Buckeye All-Americans dating back to 1914 have been so honored.

Ole Miss: *Speed Limit of 18 MPH on Campus*

In honor of former quarterback Archie Manning's number, the speed limit throughout campus is 18 miles per hour, except for on one street where the speed limit is 10 miles per hour to honor Archie's son: Eli.

University of Oregon (Various Sports): *QuackCave*

In a relatively new tradition, the University of Oregon has introduced a social media command center known as the *QuackCave*. The school believes it to be the first digital media hub in college athletics. And while Oregon may be an individual leader in digital media, the SIAC (a Division II conference of thirteen historically black colleges and universities [HBCU]), has quietly become the front-runner among conferences in this area. "What's distinctive about black college football is the pageantry and tradition—the marching bands, the tailgating, the alumni, the fraternities and sororities," Commissioner of the SIAC, Carl Moore, said. "The value added for our games is somewhat different than an Auburn or Alabama game."

Oregon State University (Various Sports): *Dads and Daughters*

Oregon State women's basketball, volleyball, and gymnastics recently announced the *Dads and Daughters Series*, a program designed to encourage dads and daughters to spend quality time together while enjoying Oregon State women's athletics. For only $25, a dad and daughter can enjoy tickets to a women's basketball game, tickets to two volleyball or gymnastics events, and t-shirts.

Peninsula College (Basketball): *Alumni Game*

Peninsula College plays their alumni in the first game of each season.

Penn State (Football): *Nittanyville*

Students camp out for football tickets, but with no bed checks, as is said to happen at *Krzyzewskiville* at Duke.

Rice University (Football): *Coaches' Table*

Years ago, coaches drank coffee daily at Ye Olde College Inn where Rice coaches and visiting coaches carved their names in a table. The original table and a duplicate (used for current signatures) are on display in the *Owl Club*.

Rose Bowl (Football): *Lawry's Beef Bowl*

A few days prior to each year's Rose Bowl, the competing Big 10 and Pac 10 teams compete in a unique way. For almost sixty years, the teams have met in *Lawry's Beef Bowl* to see which team can consume the most prime beef. Winning teams typically consume between 600 and 700 pounds of beef. But interestingly, the winner of Lawry's Beef Bowl has gone on to take the Rose Bowl 70 percent of the time.

St. John's University Minnesota (Football): *Winning with "No's"*

John Gagliardi, who over his 63-year coaching career had 489 wins—the most in NCAA history—had a *winning with no's tradition*: no whistles, no blocking sleds, no calling him "coach" (they called him "John"), no profane language, and no tackling or cut-blocking in practice. Under John's reign at Saint John's–Minnesota, they had faux calisthenics preceding their games and his players seemed to have more fun than any others in the country. John retired at the end of the 2012 season, and will be missed!

St. Joseph's University (Basketball): *Bracketology Class*

Joe Lunardi, very well known for his personal knowledge (and predictions) of teams to be included in March Madness and their seeds, teaches a *bracketology class* at St Joseph's.

University of St. Thomas (Ice Hockey): *Bowling on a Hockey Road Trip*

How do you break-up a three-hour bus ride from Minneapolis to Winona, Minnesota? If you are the St. Thomas ice hockey team, you *go bowling* before taking to the ice. Each year for thirty years, the Tommies have stopped on their way to Saint Mary's for a few frames of bowling. And it would be hard to stop this tradition, since St Thomas is 23–6–1 on the ice at Saint Mary's since combining their hockey with bowling.

Sun Bowl (Football): *Hair Dryers to Players*

Each of the college football bowls gives various gifts to the players, coaches, and school officials. The most common gifts are watches, video games, sunglasses, gift cards, headphones, etc., but the Sun Bowl (the second oldest bowl game, tied with the Sugar and Orange), has a wonderful tradition of *providing hair dryers* to the players and coaches. The hair dryers are made by Helen of Troy, a longtime supporter of the game, headquartered in El Paso, site of the game. In an age of buzz-cut-players, can you say regift?

Syracuse University (Football): *Zip Code*

Syracuse has a *zip code* of 13244 that is said to honor the number 44 worn by Jim Brown and other prominent Orange players. But can a city really choose its own zip code? We love this wonderful coincidence.

University of Tennessee (Swimming/Diving): *Coonskin Hats*

The *coonskin caps* proudly worn by Tennessee's swimming and diving teams debuted in 1971. Legendary head coach Ray Bussard took his undefeated squad to Dallas, Texas, to meet (also) undefeated Southern Methodist. Prior to leaving the visiting locker room to face a hostile crowd in excess of 2,000, Bussard gave his team a history lesson about Tennessee, Texans, the Alamo, and Davy Crockett. He then opened a box of coonskin caps and distributed them to the team. Senior All-American Jim Baer took the lead by slapping a coonskin cap on his head and letting out a yell. Adequately inspired, the Vols went out and handed SMU their first home loss since 1960. Now the coonskin cap is worn by UT teams as a proud reminder that Davy Crockett's birthplace is about one hour north of Knoxville.

Various Schools: *Babies Dressed Like College Coaches*

In one of our favorite Halloween traditions, more and more babies are going trick-or-treating *dressed like well-known college football coaches*.

Various Schools: *Obituaries*

Charles Clotfelter, a professor at Duke University's Sanford School of Public Policy, was surprised to find—while researching a book—how many obituaries mention college sports teams and the devotion people have towards them. Our favorite example includes asking mourners to dress in team colors.

Various Schools (Various Sports): *Retiring Jersey Numbers*

Most colleges/universities have *retired jerseys*, but it is unknown which school began this tradition. But certainly among the most interesting stories about a retired jersey can be found in Tim Layden's *Sports Illustrated* article of November 7, 2011. Tim describes how for five decades Williams College kept the number 50 jersey packed away in a box, unofficially retiring it even though the school did not retire numbers. Over time, no one remembered who had worn it last, or why it had not subsequently been given-out, until 2010. The story of Mike Reily and his number 50 jersey is well worth your tracking down and reading. The *Michael Meredith Reily '64 Award* is now given to the Williams football player who best exemplifies the qualities of performance, leadership, and character. But, as a gesture of respect for the many equipment managers who honored the "do not issue" written on the number 50 box, the team's current equipment manager is included (along with the players) in determining the award's winner.

Virginia Tech (Football): *Lunch Pail*

Virginia Tech's *lunch pail* has come to not only symbolize the Hokies' tireless, blue-collar approach to the game, but also to inspire current players to uphold that tradition. It all began in 1995, when then co–defensive coordinators Rod Sharpless and Bud Foster brought the pail back from New Jersey and decided to use it as a motivational tool for that season's defense. Sharpless's mother-in-law found the now-famous original lunch pail in Mercerville, New Jersey, where it had belonged to a coal miner. Throughout the season, the pail holds the players' defensive goals, weekly goals, their keys to success for the week, and a mission statement that was signed by each player before the season. And, of course, little bits of opponents' turf from road wins also have become part of the tradition.

Wake Forest University: *Former Athletes Recruited into Postgraduate Program*

It's no accident that of Wake Forest's recent class of ninety-six students enrolled in their prestigious Master of Arts in Management Program, fourteen were former student athletes. The *recruitment of former athletes* into the program began informally in 2010 and became more formal in 2011. Steve Reinemund, dean of the Wake Forest School of Business, knew from his thirty-year career that the field of business is not far from the field of play. Rather than waiting for student athletes to find his postgraduate management program, he has chosen instead to actively recruit them. Go Deacs!

Williams College (Softball): *Ephie, the Softball Team's Mascot*

At every game, Williams' dugout is clearly marked with a street sign, which the 2004 Williams team affectionately named *Ephie*. It is a yellow diamond caution sign with a purple cow (their mascot) in the center and their won/loss record from each season since the start of the Williams softball program on the back. Softball players even take Ephie on their spring trip to Florida or California every year (they get some strange looks at the airport). One of the special things about Ephie is the process by which she is handed down. A different junior carries Ephie every year and at the end of the year, the player responsible for carrying Ephie that year decides who will have the responsibility for the next year.

14

PATRIOTIC TRADITIONS

You're nine years old and going to your first *Army–Navy* game. It's early Saturday morning and Aunt Kay's driving from Rockaway Beach, New York, down the New Jersey Turnpike to Philadelphia. To Municipal Stadium, the cavernous old 100,000-seat stadium in Philly. Anchors aweigh, Aunt Kay.

We're a Navy family, blue and gold, riding in two cars to see the greatest game and rivalry in all of college football. The most patriotic, too.

It's November 28, 1959, and Army's a hefty favorite. But on a gray and drizzly day, Joe Bellino scored three touchdowns and Navy upset Army 43–12. Unbeknownst to us all, it's the dawn of the last Golden Age of the Army–Navy game.

The previous season, Earl Blaik's Army team went 8–0–1 and Pete Dawkins won the Heisman Trophy. Now Bellino's burst on the national scene in the Midshipmen's 43–12 upset of Army.

In that six-year period from 1959–1964, Navy won the first five games. Two Middies—Bellino in 1960 and later a scrambling quarterback named Roger Staubach—will win the Heisman Trophy. Bellino will lead a 9–1 Navy team to the Orange Bowl, where Navy falls to Missouri.

After Navy's 13–7 victory over Army in 1961, the sophomore Staubach introduced himself in style. *Roger the Dodger*, as he was known, ran for two touchdowns and passed for two more in Navy's 34–14 victory. In the fall of 1963, Staubach would become the last player from a service academy to win the Heisman while leading the 9–1, #2 Middies to a Cotton Bowl showdown with unbeaten Texas. The Longhorns won 28-6 and were named national champions. Roger the Dodger later won two Super Bowls with the Dallas Cowboys.

Throughout all of this, the pomp and pageantry, patriotism, and grandeur of Army–Navy were almost palpable. Especially to a kid, especially in those two years when a charismatic young president graced the game with his presence. John F. Kennedy, who served in the Navy during World War II, sat on the Army side of the stadium for the first half, then walked across the field to Navy's side.

For those of us alive at the time, we all know where we were on November 22, 1963. The day Kennedy was assassinated. I never forget the date. It was my father's thirth-ninth birthday.

With the nation in shock and in mourning, the Army–Navy game was postponed for a week. It was finally played on December 7, and thousands of us wept during a moment of silence in Municipal Stadium—which would soon be renamed John F. Kennedy Stadium.

That day, Navy fullback Pat Donnelly ran for three touchdowns and Army quarterback Rollie Stichweh couldn't get off a last second play at the goal line in time. Navy survived 21–15, in one of the *earliest games to use instant replay on TV*.

The Cadets finally prevailed 11–8 in 1964, Staubach's senior year. Even a fourteen-year-old Navy fan could live with that outcome.

By then, change was coming to the country, its service academies, and the world. The Vietnam War, the draft, the academies' five-year service requirement upon graduation all affected Army–Navy football. There would still be epic games, especially for Navy running backs Napoleon McCallum and Eddie Meyers. But times had changed, and so had the luster of the Army–Navy game for many. But not for us.

In 1999, that wide-eyed nine-year-old who saw his first Army–Navy game forty years earlier sat in the press box at the Vet—Veterans Stadium in Philadelphia, now long gone, too, just like JFK Stadium. On that Saturday, December 4, 1999, they played the hundredth Army–Navy game. The kid-turned-sportswriter saw and savored it all. Tried to capture Navy's 19–9 victory, too.

To wit: "To me, this was the Super Bowl," said Gino Marchetti, Navy's senior defensive end, who wept again for joy.

Not so for Scott Kozak, Army's senior guard: "It's a ghost I'll have to live with the rest of my life."

Charlie Weatherbie, then Navy's coach: "They made history. They can sit their grandkids on their knee someday and say, 'Hey, we beat Army in the hundredth game in that rivalry. Don't remember what the score is, but we kicked their butts.'"

What began on November 29, 1890, when Navy won the first Army–Navy game 24–0 at West Point, was grandly renewed that year. Red, white, and blue bunting adorned the Vet and its record crowd of 70,049. So did a hundredth Army–Navy logo designed especially for the centennial.

There were parachutists from both academies—the *Leap Frogs* of Navy and Army's *Golden Knights*—who all landed safely on the turf. There was the pregame *March-On*, of course, of Cadets and Midshipmen. A *flyover*, too, as always.

When the team captains and their four Heisman-winning escorts—Army's Glenn Davis and Dawkins, Navy's Bellino and Staubach—walked to midfield for the coin toss, a company of Army Rangers—some on motorcycles, all armed and wearing camouflage—roared onto the field and *secured the perimeter* around the coin toss.

If only Army had better secured Brian Madden. Navy's option quarterback rushed 41 times for 177 yards and for the Middies' only touchdown in their 19–9 win.

At times that afternoon, Navy looked like the All-Madden Team.

"The hundreth game, you get a win in," Weatherbie said, "people will remember that forever."

There was one last tradition to attend to: The singing of the alma maters, and certainly one of the finest team traditions in all of college sports, the *Sing Second*.

At game's end, both teams head to the losers' side of the field. The victors stand behind as the losing team leads its fans—either the corps of cadets or brigade of midshipmen—in the singing of their alma mater. Then the teams go back across the gridiron, where the winners sing a rousing rendition of their alma mater while the losers often weep.

Hence, Sing Second. You never want to sing first.

(Postscript: The 2012 Army–Navy game ended in Navy revelry and Army agony. For the eleventh-straight year, the Middies won—barely—to extend the longest winning streak in Army–Navy history. On Army's last drive, senior quarterback Trent Steelman led the Black Knights inside the Navy ten. But he lost a fumble in the final minute and Navy held on to win the 113th renewal, 17–13, in Lincoln Financial Field in Philadelphia. Afterward, Steelman and many other Cadets wept inconsolably. No one wants to see that. Not even that little kid in Aunt Kay's car. Now sixty-three, he knows better than ever: Army–Navy remains the greatest rivalry of all.)

PATRIOTIC TRADITIONS BY SCHOOL

Air Force (Football): *March-On*

The *Cadet Wing* marches onto the field and into the cadet seating areas twenty minutes before game time.

Air Force's Falcon.
The Air Force Academy

Army–Navy (Football): *March-On*

For pageantry and patriotism nothing compares with watching the uniformed students who make up the *corps of cadets* and *brigade of midshipmen* march into the stadium in processional before the season ending showdown. And to demonstrate that this game is very different than any other, the Navy Midshipmen march into the game through the Army tunnel, while the Army Cadets enter the stadium through the Navy tunnel.

Army–Navy (Football): *Flyover*

Each year, jets, attack helicopters, or Stealth bombers *flyover* the stadium during the National Anthem. In our fifty plus years of attending sporting events all over the world, we can say—without question—this is our very favorite sports tradition.

"A Flyover" during the National Anthem of the Army–Navy Game. *The U.S. Naval Academy*

Army–Navy (Football): *Pep Rally at the Pentagon*

All schools have a pep rally before big games, but how many schools can have their traditional *pep rally at the Pentagon* (Navy in the morning, and Army in the afternoon), followed by bands, cheerleaders, and mascots wandering through the various Pentagon offices? Of course, this only happens when *the* game is played in the DC area, but shouldn't it always be? Can't you just visualize the Navy mascot (*Bill the Goat*) with his hand on a Nuclear Launch Button?

Army–Navy (Football): *Game Doesn't Count in BCS Standings*

In the era of the Bowl Championship Series (BCS), a popular saying is "every game counts." Every game, *except* the annual Army–Navy game. Because this traditional rivalry is played after the final BCS standings, the game is actually not considered as part of any team's final standing.

Army/Navy/Air Force (Football): *Commander-in-Chief Trophy*

Divided by the Line of Scrimmage. United by an Oath. That summarizes this unique rivalry. The three-sided trophy is two-and-a-half feet tall and is engraved with each school's seals (Navy, Army, Air Force). The three mascots (Army Mule, Navy Goat, and Air Force Falcon) are also on the sides. The trophy weighs 170 pounds, which is considerably more than many schools' cheerleaders weigh.

"The Commander in Chief Trophy" is given to the winner of the Army/Navy/ Air Force yearly series.
The U.S. Naval Academy

Army–Navy (Football): *Mutual Respect Rivalry*

This rivalry game is probably the only one to not contain hate of some form. This rivalry is founded on mutual respect, and is an example of how rivalries should actually be done.

Army–Navy (Football): *Exchange of Prisoners*

During an academic year, some naval midshipmen complete their classes at Army, while some Army cadets study at Navy. Prior to the coin toss of

"The Exchange of Prisoners" prior to kickoff of the Army–Navy game. *The U.S. Naval Academy*

the annual football game, those students are freed to go cheer for their proper school.

Army–Navy (Football): *Game Ball Marathon*

A relay team from West Point—the academy's marathon team—carries the ceremonial *Army–Navy game ball* for 100-plus miles (from campus to game site). Simultaneously, a separate group from the Naval Academy's 13th Company runs another game ball for 100-plus miles. Both balls are presented prior to kickoff.

Naval Academy (Various Sports): *War Paint on Tecumseh*

An Indian figurehead, called *Tecumseh*, has been on campus since 1866. The original wooden Indian has been replaced by a bronze replica. Before each Army–Navy game in any sport, Tecumseh gets a fresh coat of war paint.

Painting "Warpaint" on
Tecumseh prior to any
Army–Navy contest.
The U.S. Naval Academy

Naval Academy (Various Sports): *Ringing of the Enterprise and Japanese Bells*

The *Japanese Bell* came from Okinawa, where its original purpose was to repel barbarians. Commodore Perry brought it to the United States in 1854, and his widow donated it to Navy in 1858. The bell rings when Navy beats Army in football and/or when Navy has an edge in the five spring sports. The *Enterprise Bell* (from the bridge of the ship by the same name) arrived in 1950. The *Enterprise Bell* rings when Navy scores a victory over Army in any sport.

Navy–Marine Corps Classic (Basketball): *Aboard the USS Bataan*

The 2012 game between Florida and Georgetown was cancelled after a brief start due to condensation on the court. The *Navy–Marine Corps Classic* was the highlight of the city of Jacksonville's *Week of Valor*.

Various Schools (Basketball): *Carrier Classic*

The *Carrier Classic* is a great tradition that began in 2011 with Michigan State playing North Carolina on an aircraft carrier. The 2012 Carrier Classic was to have involved college basketball powerhouses Marquette and Ohio State, and be played on the *USS Yorktown*, but it was cancelled after condensation on the court made it unsafe. Organizers believe they have an engineering solution to correct the court condensation issue, and have announced that the 2013–2014 will also be played on the *USS Yorktown*, and will include a women's game. The game helps raise money for the *Navy–Marine Corps Relief Society*, the *Wounded Warrior Project*, and the *Congressional Medal of Honor Society*.

(15)

PERSONAL TRADITIONS

The power of one is a powerful, wonderful thing. In college athletics, where the team concept is rightly revered—"there's no 'I' in team!"—one person can make a lasting impact without ever wearing a jockstrap or sports bra, without ever making a tackle, or teeing it up, or throwing it down, simply by being a fan, an ardent, clever, loyal fan, or an admirable example.

The state of Arizona is doubly blessed. For more than thirty years, the University of Arizona had its very own *Wizard of Ooh-Aahs*: Joe Cavaleri, the *Ooh Aah Man*, the guy who primed the McKale Center basketball crowd by spelling "A-R-I-Z-O-N-A!" while contorting his body. Cavaleri then orchestrated the "U of A!" chant throughout the arena, section by section, side by side. When he stripped down by taking off his sweaty shirt and pants, not to worry: Joe always had another layer of Wildcats clothing underneath.

In Tempe, at rival Arizona State, the marching band plays for peanuts prior to football games. Literally. Courtesy of the *Peanut People* (not their real names), Dave and Jenni Ryon shower the saxophonists and trumpeters, tuba players, and drummers with peanuts. As the band marches around Parking Lot 59—specifically detouring to pass by the Ryons—to enter Sun Devil Stadium, Dave and Jenni chuck bags of peanuts to the band for sustenance in the stands—and just for the sheer hell of it—since 1981.

For decades, Florida football was favored by the delightful *Mr. Two Bits*, as George Edmondson Jr. was known. He meandered through the stands carrying a sign and a whistle primed to pump up the volume to that most traditional of cheers. All together now: "Two bits! Four bits! Six bits a dollar! All for the Gators, stand up and holler!"

After officially retiring in 1998, Mr. Two-Bits became an honorary alum in 2005. His farewell was at the last home game of the 2008 season against The Citadel. Mr. Two-Bits went out in four-star style.

Utah State basketball has its own shirtless *Wild Bill*.

On college football Saturdays and during every *Game Day* telecast on ESPN, Washington State *proudly waves the WSU flag* thanks to an elaborate relay and nationwide network of well over 100 alumni contacts.

And at one college, the Big Man on Campus can be found in a wheelchair, fair weather or not.

No finer tradition exists in the land than in Vermont. At Middlebury College where, for more than a half century, freshmen football and basketball players have been *Picking Up Butch*. That's what they call a tradition which began in a blizzard in 1961. Butch Varno was thirteen then, born with cerebral palsy (CP) and wheelchair-bound on one snowy Saturday during a Middlebury Division III football game. Butch's grandmother, a housekeeper at the college dorms, had wheeled him to the stadium about a mile away from their home. During the game, the snow fell and kept falling, and on the way home the elderly lady had trouble pushing Butch. Roger Ralph, then a Middlebury student and football player, happened to drive by. He stopped, got out of his car, lifted Butch out of his wheelchair, and took the boy and his grandmother home. With that, a tradition was born.

Before each opening kickoff, Middlebury freshmen basketball players drive to the nursing home where Butch now lives. During hoops season, football players do the honors.

"My mom's a great mom," Butch told me in 2004. "It's hard to raise a kid with CP. CP just sucks." (Butch's mom and grandmother have each passed away.)

Freshmen lift Butch from his wheelchair and into a college-provided specialty vehicle. They sit beside him during games, helping him to his feet to stand for "The Star Spangled Banner." They converse with, and especially listen to, Butch. They hold his hands so that he doesn't get tense late in a nail-biter of a ballgame. They hand-feed Butch hot dogs and take him to the bathroom before taking him back to the nursing home.

"He always likes a hot dog and a Coke," Clark Read, then a nineteen-year-old power forward, told sportswriter Rick Reilly back in 2003, "It's kind of weird at first, sticking a hot dog in his mouth. The trick is to throw out the last bite so he doesn't get your fingers."

"Picking Up Butch" at Middlebury College. *Middlebury College*

"After thirty minutes with Butch, I felt as comfortable with him as anyone I knew," John Donnelly, a senior guard in 2004, told me. "It was nothing like I expected," Donnelly said of his first football adventure with Butch. "He was talking your head off the whole time: 'Hey, buddy, hey buddy . . .'"

"He's always got something to say," Donnelly continued. "What's amazing is how he never gets down. He's always positive. I've never heard a single negative thing out of his mouth. And he's always smiling, loves to see you, no matter who you are."

"It kind of puts into perspective how lucky we are to be at this school, playing sports, to be part of this community. He would love to be out there playing basketball, football."

"That's the hardest part about having CP: the inconvenience," Butch told me. "It took so much away from me. It just totally wiped out my damn career."

In a perfect world, in another life, Butch would have liked to be a lawyer. Why? "To help out poor people," he said, "handicapped people."

Instead, in this life, as I wrote in 2004, "He's become Middlebury's inspiration to its sons and daughters of privilege. In turn, many of them have helped Butch with his daily physical therapy, some also helping him learn to read and study and finally earn his GED."

"Without them," he told me, "I'd probably be in an institution."

Without people like Sarah Smith: "My bread and butter," Butch said one winter's day in 2004. "My motivator . . . emotional leader . . . best friend . . . my big sister."

Then a senior and pole vaulter on the track team while majoring in environmental policy, Smith was Butch's primary tutor and therapist and most ardent advocate. She organized a team of students to assist Butch.

"Totally amazing," Smith said of her four years working with Butch. For his birthday in November, 2003, Smith and some girlfriends bought Butch a more comfortable seat cushion for his wheelchair. *"Heave the Heap"* was the slogan for Smith's fundraising campaign that ultimately bought Butch a new wheelchair.

Smith's most pivotal role was in preparing Butch for the GED high school equivalency diploma exam, then enabling him to take it and pass it. "Without her, I'd be totally wiped out, confused," he said. "She had guts from day one."

Eighteen months. That's how long it took Butch to study for the GED. Smith, after finally convincing him to take the exam, tutored him in several subjects. Jeff Brown, then the Middlebury men's basketball coach, supplied Middlebury box scores so Butch could sharpen his mathematics skills. State educators balked at allowing Butch, for whom writing is very difficult, to take the test orally. Smith fought. The educators finally consented. It took Butch three days to take the tests. Science was the toughest. But Butch Varno got—no, earned—his GED.

"The damn struggle was over," Butch recalled. "I just cried. Sarah took me somewhere where I could cry. Don't mention I cried. Men really don't cry."

Middlebury threw him a graduation party. Someone found a cap and gown for him to wear. Butch flashed his Middlebury College ring, the one with his name engraved and also football and basketball logos. He smiled a lot. At least until that May, and every May—May means graduation.

"Every year, Butch is an emotional wreck," Jeff Brown told me in 2004. "His number one senior graduates, and someone else has to step into that role."

The role of the seemingly irreplaceable Smith. "Sarah, that I love," Butch told me, his eyes welling with tears. "She helped me through a lot of B.S."

"People said I couldn't do things: 'He can't read. He can't write,'" he said, weeping. "She helped me show them I could."

"These kids care what happens to me," Butch told Rick Reilly. "They don't have to, but they do. I don't know where I'd be without them. Probably in an institution."

But, as Reilly wrote, "That's not the question. The question is, where would they be without Butch?"

"It makes you think," Ryan Armstrong, then a Middlebury freshman wide receiver, told Reilly in 2003. "We're all young athletes. Going to a game or playing in a game, we take it for granted. But then you go pick up Butch and, I don't know, it makes you feel blessed."

And an amazing part of this wonderful tradition is that it's now into its second generation, with sons of students that once picked up Butch now doing the honors. How wonderful is that?

Butch Varno continues to make young athletes feel blessed. All 5-foot-3, 170 pounds of him, a 60-something-year-old man who was dealt a bad hand and persevered and triumphed. He's the better for that. So are the men and women of Middlebury. For them, for more than a half century, Picking Up Butch has been a mutually uplifting relationship. The finest tradition in all of college sports.

PERSONAL TRADITIONS BY SCHOOL

Cal State Fullerton (Baseball): *SID Shags Fly Balls*

Mel Franks, sport information director since 1980, has traveled to Omaha with the Titan baseball team fourteen of the sixteen times they have qualified (missing 1975 and 1979). As he told me in 2012, "Each time I shagged fly balls in the outfield on at least one of the Omaha off-day practice sites while wearing a pair of red Puma steel baseball cleats that formerly belonged to Bobby Bonds when he played for the California Angels, where I was employed 1973–1979 . . . he gave them to me to wear in an annual staff vs. media fun baseball game at Anaheim Stadium . . . the only other place I've ever worn them besides Omaha was at George Mason University in Fairfax, Virginia, where our 2005 team practiced after a visit to the White House for winning the 2004 NCAA championship."

Murray State University (Basketball): *Birthday Cakes for Players*

Local grandmothers send birthday cakes to players on their birthdays.

Southern Miss (Football): *Mr. Two-Bits*

Ray Crawford is easily recognizable from his t-shirt emblazoned with *Two Bits*, his megaphone, and hat with ticket stubs and pins. And, he frequently leads the inevitable cheer.

TCU (Football): *Keeper of the Frog Horn*

The Horned Frogs blow a 120-decibel train horn at key times during football (and some soccer and baseball) games. This tradition began in 1958, when two students hoisted a home-made contraption onto a railing at the stadium, and waited for the Frogs to score. When they did, the enterprising young men would wrench open a valve and everything would come to a standstill as the stadium filled with the roar of a borrowed *train whistle* that the boys had cobbled onto the end of an air canister. But turning it off wasn't so easy, and the thing blasted for fifteen minutes before the air finally ran out. The game was stopped and officials ungraciously escorted the boys from the stadium. But the Frogs beat Texas, 22–8 that day. Fast forward to 1994 when football coach Pat Sullivan asked an alumni group why they had no football traditions to get the crowd involved. Someone remembered the 1958 prank, and enlisted a few other friends to help him recreate the sound. A university trustee was CEO of Burlington Northern Railroad, and gladly agreed to help. Four hours later preliminary drawings for a new contraption were faxed for approval. A small group of men at Burlington's Springfield, Missouri maintenance shop had less than four weeks to complete the horn, but the challenge energized them. Never at the railroad had they ever built anything like this. Rumor has it that the maintenance men put about fourteen coats of paint on it. During subsequent planning meetings, the *trailer with a horn*—since patented by the railroad—expanded to include marquee lights for TCU logos, green flashing eyes, and purple theatrical smoke that poured from two chrome horns on top. Those extras, of course, meant additional equipment under the cowling, so it overheated during a test drive. Vents were added to the body, which was all hand machined in the Springfield shop. A local artist was hired to paint the face after agreeing to give the beast a ferocious look. A bell from an old steam locomotive was also added. The shiny new *Frog Horn*, weighing in at 3,000 pounds, was loaded onto a C-47 and flown to Fort Worth. The bell was rung for the first time before the 1994 home opener against Kansas. No one at TCU (including the administration) had been told about the Frog Horn, so its debut was a surprise.

TCU's "Frog Horn." *Jason Lesikar*

Since 2002, Jason Lesikar (class of 2002) has lovingly cared for TCU's famous Frog Horn, keeping it in running condition and managing it at games. Jason gets help from a spirit organization, since it takes one person to watch the game and cue a second handler to ring the bell or blow the horn at the right time (a very important task since blasts at the wrong time can violate NCAA rules), and one person to keep others at an appropriate distance. Jason recently invited me to the secret/secure facility on his ranch west of town where he handles all the maintenance and repair—mostly out of his own pocket. It's a fairly needy piece of machinery—now almost twenty-years old, after all—and parts are not only expensive, they are sometimes hard to locate. In recent years Jason crafted new fenders and replaced the fog machines and more light bulbs than he can count. Occasionally he has to crawl inside during a game to keep it blasting and flashing. "It's a big asset, but it's also a big responsibility," Jason says. "Getting to work on it has been a huge honor." One thing no one has fixed is a dent near the front that an opponent (reportedly a Texas Tech player) put there with his helmet in a moment of extreme frustration at the Frogs success on the field. "It's part of its history," Jason says, "so we've left it there."

Utah State University (Basketball): *Wild Bill*

Only a few super fans are wild and crazy enough to become as famous as the athletes they cheer for, such as the New York Jets' *Fireman Ed* and

Duke's *Speedo Guy*. *Wild Bill* can now be added to that list, and perhaps no fan has ever captured our imagination quite like him. You probably don't know which team he roots for and you certainly don't know his real name, but if you're a sports fan, you've undoubtedly seen a clip of Utah State fanatic Bill Sproat on TV or YouTube. He's the large, often shirtless student who stands behind the basket at Aggie home games and distracts opposing free-throw shooters with his ridiculous costumes that look like he's come straight from trick-or-treating. "I love to be as close to naked as possible without going to jail," Sproat said. Sproat draws most of his inspiration from Disney movies, Jack Black, and Chris Farley, dressing as everything from the Little Mermaid, to Nacho Libre, to Peter Pan to Tigger. He was even going to dress like a showgirl for a Nevada game before Utah State put its foot down (he's also not allowed to wear a Speedo or do pelvic thrusts). The publicity he's received has grown beyond his wildest expectations. He's been mentioned on ESPN's *Pardon the Interruption*, interviewed on *First Take*, profiled by *Sports Illustrated's* Seth Davis, turned into a YouTube sensation, and even visited ESPNU's offices in Charlotte—which he described as being like a "kid in a candy store." Sproat made headlines by dressing up as the teapot from *Beauty and the Beast* during a game against Nevada. It's one of the many Disney characters he's portrayed in the last few seasons. We can only hope that Bill continues his personal tradition after he graduates from Utah State. He is one-of-a-kind.

Washington State University (Football): *College Game Day Flag*

Tom Pounds proves that just one person, even with no connection to TV sports, can change what America sees on TV each week if he's a true flag-waver. Not that Pounds, an electrical engineer in Albuquerque, began with any grandiose plan. Having graduated from Washington State in 1981, he was struck by a suggestion in 2003 on the school's cougfan.com sports site from a WSU alum living in Austin. That alum had seen somebody unfurl the WSU flag at an *ESPN College Game Day* show at Ohio State and wondered, Why not have somebody wave the *WSU school flag* in the background during a *Game Day* show in Austin for a Kansas State–Texas football game? All Pounds had to do was stay up past midnight with his mom to make a flag, start at dawn to drive 800 miles to Austin, and end up getting sworn at by unwelcoming fans at the *Game Day* set who failed to grasp the idea's inherent nobility. Plus, the alum in Austin couldn't make it. (Pounds says he never met him—"I hope to someday"—and doesn't even know the identity of the man who first waved the flag at Ohio State.) The story could have furled there, but then Pounds heard from a seminary student in Minneapolis, not an alum, but a WSU fan who'd seen the flag and offered to drive it to a *Game Day* in Madison, Wisconsin. The relay went on. Pounds, having assembled an online network of 111 flag-bearing contacts, says the flag was allowed to flutter for ESPN cameras at ninety-four consecutive *Game Days*, and Pounds himself, for the sixth time, waved the flag for the show that aired before the 2011 Texas versus Texas Tech game in Lubbock. The flag relay, he says, inspired a nonprofit corporation (*Ol' Crimson Booster Club*) that's raised $10,000 to cover flag-wavers' expenses. One flag used is displayed at an alumni center at WSU. Pounds says the flag waving has provoked fisticuffs in Gainesville, Florida, and Eugene, Oregon, but now usually draws respect from crowds. I had the opportunity to personally wave the flag in 2012, as well as speak with a couple of the WSU alums doing the waving. What fun!

16

PRESEASON TRADITIONS

Lefty started it. Kentucky transformed it. Now it can be found almost anywhere: The Madness.

No, not March Madness. *Midnight Madness.*

It's become almost a secular hoops holiday, the premier preseason tradition in college basketball and, yes, all of college sports. Especially at Kentucky. For that, we can thank the ol' Lefthander: Charles G. "Lefty" Driesell.

In 1970, when Driesell was head coach at Maryland, he wanted to get a head start on the season's first practice. As Lefty later told ESPN's Darren Rovell in 2000, "The NCAA told us we could start practice on October 15. Well, I said, that means we can start practicing one minute past midnight on the 14th. So let's get a jump on everybody."

As Rovell wrote: "There were no half-court student shots for tuition, or slam dunk contests, or hip-hop music to introduce the Terps to thousands of screaming fans."

None of those things that are now staples of Midnight Madness. Instead, Lefty took his team to Byrd Stadium, the football stadium, for a one-mile midnight run.

"So we ran our mile on the football field and used the lights from our cars so no one could cut the corners," said Driesell, who actually started his Madness at 12:03 a.m. But that's OK. That's Lefty.

"It first started out as a gimmick to show that we could start practice before everyone else did," he told Rovell. "Now, everyone does it. The next year, we must have had 1,000 people watching us run the mile. And the following year, one of my players, Mo Howard, suggested that we have an intersquad scrimmage. Well, I thought that was a pretty good idea, and we had about 8,000 people watching us that year [in Cole Field House]."

Howard, however, got hurt in the scrimmage and missed the first few weeks of the season. And there were other potential pitfalls, including the Maryland faculty.

"The only bad thing," Lefty told Rovell, "was that if October 15 was on a Wednesday, and you had the practice at midnight on Tuesday, all the teachers complained that the guys couldn't study. So that's why the NCAA changed it [the starting date of practice] to the first Saturday in October."

After leaving Maryland, Driesell coached at James Madison and at Georgia State. At GSU, Lefty and his athletic director, Greg Manning, decided to schedule the first Panthers practice of 2000 on a Saturday morning. Morning Madness? Not exactly.

"I think it's great that a lot of teams started doing [Midnight Madness]," Driesell told Rovell that year. "It gets people talking about basketball." Besides, Lefty said, "College kids stay up all night anyway."

So why did he bypass Friday Midnight Madness for a morning start? "I don't like staying up to twelve o'clock," Lefty said to Rovell. "I'm sixty-eight now. I'm usually fast asleep by 12 a.m. I'll enjoy the sleep and we'll have a better practice on Saturday anyway."

A much better season, too. The following March, Lefty led Georgia State to just its second NCAA tournament, and the Panthers upset Wisconsin 50–49 in the first round. Alas, in the second round Georgia State lost to a superior Maryland team, 79–60. Lefty didn't lose any sleep over it.

More Midnight Madness moments:

In 1982, Kentucky officially promoted a preseason celebration of Midnight Madness, and has since turned it into an annual spectacle. (Much more on that to come).

In 2012, a marriage proposal at a Davenport University Midnight Madness event went viral on the internet.

In 1985, *Late Night in the Phog* debuted at Kansas in Phog Allen Fieldhouse. The Jayhawks practiced, yes, but there were giveaways for fans, classic KU videos on the overhead scoreboard screens, some players shooting half-court shots, others throwing down thunderous dunks to roars.

Most Midnight Madness schools will include a three-point shooting contest with a dunk-a-thon and long-range heaves. The Madness is now often a coed event, for both men's and women's teams, especially at colleges like UConn and Baylor, whose 6-foot-8 Brittany Greiner—the National Player of the Year in 2012 when Baylor went 40–0 and won the national title—can dunk with the big boys.

Midnight Madness, by any name, is also used as a recruiting tool. Scout .com estimated that in 2007, 160 of the top high school basketball recruits in the country attended Midnight Madness somewhere. That number has since increased exponentially. And now, in the twenty-first century, Midnight Madness has become even more lavish and extravagant, with celebrities included.

One year, Michigan State coach Tom Izzo rode onto the court at the Breslin Center astride a Harley-Davidson. Izzo was dressed like a hippy, as in *Easy Rider*. Then he posed with Sparty, the Spartans' in-costume mascot.

That Michigan State team won the 2000 national championship. The following season for Midnight Madness, the Spartans—wearing boxing gloves and green satin robes—were introduced as they stepped through the ropes of a boxing ring. Izzo? He arrived in a white stretch limousine, dressed in a black tuxedo.

Another year, Billy Donovan, the two-time NCAA-winning Florida coach, rose up out of a coffin in the O-Dome during Midnight Madness. In 2012, Izzo made another grand entrance at the Breslin Center attired in an Iron Man costume while his wife and children were dressed as other Marvel Avengers. The *IZZone* student section went bananas.

In 1994, on the University of Cincinnati campus, a student named Cory Clouse brought down the house. Having already won the slam dunk and three-point shooting contests, Clouse launched a half-court shot in *The Shoe*, as the on-campus Shoemaker Center is still known. Clouse cleanly nailed the forty-seven-footer to earn a free year of college tuition, and more. Dick Vitale jumped into his arms. And more important, in the summer of 1995, Cory Clouse won an ESPY for his Midnight Madness moment.

At Indiana, it's *Hoosier Hysteria*. *Tubby's Tipoff*, they once called it at Minnesota. In Madison, it's *The Night of the Grateful Red* at the University of Wisconsin.

At Missouri's Midnight Madness in 2012, Keion Bell dunked over six people lined up in size-order from the foul line to the basket. Wagner's Josh Thompson dunked over his parents, standing back-to-back, even if Dad got conked in the head. Brittney Griner nearly threw down a 360-degree dunk.

But nobody—and we mean nobody—does Midnight Madness like they do it in the Bluegrass at Kentucky.

In October of 1982, coach Joe B. Hall, recalling Lefty's stroke of midnight genius, invited Kentucky fans to attend *Midnight Special*, the first practice of that season. More than 8,500 fans showed up in old 12,000-seat Memorial Coliseum. It shortly became Midnight Madness. And, by any name, it's in a class all its own.

In 1986, a fire marshal ordered the doors of Memorial closed two hours before the Madness was scheduled to start. More than 12,500 Big Blue zealots were already inside, with hundreds more stuck outside.

In 1990, according to the UK website, Wildcats fans reveled in a *Big Blue New Year*. In 1991, fans lined up thirty-six hours in advance for *Back in the Spotlight*. For the first time in the Rick Pitino era, UK was off probation and again eligible for the postseason. The doors were closed for forty-five minutes after they opened, the earliest closing ever. All four Kentucky recruits who attended *Big Blue Madness* that year—Rodrick Rhodes, Jared Prickett, Tony Delk, and Walter McCarty—verbally committed to UK the next week. In 1996, Kentucky would win the NCAA title.

In 1992, *Big Boo Madness* appeared on Halloween Night. Fans began arriving five days early for the event, then seventeen. And finally there was Wally Clark, who got in line to claim his spot thirty-eight days before more Madness ensued.

Jump ahead to 2000: Some tickets—all are free—were available on the Internet for the first time. All 700 were gone in the first thirteen minutes. The remaining 8,000 were long gone in 10 minutes to those who'd waited in line.

In 2002, to celebrate the 100th season of Kentucky basketball, popular long-time equipment manager Bill Keightley jumped out of an enormous birthday cake to the delight of the UK faithful.

In 2005, *Big Blue Madness* was held in Rupp Arena for the first time, due to construction of the new basketball practice facility at Memorial Coliseum. More than 23,000 tickets were snapped-up in less than 48 hours. As the school also noted, UK fans broke the national attendance record for a practice.

Midnight Madness, or Big Blue Madness, is annually televised by ESPN on several of its networks. Telecasts can last several hours, featuring footage from several colleges around the country. Just because you can't actually be there doesn't mean you can't watch Midnight Madness.

Recently, at Big Blue Madness 2012, Kentucky raised its eighth national championship banner from its title game win over Kansas. It also celebrated its seven previous titles, raising those banners, too. There were videos, skits, dancing. When coach John Calipari told the crowd, "I came here to win national championships for you," the noise was deafening.

The court at Rupp Arena was covered by an enormous white cloth and used as a movie screen to show animations and highlights projected from high above.

Nearly 600 tents had been pitched outside Memorial Coliseum for the distribution of free Big Blue Madness tickets—four to a person—on September 22. They were gone in a half hour. Good luck with trying to scalp some, not that some folks didn't try.

And as for those four heralded freshmen? Kentucky fans got their first look at Nerlens Noel, Willie Cauley-Stein, Archie Goodwin, and Alex Poythress together in action. They, too, all four of 'em, attended Big Blue Madness the previous year.

PRESEASON TRADITIONS BY SCHOOL

Augusta State University (Basketball): *Meet and Greet*

This tradition began in 2004 with Dip Metress' arrival as a new coach. Interested fans can purchase a ticket for a meal with the team and coaches, as well as hear a preview of the upcoming season. The *meet and greet* was originally held at Metress' house, but in 2011 it moved to Christenberry Fieldhouse, where fans got the chance to do the things mentioned above, plus tour the facility and watch the teams practice. A recent wonderful moment was when Metress had his players onstage and asked each of them a couple of get-to-know-you questions. He asked the starting point guard where he had taken his high school prom date to dinner. His response? "McDonald's." Fans also get a chance to purchase season tickets and choose their seats for the upcoming season.

University of Houston (Football): *Frontier Fiesta*

Coinciding with Houston's spring football practice, there is a six-category cook-off, variety shows, and live music.

IMG Academy (Various Sports): *Unique Preseason Training*

IMG Academy is a private athletic training institute for youth, high school, collegiate, and professional athletes located in Bradenton, Florida. The academy offers programs for tennis, golf, baseball, basketball, lacrosse, soccer, football, and athletic and personal development. IMG Academy attracts more than 12,000 athletes (many of whom are college athletes conducting preseason training) from approximately 80 countries every year.

Ithaca College (Crew): *Barbecue*

Men's and women's crew programs host a *barbecue* one night a week for the entire summer at the boathouse the teams use. The barbecues are open to anyone, but geared toward alumni and families.

Marquette University (Basketball): *Training Camp*

Basketball coach Buzz Williams packs his team into a yellow school bus for three days of *old-school training camp*. The destination is Camp Mini-Kani, a thirty-minute drive from Milwaukee. Players practice in elementary school gyms and sleep in cabins (with no TV and sparse cell-phone coverage), entertaining themselves with games of Catch Phrase.

University of Minnesota (Baseball): *Steak and Beans Event*

The men's baseball team holds an annual *steak and beans event*.

Mount Aloysius College (Basketball): *Mountie Madness*

Mountie Madness is their version of Midnight Madness.

Northwestern University (Football): *Camp Kenosha*

Beginning in 1992, preseason practices were moved off-campus. The sessions, located at the University of Wisconsin–Parkside in Kenosha, are a trial-by-fire for the team, and they have their own set of traditions, including a watermelon eating contest and the final scrimmage.

Northwestern University (Football): *Preseason Games*

Beginning in 2010, Northwestern sought and received special permission from the NCAA to hold its preseason practices at two off-campus locations: Kenosha and one practice at the Great Lakes facility near Glenview, Illinois. NU's ties with Great Lakes go back to 1918, and the school is trying to establish the Wildcats as the adopted college team for the nearby servicemen.

Saginaw Valley State University (Football): *Singing for Your Supper*

As do many schools, Saginaw Valley State football players insist that new players *sing for their supper* during preseason meals.

Seton Hall University (Basketball): *Hall Hoop Hysteria*

Seton Hall's Midnight Madness is called *Hall Hoop Hysteria*.

SPIRE Institute (Various Sports): *Off-Season Training*

Located in Geneva, Ohio, this nonprofit facility (of 1,000,000 square feet) offers both weekend and week-long training programs for soccer, track and field, basketball, and softball as well as classes in nutrition, fitness, and sports psychology. More than 250,000 athletes from many prominent colleges/universities have attended as part of their preseason ritual.

University of Wisconsin–Platteville (Basketball): *The Hill*

The team has used the same hill in Platteville for over twenty-five years to not only train physically, but also mentally. This was started by former Pioneer coach, Bo Ryan.

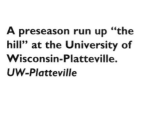

A preseason run up "the hill" at the University of Wisconsin-Platteville. *UW-Platteville*

17

TRADITIONS PROBABLY NOT
UNIVERSITY SANCTIONED

They're the traditions that help enhance the college experience. They give texture to campus life, if occasional agita to the administration:

Ah, the singing of the *alma mater*. That prize-winning float in the *homecoming parade*. The ritual *tossing of the tortillas*. Oh, those *fight song sing-a-longs*. The *flinging of mortarboards* at commencement. And what will you recall? You make the call:

A well-executed *naked bootleg* near the goal line? Or a well-appointed *naked lap* around the Carleton College quad in Minnesota's wintry chill?

Naked came the brunette biology major.

Alas, some traditions aren't university sanctioned. Some things Dean Wormer won't warm to. Double-secret probation anyone? Mr. Blutarski has no grade-point average.

Speaking of streaking of another sort and that can't-do spirit: In 1981, in the midst of a thirty-four-game football losing streak—then the longest in Division I-A history—Northwestern fans celebrated a 61–14 home loss to Michigan State by *tearing-down the goal posts* and marching through the streets of Evanston, Illinois, shouting, "We're the worst!" Then they tossed the goal post into Lake Michigan. A new tradition—and word—were born: *laking*.

On September 25, 1982, after Northwestern beat Northern Illinois 31–6 to end the streak, coach Dennis Green said, "When I woke up this morning, I knew it was a special day." Down came the goal posts. Into Lake Michigan they went. More "Laking," and much more liking.

Columbia University surpassed Northwestern's ineptitude by losing forty-four games in a row. At some point, the Columbia band began playing the *Mickey Mouse Club* theme when the Lions took the field. The football players were not amused.

And speaking of streaking of another ilk: Concordia-Nebraska University has a *Naked Man Snow Angel Run*. Denison University enjoys both *Naked Week* and the ultimate in ultimate Frisbee: *Naked ultimate Frisbee*. There's a *Naked Mile* at both Lewis & Clark College and the University of Michigan. Tufts students tough it out during a *Naked Quad Run*. We'll see your Union College *Naked Nott Ride* and raise you Vermont's *Naked Bike Ride*. William & Mary celebrates its *Naked Triathlon* while Yale revels in—what else?—*Naked Punt Returns*.

Alpha Delta Phi fraternity waits for the first snow of the year. Once the main campus bar closes, everyone heads to Old Campus, where the frat's pledges have to return punts in their thongs. Meanwhile, football players are all there to tackle them into the snow. And *all* eyes are watching.

Many happy returns? Mostly.

On a more serious note:

In 2010, Texas A&M-Kingsville banned the tradition of *tortilla tossing* at football games. The opening coin toss? Fine. Tossing touchdown passes? Better by the home team. But tossing tortillas? No more.

According to a newspaper report in *The Corpus Christi Caller-Times*, while no one knows who started the tradition, tortillas had been flying for decades. Students at other universities, including the University of California, Santa Barbara and Texas Tech, flirted with the idea of tortilla tossing in the stands. Both schools stopped it when officials threatened to penalize the home team.

The Flying Burrito Brothers? They had their music, back in the day. But the flying tortilla tossers? No more.

"Over the course of the past year, I wrestled with a difficult issue related to the spirit of the institution," Texas A&M-Kingsville president Steven Tallant said in a 2010 statement outlawing tortilla tossing. The *Caller-Times* roundly agreed in an editorial headlined "A&M-Kingsville is right to ban tortilla tossing."

It began:

Before the first kickoff of the 2010 season, Texas A&M University-Kingsville President Steven Tallant made an excellent call. On August 19 he banned tortilla tossing at Javelina football games, a quasi-tradition of questionable origin and unquestionable lack of decorum.

Tallant based his decision on three issues, according to his official statement: safety, a waste of food, and offensiveness.

On the safety issue, he noted reports of spectators hit by frozen tortillas. He also pointed out that someone could slip on a slippery tortilla and fall, and that tortilla tossing could provoke fights.

Tallant said the waste of food is inconsistent with the stewardship he expects of students and insensitive to families in need. Refraining from the tortilla tossing won't feed those families, but at least it will remove the impression that the students don't care.

The university president also took care to explain why the practice would offend: "Many people, both Hispanic and non-Hispanic, have told me they are offended by this practice. They consider it a racist gesture, and even if some people in our community do not agree with this opinion, we need to be sensitive to those who are offended by throwing tortillas."

Tallant discussed the topic of tortilla tossing at student roundtables and with the student government before making his decision. "I know that some people, especially some student groups, are disappointed by my decision to ban throwing tortillas," Tallant said in his message. "I understand their disappointment, and I hope everyone understands that I didn't make this decision lightly." Obviously he didn't. He showed tolerance and patience.

He is also offering an alternative. The school handed out free *spirit towels* at the following year's first home game September 18. Another good call.

At Dartmouth football games, *Keggy the Keg* is king. Forget the official mascot of the Big Green. Keggy, a mascot without portfolio, is the people's choice. A giant dancing keg of beer that students cheer each time he completes a lap around the field. Hey, aren't mascots supposed to *tap* into the spirit of the school?

Or would you prefer the *keg and eggs* before the opening kickoff of each *Cortaca Jug Game* between Ithaca and Cortland? And how would you like your eggs? Scrambled? But of course.

At Fredonia State, a branch of the State University of New York (SUNY), the *Naked Library Run* is a spring perennial. It has no set date. Members of the track and field teams, both male and female, suddenly appear when word gets out that it's time for another Naked Library Run. They sprint around the perimeter of the college library completely nude, running several laps before some 1,500 onlookers on this, the day of the naked lap. The participants are, in every sense, running buffs.

And don't forget Harvard's *Primal Scream*. No one who's run it, or seen it, ever has. At midnight on the last night of the reading period and before final exams begin, students streak through the Old Yard and run a lap around it. It's done in both semesters, each time in the nude. It's a great way to release stress, an even greater night to be a spectator. Especially in the dead of winter, Primal Scream is no place for the primal squeamish.

NON-UNIVERSITY-SANCTIONED TRADITIONS BY SCHOOL

Appalachian State University (Football): *Jumping in the Pond*

Appalachian State fans have been known to *jump into a local pond* after big wins.

Bucknell University (Lacrosse): *Streaking*

Streaking at lacrosse games is a Bucknell tradition.

University of California, Davis (Track): *Naked Mile*

Once a year, the Davis track team and friends streak across the campus in the late night *Naked Mile*.

UCLA (Football): *Over the Wall*

It's been an off-and-on affair for the better part of thirty years, and is known as "going over the wall," or, skipping practice after warm-ups. Seniors spontaneously decide and then subsequently all players get together for a team activity (i.e., movie). This tradition appears to have been stopped by the seniors in 2012. Will it return in the future? We hope so.

Carleton College: *Schiller*

A bust of Friedrich Schiller, known simply as *Schiller*, has made regular appearances, though briefly, at large campus events and sporting events. The tradition dates back to 1957, when a student took the bust from an unlocked storage area in the Gould Library, only to have it taken from him in turn. Possession of the bust escalated into an elaborate competition, which took on a high degree of secrecy and strategy. These days, Schiller's appearance, accompanied by the shout of "Schiller!" is a tacit challenge to other students to try to capture the bust. The currently circulating bust of Schiller was retrieved from Puebla, Mexico, in the summer of 2003. In 2006, students created an online scavenger hunt, made up of a series of complex riddles about Carleton, which led participants to Schiller's hidden location. The bust was subsequently stolen from the winner of the scavenger hunt. At commencement in 2006, the holders of the bust arranged for Schiller to graduate. When his name was called at the appropriate moment, the bust was pulled from behind the podium and prominently displayed. In March 2010, the bust of Schiller appeared on *The Colbert Report*. The appearance was organized by custodians of Schiller who contacted Peter Gwinn, a Carleton alumnus, who is a writer for the program. The bust has also appeared on a Halloween broadcast of *A Prairie Home Companion* on Minnesota Public Radio, as well as at a recent presidential debate.

"Schiller" being freed and pursued, at Carleton College. *Carleton College*

Dartmouth College (Football): *Rush the Field*

At halftime of the homecoming football game, some upperclassmen encourage freshman to *rush the field*, although no upperclassman has seen a significant rush since several injuries sustained during the 1986 rush prompted the school to ban the practice. Among the two or three students who sometimes run across the field, those who are arrested are charged with trespassing (the independent newspaper, *The Dartmouth Review*, has set up a fund to automatically pay any fines associated with freshman who rush the field). For the 2011 homecoming game, however, over forty members of the Class of 2015 rushed the field at homecoming without any action taken by Safety and Security, or the Hanover Police Department.

University of Georgia (Various Sports): *Damn Good . . .*

While a student at UGA in the late 1960s, I loved that everything was "*Damn Good . . .*" as in "Damn Good, Dawgs." But my favorite was overheard after a football stadium invocation, when the students next to me began to chant, "Damn Good, Prayer!"

Idaho State University (Football): *Potato Tossing*

Some Idaho State fans *toss spuds* at games.

Messiah College (Soccer): *Boxer Run*

Started in 1986, and also known as the *Brothers Fiesta*, the *Boxer Run* is a long-standing men's soccer team tradition. Every year in December, a group of guys brave the cold and run the entire campus in their underwear. Some also wear ties, hats, suspenders, or other costume-y items. They sing Christmas carols and scream "Merry Christmas" to every girl they pass. While on the run, they enter dorms and knock on doors asking other guys to join them. Outside, they search for a random discarded object, such as a toilet seat or kid's bicycle. A male freshman is preselected as the winner. The criteria for this selection are unknown, except that it cannot be an athlete. At the end of the run, the guys stop by that freshman's dorm room and knock. He opens the door to hundreds of screaming almost naked guys who hand him a prize. This tradition is highly anticipated by female students.

University of Missouri (Football): *Goal Posts*

Mizzou students often celebrate huge wins by *hauling the goal posts* seventeen blocks from Faurot Field to Harpo's Tavern.

Northwestern University (Football): *Marshmallows in the Tubas*

This tradition started in the 1970s and continued until the mid-1990s. The goal was to get a *marshmallow into one of the band's tubas*.

The Ohio State University (Football): *Jumping in Mirror Lake*

Ohio State students often *jump into a freezing lake* for good luck before the annual football game against Michigan. In 1990, 100 OSU students jumped in the lake at the end of a march around campus two nights before the Ohio State–Michigan game. Today, thousands of students jump into the freezing waters of Mirror Lake in November, an activity roundly discouraged by school administrators.

University of Texas at El Paso (Basketball): *Burrito Bomber*

UTEP's *Burrito Bomber*, who launched burritos at the public at Miner basketball games, was ejected from one game in 2004 after swatting a referee.

UTEP's Burrito Bomber. *UTEP / Michael P. Reese*

Various Schools: *Streaking*

Yes, *streaking* (running naked) still exists on many campuses, sometimes to even raise money for charity. Most are yearly events, although some others happen more often. On the following page are a few examples:

Cal Tech, San Luis Obispo: *Streak Hathaway*
University of California, Berkeley: *Moffitt Library*
University of California, Santa Cruz: *First Rain*
Centre College: *Running the Flame*
University of Chicago: *Regenstein Library*
Dartmouth College: *Blue Light Challenge*
Hamilton College/Colgate/Princeton/Williams: *Streak competitively against other schools*
Lawrence University: *Senior Streak*
University of North Carolina: *The Undergraduate Library*
University of Notre Dame: *LaFortune Student Center*
Penn State: *Mifflin Road*
Princeton University: *Various Running-a-Streak*
Rice University: *Baker 13*
Swarthmore College: *Dash for Cash*
University of Virginia: *Rotunda to Statue of Home*
Wheaton College: *Kingdom Run*

University of Virginia (Football): *Fourth Year Fifth*

It's a tradition that school officials have mightily tried to stop. Seniors, called "fourth years" at UVA, *drink a fifth of alcohol*—that's seventeen or so shots—during the last home football game, before kickoff.

West Virginia University: *Burning Couches*

WVU students *burn couches*. They burn them because the basketball team won. They burn them because the football team won. They burn them because the football team lost. They burn them because Bin Laden was killed. They burn them because it snowed. WVU students burn couches. It's what they do. The practice, immortalized in song and in generations of carbon patches on the roads of Morgantown, may be nearing an end. Until recently, couch burning had been a misdemeanor, with only a $1,000 fine to back it up. Now it is a felony arson charge, which carries the possibility of up to three years in prison. There is even a rhyming educational and awareness campaign: "Students Will Learn Not to Burn" from stickers, magnets, and flyers around campus, and presumably earn three to six credit hours in the freshman core curriculum.

18

RIVALRIES/THE WINNERS GET *WHAT?*

Once, while coaching the New York Jets, an exasperated Herm Edwards famously yelled at the press, "You play . . . to win . . . *the game!*"

Not just every game, folks, but especially *The Game.* THE GAME. That annual Hatfield-McCoy hate-fest against your Aggie archrivals, or the State U. snobs, or those insufferable city slickers. When there are bragging rights at stake, and more: A lovely parting gift for the winner.

"So, Don Pardo, tell 'em what they've won!"

A $30,000 Waterford crystal football? That'd be nice, but that goes to the BCS National Champion. Crystal's fine, but it's no *Floyd of Rosedale,* who sounds like a caller from Queens on WFAN radio in New York—"Floyd of Rosedale, you're on the air"—but is a trophy given to the winner of the Iowa-Minnesota football game.

A trophy of a pig. A pig named Floyd.

In 1935, the governors of Minnesota and Iowa placed a wager on the Gophers-Hawkeyes game. The previous year, the Gophers had battered Iowa's Ozzie Simmons. So tensions were running higher than the price of pork futures. Especially after Iowa Governor Clyde Herring warned, "If the officials stand for any rough tactics like Minnesota used last year, I'm sure the crowd won't."

Clyde's gubernatorial counterpart, Floyd Olson (no relation to Floyd of Rosedale) responded, "Minnesota folks are excited over your statement about Iowa crowds lynching the Minnesota football team. I have assured

"The Floyd of Rosedale Trophy" going to the winner of the Iowa–Minnesota football game. *Iowa Athletic Communications*

them you are law abiding gentlemen and are only trying to get our goat . . . I will bet you a Minnesota prize hog against an Iowa prize hog that Minnesota wins."

True to his word, Governor Herring walked into Olson's office after Minnesota's 13–6 triumph. He brought along Floyd of Rosedale, a prize-winning hog. And so began a ham-handed handoff. The ceremonial passing of the pig.

Eventually, time passed. As did Floyd, who moved on to that great sty-in-the-sky. In his memory, the winner of the Iowa-Minnesota game now claims a fifteen and half-inch high, twenty-one-inch long bronze statue of a prized porker.

Floyd of Rosedale. The sausage link to the past.

The historically black colleges and universities often play their equivalent of bowl games during the season. They're called various "Classics," and that they are . . . especially when a rivalry is involved.

You want cups? We got cups. All kinds of cups. Our cups runneth over. Everything from assorted *Governors' Cups*, including Georgia–Georgia Tech to the *Apple Cup*, which big-time rivals Washington and Washington State have fought over since 1900 to a delightfully named newbie, the *Apothecary Cup*.

It pits the Albany, New York, College of Pharmacy and the St. Louis College of Pharmacy. Two basketball teams who just don't like each other, even if the rivalry's just two years old, even if they break bread together over dinner the night before the game.

The Eutectics, as St. Louis is nicknamed, or "Euts" (not to be confused with Utah's Utes) won the first meeting in 2011. It was played in the St. Louis bandbox gym known as the *Pillbox*. Perfect. On November 17, 2012, Albany claimed the Apothecary Cup, a trophy replica of an actual apothecary cup. The Panthers edged the Euts 90–83 in double overtime.

What's a eutectic, you ask? From the *Merriam-Webster Dictionary*: "A mixture of two or more components, a eutectic alloy or solution in such proportion that their combined melting point is the lowest possible, in some cases as low as (minus?) 60 degrees C (minus? 140 degrees F)."

But then you knew that. Bottom line, these Euts have ice water in their veins.

The *Canal Cup*? That goes to the winner of the *Battle of the Bridge*, an all-sport competition between Niagara University and Canisius College, whose teams cross the Grand Island Bridge in upstate New York to play each other.

If it's history you want, you got it:

The *Red River Rivalry*: The annual bad bloodbath between Oklahoma and Texas since 1900, and first played in Dallas in 1929. The historic *Cotton Bowl* has hosted the game each October since 1937, in conjunction with the Texas State Fair. Not one, not two, but three trophies go to the winner. Read on and find out about 'em.

The most patriotic and meaningful trophy of all? The *Commander-in-Chief Trophy*, awarded to the winner of the Army, Navy, and Air Force football rivalry. If there's no outright winner, then the Commander-in-Chief Trophy stays put, until one of the service academies beats the other two in the same season.

The *1899 Territorial Cup*? That goes to the winner of the annual Arizona–Arizona State football game. What's that, you say? That's so 1899? Exactly. In 2001, the 1899 Territorial Cup received NCAA Division I-A designation as the oldest rivalry trophy in the United States, and my family and I were fortunate to see it awarded in 2013 for the victory in 2012.

On November 30, 1899, Thanksgiving Day in Tempe, the then Arizona Territorial Normal School beat Arizona 11–2 before a reported crowd of 300. The Cup had its first curator. Over the years, the prized, silver-plated antique was misplaced. So for the Big Game, as Arizona and Arizona State came to call their rivalry, other new awards sufficed. A *Governor's Trophy* (1953–1979), a *victory sculpture* by artist Ben Goo, it is a bronze *saguaro trophy*, a sculpture presented to the winning coach to display in his office for a year.

Thankfully, the 1899 Territorial Cup was finally discovered in the basement of a church that was being demolished. Ever since, to ensure its safety, the original Territorial Cup is moved from one school to another only under escort and the supervision of gloved archivists.

According to the NCAA, the previously oldest trophy was the Michigan-Minnesota *Little Brown Jug*, also from1899.

The great thing about ancient, traditional rivalries is that each year, everything old is renewed again. Sportscasters will say the old cliché, "This one's for all the marbles!" Marbles, shmarbles. Would you rather claim a rare cat's eye marble or the *Cortaca Jug*?

The *Biggest Little Game in the Nation*: That's what *Sports Illustrated* anointed the November football rivalry between Ithaca College and Cortland, two campuses in New York about twenty miles apart. As for Cortaca, CORT-land vs. ith-ACA. Get it? The Cortaca Jug is the traveling trophy between these Division III (D-III) teams who've developed one of the classic D-III rivalries.

In 1959, pals Dick Carmean and Tom Decker, captains of Ithaca and Cortland respectively, donated the Cortaca Jug to the already-heated rivalry. The Ithaca Bombers and Red Dragons of Cortland draw big crowds, often doubling the 5,000 capacity of Ithaca's Butterfield Stadium.

There's often much at stake. In 1988, in the second-to-last week of the regular season, Ithaca and Cortland were ranked first and second nationally in D-III. Cortland prevailed; but three weeks later the Bombers beat the Red Dragons in the NCAA playoffs en route to winning the Division III national championship. Nothing else, however, trumps taking home the Cortaca Jug.

In the market for household furnishings? It's almost as if college sports rivalries are an enormous, old-time general store. Or maybe if Home Depot merged with Toys 'R' Us? Need a *beanpot*, perhaps? That's Boston's revered hockey classic come February between Boston College, Boston University, Harvard, and Northeastern. How about a skillet? No ordinary frying pan. The *Iron Skillet* was first awarded to the winner of the SMU-TCU game, back in their Southwest Conference halcyon days.

A *beer barrel*, you say? Maybe not in these politically correct times. It goes to the winner of the Tennessee versus Kentucky football game. And while it is clearly a beer barrel, the sign on the side says "ice water", in deference to the temperance groups, way back when. Yet you can still hope for a keg. The *Keg of Nails*, courtesy of either Cincinnati or Louisville.

Anyone for a *war canoe*? Or an authentic *totem pole* with two names? Middle Tennessee calls it *Harvey*. To Tennessee Tech students, it's *Sin-a-Ninny*. The pigskin tradition began in the 1960s before the totem pole disappeared for several years. Harvey/Sin-a-Ninny resurfaced in 1991. Tech students were the suspected culprits. Now you, too, can claim Harvey for a limited time if your team wins.

How's this for a bucket list?

The *Bayou Bucket*, which goes to the winner of the Houston–Rice football game.

The *Old Brass Spittoon* belongs to the winner of the Indiana versus Michigan football game. It's not to be confused with the *Brass Spittoon* (New Mexico State–UTEP football).

The *Old Oaken Bucket*, which neither Indiana nor Purdue would ever spit into, dates perhaps to Civil War times. The actual bucket itself, not the game.

The *Paint Bucket*, no primer necessary.

A personal favorite of ours: The *Slab of Bacon Trophy*, which Minnesota and Wisconsin long slobbered over in football until 1948, until someone forgot to bring home the bacon. The schools first played in 1890, when Minnesota slaughtered Wisconsin 63–0. More than a half century hence, the Slab of Bacon Trophy was lost in the early 1940s following a postgame melee in which students and spectators ran wildly around the field. Wisconsin officials say that the Slab of Bacon disappeared in 1945, yet the scores of every Minnesota–Wisconsin game from 1930–1970 were written on the back of the slab.

It was replaced in 1948 by *Paul Bunyan's Axe*. On the six-foot long handle of ol' tall tale Paul's axe is emblazoned the results of each Badgers-Gophers game. That's swell, but it's not a Slab of Bacon.

And what goes better with bacon than . . . eggs. The annual *Egg Bowl* between Ole Miss and Mississippi State.

Then again, speaking of axes . . . the *Axe* goes to the winner of *The Big Game*—the annual Cal-Stanford football epic.

So, ladies and gentlemen, it's now showtime. Lights . . . camera . . . AX-tion!

"The Slab of Bacon Trophy" Going to the Winner of the Minnesota–Wisconsin Football Game. Notice how it can be viewed upside down to represent each school. *University of Wisconsin Athletic Communications*

The winner of the Minnesota–Wisconsin game receives "the Paul Bunyan Ax." *University of Minnesota*

Stanford and Cal play in "the Big Game," with the winner getting "the Axe."
Stanford University

When it comes to Cal-Stanford, think big. Really big. No, we mean Really, REALLY BIG. When it's the Cal-Stanford rivalry, everything—not just football's Big Game—is B-I-G BIG.

It's not Cal–Stanford volleyball, it's the *Big Spike*. Water polo? That's the *Big Splash*. Ice hockey? Easy: the *Big Freeze*. And Cal–Stanford Crew? That became the *Big Row*.

But in 2011, it was renamed the *Jill Row*. That was in honor of Jill Costello, the Cal coxswain who lost her year-long battle with lung cancer. In her last months in the boat, Costello helped lead Cal to a second-place finish at the nationals.

Since then, in her honor and memory, family and friends have founded *Jill's Legacy*, which has raised a significant amount of money for lung cancer research. Ironically, Jill Costello was a nonsmoker. She was also a teammate and friend, daughter and coxswain, with the very biggest of hearts.

Some treasures are nothing to shake a stick at. The *Old Hickory Stick*, for example, which goes to the Northwest Missouri State–Truman State football winner.

Other gridiron riches sound almost Olympian. Think Gold. Silver. Bronze. Think . . .

The *Golden Hat*: Oklahoma–Texas, a ten-gallon cowboy hat on a wooden
  block.
The *Silver Spade*: New Mexico State–UTEP.
The *Bronze Derby*: Newberry–Presbyterian.

These boots were made for winnin':

The *Golden Boot*: Arkansas–LSU.
The *Beehive Boot*: BYU–Utah–Utah State.
The *Bronze Boot*: Colorado State–Wyoming.

Instead of a spittoon, anyone care for a *peace pipe*?

Or the *Shillelagh*, a Gaelic war club that's gone to the winner of the
Notre Dame–University of Southern Cal football game since 1952. It's
made of oak or thorn saplings from Ireland. The only woods, so they say,
which are tougher than an Irish skull. The Shillelagh is adorned with ruby
red Trojan heads with the score and year of USC wins, and emerald-stud-
ded shamrocks for Fighting Irish victories.

In Los Angeles, the cherished *Victory Bell* goes to the winner in the
cross-town rivalry between UCLA and USC. The school gets possession of
the 295-pound Victory Bell, if only briefly. One of the least-seen trophies in
the land, the Victory Bell sits in a warehouse or vault for all but two days of
the year. It's displayed in the Los Angeles Coliseum during the first three
quarters of the UCLA–USC game, and on the Monday following the game
on the winning team's campus. Then it goes back into hiding.

There's weaponry to be won, from a *musket* to a once-upon-a-time *Kit
Carson rifle* (no longer awarded) to a *cannon* with a few screws loose.

The University of Nevada and UNLV play for the *Fremont Cannon*. At
545 pounds, it's the heaviest and among the most expensive trophies in
college football, a replica of a howitzer cannon used by explorer John C.
Fremont on an 1843 expedition in the Sierra Nevadas.

After a 1978 Nevada victory, coach Chris Ault persuaded airport security
to let his team disassemble the canyon and carry it on a plane back home
to Reno. In 2000, the cannon was refurbished after being damaged during a UNLV victory celebration. During the refurbishment, officials found
inscriptions inside the Fremont Cannon that included such anti-UNLV
graffiti as "University of Notta Lotta Victories."

Alas, the cannon, fired after each team scored, has been inoperable since
1999.

The *Sweet Sioux Tomahawk* was once awarded to the winner of the annual Illinois-Northwestern football game. In these twenty-first-century times, the tomahawk was replaced by the *Land of Lincoln Trophy*. It's a bronze replica of Honest Abe's stovepipe hat.

Speaking of hats . . . in 1993, Lycoming College and Susquehanna University turned their game into a Stagg party. The annual *Stagg Hat Game*. The trophy? The late Amos Alonzo Stagg's actual fedora he wore as the grand old man of college football coaching. Stagg won 314 games in a legendary career that began at the University of Chicago and ended at Susquehanna. His hat was bronzed and later given to the university as a gift. It sat displayed in a trophy case for several years before the Stagg Hat Game began in 1993, but the game is no longer played due to conference alignment.

And then there's the nonpareil Lafayette–Lehigh game, the most played and longest uninterrupted rivalry in college football. They've tackled each other 148 times since 1884 with one interruption, in 1896. The current streak stands at 121 games played consecutively. I witnessed the 148th rendition, and hope to also attend the 150th game scheduled soon for Yankee Stadium.

What's most remarkable about this hallowed rivalry between two Pennsylvania campuses just seventeen miles apart: the Rivalry, as it's simply known, is so ancient that it predates football trophies. How cool is that? The winning team gets the game ball, painted with the final score and date.

Lafayette–Lehigh has been the subject of several books and a PBS television documentary narrated by the late, great sportscaster, Harry Kalas.

Most schools, of course, cherish the rivalry rewards that accompany such signature triumphs. Since 1938, North Dakota and North Dakota State have slugged it out on the gridiron in hopes of winning the *Nickel Trophy*. It weighs seventy-five pounds and is a large replica of—what else—a nickel. One that's been the object of many raids and thefts, recoveries and returns over the years.

The *Chief Caddo Trophy*? Not so much. Why? You try to pilfer it. It's the biggest football trophy in the country, and goes to the winner of the Northwestern State–Stephen F. Austin football game. The Chief's a big dude, standing 7'6", weighing more than 320 pounds. He's over 50 years old, having been carved from a 2,000-pound black gum log after the 1961 rivalry game.

The statue is named in honor of the Caddos, a Native American tribe indigenous to the area. Legend has it that a Caddo chief and his two sons were responsible for settling Nacogdoches, Texas, and Natchitoches, Louisiana, each school's respective cities.

"The Chief Caddo Trophy"
going to the winner of
Northwestern State–
Stephen F. Austin football
game. *Stephen F. Austin*
University

And for one last legendary rivalry trophy, please read-on and relish the rich history of Michigan–Minnesota and the *Little Brown Jug*.

It's a prime example of the ultimate parting gift. A to-go bucket or jug, bowl, or trophy that comes at the expense of a long-time foe. Even better when you're the visitor and defeat your rival and take home the spoils of victory. For either Iowa or Minnesota, that means one thing: bringing home the bacon. Floyd of Rosedale.

RIVALRIES BY SCHOOL

Adams State University–Fort Lewis College (Football):
The Musket Game

A bunch of Indians and a group of Raiders first fought over a gun in 1966. No, it wasn't the first skirmish between actual Indians and Raiders, but it was the first scrimmage between the two in a metaphorical sense. Their team nicknames have long since changed to Grizzlies and Skyhawks, but

Adams State and Fort Lewis College still play for the same Springfield .45–70 military-issue rifle they did back in 1966, the first year of what's now come to be called the *Musket Game*. As is custom, the seniors of the winning team fire the weapon after the game, along with the head coach and occasionally some assistants and school administrators. The rifle itself actually isn't a musket in the literal sense. Although the exact model year isn't known, Springfield .45–70 rifles were in use beginning in 1873 and were used up until 1892. At this point, the victors fire blanks from the gun, and it's become customary for those who fire it to keep the shell casings as a memento.

Air Force/Colorado State University (Football): *Ram–Falcon Trophy*

The *Ram–Falcon Trophy* originated in 1980 to highlight the series between CSU and Air Force. The wood-carved trophy was produced by local artist Bill Wrage. The Air Force ROTC detachment on the CSU campus initiated the creation of the trophy. John Lorber, a retired four-star general, scored the first touchdown in Falcon Stadium history against in-state rival Colorado State. It was the only touchdown of Lorber's career. He went on to command tens of thousands of troops in the Pacific, serving thirty-five years before retiring in 1997.

University of Akron/Kent State University (Multi-sport): *Wagon Wheel Trophy/Challenge*

Since 1946, the winner of the annual Akron–Kent State football game has won the *Wagon Wheel Trophy*. But in a nice twist to this rivalry, the competition now spans fifteen sports between the two schools in the *Wagon Wheel Challenge*. With each victory, the winner earns a point for their school toward winning the series trophy.

University of Akron/Youngstown State University (Football): *Steel–Tire Trophy*

Steel and tires are these two towns' main industries, so the *Steel–Tire Trophy* goes to the winner of the Akron–Youngstown State game. The Steel–Tire Trophy was awarded, from 1940 until 1995, to the winner of the annual college football game between the University of Akron and Youngstown State University. The series was put on notice when Akron moved up to the Division I-A level (now FBS) in 1987 and ceased to be a yearly rivalry after 1995.

University of Alabama/Auburn University (Football): *Iron Bowl/Foy–ODK Sportsmanship Award*

In a series that began in 1893, the *Iron Bowl* is considered by many as an example of one of the fiercest rivalries in all of sports. Or, as my wife taught our kids to say instead using the word "hate," these two schools have little in common. The trophy given to the winner of the game is the *Foy–ODK Sportsmanship Award*. It is named after James E. Foy, an Alabama graduate and former Auburn dean of students and a member of the Omicron Delta Kappa honor society. The Foy Trophy is presented at halftime of the Alabama–Auburn basketball game later in the same academic year at the winner's home court. At the start of each season, the Student Government Association (SGA) presidents of both schools agree to bet on the outcome of the Iron Bowl by agreeing that after the trophy presentation, the SGA president of the losing team will sing the winning team's fight song. This rivalry had a forty-one-year break in the festivities (resuming in 1949). It is said that the break was over a disagreement involving an extra fifty cents in per diem money and the selection of officials.

Alabama A&M/Alabama State University (Football): *Magic City Classic*

Alabama A&M–Alabama State is one of the greatest rivalries among the historically black colleges and universities. The rivalry began in 1924 and has grown to be similar to a bowl game experience with a parade, after-game concert, large tailgate party, and halftime band action. Recently, 66,000 attended the game, with an additional 40,000 outside the stadium enjoying the festivities. Alabama Tourism Department named the game one of their Top 10 Events for 2013.

University of Alabama at Birmingham/University of Memphis (Football): *Battle for the Bones*

The two teams first played each other in 1997 with the *Battle for the Bones* beginning in 2006. The trophy is a 100-pound bronzed rack of ribs. This game is also surrounded by a barbecue contest where fans are invited to sign-up and have their grilling skills judged against fans from the rival school to determine which city has the best barbecue.

Alabama State University/Southern University (Football): *Gulf Coast Classic*

Alabama State–Southern began this rivalry in 1974. In 2007, the *Gulf Coast Classic* set a new record for the most RVs and motor homes inside Ladd-Peebles Stadium. The Classic is the only regular season college football game annually played in Mobile. The foundation that owns the Classic is a nonprofit organization and was established to directly impact the lives of the students and student athletes who reside along the Gulf Coast.

Alabama State University/Tuskegee University (Football): *Turkey Day Classic*

The Alabama State–Tuskegee series started in 1924, and is considered to be among the oldest of the Historically Black College Classics. The game has traditionally been played at the Cramton Bowl, a 26,000-seat stadium located near Alabama State's Montgomery campus. When the Hornets opened up their new on-campus facility in 2012, the *Turkey Day Classic* came with it. Like the SWAC Championship and the Bayou Classic, this game is scheduled at the same time as the FCS and Division II playoff tournaments. As a result, both Alabama State and Tuskegee have turned down playoff berths in order to preserve the history and tradition of the rivalry.

University of Alaska Anchorage/University of Alaska Fairbanks (Ice Hockey): *Governor's Cup*

This rivalry takes place during *Fairbanks Winter Carnival*, and also features an *Outhouse Race*.

Albany College of Pharmacy/St. Louis College of Pharmacy (Basketball): *Apothecary Cup*

This tradition began in 2011 and now continues with alternating sites, with women's teams planned for future years.

Albany State University/Fort Valley State University (Football): *Fountain City Classic*

While these two HBCUs have been playing each other since 1945, the rivalry morphed into the *Fountain City Classic* in 1989 when the game was

moved off-campus to A. J. McClung Memorial Stadium in Columbus, Georgia. Numerous festivities highlight the two weeks leading up to the game,
including a parade, a fun run, and a golf classic. The game itself is known for
its dynamic halftime show, which features the Albany State *Marching Rams
Show Band* and the *Marching Blue Machine* of Fort Valley State.

Alcorn State University/Jackson State University (Football): *Capital City Classic*

Alcorn State–Jackson State began their rivalry in 1993. Although the
game is typically played in Jackson, in 2012 Alcorn's administrators said
their school would exercise the home team's right to play on their home
field versus in Jackson. In language inspired by the Declaration of Independence, Alcorn's administrator said, "The facts are self-evident that the
Lorman campus is an equal and adequate venue for *any* football game,
including Jackson State. The time has come to declare our independence
from hosting the *Capital City Classic* on our rival school's home field."

Alverno College/Milwaukee School of Engineering (Women's Basketball and Soccer): *Red Rivalry Cup*

The name for the traveling trophy and game comes from the parallel in
both teams' colors. In addition to the cross-town rivalry—the two institutions
are a mere seven miles apart in the city of Milwaukee, they also have a conference rivalry—both are members of the Northern Athletics Conference.

Amherst College/Wesleyan University/Williams College (Various Sports): *Little Three*

Amherst and Williams first became league rivals in 1882, and Wesleyan
joined them in 1899 to form the *Triangular League*, or *Little Three*. This
partnership lasted only three years before disputes caused a breakup, but
it was reformed in 1910 and has been played continuously in every sport in
which each school fields a varsity team.

Amherst College/Williams College (Football): *Biggest Little Game in America*

The Amherst–Williams rivalry is so special that it has not only been featured on *ESPN Game Day*, but it was also recently featured prominently by

a regional sports network. What other rivalry in this great nation had to have its news directors decide the outcome of games played eighty years earlier? For many years, the Ephs and Lord Jeffs reported different won–loss totals until 1964 when John English of Williams and Horace Hewlett of Amherst finally resolved the scores of the games played in 1884, 1886, 1887, 1890, 1896, 1897, 1918, and 1925.

Appalachian State University/Western Carolina University (Football): *Old Mountain Jug*

The football rivalry between ASU and WCU dates back to 1932, but took on a new shape in 1976. That shape came in the form of a replica moonshine jug dubbed the *Old Mountain Jug*, or as some say, the Jug. *Sports Illustrated* once called the ASU–WCU series the best football rivalry you've never heard of.

University of Arizona/Arizona State University (Football and Basketball): *Big Game Trophy/1899 Territorial Cup/Duel in the Desert*

In the summer of 2001, officials at Arizona and Arizona State received NCAA Division I-A designation for the *1899 Territorial Cup* as the oldest trophy for a rivalry game in America. The annual Arizona–Arizona State winner obtains possession of the Cup for its hall of fame, a replica goes to the winning school's president's office, and two later trophies used over the years in the hard-fought rivalry are awarded to the winning coach and the most valuable player. On Thanksgiving Day in 1899, then Arizona Territorial Normal School defeated Arizona 11–2 in front of a reported 300 fans, and the Cup had its first curator. But over the years, the silver-plated antique prize was misplaced and supplanted by various other awards for the Big Game—the *Governor's Trophy* (1953–1979), a *victory sculpture* by artist Ben Goo, and a *saguaro trophy*, among others. To ensure the safety of the original trophy, the actual Territorial Cup is moved from one school to the other only under escort and the supervision of gloved archivists. The *Ben Goo Trophy*, awarded from 1979 to 1998 as the game trophy, became the *Bob Moran Most Valuable Player Award* in 2008. It is selected each year by covering media, in honor of the rivalry's late sportswriter. The Saguaro Trophy, a smaller bronze piece commissioned from artist Dora Perry in 1998, goes to the winning coach in the series. The games themselves have assumed various proportions in the last century depending on the annual success of both teams, but always they've been a matter of pride more

"The 1899 Territorial Cup," which goes to the winner of the University of Arizona versus Arizona State University football game. *Wikimedia Commons*

than hardware. Now, it's the oldest intercollegiate rivalry trophy game in America with a century-old silver award.

University of Arizona/University of New Mexico: *Kit Carson Rifle*

The *Kit Carson Rifle*, a Springfield rifle, is rumored to have once belonged to Geronimo. Until the end of the 1997 season, Arizona and New Mexico shared a tradition of the Kit Carson Rifle, a weapon named for the famous territorial scout. The trophy, once retained each year by the winning team, is now in Arizona's heritage center after retirement as a game emblem prior to the Insight.com bowl game, which pitted the two teams in December 1997. Officials at both schools joined in deeming the emblematic spirit of the rivalry (which began in 1907), more important than a weapon of the sort used in the Southwest against Native Americans. Arizona won the rifle twenty-one times and New Mexico ten times in the years the gun was offered as the game prize since 1938.

University of Arkansas/LSU (Football): *Golden Boot*

The *Golden Boot Trophy* is 4-feet tall, weighs 200 pounds, and has a value that exceeds $10,000. The *Battle for the Golden Boot* is a college football rivalry game played annually by the Arkansas Razorbacks and the LSU Tigers. The first game between the Razorbacks and Tigers was played in 1901. With the admission of Arkansas as a member of the Southeastern Conference in 1992, the rivalry became an annually scheduled game between fellow members of the SEC's western division. The Golden Boot Trophy, named for the combined shape of Arkansas and Louisiana, was first awarded to the game's winner in 1996. The game is usually played on the Friday after Thanksgiving.

University of Arkansas/Texas A&M (Football): *Southwest Classic*

These two schools first met on the gridiron in 1903 with Texas A&M winning 6–0. Texas A&M and Arkansas were part of the inaugural group of the eight schools that formed the Southwest Conference in 1915. From 1934 through 1991, the teams met every season as part of the Southwest Conference. Arkansas withdrew from the league in 1991 to join the Southeastern Conference, while Texas A&M joined in 2012. So now they play each other once again.

University of Arkansas at Pine Bluff/Southern University (Football): *Dallas Lone Star Classic*

This game started in 2008 and is played at the Cotton Bowl in Dallas.

Arkansas State University–University of Louisiana at Monroe (Football): *Trail of Tears Classic*

Played since 1959, the name of this rivalry stems from the fact that both teams were formerly nicknamed Indians. It remains the name of the rivalry even though ULM changed their nickname to the Warhawks in 2006 and Arkansas State changed to the Red Wolves in 2008.

Ashland University/Hillsdale College (Football): *Traveling Trophy*

The Ashland Eagles and the Hillsdale Chargers battle annually for the *Traveling Trophy*. Established in 1970, the Traveling Trophy game is one of only a few NCAA-recognized trophy games. The winner of the game gets to keep the trophy at their institution until the following year.

Auburn University/LSU (Football): *Tiger Bowl*

A match-up of teams with identical nicknames, Auburn and LSU have been in the same conference almost continuously since 1896. However, the two programs did not consider each other to be important rivals for much of their respective histories, facing each other only twenty-four times from 1901–1987 and once going twenty-five years in between match-ups. All of that changed in 1988, when LSU defeated Auburn 7–6 on Tommy Hodson's touchdown pass to Eddie Fuller on fourth-and-goal with just under two minutes remaining. The reaction of LSU's Tiger Stadium crowd was so intense that it registered as an earthquake in Baton Rouge. Things picked up even further in 1992, when the SEC split into divisional play and the two teams became yearly foes. Both programs are annual contenders for the division crown, which has resulted in the Tiger Bowl becoming one of the most anticipated games on the SEC schedule.

Augsburg College/Hamline University (Football): *The Hammer*

One of the oldest rivalries in Division III, these Twin Cities liberal arts colleges first met on the gridiron in 1926. The rivalry was given added spice in 2005, when the *Hammer* was adopted as the trophy to be awarded to the winner. It is one of five Minnesota Intercollegiate Athletic Conference trophy games.

Augusta State University/Georgia College (Basketball): *Battle of the Cats*

A battle between Jaguars and Bobcats, this hoops rivalry has been one of the best in the Peach Belt Conference since Augusta State joined in 1991. With only nintey miles between the two schools, this rivalry has maintained intensity even after the recent conference expansion placed the two teams in separate divisions.

Augusta State University/University of South Carolina-Aiken (Basketball): *Cross Border Rivalry*

It was only natural for these Peach Belt Conference powers to develop a rivalry, as the two schools are separated by a mere seventeen miles and the Georgia–South Carolina border.

Augustana College/University of Sioux Falls (Football):
Key to the City

These South Dakota city rivals have met infrequently since 1916, as Sioux Falls was a longtime NAIA school and only joined the Division II ranks as a full member in 2012. This proved to be the perfect opportunity for the two colleges to start a trophy game, as the 2012 contest marked the first time in twenty-six years that the two had met on the gridiron.

Baldwin-Wallace University/John Carroll University (Football):
The Cuyahoga

These Cleveland-area schools have been playing since 1921, but the rivalry rose in prominence when John Carroll re-joined the Ohio Athletic Conference in 1989. It was at this time that the trophy—a plaque with a rock shaped like a football—was adopted and to be held by the winning school for each year. This rivalry is known as one of the most balanced rivalries in Division III, with the majority of games being settled by ten points or less.

Ball State University/Northern Illinois University (Football):
Bronze Stalk Trophy

These two schools share the unique distinction of being the only schools in the MAC from their respective states. The rivalry, which dates back to 1941, picked up steam when the two were conference rivals from 1975–1986, then was reinvigorated when NIU rejoined the conference in 1997. It was not until 2008 that the *Bronze Stalk Trophy*—which reflects the prevalence of maize in both Indiana and Illinois—was added to further spice things up.

Bates College/Bowdoin College/Colby College (Football):
Multicollege Trophy

Perhaps the most intense gridiron match-ups in the state of Maine, Bates, Bowdoin, and Colby Colleges, have all been playing each other since the late nineteenth century. The *CBB Championship*, named for the first initial of each school, was created in 1965 as a way of strengthening the bonds between the colleges.

Baylor University/Texas A&M (Football): *Battle of the Brazos*

Football has been a way of life in the state of Texas since the nineteenth century, so it was only natural that two of the state's most prominent universities would start up a fierce rivalry. The *Battle of the Brazo* originated in 1899 and eventually became one of the premier rivalries in the Southwest Conference (SWC). Rooted in military training, Texas A&M was an all-male college until 1911, and some believe that the Aggies' rivalry with the Bears—located ninety miles away in Waco—stemmed from the fact that Baylor was the closest school that admitted women. The early days of this match-up was marked by Aggie dominance, as Texas A&M won nineteen of the first twenty-four meetings. Tragedy struck this rivalry in 1926, when a riot broke out between the two crowds and resulted in the death of an Aggie student, leading-to the rivalry not being played for four years. Things reached their competitive peak during the latter half of the SWC's history, with the Aggies holding a 16–14–1 edge from 1958 to 1990. The Aggies' dramatic 31–30 victory in the 1986 match-up was regarded as the SWC's Game of the 1980s by *Texas Football* magazine. That competitiveness—along with a governor that happened to be a Baylor grad—played a role in the Bears getting admitted into the Big 12 along with Texas A&M following the SWC's demise. Sadly, Texas A&M's jump to the SEC has caused this rivalry to go the way of the dodo, ending nearly a century of match-ups between these Lone Star State schools.

Baylor University/TCU (Football): *Holy War*

When the Southwest Conference met its demise in 1996, many of the longtime match-ups between the haves (i.e., those going to the Big 12) and have-nots (everyone else) became footnotes in the history books. Baylor–TCU, however, managed to avoid such a fate. First played in 1899, the *Holy War* matches up two of the most prominent religious schools in Texas, and historically has been one of the most evenly matched rivalries between former SWC foes. This was also originally a city rivalry, as TCU was located in Waco in its early years before relocating to Fort Worth in 1910 following a fire at the school's main administration building. TCU would follow Baylor into the SWC in 1923, and the Horned Frogs held a slight 35–32–2 edge in their games against the Bears during their time as conference rivals. The game was not played following the demise of the SWC, but the Holy War was reignited in 2006 and has once again become an annual fixture on the college football calendar with the Horned Frogs' admission to the Big 12.

This rivalry has been so evenly matched over the years that neither team has had more than a three-game edge in the overall series since the 1970s.

Bethune-Cookman University/Florida A&M (Football): *Florida Classic*

A match-up between two of the Sunshine State's most prominent HBCUs, Bethune-Cookman and Florida A&M have a longstanding rivalry that dates back to 1925. But the game turned into the *Florida Classic* when it moved to neutral-site Tampa Stadium in 1979, and the contest proved so popular that it was moved to the much-larger Citrus Bowl in 1997. It is annually among the best attended FCS football games of the year, drawing crowds upwards of 70,000 people. But for many fans, the football game itself is a secondary event, as the halftime show put on by B-C's marching band and FAMU's *Marching 100* is often cited as the reason for the game's high attendance. Both bands are also prominent in the other events of the Florida Classic, including a *Battle of the Bands* competition the night before the game.

Big 10/Pac-12 (Football): *Rose Bowl*

Nicknamed the "Granddaddy of Them All," the *Rose Bowl* is the oldest postseason game in college football. The game, long known for its scenic setting, frequently ends just as the sun goes down over the Arroyo Seco on New Year's Day. It is also preceded by the *Tournament of Roses Parade*, which draws upwards of 700,000 spectators every year. Contrary to popular belief, the Rose Bowl was not always a grudge match between the Pac-12 (or its predecessor, the PCC) and the Big Ten. The first Rose Bowl, a 49–0 Michigan victory over Stanford that was called midway through the third quarter, was considered such a failure that the game was not played again for fifteen years. Once football was reinstated, the Tournament of Roses Committee was not exactly eager to invite Big Ten opponents. The next thirty Rose Bowls included only two current members of the conference, one of which (Penn State in 1923) was an independent at the time. It was not until 1947 that the Rose Bowl became an annual match-up between the two conferences, with the two champions guaranteed to meet in Pasadena every year until the advent of the BCS in 1998. For many years, the Rose Bowl was the largest football stadium in the country, holding a maximum capacity of 104,091 at its peak. While it has since been lowered, it is still the largest stadium that hosts a bowl game and remains one of the most coveted tickets of the college football postseason. The Rose Bowl also introduced television to the sport, as the 1952 game between Illinois and Stanford was among the first to be seen by a national audience.

Big 10/Pac-12 (Football): *Beef Bowl*

Not all of the competitions between the Big Ten and Pac-12 take place on the field. Prior to the 1957 Rose Bowl between Oregon State and Iowa, Lawry's Restaurant in Beverly Hills decided to entertain the two teams with a dinner that featured their signature prime rib. It did not take long for this to become an annual tradition, with the restaurant hosting each team on different nights and holding a contest to see which team could consume more prime rib in a single sitting. The winner of the eating contest has gone on to win the Rose Bowl game approximately 70 percent of the time.

Black Hills State University/SD School of Mines and Technology (Football): *Homestake Trophy*

One of the most frequently played college football rivalries west of the Mississippi River, Black Hills State and the South Dakota School of Mines have been butting heads on the gridiron since 1895. This rivalry is so engrained that both schools elected to transition from the NAIA ranks to the NCAA Division II in an effort to preserve the history. The *Homestake Trophy* is named for a mine in the Black Hills area.

Boise State University/Fresno State (Football): *The Milk Can*

The *Milk Can*, a chromed, ten-gallon, old-school milk can is a fairly new trophy that began in 2005. The Dairymen in Fresno and Boise thought up the trophy to make the rivalry official and, of course, to shamelessly promote the benefits of milk. This rivalry rose to prominence while these two programs dominated the WAC in the 2000s and has followed the teams into the Mountain West Conference.

Boise State University/University of Idaho (Football): *Gem State Game*

When this series began in 1971, many Idaho faithful scoffed at the idea that Boise State—just a few years removed from junior college status— could ever become a legitimate rival. Idaho fans, however, were forced to eat their words when the Broncos handed the Vandals a 42–14 defeat in the inaugural game and wound up taking eight of the first eleven meetings. The Vandals would go on to dominate this rivalry for much of the 1980s and '90s, but Boise State has been in complete control since both schools made the jump to FBS status in 1996. The *Governor's Trophy* was adopted in 2001, but it never left the stadium with the Smurf Turf. After winning twelve meetings in a row by increasingly large margins, it was the Broncos' turn to scoff at the rivalry, electing to cancel the yearly series upon moving to the Mountain West following the 2010 season.

Boston College/Boston University/Harvard/Northeastern University (Ice Hockey): *Beanpot Trophy*

The city of Boston has long been the center of the college hockey world, as evidenced by competition between the four area college teams for the *Beanpot Trophy*. The first Beanpot was held in December of 1952, but all subsequent competitions have taken place over a two-weekend period in February, with every game played on the home ice of the NHL's Boston Bruins. All four schools are known for bringing raucous crowds, and the Beanpot often results in some of the highest attendance numbers of the college hockey season. BC and BU have historically dominated the Beanpot, but Wayne Turner's overtime goal in the 1980 championship game (the *Shot Heard 'Round the Beanpot*) gave Northeastern its first-ever title and is often considered the tournament's most memorable moment.

Boston College/Boston University (Ice Hockey): *Green Line Rivalry/Battle of Boston*

Boston University and Boston College are prestigious ice hockey colleges. The clash between the two is known as the *Battle of Boston* or the *Green Line Rivalry* (after the trolley line linking the two colleges). The contest is played out over three games, each drawing more than 60,000 spectators. The University Terriers in white and scarlet challenge the College Eagles in gold and maroon in meetings dubbed as one of the greatest rivalries in all of sports by *Sports Illustrated*.

Boston College/Clemson University (Football): *Battle for the Leather Helmet*

Many figured that Boston College was an odd fit for the ACC when they joined the conference for the 2005 season. Clemson, which had played BC fourteen times since the 1940 Cotton Bowl, was one of the few teams that had a significant history against the Eagles and were one of the few conference members to welcome the newbies with open arms. This led to the creation of the *O'Rourke-McFadden Trophy* in 2008, which features two leather helmet replicas of star players from the inaugural Cotton Bowl match-up. Five of the first six meetings between the two schools as conference foes were decided by a touchdown or less, making this rivalry one of the most memorable of the twelve-team era of the ACC.

Boston College/Holy Cross University (Football): *Holy War*

In the first half of the twentieth century, this was considered the most intense rivalry in the entire New England area. Separated by a mere thirty-six miles, Boston College and Holy Cross first met on the football field in 1896 and faced each other on a yearly basis for much of the next century. Boston College holds a 48–31–3 all-time advantage, but Holy Cross' 55–12 upset in the 1942 meeting is often regarded as the most famous meeting. The loss not only resulted in the ruining of BC's perfect season, but also the cancellation of their victory celebration in the Coconut Grove nightclub, meaning that the Eagles were not there when the club caught fire later that evening. The series died out when Holy Cross declined as a football powerhouse, eventually being cancelled altogether when the Crusaders moved to the 1-AA Colonial League in 1986.

Boston College/UMass (Basketball): *Commonwealth Classic/ Commonwealth Cup/Governor's Cup*

While they first met in 1905 and are separated by less than a hundred miles, Boston College and UMass had rarely faced each other on the hardwood for much of their respective histories. To remedy that, the *Commonwealth Classic* was instituted in 1995 and became one of college basketball's finest nonconference hoops rivalries for nearly two decades. UMass dominated much of the 1990s, with John Calipari running the show and Marcus Camby leading some of the Minutemen's finest teams. BC's rise to power in the 2000s included dominance in the Commonwealth Classic, and the rivalry ceased to be an annual match-up following the 2012 match-up.

Boston College/University of Notre Dame (Football):
Ireland Trophy/Holy War/Frank Leahy Bowl

As the only Catholic universities playing major college football, the *Holy War* holds a special significance on the schedule of each school. Boston College and Notre Dame had met three times prior to the series becoming a yearly event, with the eighth-ranked Fighting Irish handing the ninth-ranked Eagles a humiliating 54–7 defeat. BC would get its revenge in a big way the following year, stunning top-ranked Notre Dame 41–39 on David Gordon's forty-one-yard field goal as time expired. "God is Good . . . and so was Gordon's Kick" became a popular saying on the Boston College campus for much of the next year. There were fears that the rivalry would be cancelled when Boston College left the Big East for the ACC, but efforts were made on both sides to preserve the annual late season meeting. The winner of this game receives the *Ireland Trophy*.

Bowling Green State University/Kent State University:
Anniversary Game

These cross-state MAC rivals have been battling for supremacy in Ohio since 1921, with Bowling Green often finding itself on the winning sideline. The *Anniversary Award* was instituted in 1985, commemorating the seventy-fifth anniversary of the founding of each school.

Bowling Green State University/University of Toledo (Football):
Peace Pipe/Battle of I-75

A *peace pipe* goes to winner of this football game, which started with a basketball rivalry in 1947–1948. The Peace Pipe, which was awarded to the winner from 1948–1969 and from 1980 until recently, has been replaced by a trophy that says *Battle of I-75*, referring to the interstate highway that connects the two cities, which are roughly twenty-five miles apart.

Bridgewater State University/Mass Maritime (Football):
Cranberry Bowl

These Southeastern Massachusetts Division III rivals have been facing each other since 1978, with the winner of the rivalry receiving the *Cranberry Scoop*.

Brown University/University of Rhode Island (Football):
Governor's Cup

The oldest college football rivalry in the nation's smallest state, FCS schools Brown and Rhode Island have been doing battle since 1909.

Butler University/University of Indianapolis (Football):
Top Dog Trophy

While their first meeting occurred in 1930, the match-up of these city rivals did not become a yearly event until 1969—the year before Indianapolis joined the Indiana Collegiate Conference. The *Top Dog Trophy* was awarded every year from 1971 to 1992, and the rivalry ended for good when Butler moved up to Division I-AA in 1993. Butler won nineteen of the twenty-eight meetings between the two schools.

Butler University/Valparaiso University (Football):
The Hoosier Helmet

The *Hoosier Helmet* was established as the trophy helmet for the rivalry football game played between Butler and Valparaiso University. The Hoosier Helmet was created prior to the 2006 season to commemorate the football rivalry that has existed since 1921. These two Indiana private schools have been conference foes almost continuously since 1925.

BYU/University of Utah (Multisport): *Desert Dual Trophy*

The tone for this rivalry was set in the very first sporting event between these two schools, as the inaugural baseball game in 1895 ended with a bench-clearing brawl. Despite this unceremonious beginning (or perhaps because of it), BYU and Utah decided that more match-ups in a variety of sports would be a good idea. This resulted in the Cougars and Utes developing longstanding rivalries not only in baseball, but in virtually every other sport played by both schools. In 2008, the multisport rivalry became a formalized competition called the *Desert First Duel*, named for a credit union based in Salt Lake City. Points are awarded to the victors of each match-up between the two schools in twelve different sports: winners in football and men's basketball get ten points apiece, while baseball, women's basketball, gymnastics, softball, volleyball, soccer, men's and women's swimming, and men's and women's tennis each get three points. This challenge was so important that both schools elected to continue scheduling each other in all sports even after Utah went to the Pac-12 and BYU to the WCC.

BYU/University of Utah (Football): *Holy War*

There is some dispute as to when this *holy war* actually began. Utah begins the rivalry in the year 1896, with the schools splitting six meetings played in the 1890s. BYU, on the other hand, does not recognize these six match-ups because they were known as Brigham Young Academy at the time and had also dropped football after the 1899 season. They place the beginning of the rivalry in 1922, when the football team resumed play as part of Brigham Young University. At the time, Utah considered Colorado to be their chief football rival, and BYU did not help matters by winning only eight of their first fifty-three meetings with the Utes. But all that changed in 1972, when LaVell Edwards took over at BYU and turned the Cougars' football fortunes around. Edwards would win 257 games in 29 seasons as head coach, racking up a 22–7 record against Utah during his career. Since Edwards' retirement, the Holy War has become known for last second finishes. Ten of the first twelve games of the new millennium were decided by a touchdown or less, and the ending to the 2012 game was so crazy that Utah fans rushed the field three times before the game was over. Utah's recent admittance to the Pac-12 and BYU's subsequent push for independence in football has put the future of this rivalry in doubt, but it is difficult to imagine that the fan bases on either side of the field would want to see this rivalry end. This game is also a part of both the *Desert First Duel* and the *Beehive Boot* contests.

BYU/Utah State University (Football): *Wagon Wheel*

Believe it or not, Utah State was not always the little brother program in this rivalry. In fact, the Aggies managed to win thirty of their first fifty match-ups with the Cougars. But like all things BYU, the Cougars' fortunes in this rivalry turned around when LaVell Edwards took over the program, as the legendary coach went 21–6 in this series during his legendary tenure in Provo. BYU has essentially been in control of the rivalry since, and this is no longer a match-up that is guaranteed to be played every year. The *Wagon Wheel*, which is a tribute to the pioneers who settled Utah in the mid-1800s, was adopted as a trophy in 1948. It has a long history of being stolen by fans of the losing school, sometimes disappearing for years at a time.

BYU/University of Utah/Utah State University (Football): *Beehive Boot*

They take their college football seriously in the state of Utah, with a number of programs vying for supremacy over the years. The *Beehive Boot*—a trophy made from authentic pioneer footwear—was created to help settle the issue. This has primarily been a contest between Brigham Young, Utah, and Utah State, as those are the three FBS programs that reside within the state. An FCS school, Weber State, was originally eligible to win the award when it was created in 1971, but the Wildcats are no longer factored into the running. Traditionally, the Beehive Boot has been awarded to whichever of the three schools had the best record against their in-state rivals; in case of a tie, the winner is decided by in-state media outlets. There is some concern over whether this contest will continue in the future, as Utah has moved into the Pac-12 Conference and is hesitant to schedule both BYU and Utah State as nonconference opponents.

BYU/University of Utah/Utah State University (Basketball): *Oquirrh Bucket*

The basketball equivalent of the Beehive Boot, the *Old Oquirrh Bucket* was created in 1974 to award the best college basketball team in the state of Utah based on head-to-head match-ups. This award is open to schools beyond the Big Three, with Weber State (a four-time champion), Utah Valley, and Southern Utah also included in the competition. The trophy itself, which is named for the Oquirrh Mountains west of Salt Lake City, was retired following the 2010 season because of a number of in-state schools moving to new conferences.

Cal/Stanford University (Football): *The Big Game/Stanford Ax*

Perhaps the most famous rivalry in the West, California and Stanford first met on the gridiron in 1892 and have played on a yearly basis since the end of World War I. Both schools built 75,000+ capacity stadiums specifically for this rivalry, although most years, the *Big Game* was often the only time that either school ever came close to a sellout. It is also one of the first rivalries to adopt a traveling trophy. The *Stanford Axe*, which was originally associated with the Stanford baseball team, was stolen by Cal students in 1899 and held on the Berkeley campus as a prize of conquest for thirty-one years. But in 1930, a daring group of Stanford students (the

Immortal 21) stole it back, and the Axe was adopted as the trophy for the Big Game three years later. Traditionally, the Stanford Axe is brought to the fifty-yard line by the winning team from the previous year, and students from both schools engage in the *Stare Down* until the end of the game. But no discussion of the Big Game is complete without mentioning *The Play*. California concluded the 1982 match-up with a five-lateral kick return for a touchdown that ended with the Golden Bears' Kevin Moen dodging Stanford band members and running over trombone player Gary Tyrrell in the end zone. Many consider The Play to be the most famous in college football history, and the loss ensured that quarterback John Elway would never play in a bowl game while wearing a Stanford uniform. Not that Stanford recognizes the outcome. To this day, Cardinal students believe that The Play was illegally carried out, and the listed score of the 1982 game on the Stanford Axe is modified by whichever school is in possession of the trophy.

Cal/Stanford University (Volleyball): *The Big Spike*

The rivalry between California and Stanford is hardly limited to football, as both schools have an impressive athletic tradition in a variety of sports. One of the biggest is the *Big Spike*, which has been the name of the annual home-and-home volleyball series between the two schools since the sport was added to the docket in 1976. Stanford, which is often regarded as the preeminent volleyball program in college athletics, has a sizable advantage in the all-time series, but Cal has also had seasons as a powerhouse and is an annual contender for the NCAA Tournament. Perhaps the biggest game in this rivalry was their first match-up in 2011, as Cal and Stanford sat in the top two spots of the national rankings at the time.

Cal/Stanford University (Water Polo): *The Big Splash*

In 1969, water polo officially became an NCAA sport. This was welcome news for Cal and Stanford, whose fierce rivalry in the sport actually dates back to the 1920s. Not surprisingly, the Golden Bears and Cardinal have become two of the nation's preeminent water polo teams. The *Big Splash* is the name of the match-up between the two powers that is held the same weekend as the Big Game. The winner of the Big Splash receives the *Steve Heaston Trophy*, which was established in 1999, and named for the former Cal coach who passed away that year.

Cal/Stanford University (Crew): *Formerly The Big Row, now The Jill Row*

Renamed in 2011 in honor of Jill Costello (Cal coxswain) who lost a yearlong struggle with lung cancer. In her final months, she helped lead Cal to second place at the nationals, and since then her friends and family founded *Jill's Legacy*, which has raised a substantial amount for lung cancer research. (Jill was a nonsmoker.)

Cal/Stanford University (Ice Hockey): *The Big Freeze*

The Cal–Stanford rivalry even extends to club sports, as the *Big Freeze* is the name given to the annual home-and-home match-ups between the hockey teams of both schools. These games get plenty of attention from both schools, as attendance for the Big Freeze ranks behind only football and men's and women's basketball among the rivalry games between the two schools.

University of California, Davis/Sacramento State (Football): *Causeway Classic*

Separated by a mere 20 miles, UC-Davis and Sacramento State have been squaring off on the gridiron since 1954 and have played yearly even when the Aggies and Hornets were in different leagues and classifications. The game is named after the Yolo Causeway, which is the bridge on I-80 that connects the two cities. Cement from the Causeway is used in the trophy that is given to the winner of the match-up.

Cal Poly/UC Davis (Football): *Golden Horseshoe*

Cal Poly and UC Davis first played in 1939 and began meeting on a yearly basis in the 1970s. In 2004, the two schools decided to spice up the rivalry with a brand-new trophy. Each school created a trophy for the game, and the *Golden Horseshoe* was adopted as a permanent trophy when UC Davis prevailed in the 2004 match-up. This has never pleased Cal Poly students, who modify the trophy whenever it is in their possession by adding blue and green gems. UC-Davis removes those gems when they hold the trophy, believing that it should be preserved in its original condition.

Cal Poly/Fresno State (Football): *Victory Bell*

These two schools first met in 1922 and played each other on an almost yearly basis following the end of World War II. The *Victory Bell* was added to spice up the rivalry around 1956, though constant thefts by overzealous fans resulted in the trophy being retired in 1975. Ten years later, the rivalry itself came to an end as Fresno State—which had a commanding lead in the series—made the jump to Division 1-A status.

Cal Poly/University of California, Santa Barbara (Various Sports): *Blue–Green Rivalry*

The *Blue–Green Rivalry* is based on UCSB Gauchos and Cal Poly Mustangs competing in sixteen sports. Each winner receives one point per win (regular season) with two points being awarded to the series winner in baseball and softball. The overall winner is announced each spring. The creative angle of using games to promote campuses' sustainability and recycling efforts is the first of its kind in college athletes. Both Cal Poly and UCSB plan expanding marketing of the innovative rivalry series to include sponsor messages, recycling challenges, and additional promotional platforms in upcoming years.

UCLA/USC (Football): *Victory Bell*

The winner of the annual UCLA–USC football game, perhaps America's greatest cross-town rivalry, is given year-long possession of the *Victory Bell*. The 295-pound bell originally clanged from atop a Southern Pacific freight locomotive. It was given to UCLA in 1939 as a gift from the UCLA Alumni Association. On Nov. 12, 1942, the bell was wheeled in front of the *Tommy Trojan* statue and the student body presidents of both schools signed an agreement stating that thereafter the annual winner of the Bruin–Trojan gridiron clash would keep the bell for the following year. In the case of a tie, the bell would be retained by the school that won the previous year's game. The USC Alumni Association later repaid the UCLA Alumni Association for half the cost of the bell. Although the Victory Bell is one of college football's most famous trophies, it is probably the least seen. For all but two days of the year, the bell sits in a warehouse or a vault. The universities only display the bell during the first three quarters of the UCLA–USC game and on the Monday following the game, when it is delivered to the winning school's campus. Then the Victory Bell, which gained its reputation from being hidden, goes back into hiding.

UCLA/USC (All Sports): *Crosstown Gauntlet*

To highlight the yearlong all-sports competition between cross-town rivals UCLA and USC, the *Crosstown Gauntlet Trophy* is awarded annually to the school with the most successful athletic year against the other. Points are awarded to the winner of each Bruin-Trojan head-to-head contest and the Gauntlet is awarded to the school with the most points at year's end.

California University of Pennsylvania/Indiana University of Pennsylvania (Football): *Coal Bowl*

This is more than just a match-up of Pennsylvania colleges that share names with other states: it is also a Division II rivalry that dates back to 1918. The rivalry was christened the *Coal Bowl* in 2009, and the winner receives the *Coal Miners Pail Trophy* in tribute of the Pennsylvania Coal Association.

Calvin College/Hope College (Basketball): *One of the Best D-III Basketball Rivalries*

This rivalry began in either 1917, or 1920, depending on which school you believe. Through the first 185 games, a total of only 88 points separated the two teams. In 2005, the staff at ESPN listed this rivalry as the fourth-best in college basketball and the greatest of all match-ups in Division III.

Canisius College/Niagara University (All Sports): *Battle of the Bridge/Canal Cup*

The *Battle of the Bridge*, the all-sports competition between cross-town rivals Niagara University and Canisius College, enters its eighth season in 2013–2014. During the 2006–2007 athletics season, Niagara and Canisius developed an all-sports competition in an effort to enhance the historic rivalry between the Purple Eagles and the Golden Griffins. The bridge referenced in the Battle of the Bridge is the Grand Island Bridge, which both teams cross when traveling to the other's campus. Points are awarded to the winner of regular season contests, except for cross-country, golf and swimming and diving, which are determined by Metro Atlantic Athletic Conference Championship standings. The *Canal Cup* is awarded to the victor each year. Records indicate the two schools first met on the basketball court in 1904. Currently, Niagara and Canisius compete in baseball, men and women's basketball, men and women's cross-country, golf, men's ice hockey, women's lacrosse, men and women's soccer, men and women's swimming and diving, softball, and volleyball.

Carleton College/Macalester College (Football): *Book of Knowledge*

Informally dubbed the Brain Bowl, this Division III rivalry is between two of the top academic institutions in the state of Minnesota. The *Book of Knowledge* was adopted as a trophy in 1998, and it has rarely left the Carleton campus since.

Carleton College/St. Olaf College (Football): *The Goat/Cereal Bowl Trophies*

One of the oldest rivalries in Division III, cross-town rivals Carleton and St. Olaf kicked off their rivalry with three games during the 1918 season and have met on an annual basis almost every season since. Recently dubbed the *Cereal Bowl* in honor of the local Malt-O-Meal production facility, the winner of this game receives both a silver *Cereal Bowl Trophy* and the traditional *Goat Trophy* that was created by a St. Olaf carpenter in 1931. The 1977 match-up is without question the most famous of the rivalry, as the *Liter Bowl* is the only NCAA-sanctioned football game ever to be played on a field that used meters instead of yards.

Carnegie Mellon University/Case Western Reserve University (Football): *Academic Bowl*

These Division III scholastic powerhouses met on the football field for the first time in 1970, and their rivalry was dubbed the *Academic Bowl* in 1986. This game also doubles as a border battle, featuring the best of Pittsburgh taking on the best of Cleveland.

Case Western Reserve University/The College of Wooster (Football): *Baird Brothers Trophy*

Fishing and football don't ordinarily go together, but don't tell that to Case Western Reserve University and the College of Wooster. When the Spartans and the Scots meet on the gridiron, the winner claims one of the most unique trophy traditions in college sports, the *Baird Brothers Trophy*.

This trophy, noted in a 1995 issue of *Sports Illustrated* magazine as one of the most unique trophies in college football, consists of a golden fishing stringer with carved brass fish representing each meeting. The trophy's beginnings date back to 1984 when Bob Baird, an economics professor at CWRU, and his brother Bill Baird, an economics professor at Wooster, came up with the idea. The winner of the game gets to keep the stringer for the year and add a new fish for that year's contest. Each added fish is representative of how the game was played, with the score and winner engraved on the side. The original fish is a four-inch blue gill symbolizing the narrow last second Case victory, 21–14. A big northern pike denotes the Spartans 37–0 victory over the Scots in 1985. Other fish included on the trophy are a flounder, a carp, a walleye, a catfish, a rainbow trout, a sturgeon, a sucker, a crappie, a muskie, a sheepshead, a gar, a largemouth bass, and a smallmouth bass. The Baird brothers originated the trophy in 1984 when Wooster and Case first met as members of the North Coast Athletic Conference. The brothers, economic professors at the rival schools, were taught by their father to fish at an early age and thought the fish theme would be a fitting reward to the victors. Bob Baird passed away a few years ago, but his brother Bill still carries on the tradition of presenting the trophy to the winning team at the conclusion of the game. The two schools have met about twenty-five times, with Wooster currently holding a slight advantage.

The Baird Brothers Trophy is given to the winner of the Case Western–College of Wooster football game. *Case Western University*

Catholic University/Georgetown University (Football): *Steven Dean Memorial Trophy*

This trophy series was dedicated in 1976 and named for the late Steven Dean, a former GU team manager and Catholic University sports information director afflicted with cerebral palsy. The rivalry ended in 1993 when Georgetown football jumped to Division I-AA status while Catholic remained at Division III.

University of Central Arkansas/McNeese State University (Football): *Fifty-Pound Iron Pot/Red Bean and Rice Bowl*

Starting in 2008, the *Red Beans and Rice Bowl* has highlighted how important rice and red beans are to both Arkansas and Louisiana. And the tailgating extravaganza includes free red beans and rice for all! Winner of the contest carries home the *Fifty-Pound Iron Pot*.

Central Connecticut State University/Southern Connecticut State University: *Governor's Trophy*

These two teams first matched up in 1949 and met on an almost yearly basis for the next half century. The rivalry began to lose steam after Central Connecticut moved up to Division I status in all sports in 1986 and was discontinued altogether following the Huskies' 30–23 win in 1999. The winner of this game was traditionally awarded the *Governor's Trophy*, which now resides in the Central Connecticut Coaches' office. The players see it when they pick-up their mail.

University of Central Florida/ University of South Florida (Football): *War on I-4*

Seldom does one school indicate the importance of a rivalry considerably more than the other school. But UCF seems to view this game as more of a rivalry than does USF. Two of the youngest programs at the FBS level, the *War on I-4* (named for the road connecting Orlando and Tampa) began as a four-game series in 2005 but wasn't played after four consecutive South Florida victories convinced the Bulls athletic department to pursue more competitive nonconference games. This rivalry is set to resume in the future when Central Florida joins the American Athletic Conference and makes this match-up a conference game.

Central Michigan University/Western Michigan University (Football): *Cascade Cup*

This highly competitive Michigan rivalry dates back to 1907 and has been played almost continuously since 1925, kicking into high gear when Central Michigan joined the MAC in 1971. The winner of the contest receives the *Victory Cannon*, which was created in 2008. Western Michigan dominated the early days of this series, winning twenty-four of the first twenty-seven meetings and giving the Broncos an edge that they enjoy to this day.

Central Michigan/Eastern Michigan/Western Michigan Universities (Football): *Michigan MAC Trophy*

While the directional Michigan schools have all been together in the Mid-American Conference since 1971, it was not until quite recently that the three schools decided to have a formal competition for state MAC supremacy. Central, Eastern, and Western Michigan began competing for the *Michigan MAC Trophy* in 2005, and each of the three schools has taken its turn in hoisting the trophy since its inception. The competition was also adopted for men's basketball in 2006.

Central State University/Kentucky State University (Football): *Kentucky Heritage Classic*

A match-up of HBCUs from neighboring states, Central State (Ohio) and Kentucky State first met on the gridiron in 1947 and have forged a rivalry that managed to withstand the absence of a CSU football program from 1996–2004. The Division II rivalry has since joined the list of annual *HBCU Classics* and is often played in late November.

Cheyney University/Lincoln University (Football): *Battle of the Firsts*

Both of these Pennsylvania Division II schools lay claim to being the very first historically black university in the United States. In 2009, a mere three years after Lincoln revived its football program, these schools agreed that the feud was best played out on the gridiron in the annual *Battle of the Firsts*.

University of Chicago/Washington University in St. Louis (Football): *Founders' Trophy*

These academic stalwarts met for the first time in 1933, when Chicago was still a member of the Big Ten Conference. However, the modern rivalry began in 1983, when the Maroons and Bears played the first game in the history of the brand-new University Athletic Association. That match-up was commemorated in 1987 with the introduction of the *Founders' Cup*, which is awarded to the winner of the annual game.

Chico State University/San Francisco State University (Football): *Dan Farmer Trophy*

This Bay Area rivalry began in 1940 and ended when San Francisco State dropped football in 1995 and Chico State followed two years later. The *Dan Farmer Trophy* was named after a former Chico State alum that later became a prominent figure in the San Francisco State athletic department, as both a coach and administrator.

University of Cincinnati/University of Louisville: *Keg of Nails*

As big-city schools separated by roughly a hundred miles, Cincinnati-Louisville is a fierce rivalry no matter what conference the teams happen to be in. The two schools first met in 1929, and with the exception of a brief period in the mid-1990s, they have met every year since 1966. The *Keg of Nails trophy* is said to have been initiated by fraternity members of each school, signifying the tough-as-nails nature of the winning team. However, the trophy exchanged between the two schools is actually a replica, as the original was misplaced by Louisville during the construction of their athletic offices. With Louisville set to join the ACC, there is some concern that this rivalry may come to an end in the near future; others are not so worried, considering that the Bearcats and Cardinals have been members of the Missouri Valley Conference, the Metro Conference, Conference USA, the Big East, and independents during the course of their rivalry.

University of Cincinnati/Miami University of Ohio (Football): *Victory Bell*

The original bell hung in Miami's Harrison Hall (Old Main) near the site of the first football game in 1888 and was used to ring-in Miami victories.

The traveling trophy tradition began in the 1890s when some Cincinnati fans borrowed the bell. The bell went to the winner of the annual game for the next forty years until it mysteriously disappeared in the 1930s. The original bell reappeared in 1946 and is on display in the lobby of Miami's Murstein Alumni Center. The current trophy is a replica of the original bell and is kept in the possession of the winning team each year. One side of the bell is painted red and black and shows Cincinnati's victories, while the other side is red and white and shows Miami's victories. Miami currently leads the series. The Miami–Cincinnati series ranks fifth on the list of most played rivalries in college football and is one of the oldest rivalries west of the Allegheny Mountains.

University of Cincinnati/University of Pittsburgh (Football): River City Rivalry/Paddlewheel Trophy

The *River City Rivalry* is the name of the football game played every season between the University of Cincinnati Bearcats and the University of Pittsburgh Panthers for the right to claim the *Paddlewheel Trophy*. The history of this rivalry technically dates back to October 15, 1921, when these two football programs first played each other. The result of that first meeting between the two colleges ended with a University of Pittsburgh win by a score of 21–14 at a game played in Pittsburgh. Despite the fact that these two teams first played each other roughly 90 years ago, the River City Rivalry is relatively new by college football rivalry standards, as it only dates back to 2005. Prior to 2005, the two schools had played each other only four times. Each of those four occurrences resulted in University of Pittsburgh victories. The Paddlewheel Trophy that travels to whichever campus won the most recent head-to-head competition between these two schools was created in 2005 when the University of Cincinnati joined the Big East Conference. Cincinnati and Pittsburgh are geographically in close proximity with one another and have historical rivalries between the professional sports teams in the two cities. The idea behind the Paddlewheel Trophy was to jump-start the college football rivalry between these two cities in an attempt to drum-up interest and ignite a friendly rivalry that everyone could enjoy. The name Paddlewheel Trophy refers to the paddle wheel style boats that were mainstays on American rivers in 1800s and early 1900s. The Ohio River separates these two cities and aids the geographic landmark theme of the River City Rivalry and Paddlewheel Trophy. The dimensions of the traveling trophy are quite large at forty-six inches in height, and a weight of ninety-five pounds. The intricate design of the trophy is said to have taken more than 175 man hours to complete between both labor and design.

University of Cincinnati/Xavier University (Basketball): *Crosstown Classic (formerly Shootout)*

This is one of college basketball's best rivalries. The schools are separated by just three miles: one is a small, private, Jesuit University, while the other is a large public university. The rivalry began in 1928, and has been played each year since 1945–1946. During game week, *Skyline Chili*, the world-famous restaurant chain, has been known to serve different types of chili to each school's fans.

The Citadel/Virginia Military Institute (Football): *Silver Shako*

A match-up of two military colleges, the Military Classic of the South was first played in 1920 and has been played almost annually since the end of World War II. In 1976, the Silver Shako was introduced as a traveling trophy. This series ranks as one of the oldest college football rivalries at the FCS level.

Clemson University/North Carolina State University (Football): *Textile Bowl*

One of the ACC's classic rivalries, Clemson–NC State was first held in 1899 and has been played without interruption since 1971. This rivalry was important enough to both schools that the ACC elected to preserve it as an annual series when the conference expanded to twelve teams. The name *Textile Bowl* was adopted in 1981 and pays tribute to the role that textiles played, both in the development of the Carolinas, and in the founding of each school. Clemson and NC State are among the largest university-level textile schools in the world.

Clemson University/University of South Carolina (Football): *Palmetto Bowl*

One of the great state rivalries in college football, the *Palmetto Bowl* (also called the *Battle for the Palmetto State*) began in 1896 and has been played every year since 1909. Clemson-South Carolina is one of the very few rivalries that was played throughout World Wars I and II and is one of the longest uninterrupted rivalries in the South. The bitterness between the two schools predates either football team and stems from the controversial nature in which Clemson received its charter (and state support) at the Gamecocks' expense. It did not help that Clemson had so much success in the rivalry, despite the fact that South Carolina hosted every single meeting until 1959 on the Thursday of the South Carolina State Fair. The game was mandated a yearly event by state law in 1952, and it was transformed from a *Big Thursday* in Columbia event into a home-and-home Saturday rivalry in 1960. It has since become a part of the annual ACC–SEC showdown during the final week of the regular season. The two schools also compete away from the field, holding an annual blood drive the week before the football game.

Coast Guard Academy/Merchant Marine Academy (Football): *Secretaries' Cup*

The *Secretaries' Cup* has taken place since 1949.

Coe College/Cornell College (Nineteen-Sport Competition): *Bremner Cup*

Beginning in the fall of 2012, the *Bremner Cup* is a new fixture in the Coe–Cornell athletics rivalry. The long-time rivals compete for an all-sport traveling trophy named in honor of Barron Bremner, a legendary coach and administrator with forty-two collective years of service at the two institutions. "The advent of the Bremner Cup is a tremendous opportunity to recognize in perpetuity a man who has meant so much to so many people on both campuses," Cornell director of athletics John Cochrane said. "Barron is an adored figure, having touched the lives of two generations of students in immeasurable ways, as individuals and as athletes." The Rams and Kohawks have developed storied rivalries in multiple sports. The teams have met 121 times on the gridiron, holding claim to one of the oldest college football rivalries west of the Mississippi River. The men's basketball series dates back to the 1909–1910 season. The two nationally ranked wrestling programs have squared off in dual meets every season since 1966. Bremner had a positive effect on the lives of thousands of student athletes at both schools, where he is a member of their respective athletic halls of fame. The Iowa Falls native and University of Iowa graduate began his career at Cornell in 1959 as head wrestling coach and assistant football and tennis coach. Over 12 years, he coached six sports, taught, was dean of men, director of housing, and director of placement. In 1971, Bremner left for Coe to become athletic director, chair of the physical education department, and head wrestling coach. He went back to Cornell in 1978 as the college's athletic director, wrestling coach and assistant to the president. Four years later he gave up his athletic duties, and by 1985 was named vice president for institutional advancement and director of the $62 million Program for Cornell, which included the Small Multi-Sport Center. Bremner made his final career move in 1993, returning to Coe as athletic director and assistant to the president. He retired in 2001.

University of Colorado/Colorado State University (Football):
Rocky Mountain Showdown

First played in 1893, the *Rocky Mountain Showdown* is one of the few rivalries that means a whole lot more to one of the participants than to the other. Colorado has always seen Colorado State as more of a little brother rather than a rival. The two teams have been in separate conferences since 1948, and the Buffaloes dominated the early years of this rivalry to such a degree that the game was not played from 1959 to 1982. It was not until 1983 that the series was revived, with Colorado continuing to dominate the series while also hosting a disproportionate number of match-ups. The game became an annual event in 1995 and became a neutral-site match-up in Denver three years later, with Colorado still hosting an occasional game for good measure. As a result, Colorado has played only three games at Colorado State since the series was reborn and has not set foot in Fort Collins since 1996. The winner of this game is awarded the Centennial Cup, which is a tribute to the state's nickname.

University of Colorado/University of Utah (Football):
Rumble in the Rockies

For the first half of the twentieth century, many considered the annual match-up between Colorado and Utah to be the most intense rivalry in the Rockies. The two teams first squared off in 1903 and were league rivals from 1910–1947, winning a combined twenty-seven conference championships during that time. Future Supreme Court Justice Bryan "Whizzer" White cemented his legacy as a Colorado legend by scoring five touchdowns in the 1936 match-up between the two schools. Colorado left for the Big Seven in 1948, but the rivalry was so big that it continued as a non-league match-up for another fourteen years. The rivalry was discontinued following back-to-back Utah upsets in 1961–1962, with the 1961 game likely costing the Buffaloes a share of the national championship. At the time of cancellation, Colorado and Utah were each other's second most frequent opponent; however, the rivalry remained dormant for the next four decades until it was reborn when both schools joined the Pac-12 in 2011. Utah has replaced Nebraska as Colorado's traditional Black Friday opponent, and there is a very good chance that the *Rumble in the Rockies* will return to its former glory.

Colorado State University/University of Wyoming (Football): *Border War/Bronze Boot*

The Border War featuring CSU and Wyoming—the longest rivalry in each school's history—dates back to 1893. Since 1968, the schools have battled for possession of the *Bronze Boot* traveling trophy. The bronzed battle boot was worn in Vietnam by CSU ROTC instructor Dan Romero. The annual Wyoming–Colorado State football game has evolved into one of the most bitterly contested rivalries in college football. The teams have waged the Border War ninety-seven times since the schools began playing in 1899. In fact, this is one of the oldest interstate rivalries west of the Mississippi River. The series is the oldest rivalry for both schools and the Border War has been played in three different centuries. In 1968, the ROTC detachments of the respective schools initiated the Bronze Boot, a traveling trophy awarded to the winner of the contest each year. Each year leading up to the Colorado State–Wyoming game, the game ball is carried sixty-five miles on foot in a shuttle relay by the ROTC detachment of the visiting team to the Colorado–Wyoming state border, where the home team's ROTC detachment receives it and runs the game ball to the stadium hosting the game. The Boot has rested in the UW athletics department in twenty-two of the forty-three years since its inception. The Bronze Boot has become one of the most famous traveling trophies in college football.

Columbia University/Fordham University (Football): *Liberty Cup*

This rivalry, dating back to 1890, is for New York City bragging rights. Although the two schools have played each other for over a hundred years, the *Liberty Cup* only has been in existence since 2002. The Cup was created in tribute to those who lost their lives in the 9/11 attacks, including seventy-eight total members from the schools' alumni bases. Unlike other trophies, which rest in trophy cases, when Fordham wins the Cup, it sits in the team's locker room throughout the year, and then is brought-out to practice (displayed on the sideline) throughout the week leading up to the game.

UConn/University of Rhode Island (Football): *Ramnapping Trophy*

As state flagship universities separated by a mere sixty miles, it was only natural that Connecticut and Rhode Island would start a rivalry on the gridiron. These schools first met in 1897, and the rivalry gained an award after the creation of the *Ramnapping Trophy* in 1935. The name of the trophy is in reference to UConn's kidnapping of Rhode Island's Ram mascot in 1934, which was referred to as "ramnapping" by both sides. UConn would win forty of the sixty-two games that were played for the Ramnapping Trophy, with the series ending in 1999 following the Huskies' move into the Big East in all sports.

Cornell University/University of Pennsylvania (Football): *Trustee Cup*

Every Ivy League match-up qualifies as a longtime rivalry, but Cornell-Penn stands out from even that crowd. Originating in 1893, the rivalry between these two schools has been continuously played since 1919 and is the fifth oldest in all of college football. Discussions from both sides resulted in the 1994 creation of the *Trustee Cup*, named in honor of the high degree of support that both schools bring to the rivalry.

Dartmouth College/Princeton University (Football): *Governors' Trophy/Sawhorse Dollar*

One of the Ivy League's most storied gridiron rivalries, Dartmouth and Princeton first played each other in 1897 and have missed playing only one time since 1933. Princeton hosted almost all of the games during the first century of the rivalry, as the Tigers did not make their first trip to Hanover until 1946 and played only five times away from Princeton, until the rivalry became a true home-and-home series in 1980. The winner of this game receives both the *Governor's Trophy* and the *Sawhorse Dollar*, which is an authentic note featuring the images of both George Washington and Christopher Columbus.

Dartmouth College/University of New Hampshire (Football):
Granite Bowl

These state rivals first met in 1901, and the series has been played inter-mittently since. Dartmouth dominated play early on, winning seventeen of the first eighteen games. New Hampshire, however, has since evened out the series. The Big Green's membership in the Ivy League make it difficult to keep regular nonconference rivals, but these two teams expect to make the effort to face each other as often as possible in the coming years. The winner of this game receives the *Granite Bowl Trophy*, which is a tribute to the state's nickname.

Dartmouth College/University of New Hampshire (Ice Hockey):
Riverstone Cup

Ice Hockey is a very big deal in New Hampshire, making this match-up of two of the state's largest college hockey programs, one of the biggest events on the local sports calendar. Games between the two schools are moved to the Verizon Wireless Arena in Manchester and rank among the best-attended games in all of college hockey. The winner of the game re-ceives the *Riverstone Cup*.

University of Dayton/Xavier University (Football):
Governor's Cup

University of Dayton football team captain Jake Burkhardt lifted the *Governor's Cup* above his head as he ran off Baujan Field in victory having defeated archrival Xavier University 31–13. That was Nov. 4, 1972. Thirty years later, in 2002, the trophy Burkhardt carried off the field was sitting in a dumpster with other UD athletic memorabilia as renovations occurred inside UD Arena, according to Tony Caruso. Caruso has been the head equipment manager for the athletics department since the late 1980s. Ca-ruso said he took the corroded keepsake inside and sat the Governor's Cup on top of a tall, wooden cabinet on the wall outside his office in the football locker room inside UD Arena where it remains today. After Burkhardt car-ried off the trophy in the 1972 UD victory, Dayton and Xavier played again in Cincinnati on Nov. 3, 1973. The game was a 28–28 tie so the trophy remained with Dayton. Xavier dropped its college football program in the spring of 1974.

University of Delaware/Delaware State University (Football): *First State Cup*

One of college football's newest state rivalries is located in the country's very first state. Delaware and Delaware State met for the first time in 2007 in the I-AA playoffs, and as a result, an annual rivalry has been created between the state's two largest universities.

University of Delaware/Villanova University (Football): *Battle of the Blue*

Although they first met in 1895, Delaware and Villanova did not start meeting regularly on the gridiron until 1962. The rivalry nearly ended when Villanova dropped football in 1981, but quickly reemerged when the Wildcats revived their program eight years later. It has been played annually since, and has become one of the marquee regular season match-ups at the FCS level, with both schools having emerged as perennial contenders for the national championship. The game became known as the *Battle of the Blue* in 2007, and the winner receives a trophy that features each team's logo and preferred shade of blue.

Delaware Valley College/Widener University (Football): *Keystone Cup*

These Division III schools met for the first time in 1977 and have met almost every year since.

Delta State University/Mississippi College (Football): *Heritage Bell*

This Magnolia State gridiron rivalry dates back to 1936 and was played intermittently until 1979, when the *Heritage Bell* became a permanent fixture. The two schools discontinued the rivalry in 1993 after Mississippi College was found to have committed NCAA violations, and decided to move from Division II to Division III four years later.

DePauw University/Wabash College (Football): *Monon Bell*

This is one of the oldest uninterrupted rivalries west of the Alleghenies (since 1910), with the winner receiving the *Monon Bell* (since 1932). On one Saturday each November, DePauw University and Wabash College meet on the gridiron in one of college football's oldest and most colorful rivalries. The two west central Indiana schools have faced each other about 120 times with Wabash holding a slight lead. The teams not only play for pride but also for possession of the 300-pound Monon (pronounced MOE-non) Bell, the trophy that goes to the winning team. The two schools, on the Monon Railroad Line (now L & N), have met each of the last 102 years dating back to 1911. The actual bell entered the famed series in 1932. The 300-pound bell was a gift of the Monon Railroad, taken from one of the railroad's locomotives. The bell has been stolen at least eight times from its temporary owners, but the most famous thefts may have occurred in the mid-1960s. In 1965, a Wabash student appeared on the DePauw campus posing as a Mexican dignitary and interested in developing an exchange program with DePauw. While meeting with the university president he asked to see the bell. After learning of its whereabouts, the student returned with friends later and stole it. DePauw got the bell back in time for the game which the Tigers won 9–7. DePauw students, hoping to keep the bell safely under wraps, stole it from their own school the week after the game and secretly buried it for 11 months in the north end zone of Blackstock Stadium. Only a handful of DePauw students knew of its location. But an unexpected problem arose prior to the big game. The ground froze that week in Greencastle, and the students were barely able to recover it in time for the Wabash team to claim it as the game ended in near darkness. The Monon Bell game is more than just a game. The week preceding the annual contest has included shared activities between the two schools, such as concerts, debates, an intramural all-star football game, an alumni football game the morning of the varsity contest and other events. In 1985, Jim Ibbotson, a member of the Nitty Gritty Dirt Band and a 1969 graduate of DePauw, arranged and recorded "The Ballad of the Monon Bell" which was written by 1968 DePauw graduate and football player Darel Lindquist. Nancy Ford Charles (class of 1957) wrote the original music for the ballad. A video was also produced with the ballad. The media have long understood the special nature of this famous small college battle. In addition to *Sports Illustrated*'s extensive coverage in 1973, CBS-TV's Charles Kuralt did a feature on the game during his *Sunday Morning* show in 1979, ABC-TV aired it as a regional telecast in 1977 and *The Christian Science Monitor* praised it in a 1981 feature. The November 13, 1987, edition of *USA Today* highlighted the rivalry in a feature story in its sports section and in 1988 the CBS Radio Network aired a feature on the rivalry throughout the nation. The 1998 contest was covered as a feature in the *Wall Street Journal* and the 1999 contest was featured on Fox Sports Net's weekly show, *The*

Slant. The centennial game also was featured in the November 22, 1993, issue of *Sports Illustrated.* The game is regularly telecast live to combined alumni meetings of the two schools in cities across the country and on networks including ABC-TV in 1977, ESPN2 in 1994 and HDNet in 2003 and 2006 through 2011. The 2004 and 2005 games were telecast nationally on DirecTV.

Dickinson College/Franklin & Marshall College (Football): *Conestoga Wagon*

One of the ancient rivalries at the Division III level, these two schools have faced each other more than 100 times since their inaugural meeting in 1899. The *Conestoga Wagon*, which is a model of the wagon that transported the two teams to play each other in the early days of the rivalry, was adopted as a trophy in 1963.

Dickinson College/Gettysburg College (Football): *Little Brown Bucket*

Although Dickinson has not played Gettysburg quite as often as they have Franklin & Marshall, their gridiron rivalry with the Bullets is actually eight years older. These two teams also have one of the oldest trophies in the sport, having played over the *Little Brown Bucket* since 1938. It is surprising that the Little Brown Bucket has endured despite the rivalry going through multiple dry spells, including a twenty-five-year stretch between 1953 and 1978.

Duke University/University of North Carolina (Football): *Victory Bell*

Although it is often overshadowed by their battles on the hardwood, Duke and North Carolina also have a longstanding football rivalry. Duke's program began with two games against North Carolina during the 1888–1889 season, and the two schools have played on an annual basis since 1922. This rivalry is important enough to both that it helped influence the alignment of the ACC, as the Blue Devils and Tar Heels were both placed in the Coastal Division to ensure the game was played every year. The *Victory Bell*, which became a part of the rivalry in 1948, was created by a cheerleader from each school and is modeled after an old railroad bell. It is a tradition for the winning team to spray paint their school colors on the platform of the trophy at the game's conclusion.

Duke University/University of North Carolina (Basketball): Battle of the Blue/THE Rivalry

The Duke–UNC rivalry is one of the most important rivalries in college basketball. Many season ticket holders give the $5,000 (minimum) annual contribution and buy tickets to all home games, but only attend this one game. *Sports Illustrated* has ranked Duke–North Carolina as the greatest rivalry in college sports, while ESPN has it listed as the third-greatest rivalry in *all* of sports. The rivalry was born out of a combination of proximity and dominance, as the two schools are located about ten miles apart and rose in stature as the basketball programs became national powers. This intensified when Mike Krzyzewski took over the Duke program, giving the Blue Devils a coach that was fully capable of matching wits with the likes of Dean Smith and Roy Williams at North Carolina. These two schools currently have a combined nine NCAA titles and forty-seven ACC championships, and their annual match-ups draw some of the highest television ratings of any regular season games in college basketball. And another reason why it might be called a rivalry is that, as of the 2013 season, Mike Krzyzewski has coached seventy-five games against North Carolina. He has won thirty-eight and lost thirty-seven. And, a recent Turnkey Sports Poll indicated that 84 percent of the senior-level sports industry executives interviewed rated this rivalry as the best in college basketball. And that 33 percent in this same survey "wished that they could both lose."

Duke University/North Carolina Central University (Football): Bull City Classic

While many fans frown on their favorite team scheduling FCS foes, there are some who are doing their state a favor by scheduling local brethren. This is why Duke added North Carolina Central to their schedule for the *Bull City Classic* beginning in 2009.

East Carolina University/North Carolina State University (Football): Victory Barrel

Located approximately eighty-three miles apart on Highway 264, East Carolina and North Carolina State played each other annually from 1970 until 1987. The series was cancelled after East Carolina fans, who had been warned about minor vandalism in previous years, tore down the goal posts at Carter-Finley Stadium following a 32–14 victory in the 1987 match-up. The two schools would not meet again until the 1992 Peach Bowl, and the regular season series was partially revived in 1996 at the new pro football stadium in Charlotte, rather than at the campus venues. One year later, the state legislature proposed a bill mandating that both North Carolina and NC State must play East Carolina on a regular basis, and the two schools have met every couple of seasons since.

East Texas Baptist University/Louisiana College (Football): *Border Claw Trophy*

Now a re-emerging Division III rivalry in the Southeast/Southwest, East Texas Baptist and Louisiana College were regular opponents prior to Louisiana College dropping football in 1968. But the rivalry was rekindled when the Wildcats started playing again in 2000. They have played every year since, and the *Border Claw Trophy* is considered the biggest prize for either team's regular season.

Eastern Illinois University/Illinois State University (Football): *Mid-America Classic*

The oldest rivalry in the state of Illinois, these two schools have been butting heads since 1901 and have played each other more than 100 times since. It was renamed the *Mid-America Classic* in 2011 in honor of the 100th meeting. The rivalry continued, even after the two stopped playing as conference rivals in 1996.

Eastern Kentucky University/Western Kentucky University (Football): *Battle of the Bluegrass*

As the name implies, this game was a longtime battle between two of the Bluegrass State's oldest programs. Many years, it was one of the biggest games on the Ohio Valley Conference schedule. This rivalry was one of several that Western Kentucky left behind when it made the jump to FBS football in 2008. It concluded with the Hilltoppers holding a 46–35–3 lead in the all-time series.

Eastern Washington University/University of Montana (Football): *Governors' Cup*

This rivalry dates back to 1938 but did not become an annual fixture until 1983, when EWU made the transition from Division II to I-AA. It became a league game when the Eagles joined the Big Sky Conference four years later, and by the new millennium it had become a game with playoff implications annually on the line. Montana has a sizable lead in the overall rivalry, but part of the reason is that EWU moved the game against the Grizzlies to Spokane, when it was their turn to host from 1967–2004.

Eastern Washington University/Portland State University (Football): *Dam Trophy*

These border rivals have been regulars on each team's schedule since their first meeting in 1968, with the match-ups becoming league games starting in 1996. The trophy's name is a reference to the four dams that a driver would pass on the 339-mile drive between the two campuses. It is also a part of the larger competition between the two schools for the *Dam Cup*, which incorporates soccer, volleyball, and basketball as well as football.

Edward Waters College/Shaw University (Football): *Willie E. Gary Classic*

This match-up of HBCUs from Florida and North Carolina was started in 2002, following the recent revivals of both football programs after lengthy periods of not playing. Founded by the flamboyant trial lawyer who provided financial assistance for both schools, the *Willie E. Gary Classic* was played annually at the home of the NFL's Jacksonville Jaguars, which is not far from the Edward Waters College campus. The Classic was discontinued in 2009.

Elizabethtown College/Messiah College (Soccer): *Marshmallow Bowl*

This contest rotates between Messiah College and Elizabethtown, during the first men's soccer game each year. After the home team scores its first goal, marshmallows are launched by their fans! Getting the marshmallows into the stadium requires some creativity though—marshmallows have been banned from this game, and every student is searched upon entry. However, both Messiah and E'town soccer fans never fail to use their imagination and sneak tons of marshmallows in.

Elon University/Guilford College (Football): *Battle of the Christians and Quakers*

Less than 20 miles separates these longtime rivals, who first butted heads on the gridiron in 1919. The name of the rivalry is a reference to each school's use of its religious heritage as a mascot. Elon was known as the Fighting Christians prior to changing their mascot to the Phoenix in 2000, while Guilford continues to use the Quakers nickname to this day.

Fayetteville State University/UNC Pembroke (Football): *Two Rivers Classic*

Unlike many of the other college football classics, Fayetteville State-UNC Pembroke is not a match-up of historically black colleges. While Fayetteville State is an HBCU, UNC Pembroke was originally founded as a school for Native Americans. The two schools, separated by a mere forty-seven miles, created the *Two Rivers Classic* in 2009 and have traditionally made it the first game of each team's respective season.

Ferris State University/Grand Valley State University (Football): *Anchor Bone Trophy*

These two schools have been playing since the Grand Valley State football program was born in 1971. GVSU has largely dominated this rivalry, which should be no surprise considering the Lakers developed into a juggernaut in the 1990s under the direction of future Notre Dame coach Brian Kelly. The *Anchor Bone Trophy* made its debut in 2002 but not as a prize to the winner. It was awarded that year to Ferris State to honor the memory Matt Sklom, a player who passed away the week before the game.

University of Florida/Florida State University (Football): *Sunshine Showdown*

While this series only began in 1958, the seeds of the rivalry were actually planted several decades earlier. Florida State College in Tallahassee first sponsored a football team from 1902 to 1904 and was considered the best team in the state at the time, but the state legislature passed the Buckman Act, which turned the campus into an all-women's college, and abolished the football program at the school. FSC's last coach, Jack Forsythe, moved on to become the head coach of the new program at the University of the

State of Florida in 1906. Several of Forsythe's former players followed him to Gainesville, so in a way the University of Florida owes a debt to Florida State for the creation of its football program. FSU would become a coed school again in 1947, but they would not have the opportunity to play Florida on the gridiron for more than a decade. The Gators won sixteen of the first nineteen contests, but the arrival of Bobby Bowden in Tallahassee in 1976 changed this rivalry forever and ensured that the series would be evenly matched from then on. By the 1990s, both programs had become national powerhouses and annually resided in the top five of the rankings, making their yearly end of season grudge match one of the most anticipated games of the college football schedule. But the most famous game in the series, so far, is what FSU fans call the *Choke at Doak* in 1994. Florida held a 31–3 lead heading into the fourth quarter but could not stop a frenetic Florida State rally that saw the Seminoles pull even with under two minutes remaining. FSU drove into Gator territory on the final drive but was unable to stop the clock in time, and because there was not yet overtime in college football, the game ended in a 31–31 tie.

University of Florida/University of Georgia (Football): *World's Largest Outdoor Cocktail Party/Okefenokee Oar*

Certainly one of the most famous neutral-site rivalries in college football, the *World's Largest Outdoor Cocktail Party* between Florida and Georgia is an annual SEC showdown that, aside from a two-year period from 1994–1995, has taken place in Jacksonville since 1933. Both teams have long been averse to going to the other's campus. Since the rivalry debuted in 1904 (or 1915, depending on which alum you ask), the game has been held in Athens a mere five times and in Gainesville on only two occasions. This is rather amazing, considering the notorious aversion that both teams have to playing away from home. The game itself is a huge event for the city of Jacksonville, with alumni from both schools setting up camp several days before the big game and putting on a massive tailgating scene. This led to the nickname of the World's Largest Outdoor Cocktail Party, which was attached to the rivalry in the 1950s. The *Okefenokee Oar trophy* debuted in 2009, but it's actually a bit older. The oar was created from a 1,000-year-old cypress tree that grew in the Okefenokee Swamp—the one that straddles the Florida-Georgia border. But unlike most rivalry trophies, the Okefenokee Oar is not actually presented at the game. It is awarded to the student body president back on the winner's campus.

University of Florida/University of Miami (Football): *War Canoe*

This match-up actually precedes both schools' rivalries with Florida State, as Florida and Miami first went to battle in 1938. As such, this was the biggest Sunshine State rivalry for many years. Florida discontinued the rivalry in 1987, claiming that the SEC's demands for an eight-game schedule left no room for annual opponents that wanted a home-and-home arrangement (aside from Florida State, of course). Miami fans, who have noted that Florida got out of the series just as the Hurricanes were becoming a superpower, remain bitter about the decision to this day. The two teams have played sporadically since. Debuting as a trophy in 1950 and celebrating the traditions of the Seminole Indians, the *War Canoe* is hand carved and painted from a 200-year-old tree felled by lightning. It now resides at UM's Sports Hall of Fame on campus.

University of Florida/Florida State University/University of Miami (Football): *The Florida Cup*

This cup is awarded to the majority winner of the Florida, FSU, and Miami games, on the years when they all play each other.

Florida A&M/Tennessee State University (Football): *Atlanta Football Classic*

Established in 1989, this HBCU classic made its debut with Florida A&M and Tennessee State but has not always featured those two teams. South Carolina State and Southern were both given their opportunities before the Rattlers and Tigers became de facto permanent opponents in 1998. The game is presented by 100 Black Men of Atlanta, an organization dedicated to providing, supporting, and improving the quality of life for African Americans in the Atlanta community.

Florida Atlantic University/Florida International University (Football): *Shula Bowl*

Every year Florida Atlantic University plays Florida International University in the *Shula Bowl* at Sun Life Stadium, home of the Miami Dolphins. The Shula Bowl, coined after Don Shula, former coach of the Miami Dolphins and record holder of the most NFL wins, gives bragging rights to a south Florida team. Florida Atlantic University acquired a DI-AA football team in 2001 and Florida International University acquired that same status in 2002. Since both universities have acquired FBS status, this rivalry has strengthened.

Florida State University/University of Virginia (Football): *Jefferson–Eppes Trophy*

Although not the biggest rivalry on the schedule of either school, FSU-Virginia picked up steam in the mid-1990s after the Cavaliers became the first ACC team to defeat the Seminoles in league competition. The *Jefferson –Eppes Trophy*, which made its debut in 1995, is named after President and UVA founder Thomas Jefferson and grandson Francis W. Eppes VII, a former mayor of Tallahassee and former president of the Board of Trustees of the West Florida Seminary (which became FSU). This rivalry was played annually from 1992 to 2005 but was moved to a semiannual basis when the Seminoles and Cavaliers were placed in different divisions within the ACC.

Franklin College/Hanover College (Football): *Victory Bell*

These Division III rivals have been playing each other since 1896, and their incorporation of the *Victory Bell* in 1938 as a season ending prize to the victor gives this rivalry the distinction of having one of the oldest trophies in the sport. The series was briefly interrupted from 1971–1988, but anyone who has attended any of the games since will tell you that no love was lost between the two rivals during that time.

Fresno State/Louisiana Tech (Football): *Battle for the Bone*

In one of the thriving rivalries in the last days of the WAC, Fresno State, and Louisiana Tech met every season from 2001 to 2011. It was nicknamed the *Battle for the Bone* due to both teams being nicknamed the Bulldogs. Fresno State's move to the Mountain West in 2012 suspended this rivalry, while Louisiana Tech's departure for Conference USA also put its continuation in further doubt.

Fresno State/University of Hawaii (Football): *Golden Screwdriver*

This rivalry originated in 1970 but really picked up steam when Fresno State joined Hawaii in the WAC, where the two schools remained for the next two decades. The notorious rowdiness of each school's fan base has contributed to rumors of abusive behavior over the years, which combined with the success of both programs to make this one of the WAC's most intense match-ups. It looks like this rivalry will be around for the long term, as both schools elected to join the Mountain West following the demise of the WAC. Thankfully, this match-up was not one sacrificed to the gods of realignment.

Fresno State/San Jose State University (Football): *Battle of the San Joaquin Valley*

As fellow members of the California State University system, foes Fresno State and San Jose State are almost obligated to have a gridiron rivalry. The two first met in 1921 and have faced each other on a regular basis since, with San Jose State dominating much of the rivalry before Fresno State gained its footing in the 1990s. Both schools were members of the WAC during its final days, and San Jose State's admittance into the MWC ensures that this will be a regular fixture for the foreseeable future.

Frostburg State University/Salisbury University (Football): *The Regents Cup*

Maryland's only football-playing Division III schools, Frostburg State and Salisbury, have played every season since 1973. The *Regents Cup* was added in 1999 to signify the only rivalry game between members of the University System of Maryland. This rivalry got an added twist in the 2000s when Frostburg State hired Rubin Stevenson as head coach, as Stevenson is not only a Salisbury alum but also the former college roommate of Sea Gulls head coach Sherman Wood.

University of Georgia/Georgia Tech (Football): *Governor's Cup*

Some rivalries are named so perfectly that very little else needs to be said. This is the case with Georgia–Georgia Tech, who have been engaged in a battle of "Clean, Old-Fashioned Hate" since the two schools first met for Peach State supremacy in 1893. The seeds of this rivalry were planted a couple of years before their first match-up, when UGA was debating whether or not to use old gold as a school color and eventually decided against it because it looked too close to yellow. In response, Georgia Tech decided to adopt old gold as one of their colors as a proverbial slap in the face to the UGA program. Things further intensified during the World

War I years, when Georgia elected not to field a football team due to a manpower shortage. Georgia Tech, on the other hand, was a military training ground at the time and had no such issues fielding a team. This move outraged Bulldog faithful to such a degree that the two schools did not meet again on the gridiron until 1925. The rivalry has continued unimpeded ever since, continuing as a season-ending affair even after Georgia Tech withdrew from the SEC in 1963. The hatred between the two schools has only grown. Both schools' fight songs mention that the other can go to hell, and items that symbolize the pageantry of each school's program (the *Ramblin' Wreck* and the *Chapel Bell*, for example) are often the subjects of theft or mischief. The winner of the game receives the *Governor's Cup*.

Grambling State University/Prairie View A&M (Football):
State Fair Classic

One of the oldest games of its kind, the *State Fair Classic* has been a celebration of HBCU football since the game's founding in 1925. The game is held at the Cotton Bowl during the Texas State Fair and often falls on the weekend before the Red River Rivalry between Oklahoma and Texas. This game was originally a match-up between Wiley College and Langston University, with Prairie View stepping in as a replacement for Langston in 1929. Prairie View would become a regular at the Classic, playing a variety of HBCUs at the Cotton Bowl before settling on longtime SWAC rival Grambling in the mid-1980s. Grambling held the Classic together when Prairie View temporarily disbanded its football program in 1990, but the program was quickly restored and the Classic has continued without interruption since 1992. The State Fair Classic is often cited as a forerunner for *Monday Night Football*, as the contest was held on a Monday night well into the 1960s.

Grambling State University/Southern University (Football):
Bayou Classic

While it is not the oldest game of its kind, many people regard the *Bayou Classic* between Grambling and Southern as the most famous of all the HBCU Classics. The rivalry between the two schools began in 1959, one year after Grambling joined Southern as a member of the SWAC. Both programs became powerhouses in the conference, and in 1974 their annual grudge match was moved off-campus to New Orleans and transformed into the Bayou Classic. Numerous events surround this game, the most famous of which is a battle of the bands. These two marching bands have two performances during the festivities: one the night before the game, and the other at halftime. The competition between the rival bands is every bit as intense as the game and has resulted in fistfights on the field and in the stands on more than one occasion. The Bayou Classic annually has some of the best attendance of any HBCU game and is the only FCS football game that is regularly shown on national television, leading fans to informally refer to the game as the *Black Super Bowl*.

Grand Valley State University/Saginaw Valley State University (Football): *Battle of the Valleys*

One of the most tradition-laden season finales in all of Division II, the *Battle of the Valleys* has been a circle-the-date match-up between Grand Valley State and Saginaw State since the two began playing in 1975. The rivalry has actually been kicked up a notch in the new millennium, as the Lakers and Cardinals also met in the Division II playoffs three times from 2001–2005.

Grand Valley State University/Wayne State University (Football): *Wooden Shoes Trophy*

Although not quite as engrained as Grand Valley State's other rivals, the Lakers have played cross-state foe Wayne State in nearly every season since 1975. The winner of this game receives the *Wooden Shoes Trophy*, but it tends not to do much traveling. As of 2012, Grand Valley State has not lost a meeting with Wayne State since 1984.

Greensboro College/Guilford College (Football): *Gate City Soup Bowl*

These two schools have traditionally opened the season against each other since Greensboro added football in 1997. Right from the beginning, the *Gate City Soup Bowl* has been an event. The colleges also use this game as a massive food drive competition, which results in approximately 8,000 nonperishable items being donated annually by the two student bodies.

Grove City College/Thiel College (Football): *Mercer County Cup*

One of the oldest rivalries in Division III, Grove City and Thiel first met on the gridiron in 1892 and have played in nearly every season since World

War II. In 1983, the two sides started playing for the *Mercer County Cup*. Grove City has a commanding lead in the overall series.

Hamilton College/Middlebury College (Football): *Mac-Jack Rocking Chair*

This rivalry dates back to 1911 and has been played on an annual basis since 1966. In 1980, the game turned into the *Rocking Chair Classic*, with the *Mac-Jack Rocking Chair* (named for the two men who thought of the idea) going to the winner. Middlebury has long held dominance in the overall rivalry.

Hamline University/Macalester College (Football): *Old Paint Bucket*

The third oldest rivalry in Division III, Hamline and Macalester first met on the gridiron in 1887 and have been battling for the *Old Paint Bucket* since 1965. These St. Paul, Minnesota schools are literally down the street from each other, separated by a mere two-mile stretch along Snelling Avenue.

Hampden-Sydney College/Randolph-Macon College (Football): *Jacket-Tiger Cup*

The game is often referred to as the Oldest Small-College Rivalry in the South. Hampden-Sydney and Randolph-Macon first played each other in 1893, and have played in nearly every non–World War year since. The rivalry got its start as the result of Hampden-Sydney hoping to fill its schedule with only home games, as the university president had banned the team from traveling. Randolph-Macon, located a mere seventy-eight miles away and only a short drive from Richmond, was one of the few schools willing to play the Tigers without the guarantee of a return trip. The Yellow Jackets won the game 12–6, and the travel ban at Hampden-Sydney was eventually lifted so this rivalry could move to a home-and-home format. This game is known for the huge bonfire at Hampden-Sydney before this game, which is often referred to as the *Beat Macon Bonfire*. The winner of this game receives one of the most unique trophies in all of college football: the game ball.

Hampton University/Norfolk State University (Football): *Battle of the Bay*

Separated by about sixteen miles of land and water, the *Battle of the Bay* between Hampton and Norfolk State started in 1938 and has been played on a near annual basis since 1963, when the two became league foes. Like many HBCU rivalries, the Battle of the Bay is well known for the competition between the two marching bands, both of which gained acclaim in the 1980s. This rivalry withstood both schools' transition to Division I-AA in the mid-1990s.

Harvard/Yale University (Football): *The Game*

In many respects, the game between Harvard and Yale is the original template by which all other college sports rivalries are based. The first match-up between the two schools occurred in 1875, in what historians consider to be the second college football game ever played. There have been a total of ten years since when the rivalry was not played, and four of those were due to World Wars I and II. As early as 1898, fans of both sides were referring to it as *The Game*. This rivalry also started the stadium construction boom. Harvard Stadium, built in 1903, is the oldest permanent concrete structure in the country, while the Yale Bowl (1914) became the model for numerous college football stadiums that followed. Harvard–Yale has declined in national relevance from its heyday in the early twentieth century, but The Game is still capable of making noise on occasion. In fact, the most famous meeting between these two schools happened in 1968, when both teams entered The Game with perfect 8–0 records and the meeting ended in a tie thanks to a miraculous sixteen-point Harvard comeback in the final forty-two seconds of play. "Harvard Beats Yale, 29–29" headlined the Harvard Crimson student newspaper the next day and would go on to become one of the most famous sports headlines of all time.

University of Hawaii/University of Wyoming (Football): *Paniolo Trophy*

Hawaii and Wyoming reunited in the Mountain West Conference in 2012 in a rivalry that doesn't garner much interest outside of Laramie or Honolulu. With the resurrection of this rivalry, there is one small problem: the rivalry trophy has gone missing. The *Paniolo Trophy*, a tradition dating back to 1979, was last won by Wyoming. But it is clear the Cowboys' coaching staff didn't think too highly of the trophy, as representatives stated they have no idea where it is. Wyoming won the Paniolo back in the late 1990s—not too long ago. Athletic director Kevin McKinney believes it may have been broken, sent to a repair shop, and then who knows. Fortunately, just like the series, this trophy doesn't carry much historical value, or lore, as do some of the other big game rivalry trophies.

Henderson State University/Ouachita Baptist University (Football): *Battle of the Ravine*

One of the oldest college football rivalries in Division II, Henderson State, and Ouachita Baptist first played each other in 1895 and eventually turned the game into a Thanksgiving Day staple in the state of Arkansas. These two schools are within walking distance of each other in the city of Arkadelphia, meaning that the students of both campuses have plenty of interaction throughout the year. Hijinks are a common occurrence in the *Battle of the Ravine* and actually contributed to the rivalry not being played from 1952–62. This is also one of the most evenly matched rivalries in college sports, as nearly half of the meetings have been decided by a touchdown or less.

Hobart College/University of Rochester (Football): *Centennial Cup*

An ancient Division III rivalry from upstate New York, Hobart and Rochester first met in 1892 and generally play each other to end the regular season. The *Centennial Cup* was added to the rivalry in the year 2000, though that was neither the 100th anniversary nor the 100th showdown between the two schools.

Hope College/Kalamazoo College (Football): *Wooden Shoes Rivalry*

The Hope–Kalamazoo football series is known as the *Wooden Shoes Rivalry*. The teams have been football rivals since 1910. The traveling trophy, a pair of hand-carved Dutch wooden shoes, has been part of the rivalry since 1931. For years, the wooden shoes were viewed as unique among intercollegiate trophy games because when a tie occurred, the head coach of each team could have one of the pair until the next year's game. That happened six times until the NCAA eliminated the tie game ending in 1996. The teams will play for the ninety-third time in 2013.

University of Houston/Rice University: *Bayou Bucket Classic*

This is a rivalry that was birthed from geography, as the schools are located about five miles apart, and inside Houston's Inner Loop. This makes Houston-Rice one of the very few cross-town rivalries in major college football. The two schools met for the first time in 1971, just six years before Houston joined Rice as a member of the Southwest Conference. It was officially christened the *Bayou Bucket Classic* in 1974, and Houston would frequently move the game to the Astrodome whenever it was the Cougars' turn to host. The 1995 match-up between the two schools was the very last football game played in the SWC before the conference disbanded. Rice and Houston then went their separate ways, with the Owls going to the WAC and the Cougars to Conference USA. After a temporary period of inactivity, the rivalry was rekindled in 1999 and became a league game once again when Rice joined Conference USA in 2005. The winner of this game receives the Bayou Bucket, a bronzed bucket atop a wooden base.

Howard University/Morehouse College (Football): *Nation's Football Classic*

This rivalry originated in 1923 and was an important part of both team's football schedules from the mid-1950s to 1970. It was rekindled from 1985–1997 and again in 2011, when the *Nation's Football Classic* was created and moved to RFK Stadium in Washington, D.C.

University of Idaho/University of Montana (Football): *Little Brown Stein*

A match-up of flagship universities in the inland Northwest, Idaho and Montana first met on the gridiron in 1903, as they developed their rivalry as founding members of the NWIAA. Both schools eventually moved on to join the PCC, where they were consistently at the bottom of the conference standings and had trouble drawing any conference members (apart from each other) to their respective campuses. Montana left for the Mountain States Conference in 1950, but the two schools continued to maintain their rivalry as nonconference foes until the dissolving of the PCC in 1959. Four years later, the two became charter members of the Big Sky Conference, where the rivalry developed into one based on success instead of shared failure. They remained conference foes until Idaho elected to follow Boise State into Division I-A in 1996, and as a result, have played only a handful of times since. Idaho leads the overall series 55–27–2, but Montana has won eight of the last ten meetings, and has been in possession of the *Little Brown Stein* since 2003.

University of Idaho/Washington State University (Football): *Battle of the Palouse*

The name of the rivalry is derived from the Palouse, the rolling agricultural region in which both schools are located. The two land-grant universities are in different states, yet less than eight miles apart. There was once a tradition called the *Loser's Walk*, where students of the losing school walked from the winner's campus back to their own. In 1954, the Walk made national news when about 2,000 students from Washington State College made the trek after the Cougars lost to Idaho for the first time in 29 years. But losses have been few and far between for WSU in this rivalry, as the Cougars have won over 78 percent of their meetings with the Vandals since the series began in 1894. The rivalry was discontinued when the Division I split in 1978 left WSU and Idaho in different classifications but was rekindled in 1998 after the Vandals moved up to I-A status. All but one of the games since then have been played at WSU's Martin Stadium, though Idaho has actually been the home team for a handful of those games in order to boost up attendance numbers in compliance with the NCAA.

University of Illinois/Michigan State University (Gymnastics): *The Victory Plank*

Illinois and Michigan State recently started a gymnastics tradition with the unveiling of the *Victory Plank*. This is the first gymnastics rivalry trophy in the Big Ten and is often hosted in conjunction with Breast Cancer Awareness activities, with both teams often donning pink leotards during the meet.

University of Illinois/University of Missouri (Basketball): *Braggin' Rights Game*

The *Braggin' Rights Game* between Illinois and Missouri has been a staple of both teams' nonconference hoops schedules since 1980. It is held annually in St. Louis, which is considered a halfway point between the Champaign and Columbia campuses. Mizzou made preserving this matchup a priority when the Tigers jumped to the SEC in 2012, which can't be

"The Victory Plank Trophy," which goes to the winner of the Illinois–Michigan State gymnastics series. *University of Illinois Athletics*

said for some of the Tigers' other long-term rivalries. Unlike a lot of other NCAA events, this one is sponsored by a prominent light beer. Could that be the Missouri connection, since one of the world's largest brewers has its headquarters in St Louis?

University of Illinois/University of Missouri (Football): *Arch Rivalry Game*

These two schools first met on the gridiron in 1896 and began playing each other on a regular basis in 1966. Recent match-ups have eschewed campus venues in favor of St. Louis which was the site of the first match-up and is also home to large alumni bases for both schools. While this is nicknamed the *Arch Rivalry Game* (a tribute to St. Louis), it is generally considered one of the friendlier nonconference rivalries in the sport. With Mizzou abandoning all of its Big 12 rivalries after joining the SEC, it would not be a surprise to see the Tigers and Illini playing on an annual basis in the near future.

University of Illinois/Northwestern University: *Sweet Sioux Tomahawk/Land of Lincoln Trophy*

One of the Big Ten's oldest rivalries, Illinois and Northwestern played their first game in 1892, and have met each other in almost every year since. Unlike the Big Ten's other two state rivalries, Illinois-Northwestern was not protected by divisional placement when the conference divided up for the 2012 season. Instead, the Fighting Illini and Wildcats are each other's permanent cross-division rival, meaning they will still play each other every year. The 2010 meeting between the two schools at Wrigley Field in Chicago became one of the more infamous games in college football history, as the NCAA determined that the field was too small to allow for adequate space in the end zones and resulted in both teams going away from the outfield wall when they had the ball. But fans sitting along that wall were not disappointed, as Northwestern's Brian Peters ran back a pick-six in the first quarter. The *Sweet Sioux* was originally a large wooden statue of an Indian, similar to old cigar store statues. The statue was replaced in 1947 with a more mobile tomahawk, the final version of which was housed inside a frame. Due to political correctness, Illinois was forced by the NCAA in 2008 to terminate the tradition. The *Tomahawk* rests forever at NU. In 2009 the two schools initiated the *Land of Lincoln Trophy*, a bronze replica of Lincoln's stovepipe hat.

University of Illinois/The Ohio State University (Football): *Illy Illibuck*

One of the Big Ten's many trophy games, Ohio State and Illinois have been playing each other since before the Buckeyes became a member of the conference. The first game was in 1902, and the tradition between the two schools was strong enough that the Fighting Illini were placed in the same division as Ohio State and away from state rival Northwestern when the Big Ten expanded to twelve teams. The winner of this game receives the *Illibuck*, a carved wooden turtle named after the mascots for both schools. When the tradition began in 1925, the trophy was a live turtle. The turtle was chosen for its long life expectancy as a symbol of the long life of the rivalry. That was short-lived, though, when the trophy passed away just two years later. The Illibuck is the second oldest of the active Big Ten trophies.

University of Illinois/Purdue University (Football): *Purdue Cannon Trophy*

These Big Ten border rivals have been playing on a regular basis since 1892. The origins of the *Purdue Cannon* can be traced back to 1905, when a group of Purdue students brought it to Champaign with the intention of firing it after a Boilermaker victory. Illinois supporters, however, discovered the cannon before it could be fired and hid it away for the next four decades. When the rivalry resumed in 1943 after a twelve-year absence, it was adopted as a traveling trophy. Clearly, Illini faithful knew exactly where the cannon had been hidden the entire time.

Indiana University/Michigan State University (Football): *The Old Brass Spittoon*

These two teams first played in 1922 and were designated as permanent cross-divisional rivals following the Big Ten's recent expansion. This is the most one-sided of the rivalries that received such a distinction. Only one explanation could possibly make sense: the wacky trophy that's at stake whenever the two take the field. The *Old Brass Spittoon* was the brainchild of Gene McDermott, who was the junior class president at Michigan State in 1950 and a rabid supporter of Spartan football. Many were expecting Michigan State to put forth a letdown performance against Indiana that year, as the Spartans had just defeated Notre Dame and were climbing up the national rankings. Determined to help the team avoid a letdown, McDermott went to an antique shop looking for a rivalry trophy and discovered a beat-up brass spittoon that had been used by trappers from both Michigan and Indiana at an East Lansing trading post in the early 1800s. McDermott thought it was perfect, and he eventually sold the concept to both Michigan State coach Biggy Munn and the IU student council. The trophy has endured even as the rivalry remains one-sided in favor of the Spartans.

Indiana University/Purdue University (Football): *Old Oaken Bucket*

This rivalry is between the two largest public universities in Indiana, and the Bucket—which is more than 100 years old—was first awarded in 1925. After the idea for this particular trophy was proposed, it was decided that, literally, an oaken bucket should be taken from some well in Indiana. Every year, either an "I" or a "P" link is added to the chain attached to the bucket. Ironically, the very first game in the *Old Oaken Bucket* era ended in a tie, resulting in an "I-P" link in the chain. The rivalry itself dates back to 1891 and is the most played match-up in the Big Ten between in-state foes. The bucket itself is said to have been used during the Civil War by Confederate General Morgan's command during an incursion into Indiana.

Indiana University/Purdue University (Volleyball): *The Monon Spike*

These two teams began playing each other in volleyball in 1975, with the *Monon Spike* added as a traveling trophy in 1981. As with its sister trophy (the Old Oaken Bucket), a "P" or an "I" is added to a chain signifying the game's winner.

Indiana University/Purdue University (Basketball): *Basketball Mad*

In a basketball-mad state, these two schools playing each other takes on an aura of something special. What other game could have made Bobby Knight throw his chair? Yep. Okay, a lot of games could put Knight in a chair-chucking mood, but few ever did, on such a consistent basis as the Indiana–Purdue rivalry. The first game between the two schools occurred in 1901, which ended in a 20–15 Purdue victory. The Boilermakers also won the second game that season 23–19 in West Lafayette, but Indiana denies that this game ever took place. Things only escalated from there. This rivalry consists of two very different perceptions: to outsiders, Indiana's five national championships and lead in NCAA Tournament appearances makes it look like the Hoosiers dominate this rivalry. Insiders, however, note that the Boilermakers actually have a comfortable lead in head-to-head match-ups and have actually won more Big Ten titles.

Indiana University/Purdue University (Women's Basketball): *Barn Burner Trophy*

Beginning with the 1993–1994 season, Indiana and Purdue's women's basketball teams have played for the *Barn Burner Trophy*—a wooden plaque with a drawing of a barn and an attached basketball hoop, which best describes basketball in Indiana.

Indiana University/Purdue University (Women's Soccer): *Golden Boot Trophy*

Beginning around the new millennium, these two schools began playing for the *Golden Boot*—a gold-dipped soccer shoe, with the obligatory

"I's" and "P's" that other sports of these two schools add to their related trophies.

University of Iowa/Iowa State University (All Sports): *Cy-Hawk Series*

While the Iowa and Iowa State athletic programs both date back to the late 1890s and are located only two hours apart, the Hawkeyes and Cyclones have never actually been in the same conference. The two competed in a variety of sports, but Iowa was always more preoccupied with Big Ten rivals while Iowa State was more focused on the Big 12. To spice things up in-state, the *Cy-Hawk* series was created in 2004 and incorporated a total of thireen sports that are played by both schools. The rivalry has been so evenly matched that neither has been able to hold the trophy for consecutive years.

University of Iowa/Iowa State University (Wrestling): *Intrastate Tussle*

Iowa–Iowa State is one of the great rivalries in college wrestling. Long-time nonconference rivals Iowa and Iowa State have been hitting the mats since the NCAA first awarded wrestling championships in 1928. The rivalry is dominated by the legendary Dan Gable, who was an NCAA champion at Iowa State before guiding Iowa to 16 NCAA Championships from 1978–1997. Dual meets between the two schools are broadcast across the state, and the 2008 meeting set a new NCAA record with 15,955 in attendance.

University of Iowa/Iowa State University (Football): *Cy-Hawk Trophy*

On the surface, this should be one of the great in-state nonconference rivalries in college football. But Iowa has always scoffed at the idea of this annual series, perhaps because the Hawkeyes dominated the early days of the rivalry and refused to play the Cyclones on an annual basis after 1920. It would be fifty-seven years before the annual series started back up, and the two schools have now played each other every season since 1977. Iowa backed up their skepticism by winning fifteen in a row from 1983–1997, but Iowa State has since evened things out and made this game one of the most exciting September rivalries in the sport. The *Cy-Hawk Trophy* has experienced an identity crisis in recent years, as the original was retired in

2010 in favor of a sculpture of a family with small children huddled around a basket of corn. It was ridiculed almost immediately, both by alumni of the schools and the national media, and it was replaced a year later by a trophy featuring a raised football and the logos of both schools—with corn merely making up the background.

University of Iowa/University of Nebraska (Football): *Corn Bowl/ Heroes' Trophy*

The trophy looks just like it sounds: a golden bowl filled with dry field corn, attached to a wooden base. Hawkeye and Husker logos adorn the sides of the bowl. When Nebraska made the jump from the Big 12, for the Big Ten, the Cornhuskers put out feelers to see which of their new league members would be interested in a season ending rivalry game. Nebraska has a long tradition of playing on Black Friday, and the new conference was more than willing to accommodate that tradition as long as the opponent was okay with the arrangement. Iowa, whose history against Nebraska stretched back to 1891, eagerly volunteered to be the new Black Friday opponent, and the two schools began ending the regular season against each other in 2011. The winner of this game receives the *Heroes Trophy*, which is a tribute to the men and women in uniform at both schools.

University of Iowa/University of Wisconsin (Football): *Heartland Trophy*

These border rivals met for the first time in 1894, and the rivalry was important enough to both schools that the game was listed among the Big Ten's protected match-ups when the conference added Penn State in the early 1990s. The *Heartland Trophy*, which is a brass bull atop a trophy stand, made its debut in 2004. It is one of the newest of the Big Ten trophy games, though the divisional realignment in the wake of conference expansion, means that this rivalry will not take place every year. Historically, it is one of the most evenly matched rivalries in the conference, with the record standing at forty-two wins apiece after their most recent meeting in 2010.

Iowa State University/Kansas State University (Football): *Farmageddon*

While these two teams have played each other every year since 1917, for many years it was regarded as an annual match-up between Big Eight bottom-feeders. It did not become a major rivalry within the conference until the Big Eight morphed into the Big 12 in 1996. When that happened, both the Cyclones and Wildcats were placed in the north and experienced upticks in competitiveness on the national level. Kansas State, in particular, became a national powerhouse, with the Wildcats making-up the significant winning deficit they had to Iowa State prior to the 1990 season. It was given the nickname "Farmageddon" in 2009 as a reference to both schools' status as agriculture-oriented land-grant universities.

Iowa State University/University of Missouri (Football): *Telephone Trophy*

This series began in 1896, with the trophy originating in 1959. Before the 1959 game, field testing showed that the telephones the two schools used to communicate with their coaches in the coaches box were wired so that either school could hear what was happening on the other sideline. The problem was fixed before the game, but neither of the two coaches knew that. Northwestern Bell Telephone Company decided to have a trophy made (with half of each team's colors) to commemorate the incident. Missouri's departure for the SEC in 2012 brought this rivalry to its conclusion, with the Tigers in possession of a 61–34–9 lead in the overall series.

Jackson State University/Southern University (Football): *Jackson State/Southern Rivalry*

Southern put up a 98–0 thrashing in the first meeting between these two schools in 1929. They would not play again until 1958, when this became a yearly rivalry game after Jackson State joined the SWAC. Like many HBCU Classics, the Jackson State-Southern rivalry is generally played at a large, off-campus venue and annually draws some of the largest crowds in FCS football. It is also known for the *battle of the bands* between Jackson State's Sonic Boom of the South and Southern's Human Jukebox.

Jackson State University/Tennessee State University (Football): *Southern Heritage Classic*

One of many recent additions to the list of HBCU Classics, Jackson State and Tennessee State moved their rivalry to Memphis in 1990 and have since turned the *Southern Heritage Classic* into one of the Liberty Bowl's biggest annual events. Among the festivities associated with the game include a battle of the bands and a golf tournament hosted by NFL legend Ed "Too Tall" Jones, a Tennessee State alum.

Jacksonville State University/Troy University (Football): The Ol' School Bell

For many years, Jacksonville State–Troy was one of the most intense small-school rivalries in the state of Alabama. These two teams first met in 1924, and it had become an annual grudge match by the end of World War II. The *Ol' School Bell trophy* pays tribute to the origins of both schools as teachers' colleges. This rivalry died out when Troy made the jump to FBS football but could be revived in the very near future, as Jacksonville State is considering making the jump themselves.

Jamestown College/Valley City State University (Football): The Paint Bucket

In what is one of the longest running college football rivalries in North Dakota, Valley City State University and Jamestown College reunite every year (currently 108+ games), with the winner taking home the *Paint Bucket*. The first meeting between the two gridiron teams was in 1909 with then Valley City State Teachers College being the victor with a score of 16–0. The rivalry continued throughout the years, with the intensity growing to unsportsmanlike levels between the two universities located only thirty-seven miles apart. The Paint Bucket started years ago after Jamestown beat Valley City for the first time in six years, and someone painted the score (21–14) on the stadium wall. The guy was caught and he had to clean it off. Hence the Paint Bucket Trophy started. As a result, in 1961, the presidents of the two universities created a plan to try and curb the negativity that came as a result from the heated, but passionate, rivalry. The *Paint Bucket Series* was created. An original document stating the intent of the series is printed and found in the commons area of the W. E. Osmon Fieldhouse and reads:

> In the light of the unsportsmanlike rivalry existing between the Jamestown College student body and the Valley City State Teachers College student body preceding the annual football contest in the fall, the respective student associations met in January of 1961 and established a program intended to direct this rivalry to more sportsmanlike and less destructive activities. A trophy, symbolic to the rivalry of past years, shall be presented to the team emerg-

ing victorious in the annual football game. This trophy shall have the year and that school's name engraved on the base and remain in the possession of that school until the following year and game when it, as in years to follow, will again be presented to the school emerging victorious. Let it therefore be known that, on the twenty-eighth day of October in the nineteen hundred and sixty-first year of our Lord that the football game between Valley City State Teachers College and Jamestown College, the heretofore described Paint Bucket Series, shall commence.

Johns Hopkins University/McDaniel College (Football): *Maryland Railroad Lantern*

One of the oldest rivalries in college football, Johns Hopkins–McDaniel dates back to 1894 and has been played annually since 1947. The *Maryland Railroad Lantern*, however, is a relatively new addition. An authentic metal railroad lantern with four lenses, it was the brainchild of McDaniel alum Vincent Chesney and pays tribute to the railroad that connected Westminster to Baltimore.

Johns Hopkins University/University of Maryland (Lacrosse): *Mid-Atlantic Rivalry*

Widely regarded as the finest lacrosse rivalry in college sports, Johns Hopkins and Maryland have been doing battle since 1894. The state of Maryland has historically been a hotbed for lacrosse talent, which puts both schools in perfect position to land many of the nation's top amateur lacrosse players. This rivalry is intensified by the fact that both are national powerhouses in the sport, and that it is the only sporting event in which the two schools compete, as Johns Hopkins is a Division III school in all other sports. A 2003 Harris Interactive poll revealed that Marylanders considered it the fourth-biggest rivalry in the state in any sport. *Sports Illustrated* considers this rivalry to be the lacrosse equivalent of Michigan–Ohio State in football. In short, this game is a big, big deal.

Juniata College/Susquehanna University (Football): *Goal Post Game*

The oldest rivalry tradition in Susquehanna sports history is the *Goal Post Game* against Juniata College. The prize in the competition is an actual piece of goal post taken from Susquehanna's old University Field by Juniata fans following their team's 12–7 upset of the Crusaders in 1952. That season was the last coached at Susquehanna by the legendary Amos Alonzo Stagg Sr., the Grand Old Man of Football. The 1953 season then started the Goal Post Game tradition in which each team would defend the six foot tall piece of wood against its rival.

University of Kansas/Kansas State University (Football): *Governor's Cup*

Often referred to as the *Sunflower Showdown*, Kansas and Kansas State first met on the gridiron in 1902 and have played continuously since 1910, giving the Jayhawks and the Wildcats one of the longest continuously-played rivalries in college football. Kansas dominated the rivalry early on, winning 17 of the first 19 meetings and holding a 45–17 lead before the incorporation of the *Governor's Cup*. Kansas State's rise to power in the 1990s has balanced things out. The trophy was first awarded in 1969. The Cup is actually the third trophy associated with the rivalry. In the early years, a Governor's Trophy was given to the winning team. Then, beginning with the 1940 football season, the winner of the Kansas–Kansas State contest received the *Peace Pact Trophy*, which was a pair of miniature bronze goalposts. The Peace Pact Trophy was intended to keep the winning team's student body from tearing down the loser's goalposts.

University of Kansas/University of Missouri (Football): *Indian War Drum/Border War*

The rivalry between the states of Missouri and Kansas actually predates the admission of Kansas to the Union, and armed towns in the two states shed significant blood against each other during the Civil War. These battle scars never really healed, and the animosity between these two states persisted until recently, and served as the historical basis for the *Border War* between the flagship universities of each state. Kansas and Mizzou first met on the gridiron in 1891, and the two schools never took a break from playing each other for any reason over the next 120 years, giving them the longest continuous rivalry in major college football over that span and the second most played game overall. But things came to a head in 1960, when the Jayhawks handed Missouri a 23–7 loss that ended up costing the Tigers a national championship—only to have the Jayhawks later forfeit the game and the Big 8 title back to Mizzou for using an ineligible player. The bitterness between the two schools has never really died down. The name of the rivalry was changed to the *Border Showdown* in 2004 in an attempt to reduce tensions (and for political correctness), and the rivalry had to be moved to Kansas City in 2007 in order to prevent excessive vandalism on either campus. That 2007 game would prove to be one of the biggest in the series, as the Tigers defeated the Jayhawks 36–28 in the first-ever meeting between the two teams as top-five opponents. Unfortunately, Missouri's recent jump to the SEC (and lack of desire to continue playing Kansas) has brought this rivalry to a close. How evenly matched were these two teams? Missouri leads the overall series 57–54–9 (depending on who you ask), and this is the largest lead that either team has had in the rivalry since 1992. The winner of this game received the *Indian War Drum*, an authentic tom-tom that was built by the Osage Indian tribe and incorporated into the rivalry in 1937. It had to be replaced more than once over the years, and the *Lamar Hunt Trophy* (named after the Chiefs' owner) was also added in 2007 for the winner of the games in Kansas City.

University of Kansas/University of Missouri (Basketball): *Border War*

In some respects, the hoops version of the *Border War* between Kansas and Missouri was actually a bigger deal than the celebrated football match-up. Both the Jayhawks and Tigers have decidedly stronger basketball traditions, as the two schools were the dominant powers in both the Big Eight and Big 12 for much of their history. The rivalry dates back to the 1906–1907 season and as of 2012 has been played a total of 267 times, with Kansas holding a 172–95 edge. But like the football rivalry, the hoops series between these two schools has likely come to an end with Missouri's jump to the SEC and the reluctance of both schools to add each other in a nonconference game.

University of Kentucky/University of Louisville (Football): *Governor's Cup*

When this series began in 1912, it looked like an annual match-up between Kentucky and Louisville could develop into a fantastic in-state nonconference rivalry. Six shutouts by the Wildcats later, however, led both sides to put this one on the backburner. It would not be revived again until 1994, when Kentucky alum Howard Schnellenberger was coaching at Louisville and had put the Cardinals in a much better position to handle the Wildcats. The *Governor's Cup* was also added that year to sweeten the deal, and this rivalry has taken its place alongside the SEC's other great in-state nonconference affairs.

University of Kentucky/University of Louisville (Basketball): *Bluegrass Battle*

Basketball will always be numero uno in the Bluegrass State, and that fact is reflected in how the Commonwealth has traditionally supported its two most prominent programs. Kentucky and Louisville first played each other in 1913 and met sporadically over the next few decades before the rivalry was given new life in the 1983 NCAA Tournament. That game, an 80–68 victory by the Cardinals in the Elite Eight, whetted appetites for the two schools to start meeting on an annual basis, and the two schools have met in the regular season around Christmastime every year since. Both Kentucky and Louisville rank among the best supported college basketball programs in the country, ensuring that both school's 22,000+ seat arenas are always filled to capacity whenever these two teams hit the hardwood.

King College/Virginia Intermont College (Volleyball): *Retro-Night*

In 2012, King College played in decades old uniforms in a gym they seldom now use, for *Retro Night*. King and Virginia Intermont are crosstown foes in this volleyball rivalry.

King's College/Wilkes University (Football): *Wilkes-Barre Mayor's Cup*

These Division III cross-town rivals first met in 1946 and rekindled their rivalry when football returned to King's College in 1993. They have played yearly since, and in 1996 it became an official rivalry for town supremacy with the addition of the *Wilkes-Barre Mayor's Cup*. The game is now often broadcast on local television.

King's College/Marywood University/University of Scranton/ Wilkes University (Basketball): *Cross-County Challenge*

Sometimes, the best way to ring in the New Year is by issuing a challenge to your rivals. The *Cross-County Challenge* is a basketball tournament that got its start in 2012 and features four prominent Division III universities from Luzerne and Lackawanna Counties. All of the games take place at one location, with each of the four participants set to host the tournament during a four-year stretch.

Knox College/Monmouth College (Football): *Bronze Turkey Trophy*

The second oldest rivalry in Division III, Knox and Monmouth have been butting heads on Thanksgiving Day since 1888. So it only makes sense that the two teams should be battling over a turkey, right? The *Bronze Turkey* was added as a trophy in 1928 and is one of the oldest trophies in all of college football.

Lawrence University/Ripon College (Football): *Doehling-Heselton Memorial Trophy*

Dating back to 1893, the Lawrence-Ripon rivalry is the oldest in the state of Wisconsin and the fourteenth oldest in all of college football. Each team has taken its turn in dominating the series, but overall the records are fairly evenly matched. The early days of this rivalry were particularly brutal, with the 1901 game marred by Lawrence players having to dodge spectators on the way to the end zone. In the 1950s, the two teams played over a trophy called the *Old Paint Bucket*. The *Doehling-Heselton Memorial Trophy*, named for legendary coaches on each side, was instituted in 1988.

Lewis & Clark College/Willamette University (Football): *Wagon Wheel*

These Division III schools first met in 1948 and have one of the oldest rivalries in the Pacific Northwest. The *Wagon Wheel* was incorporated as a trophy only a year later, making it one of the few rivalry games that had a trophy almost from the beginning.

Long Island University/St. Francis University (Basketball): *Battle of Brooklyn*

The schools are about eight blocks apart in Brooklyn and the teams walk to the games. They play twice a year as per conference rules, but only one game counts as the *Battle of Brooklyn* and it alternates sites every other year. An MVP trophy is given after each game as well.

University of Louisiana at Lafayette/Lamar University (Football): *Sabine Shoe*

Border rivals in the states of Texas and Louisiana, these two schools first started playing in 1923. The *Sabine Shoe*, which is named for the river that forms part of the border between the two states, was first awarded in 1937. This rivalry was played on an annual basis from 1965 to 1983 but ended when Louisiana-Lafayette (then known as Southwestern Louisiana) moved up to Division I-A football.

University of Louisiana at Lafayette/University of Louisiana at Monroe (Football): *Battle of the Bayou*

The biggest rivalry between members of the Louisiana university system, Louisiana-Lafayette and Louisiana-Monroe have been playing each other since before either school had its current name. The rivalry began in 1951, when Northeast Louisiana State (now ULM) handed Southwestern Louisiana (ULL) a 13–7 defeat. It is a rivalry that has withstood numerous conference and classification changes on both sides, though it appears to have settled into a groove as both have been members of the FBS-level Sun Belt Conference since 2001.

University of Louisiana at Lafayette/McNeese State University (Football): *Cajun Crown*

Separated by a mere 75 miles down I-10, these two teams met every year from 1951 to 1986, during which time McNeese State held a 19–15–2 series lead. The rivalry came to a close just a few years after Louisiana-Lafayette (then known as Southwestern Louisiana) made the jump to Division I-A football.

University of Louisiana at Lafayette/Southeastern Louisiana University (Football): *Cypress Mug*

These state rivals played on a nearly annual basis until 1981, when Louisiana-Lafayette (then Southwestern Louisiana) moved up to Division I-A status. This rivalry has not been played since, so the *Cypress Mug*—a turned, polished mahogany mug that served as the trophy—will likely remain on the Southeastern Louisiana campus.

LSU/Ole Miss (Football): *Magnolia Bowl*

Although it may not seem like much now, the *Magnolia Bowl* between LSU and Ole Miss was once among the fiercest annual events in the SEC.

The Tigers and Rebels played their first game in 1894 and quickly gained favored status on both the Baton Rouge and Oxford campuses. Regional divides defined the SEC for much of the twentieth century, which further cemented LSU-Ole Miss as an annual regional rivalry within the conference. The heyday of this rivalry was clearly the 1950s and 60s, when the two programs were regularly contending for both conference and national championships. It was officially christened the Magnolia Bowl in 2008, named after the state flower of both Louisiana and Mississippi.

LSU/Tulane University (Football): *Battle for the Tiger Rag/ Victory Flag*

This series began in 1893, and ended in 2009. The winner was awarded a satin trophy flag known as the *Tiger Rag* at LSU and the *Victory Flag* at Tulane. The flag was divided diagonally, with the logos of each school placed on opposite sides and the Seal of Louisiana in the center. LSU's name for the flag came from their fight song—"Tiger Rag." This was an annual rivalry from 1919 to 1994 and continued unabated even after the Green Wave withdrew from the SEC in 1966. However, long stretches of LSU dominance has convinced the Tigers' athletic department that they no longer need to schedule Tulane on an annual basis.

Louisiana Tech/Southern Miss (Football): *Rivalry in Dixie*

An original rivalry born from the Southern Intercollegiate Athletic Association, Louisiana Tech and Southern Miss first met in 1935 and played on a nearly annual basis until 1992. It got its name in 1976, after Louisiana Tech coach (and USM alum) Maxie Lambright declared, "This is the finest rivalry in Dixie" following the Bulldogs' 23–22 victory. The rivalry took a break when Louisiana Tech joined the Big West in 1993 but was rekindled in 2010, and the Bulldogs' recent admittance into Conference USA ensures that it will once again be a big deal in Dixie.

Lycoming College/Susquehanna University (Men's Soccer): *Battle of the Boot*

The contest was born in 2001 when both coaches came up with a bronzed and mounted soccer shoe trophy. As with the *Stagg Hat* (for football), the winning team defends the *Boot* every year.

Lycoming College/Susquehanna University (Women's Soccer): *River Derby Cup*

Susquehanna and Lycoming compete for the *River Derby Cup* each year. The rivalry began in 1994, and the trophy was incorporated in 2007.

Lycoming College/Susquehanna University (Softball): *Cancer Cup*

The 2009 softball season brought the first *Cancer Cup*, a community-service doubleheader between the Crusaders and Warriors softball teams designed to promote breast-cancer awareness. Both squads wear pink shirts made especially for the event and collect donations for the American Cancer Society.

University of Maine/University of New Hampshire (Football): *Brice-Cowell Musket*

People generally do not think of the Northeast when it comes to long-standing college football rivalries, but do not tell that to the good folks at Maine and New Hampshire. These border rivals have been battling almost continuously since 1903, with the rivalry reaching its 100th meeting in 2010. The *Brice-Cowell Musket*, an authentic flintlock rifle that dates back to the mid-1700s, is named for the longtime coaches at both schools.

Maine Maritime Academy/Mass Maritime (Football): *Admiral's Cup*

This Division III rivalry got its start in 1946 and has been played on an annual basis since 1973, when the *Admiral's Cup* was adopted as a trophy. The cup celebrated its fortieth anniversary in 2012.

Manchester University (IN)/Anderson University (IN) (Football): *Bronze Ball*

These two Heartland Collegiate Athletic Conference Rivals have met annually since the year 2000, with the *Bronze Ball Trophy* at stake.

Marquette University/University of Wisconsin–Milwaukee (Soccer): *Milwaukee Cup*

This battle for city supremacy began in 1973 and has featured a trophy right from the beginning. But things really kicked up a notch when Marquette hired coach Louis Bennett away from UW-M in 2006. It has since become one of the great cross-town rivalries in all of college soccer, helped by the fact that neither school fields a football team.

Marshall University/Ohio University (Football): *The Bell*

Located about 80 miles apart, border rivals Marshall and Ohio first started playing in 1905 and played nearly every season from 1949–1980. The two schools were MAC rivals from 1954–1969, and Ohio kept Marshall on the schedule as the Thundering Herd recovered from the tragic plane crash of 1970. Marshall rejoined the MAC from 1997–2005, during which time the *Bell* was adopted as a trophy that would ring with the teams and fans. They have continued to maintain their rivalry even after the Thundering Herd departed for Conference USA in 2006.

Marshall University/West Virginia University (Football): *Governor's Cup/Friends of Coal Bowl*

Although these two football programs each date back to the early twentieth century, Marshall and West Virginia never developed a rivalry for state supremacy. West Virginia won the first four meetings between 1911–1923 by progressively larger margins, convincing the Mountaineers that there was no real need to continue scheduling the Thundering Herd. They would not play again until 1997, when a last minute Mountaineer victory over Randy Moss's Marshall squad led to bad blood between the two athletic departments and controversy over future schedules. They finally came to an agreement on a new series in 2006, which was designated the *Friends of Coal Bowl* and hosting duties split two-to-one in favor of Morgantown over Huntington. Marshall is still looking for its first victory over West Virginia in the rekindled series.

University of Maryland/Naval Academy (Football): *Crab Bowl Trophy*

Separated by about thirty miles, Maryland and Navy first met on the gridiron in 1905 and have had a sporadic rivalry since then. This is a rivalry fueled by both geography and stereotypes, as the heavily structured Naval Academy historically thumbed their noses at the nearby public school that they perceived to be full of redneck coal miners. There is enough bad blood between the two schools that the rivalry is unlikely to ever be played on a regular basis, even after the creation of the *Crab Bowl Trophy* (a large pewter bowl overflowing with replicas of Chesapeake Bay blue crab) in 2010.

University of Maryland/University of Virginia (Football): *Tydings Trophy*

This rivalry has been played since 1919 and has gone uninterrupted since 1957. Separated by a mere 129 miles, Maryland has played Virginia more frequently than any other opponent. This rivalry was specifically protected when the ACC expanded to twelve teams, as the two schools were placed in separate divisions but designated as each other's permanent cross-divisional rival. The *Tydings Trophy*, named for Maryland alum Millard Tydings, was adopted in the 1920s but was retired in 1945 and never replaced. Unfortunately, this rivalry will likely be discontinued when Maryland makes the jump to the Big Ten in 2014.

UMass/University of New Hampshire (Football): *Colonial Clash*

A once intense FCS rivalry in the Northeast, Massachusetts and New Hampshire first met in 1897 and had an uninterrupted series from 1952 to 2011. UMass leads the overall series 43–28–3, but New Hampshire held a 14–9 advantage from 1990 on. The rivalry came to an end when UMass announced it was making the jump to FBS football in 2012.

University of Memphis/Southern Miss (Football): *Black & Blue Bowl*

Despite the many tectonic shifts that college football has seen over the past half century, Memphis and Southern Miss have never been far apart. This rivalry began in 1935 and has been played in nearly every season since 1952, with many of their meetings coming independent of any conference affiliation. The name *Black and Blue Bowl* refers both to the colors of each team, as well as the intensity of this rivalry over the years. It has been a conference game since the founding of Conference USA in 1996, but that could change when Memphis joins a new league in 2013.

Merchant Marine Academy/St. Lawrence University (Football): *Hoffman Cup*

This trophy got its start as a birthday present, as St. Lawrence grad Tom Hoffman created the cup to honor his father Richard, a graduate of the Merchant Marine Academy. It has been played annually since 2003.

Merchant Marine Academy/SUNY Maritime College (Football):
Seafaring Scuffle

The *Seafaring Scuffle* got its start in 2009 as a friendly rivalry between schools whose alumni often wind up working side-by-side around the world.

Miami University of Ohio/Ohio University (Multisport):
Battle of the Bricks

The *Battle of the Bricks* is an annual all-sports series between the Ohio University Bobcats and the Miami University RedHawks. Founded in 1804 and 1809 respectively, both Ohio and Miami are well known for their beautiful red brick campuses, as well as their competition in both the classroom and on the athletic field. The official Battle of the Bricks Series started in 2002–2003 as a means to further strengthen and promote the historic competitive rivalry between Ohio University and Miami University.

University of Michigan/The Ohio State University (Football):
The Big Game

This rivalry is one of many called the *Big Game*. Unlike most rivalry games, the winner of the annual game between Michigan and Ohio State does not receive a trophy for the triumph. Rather, there is often something much bigger on the line when these two teams match up, be it a conference title, a Rose Bowl berth or even a national championship. The two national powers have met every year since 1918, a streak which ranks 11th in NCAA Division I-A history for the longest uninterrupted series. Since 1935, the Michigan-Ohio State game has been played on the final Saturday of the Big Ten season. A gold miniature charm depicting a pair of football pants is given to all Ohio State players and coaches following an Ohio State victory over the Michigan Wolverines. The tradition began as the result of a comment to reporters by newly hired head coach Francis Schmidt on March 2, 1934: "How about Michigan? They put their pants on one leg at a time, the same as we do!" The first gold pants, which were a creation of Simon Lazarus (president of the Lazarus chain of department stores) and Herbert Levy, were awarded that year for a 34–0 defeat of the Wolverines.

University of Michigan/The Ohio State University (Track): *The Dual*

On January 19, 2008, the University of Michigan hosted the Ohio State University in an indoor dual track and field competition renewing college athletics greatest rivalry that began outdoors on May 18, 1907, in Ann Arbor and had not been contested since 1993. The teams now square off each year in one indoor dual meet in Ann Arbor, and one outdoor dual in Columbus, Ohio. Both programs have cultivated a century of great champions in the sport. While the dual meet rivalry was primarily contested in the 1920s thru the 1950s, the Wolverines and Buckeyes have met consistently at major invitationals, Big Ten championships, NCAA Championships and Olympic Games. As collegiate track and field has evolved, the time was right to renew this best of intercollegiate competition and team spirit. *The Dual* has added to the already storied history of UM–OSU athletic battles and created new legends for future Maize 'n Blue and Scarlet 'n Grey supporters to discuss and emulate. This meet provides a unique opportunity that only UM–OSU student athletes, coaches, and supporters can experience: a passion to compete head on against a respected rival who will give their best effort in an atmosphere of fair play and good sportsmanship. In addition, a traveling trophy, The *Dual Pennant*, is awarded to the winning team.

University of Michigan/Michigan State University (Football): *Paul Bunyan Trophy*

The annual Michigan–Michigan State game not only gives the winner state bragging rights, but also ownership of the mammoth *Paul Bunyan Trophy*. The four-foot wooden statue, donated by then Governor G. Mennen Williams in 1953, portrays the legendary figure astride an axe with feet planted on a map of the State of Michigan. Two flags—one with the Michigan "M" and the other with the Michigan State "S"—are planted on either side of Bunyan. A five-foot stand supports the statue.

University of Michigan/Michigan State University (Soccer): *Big Bear Trophy*

When the Wolverines and Spartans meet on the pitch, more than state pride is on the line. The two teams battle for the *Big Bear Trophy*, a wooden sculpture UM head coach Steve Burns purchased to commemorate the rivalry between the schools. The traveling hardware has been up for grabs in each regular season meeting between the two schools since 2000.

University of Michigan/Michigan State University (Volleyball): *State Pride Series*

The University of Michigan and Michigan State University share a long history of rivalries, in academics and athletics. To celebrate the volleyball rivalry, the two state of Michigan and Big Ten Conference institutions sponsor a *State Pride* season series with each university hosting a *State Pride Night* when the teams meet during the regular season. A state of Michigan flag bearing the motto "Tuebor" or "I will defend" serves as a symbol of the Michigan-Michigan State volleyball rivalry. The winner of the season's two head-to-head matches retains possession of the flag for the year. The flag flew above the State Capital in Lansing on September 18, 1990, the first season of the State Pride battle. In addition to the state flag, each school's winning year is listed on its half of the special Michigan–Michigan State banner which hangs in each university's home arena. A new chapter of the State Pride Series was written in 2005 when Michigan head coach Mark Rosen designed and built a custom trophy case for the original state flag and had each team's winning years engraved on its face. The winner of each State Pride Series holds the trophy in its possession until the following year's contest is decided.

University of Michigan/University of Minnesota (Football): *Little Brown Jug*

This tradition dates back to 1903 between Michigan–Minnesota. Michigan had won twenty-eight straight games going into their game against the Gophers (Minnesota had one of their best teams in history), so many were expecting a great game. 20,000 spectators watched the game in bleachers, atop telephone poles and trees, and when the Gophers scored a second half touchdown to tie the score 6–6, the crowd went wild (the game had to be called because there was so much pandemonium). Following the game, Minnesota custodian Oscar Munson carried an earthenware water jug, belonging to Michigan head coach Yost, to the office of L. J. Cooke, the head of the athletics department. They decided to keep the jug—still giddy from the thrilling tie—and painted on its side "Michigan Jug—Captured by Oscar, October 31,1903," and the score "Minnesota 6, Michigan 6." Michigan's Coach Yost sent a letter asking for Minnesota to return the jug. Cooke wrote back "if you want it, you'll have to win it." Dating back to 1909, the battle for the *Little Brown Jug* between Michigan and Minnesota is among the nation's oldest FBS trophy games. NCAA Division I-A football teams annually compete in over sixty-five regular season trophy games, and each of those games owes its beginning to the University of Michigan, the University of Minnesota, some misgivings about water and a thirty-cent, putty-colored jug.

University of Michigan/University of Minnesota (Tennis): *Little Brown Jug*

The sports rivalry between Michigan and Minnesota is hardly limited to the gridiron, with the tennis rivalry between the two schools being particularly intense. This led to the two schools creating a tennis version of the *Little Brown Jug* in 2006. Unlike the football version, this match-up is guaranteed to be played every single year.

Michigan State University/University of Minnesota (Ice Hockey): *Bessone–Mariucci Trophy*

The trophy is named after two coaches (Bessone at MSU and Mariucci at Minnesota). It consists of both team's logos underneath a metallic image of each legendary coach, with a stick and puck at the trophy's base.

Michigan State University/University of Notre Dame (Football): *Megaphone*

A rivalry that was started by geography and developed into something much greater, Michigan State and Notre Dame first met in 1897 and have met in almost every season since 1948. The *Megaphone Trophy*, which is painted blue on one side and green on the other, was first awarded the following year and has symbolized how the rivalry grew into one of the most balanced in college football in the ensuing years. But no conversation about this rivalry can happen without mentioning the 1966 Game of the Century, when the top-ranked Fighting Irish and the second ranked Spartans met in East Lansing and battled to a 10–10 tie after Notre Dame elected to run the final minute off the clock rather than go for the win. Notre Dame coach Ara Parseghian believed that the Fighting Irish's resume was such that the team could withstand a season ending tie and still be voted national champs, and the Irish and Spartans ended up splitting the title that year while also shutting out defending champ (and unbeaten) Alabama. Many consider this game to be the starting point of modern college football, as it created pressure on both Notre Dame and the Big Ten to adjust their rules on bowl games that resulted in both teams being shut out of the postseason. This game is also considered by historians to be what kick started the push for a college football playoff.

Michigan State University/Penn State (Football): *Land Grant Trophy*

In an odd case of history meeting sports, this trophy's name honors the Morrill Land Grant Act. The bill used the sale of public land to develop schools of agriculture, and both Michigan State and Penn State are land-grant universities. Perhaps the most forced of the Big Ten's many trophy games, Michigan State and Penn State were the two newest members of the Big Ten when the Nittany Lions joined the conference in 1993 and were therefore assigned to each other as permanent rivals by the league scheduling office. Neither Michigan State nor Penn State has a particular attachment to this rivalry and little effort was made to preserve it when the conference went to divisional play in 2011.

Michigan Technological University/Northern Michigan University (Football): *Miner's Cup*

Isolated on the state of Michigan's upper peninsula, Michigan Tech and Northern Michigan have been playing each other on a regular basis since 1921. The *Miner's Cup*, created by the Michigan Tech Athletics Department and its Army ROTC, was added in 2002 and consists of an antique miner's helmet mounted on a wooden base.

Middle Tennessee State University/Troy University (Football): *The Palladium Trophy*

These two programs met eight times from 1936 to 1953, with Middle Tennessee winning each and every match-up. It did not become a real rivalry until the series was rekindled forty-six years later, when Troy recorded its first victory over the Blue Raiders and began the push to Division I-A football status. In 2003, the *Palladium Trophy* was added to intensify the rivalry and pay tribute to each school's mascot being rooted in Greek mythology. It consists of a wooden replica of the statue of Athena that legend says fell from the heavens into the city of Troy but was stolen by the Raider Odysseus during the Trojan War.

Miles College/Stillman College (Football): *Steel City Classic*

A rivalry between HBCUs in the state of Alabama, Miles and Stillman played each other regularly from 1930 to 1950 but was interrupted when Stillman elected to drop football. They revived their program in 1999, and the rivalry between the two schools was turned into the *Steel City Classic* in Birmingham in 2001. Legion Field played host to the next six games between the two schools before the Classic was ended in 2006.

Millsaps College/Mississippi College (Football): *Backyard Brawl*

The Division III version of the *Backyard Brawl* dates back to 1920 but had to be cancelled in 1960 after a fight broke out during a basketball game between the two schools the year before—over a stolen flag from a Millsaps fraternity. The two schools did not play each other in any sport for the next several years, and the football rivalry would not be restored until the turn of the millennium.

University of Minnesota/University of Minnesota-Duluth (Women's Ice Hockey): *Northern Star Trophy*

Since the University of Minnesota-Duluth joined the Western Collegiate Hockey Association in 1999, they have participated in a trophy game against the Gophers. The *Northern Star Trophy* is passed to the team who sweeps a regular season series. If the series is split, the trophy remains with the previous year's winner.

University of Minnesota/Penn State (Football): *Governors' Victory Bell*

Similar to *Floyd of Rosedale*, the *Governors' Victory Bell* was also founded by a pair of state governors. This trophy started with the first game of the series in 1993, as a way to signify the inaugural Big Ten game for the Nittany Lions. With the addition of the Governors' Victory Bell, the Gophers have four active trophy rivalries on their schedule, more than any other college football program in the country.

Minnesota State University/St. Cloud State University (Football): *The Trainer's Kit*

The oldest Division II rivalry in the Land of 10,000 Lakes, Minnesota State and St. Cloud State have a near continuous rivalry since the two schools first met on the gridiron in 1923. In 1978, the rivalry added a *Traveling Trainer's Kit* as a trophy that is painted in MSU purple on one side and St. Cloud red on the other. ESPN's Jeff Merron declared it to be the second most bizarre rivalry trophy in college football in 2004.

University of Missouri/University of Nebraska: *Missouri–Nebraska Victory Bell*

As the only major football programs in either state, Nebraska and Missouri always had a shared connection that was unlike any other in the Midwest. The two schools first met on the gridiron in 1892 and played on an annual basis from 1922–2010 in a rivalry marked by stretches of extreme dominance on both sides. Nebraska controlled the early days of the rivalry, winning twenty-two of the first thirty-one meetings. But Missouri would take control during the dark ages of Nebraska football, and by 1962 the Cornhuskers' lead was down to just 28–25–3. Missouri would remain a thorn in Nebraska's side for the next sixteen years, but the Cornhuskers finally took control in 1979 and would win the next twenty-four meetings. The *Victory Bell*, which was taken by Nebraska fraternity members in 1892 (the year of the first Nebraska–Mizzou match-up), was adopted as a trophy in 1926 and is engraved with the letters "M" and "N" on either side. But this rivalry appears to be another casualty of realignment, as Nebraska's departure to the Big Ten (much to the annoyance of Missouri) and the Tigers' subsequent departure to the SEC resulted in the cancellation of the series in 2010. Nebraska won the last meeting, so the Victory Bell is likely to reside in Lincoln for a very long time.

Missouri Southern State University/Pittsburg State University (Football): *Miner's Helmet & Ax*

Another example of the intense state rivalry between Kansas and Missouri, these two teams have played since Missouri Southern became a four-year school in 1968. The *Miner's Bowl Trophy* was added in 1986 and has been monopolized by Pittsburg State, who have lost the trophy on only a single occasion. This game is a part of the nine-sport *Sonic Trophy Series* between the two schools.

University of Mobile/Spring Hill College (Basketball): *Badger Brawl*

These schools are located just eleven miles apart. Before the basketball games, on the SHC side, it's a week-long festival known as *Badger Brawl* during which the students have dances, concerts, pep rallies, and other events on campus leading up to the big game. The Badger Brawl also extends into other sports between the two schools, including a head-to-head duel for supremacy in cross-country.

University of Montana/Montana State University (Football): *The Great Divide Trophy*

When Montana State visits Montana for a football game, about 40 percent of Missoula's population turns-out (25,217). Every home game with this rival has been sold-out since 1986. These two began playing in 1897 and have the fourth oldest rivalry in FCS football. The trophy, which was created in 2001, is a nod to the two teams being on opposite sides of the Continental Divide.

Morehouse College/Tuskegee University (Football): *Morehouse–Tuskegee Classic*

The grand daddy of all HBCU Classics, the rivalry between these two schools dates back to 1902, but only became the *Morehouse–Tuskegee Classic* in 1936. Held annually in Columbus, Georgia, the Classic serves as a fundraiser for scholarships to allow young men and women to attend both schools. It also includes an annual parade, a golf tournament, and a battle of the bands competition.

College of Mount St. Joseph/Thomas More College (Football): *Bridge Bowl*

Both of these programs were birthed in 1990, which naturally led to the creation of this Ohio–Kentucky border battle. The trophy features a half of a football situated over a suspension bridge.

University of Mount Union/University of Wisconsin–Whitewater (Football): *Stagg Bowl Foes*

It is not a rivalry in the traditional sense, as Mount Union and Wisconsin–Whitewater have met exactly one time in the regular season in the entire history of the two programs. Instead, this is a rivalry that was bred from success, as these two teams met in the Division III Championship Game seven consecutive years from 2005–2011.

Murray State University/Western Kentucky University (Football): *Red Belt Trophy*

For much of the twentieth century, the annual match-up between Murray State and Western Kentucky was one of the marquee events in the Bluegrass State. These two schools first met in 1931, and by 1939 the game had become the annual regular season finale for both teams. The rivalry gained a trophy in 1978, when WKU trainer Bill Edwards realized he had forgotten his belt while at a district meeting and had to borrow one from Murray State's Tom Simmons. After the meeting, Edwards told Simmons that he could have the belt back if Murray State won the football game that year. The annual rivalry came to an end when Western Kentucky left the Ohio Valley Conference for the Gateway Football Conference, and it is unlikely to ever again be played on a regular basis now that the Hilltoppers have moved up to FBS status.

Naval Academy/University of Notre Dame (Football): *Emerald Isle Classic*

Navy and Notre Dame have been playing each other annually since 1927, making this one of college football's longest-running nonconference series. They played the game most recently (in 2012) in Ireland, with the influx of fans going to Ireland for the game, the largest for any single-day sporting event in Ireland's history.

Naval Academy/SMU (Football): *Gansz Trophy*

Southern Methodist University has long had great respect for the football team from the United States Naval Academy, with the two teams scheduling numerous home-and-home match-ups since the first meeting between the two teams in 1930. In 2009, the rivalry incorporated the *Gansz Trophy*, which is named after a former Midshipmen linebacker who later served on the SMU coaching staff.

University of New Mexico/New Mexico State University (Football): *Battle of I-25/Maloof Trophy*

The *Battle of I-25* features New Mexico–New Mexico State. Although these aren't very prominent college football games, their rivalry is one of the oldest on record, with the first meeting between the two schools occurring in 1894. The teams play for the *Maloof Trophy*. When this game is hosted by New Mexico, a *Red Rally* is held the Thursday night before the game. A bonfire engulfs a twenty-five-foot replica of rival New Mexico State's *Pistol Pete* and Lobos captains also speak to the pep rally crowd. This rivalry is also referred to as the *Rio Grande Rivalry*.

University of New Mexico/New Mexico State University/UTEP: *Rio Grande Champion*

Before the breakup of the Western Athletic Conference, these three schools often played each other, with the winner of the series among the three schools earning the title of the *Rio Grande Champion*.

New Mexico State University/UTEP (Football): *Silver Spade & Brass Spittoon*

When the Miners and the Aggies meet during football season, the winner receives a pair of traveling trophies—the *Silver Spade* and the *Brass Spittoon*. The first spade used for this purpose was an old prospector's shovel dug up from an abandoned mine in the Organ Mountains near Las Cruces in 1947. The current Silver Spade was initiated by UTEP Student Association in 1955, and each year the score of the game is engraved on the blade. The Brass Spittoon, officially known as the *Mayor's Cup*, came into existence in 1982 when the mayors of the universities' cities decided to present another traveling trophy to the winner of the NMSU–UTEP game. The rivalry was first played in 1913 and has since been christened the *Battle of I-10*, after the interstate that connects the two campuses.

Newberry College/Presbyterian College (Football): *Bronze Derby*

The winner of this annual football game received the *Bronze Derby*, which actually got its start as a basketball trophy following a heated game during the 1946–1947 match-up. Prior to the start of the game, Presbyterian students unveiled a banner that read "Beat H . . . Out of Newberry" on the wall over the Blue Hose student section. A group of Newberry students climbed the outside of the gym wall and stole the banner, which Presbyterian fans demanded to be returned after the game. Their request was denied, and the resulting melee saw a derby hat stolen from the head of a Presbyterian student. After a discussion between the two schools, the hat was bronzed and turned into a rivalry trophy, and during the early years it was exchanged after every sporting event. After a few years, however, it was decided that the Bronze Derby would only be awarded to the winner of the annual Thanksgiving Day football game, which was later moved to earlier in the season in order to avoid conflict with the Division II playoffs. The series, which originated in 1913, has been put on hold while Presbyterian transitions to the Division I level but hopefully will return in the near future.

Nicholls State University/Southeastern Louisiana University (Football): *River Bell Trophy*

This rivalry originally began in 1972 and was played on an annual basis until Southeastern Louisiana dropped football in 1985. The Lions brought back football in 2005, and the rivalry resumed as if it had never stopped. It is traditionally the final game of the season for each school, which are separated by less than 100 miles in Louisiana. The winner of the game receives the *River Bell Trophy*, which is a ship's bell under a wooden arch.

Nicholls State University/Texas State University (Football): *Battle for the Paddle*

It is not often that a rivalry game gets its name from a mild natural disaster. Nicholls State and Texas State, who first started playing in 1980, were set to meet in San Marcos in 1998 when heavy rains flooded the Texas State football field and resulted in the postponement of the game. Both teams joked that they would need to use a boat and a paddle in order to get to the game, and from that moment on the rivalry was known as the *Battle for the Paddle*. This rivalry, which originated in 1980, met its end when Texas State elected to make the jump to FBS football. Nicholls State, however, gets the last laugh, as the series concluded with the Colonels holding 16–14 edge.

Norfolk State University/Virginia State University (Football): *Labor Day Classic (Virginia)*

Two of Virginia's most celebrated HBCUs, Norfolk State and Virginia State have met every year since 1963. The rivalry morphed into the *Labor Day Classic* in 1991 and became a fixture of the opening weekend of lower-division college football for many years. Unfortunately, time may have run out on this Classic. An NCAA bylaw prohibits Virginia State, which is at the Division II level, from starting their season before Labor Day and resulted in the cancellation of the series in 2013. It remains to be seen whether or not these two schools can continue their rivalry as a regular series.

North Carolina A&T/North Carolina Central University (Football): *Aggie–Eagle Classic*

The two largest HBCUs in the state, NC A&T and NC Central met for the first time in 1924 and have played almost every season since. In 1994, the game was transformed into the *Aggie–Eagle Classic* and was moved to Carter-Finley Stadium in Raleigh, which is the regular home of North Carolina State University. A&T would go on to win ten of the twelve Classics, which ended in 2005 after the contract with the city of Raleigh was not renewed. After a one-year gap, the rivalry resumed in 2007 using a home-and-home format and gained greater importance when NC Central rejoined the MEAC in 2010.

North Carolina A&T/South Carolina State University (Football): *Rivalry Classic*

One of many border wars between their respective states, North Carolina A&T and South Carolina State first met on the gridiron in 1924, and this game has been an intense Mid-Eastern Athletic Conference battle since the conference was founded in 1970.

North Central College/Wheaton College (Football): *Little Brass Bell*

While these two schools have been playing since 1900, the series is as much a battle between rival towns as anything else. The *Little Brass Bell*, which was brought to the area by a New England family that settled in the area in 1839, became a symbol of the battle between Naperville and Wheaton over the location of the new DuPage County Courthouse. Wheaton successfully gained leadership, but Naperville refused to turn over county court records. This resulted in a raid of the courthouse by Wheaton, and the Little Brass Bell was taken along with the documents. Eventually, the bell fell into possession of a local farmer whose two sons wound up attending each school. The son attending North Central inherited the bell, thus turning it into the subject of night raids and collegiate hijinks until it was hidden in a Naperville home by the North Central brother. It turned up again in the early 1940s, and in 1946 it was adopted as the trophy for the annual North Central–Wheaton football game. North Central won twenty-two of the first twenty-nine games between the two schools prior to the Little Brass Bell trophy. Wheaton has dominated the series since.

North Dakota State University/South Dakota State University (Football): *Dakota Marker*

These two border rivals have played over a hundred times since their first meeting in 1903, and the rivalry gained added importance in 2004 when both schools left their in-state brethren behind and elected to make the jump from Division II to Division I. The Bison and Jackrabbits marked the occasion by adopting the *Dakota Marker*, which is a model replica of the quartzite monuments that marked the original border between North and South Dakota in 1891.

Northwest Missouri State University/Pittsburg State University (Football): *Fall Classic*

Arguably the biggest rivalry in Division II, NW Missouri State and Pittsburg State (Kansas) have been engaged in a border war since 1932 and have been playing on an annual basis since 1973. In 2002, the rivalry was kicked up a notch when it became the *Fall Classic* and was moved to Arrowhead Stadium in Kansas City. With crowds upwards of 20,000 people, the Fall Classic is annually one of Division II's best-attended football games. This rivalry could assume even more significance in the future, as the demise of the Kansas-Missouri rivalry leaves this match-up as the biggest game between two states whose rivalry extends well beyond the gridiron.

Northwest Missouri State University/Truman State University (Football): *Old Hickory Stick*

Since 1931, teams of Northwest Missouri State University and Truman State University have played for possession of a thirty-inch piece of hickory. It represents one of the most intense rivalries in college football. The *Old Hickory Stick* game has the distinction of being one of the oldest traveling trophy games in Division II college football. In 1930, U. W. Lamkin, president of Northwest Missouri State University, sent President Eugene Fair of Truman State University the stick of wood that would soon receive the fitting name the Old Hickory Stick. President Lamkin found the stick on the very farm where Fair was born, located within the Northwest

Missouri State district. The stick had been turned in the woodworking shop at Northwest, and the lettering on the stick listed the scores of every football game between the two colleges from 1908 to 1930. The symbolism of the Old Hickory Stick is that both schools can claim ownership of the trophy, since it was found in an area connected to both Northwest and Truman. In 1931, the annual football game between the two schools was inaugurated as a means of determining who would own the trophy for the following year. After the game, the winner dips one end of the stick in paint of their school color.

University of Notre Dame/Purdue University (Football): *Shillelagh Trophy*

It is easy to see why Purdue is Notre Dame's oldest annual foe, as the two Indiana-based schools first met on the gridiron in 1896, and the game is one of the most played rivalries in college football between teams that have never been conference foes. It became a yearly rivalry in 1946, and the *Shillelag Trophy*—a club from Ireland donated by Notre Dame fan Joe McLaughlin—was first presented in 1957. While this series is historically one-sided in favor of Notre Dame, the Irish have played Purdue more frequently than any other Big Ten opponent, making this the most likely of those rivalries to be saved should the Irish ever join a football conference as a full member.

University of Notre Dame/Stanford University (Football): *Legends Trophy*

The first meeting between these schools was in 1925 and played an important role in Notre Dame's history, as the Irish's victory in the Rose Bowl that year resulted in the program's first-ever national championship. It also may have inspired coach Knute Rockne to make trips to the Los Angeles area on a regular basis, leading the Irish into a wonderfully long series with USC. But the modern series between Notre Dame and Stanford began much later after Notre Dame's scholastic profile began to rise, resulting in a push for the school to play more opponents with similarly high academic standards. As perhaps the best combination of academics and athletics in college sports, Stanford was a natural fit and began playing a home-and-home series with the Irish in 1988. Originally, this series was traditionally played during the first Saturday in October. This was partially changed for the BCS era, as the two schools adjusted their schedules so that they ended the regular season against each other whenever Stanford hosted the game. This allows the Fighting Irish to end every season in California, with USC hosting Notre Dame in the years when the Irish host the Cardinal. The winner of this contest receives the *Legends Trophy*, which is an Irish crystal chalice on a California redwood base.

University of Notre Dame/USC (Football): *Bejeweled Shillelagh*

Widely regarded as the finest intersectional rivalry in all of sports, Notre Dame and USC first met on the gridiron in 1926 and have played annually in every non-WWII year since. Legend has it that this rivalry was the result of a conversation between the wives of Notre Dame coach Knute Rockne and USC athletic director Gwynn Wilson. USC, looking to make a name for itself on the national stage, after ascending to PCC power status, sought out Notre Dame as a national rival when the Irish were playing at Nebraska on Thanksgiving Day. Mr. Rockne initially resisted the idea due to the travel involved, as this was the days before teams could easily travel by air. Mrs. Rockne, however, was sold by Mrs. Wilson on the idea of a November trip to sunny Southern California every other year. Another version of the story claims that Rockne became interested in making trips to Los Angeles when the Irish's appearance in the 1925 Rose Bowl was well received by west coast alumni. Notre Dame began prohibiting bowl trips the following year in an effort to fight the growing commercialization of the sport, so Rockne added a home-and-home series with USC in order to justify trips out West. Whatever the reason, the decision to keep the rivalry proved to be a boon for both schools, considering they have won a combined twenty-one championships since the series began. On the end of the jeweled shillelagh (awarded to the winner) is engraved, "From the Emerald Isle." The victor of the Notre Dame–USC game gains year-long possession of the trophy. Initial presentation of the shillelagh was in 1952.

Occidental College/Pomona-Pitzer Colleges (Football): *Sagehen Burial*

From the 1930s to the 1950s, after each football victory over Pomona College, a replica of Pomona's mascot—the *Sagehen*—had a funeral and formal burial on the Occidental campus. This took place on the Monday after the game—a day designated a campus holiday. The event typically began with a service in Alumni Chapel, followed by a procession to the gravesite, where members of the football team served as pallbearers, while dressed in black gowns. Appropriate words were spoken during the service and at the grave. In 1941 the alumni associations from both schools got together and came up with the idea of playing for the *Drum*, which is awarded to the winner of the annual Occidental–Pomona-Pitzer football game.

Occidental College/Whittier College (Football): *Battle for the Shoes*

Since 1946, the Poets and Tigers have played for a pair of *bronzed cleats*. These cleats were worn by 1940 Whittier graduate Myron Claxton, in a rivalry game that has grown to be called the *Battle for the Shoes*. Occidental and Whittier first met on the gridiron in 1907 and have played more than 100 times since, making this rivalry one of the oldest in Division III.

University of Oklahoma/University of Missouri (Football): *Tiger-Sooner Peace Pipe*

This rivalry got its start in 1902, just as the Midwest was starting to find its footing on the gridiron. It became a yearly event beginning in 1910, and the rivalry increased in importance when Oklahoma joined Missouri as a member of the MVIAA (later the Big Eight) in 1919. The *Peace Pipe trophy* was first awarded in 1929, but it was replaced when Mizzou alum Dr. John S. Knight donated a genuine Indian peace pipe that was believed to be over a century old. Unfortunately, the pipe was lost by the Oklahoma athletic department during the mid-1970s and has yet to be recovered. This rivalry ceased to be a yearly event in 1996, as the Big Eight morphed into the Big 12 and the two teams were placed in separate divisions. Missouri's departure to the SEC in 2012 makes it unlikely that the peace pipe will ever be awarded again, even if it were recovered. But considering Oklahoma holds a 65–25–5 lead in the overall series, perhaps it is for the best.

University of Oklahoma/Oklahoma State University (Various Sports): *Bedlam Series*

Bedlam. It's been the word of choice to describe the Oklahoma–Oklahoma State rivalry since the very first football game between the two schools in 1904. That game, played in cold and windy conditions, saw a punt carry over the Cowboys' return man and roll down a hill into an icy creek. Both teams dove in to recover the ball, and the Sooners eventually came up with it and scored a touchdown as a result. Why Oklahoma fought so hard for that ball in a game in which they won 75–0 is a mystery, but the tradition of craziness between these two rivals was born. It eventually came to incorporate a total of seventeen other sports, with the wrestling matches between the two national powerhouses being a marquee event. The *Bedlam Series* was officially formalized in 1999, with the winner of each head-to-head competition receiving points. In sports where there is no head-to-head match-up, the Big 12 final standings are used instead. No one sport can dominate the rivalry, which is a good thing, considering that Oklahoma has a nearly five-to-one lead in the all-time series on the gridiron.

University of Oklahoma/University of Texas (Football): *Red River Rivalry/Three Trophies*

First played in 1900, the showdown between the Longhorns and Sooners—known far and wide as the *Red River Rivalry*—has become one of college football's best and most bitter rivalries. Though the Oklahoma-Texas series officially began in 1900, the game truly arrived in 1929—the year it was first played in the neutral-site city of Dallas. The city is located approximately halfway between Norman, Oklahoma (home of the Sooners) and Austin, Texas (home of the Longhorns). The storied old Cotton Bowl has played host to the game since 1937. On game day—which is always scheduled in early October, during the Texas State Fair—the stadium is split in half, with Texas fans on one side of the fifty-yard line and Sooners fans on the other. The scene is similar to the one that plays out each year in Jacksonville, Florida, where Florida battles Georgia in another classic neutral-site rivalry. The good news is that the Red River Rivalry figures to remain in Dallas for a few years to come. In 2007, Oklahoma, Texas, and the City of Dallas came to an agreement that would keep the game in the city at least through 2015. The schools had complained about the state of the Cotton Bowl, and had publicly contemplated making the rivalry into a traditional home-and-home affair. The agreement increased the payout to each school for each game to $850,000 and also committed Dallas to a massive renovation of the Cotton Bowl. The Red River Rivalry gets its name from—what else—the Red River, which separates the states of Texas and Oklahoma. For decades, the game was called the *Red River Shootout*, but starting in 2005, the name was officially changed to the SBC Red River Rivalry. The next year, it was changed once more, to the AT&T Red River Rivalry. No matter what it's called, however, this much is certain: the game is always a knock-down, drag-out affair between two schools that truly don't like each other. The series has been made especially bitter because of the fact that, dating all the way back to Oklahoma's Bud Wilkinson glory days in the 1950s, much of the Sooners' top talent has been recruited out of Texas. As former Oklahoma coach Barry Switzer once told *USA Today*: "No game carries with it the atmosphere, the excitement, the energy level that the Oklahoma-Texas game does. When you hit the floor of the Cotton Bowl, there's electricity. And if you don't feel it, you ought to have your saliva checked." The winner of the Red River Rivalry takes home, not just one but, three different trophies. The oldest is the *Golden Hat*, a bronzed ten-gallon hat, which is given to the athletic department of the winning school. The *Red River Rivalry Trophy*, first created in 2003, is given to the student government of the winning school. And the *Governors' Trophy* is exchanged by the governors of each state.

Old Dominion University/College of William & Mary (Football): *Battle for the Silver Mace*

When Old Dominion recently revived its football program after a seventy-year absence, one of the first things it strived to do was start up a rivalry with nearby William & Mary—a longtime rival in numerous other sports. The two met for the first time in 2010, and the following season saw the creation of a replica of the historic *Norfolk Mace* serve as the trophy. Alas, this has proven to be a very short-lived rivalry, as Old Dominion's pending move to Conference USA will bring an end to this series in 2014.

Ole Miss/Mississippi State University (Football): *Egg Bowl/Golden Egg Trophy*

The most prominent rivalry in the Magnolia State, Ole Miss and Mississippi State have been playing each other since 1901. Mississippi State dominated the early days of the rivalry, winning seventeen of the first twenty-three meetings and putting together a thirteen-game winning streak heading into the 1925 match-up in Starkville. So when Ole Miss pulled off a 7–6 upset, excited Rebels fans were in such a frenzy that they rushed the field and tried to tear down the goalposts, much to the chagrin of Bulldog fans. In order to avoid further property damage, the two schools created the *Golden Egg*, a trophy that has been awarded to the winner since. That 1926 meeting also marked the end of Mississippi State's dominance in the rivalry, as Ole Miss has won the *Egg Bowl* 67 percent of the time since the trophy was instituted.

Oral Roberts University/University of Tulsa (Basketball):
Mayor's Cup

This hoops battle for city supremacy began in 1974 and is known for its long winning streaks, with Oral Roberts taking eight in a row from 1976–1980 and Tulsa winning twenty-four of the next twenty-seven over the next two decades. For many seasons, this once was a rare nonconference rivalry that was played on a yearly home-and-home basis. However the two schools have not met twice in the same season since 1992–1993.

University of Oregon/Oregon State University (Football):
Civil War/Platypus Trophy

In the oldest college football rivalry in the Pacific Northwest, Oregon, and Oregon State have been engaged in a *Civil War* since they first met in 1894. This rivalry has seen both the lowest-of-lows and highest-of-highs: the 1983 game, commonly referred to as the *Toilet Bowl*, featured sixteen turnovers and four missed field goals and was the last college football game to end in a 0–0 tie. On the other side of the coin, the 2009 game—a 37–33 Oregon victory—was the first in series history in which the winner was guaranteed a spot in the Rose Bowl. The winner of this game receives the *Platypus Trophy*, which is an animal that depicts the features of both a duck and a beaver. For three years, from 1959 to 1961, the trophy was awarded to the winning school. The trophy was lost for more than forty years before being rediscovered in 2005 and proposed as the game's unofficial trophy in 2007. It is currently awarded to the alumni association of the winning school.

Philadelphia Big 5 (Basketball): *Basketball Round Robin*

Philadelphia's Big 5 are LaSalle, Penn, St. Joe's, Temple, and Villanova. The Big 5 always played each other from 1954 until recently in the musty, high-ceilinged Palestra on Penn's campus. Now versus all the round-robin games being played at the Palestra, only the Penn home games (and occasional double headers) are. And, with Philadelphia's well-known reputation as the "City of Brotherly Taunting," there isn't much love lost between the teams and their fans. Among the most entertaining parts of the rivalries, for many years, were the rollouts, banners brought in by fans that often include unprintable insults.

University of Pittsburgh/West Virginia University (Football):
Backyard Brawl

One of the Rust Belt's most legendary college football rivalries, the *Backyard Brawl* traces its origins all the way back to 1895 as both Pittsburgh and West Virginia (separated by seventy-five miles) looked to fill their schedules with local rivals. Pittsburgh dominated the rivalry for the first half of the twentieth century, helped by the fact that they hosted the vast majority of games. Because of this, Panthers faithful often thought of Penn State and Notre Dame as their primary rivals, and considered West Virginia to be more of an afterthought. But this rivalry became far more competitive when it switched to a home-and-home format in 1962, with West Virginia actually having a slight current advantage in the head-to-head series. The Backyard Brawl became one of the marquee events on the Big East calendar when both teams joined the conference for football in 1991, and as a result, the game was moved to the end of the season in order to have maximum impact on the conference standings. No game in series history was bigger than the 100th game, as Pitt's 13–9 upset knocked the second ranked Mountaineers out of the BCS Championship hunt. Sadly, this is another rivalry that has been lost to recent conference realignment. The writing was on the wall when Pitt announced it was leaving for the ACC and was officially cancelled when West Virginia jumped to the Big 12. But considering the popularity of the game with both alumni bases, you shouldn't be surprised if the Backyard Brawl ends-up staging a return at some point in the future.

Prairie View A&M/Texas Southern University (Football):
Labor Day Classic (Texas)

Separated by a mere fifty miles down I-290, Prairie View A&M and Texas Southern had played each other for over thirty years when the two schools decided to take their rivalry up a notch. In 1984, this game joined the ranks of HBCU Classics when it was moved to the beginning of the season, and since then it has been played on Labor Day weekend during most seasons.

Rensselaer Polytechnic Institute/Union College (Ice Hockey):
Governor's Cup

This hockey rivalry began in 2006 and was intended to increase interest in the ECAC Hockey League. Rensselaer and Union participate in the tournament each year, and two other teams (usually from the ECAC Hockey League) are also invited to complete the field.

Rensselaer Polytechnic Institute/Union College (Football): *Dutchman's Shoes*

One of the oldest rivalries in Division III, Rensselaer Polytechnic and Union College have played since 1886, and have the oldest football rivalry in the state of New York. The *Dutchman's Shoes*, named after the Union mascot, were adopted as a trophy in 1950 and have not left Union College very often in this rivalry.

Rensselaer Polytechnic Institute/Worcester Polytechnic Institute (Football): *The Transit Trophy*

Believe it or not, Union is not the only team that RPI has faced on more than 100 occasions. They also have a history against border rival Worcester Polytechnic that dates back to 1890, and this battle of engineers is far more evenly matched historically than the one with Union. The *Transit Trophy*, named for both schools' history of engineering, was adopted in 1980.

Rhodes College/Sewanee (Football): *Edmund Orgill Trophy*

One of the oldest rivalries in the Deep South, Rhodes and Sewanee first met on the gridiron in 1899 and have played for the *Edmund Orgill Trophy* since 1954. Orgill had close ties to both schools, having been a trustee at Rhodes and Chairman of the Board of Regents at Sewanee.

Rice University/SMU (Football): *Mayors' Cup*

SMU's first game against Rice was not the prettiest of affairs, as the Owls handed the Mustangs—in just their second year of existence at the time—a 146–3 defeat. Thankfully, none of the games since then have come close to that ugliness, and Rice–SMU has turned into one of football's most enduring rivalries. Originally, a match-up of the two smallest SWC schools, Rice and SMU have maintained their rivalry through several conference changes and have kept things very evenly matched throughout the years. In 1998, it became the *Battle for the Mayors' Cup,* named in honor of the mayors of both Dallas and Houston. Unfortunately, this rivalry has recently been put in danger, as SMU is bound for the Big East and has no immediate plans to add Rice to future schedules.

University of Richmond/College of William & Mary (Football): *Capital Cup*

Many people refer to North Carolina–Virginia as one of the South's oldest rivalries since the series began in 1892. But Richmond–William & Mary, which started in 1898 and has actually been played on more occasions, also is among the oldest rivalries. A mere fifty miles separates these rivals. For many years, this game was often referred to as the *I-64 Bowl* after the interstate that connects the two schools. It was renamed the *Capital Cup* in 2009.

University of Rochester/St. John Fisher College (Football): *Courage Bowl*

Since this series began in 1989, it has been defined by two very distinct periods: Rochester won each of the first seven games, including the first two of what became a yearly rivalry in 2000–2001. St. John Fisher has won each game since, including a perfect record in the game since it became the *Courage Bowl* in 2005.

Sam Houston State University/Stephen F. Austin State University: *Battle of the Piney Woods*

One of the oldest Lone Star State rivalries that does not involve former SWC schools, Sam Houston State and Stephen F. Austin first faced each other in 1923 and have played each other in every non-WWII year since. There is a strong military tradition with both universities, as each school's ROTC members participate in a relay to bring the ball to the host stadium prior to game time. Originally, the winner of this game received a pair of Colt Walker Pistols as a trophy. But these pistols have since been lost, and in 2007 a new trophy that features replica pistols nailed to a twenty-one-pound cedar tombstone was created.

San Jose State University/Stanford University (Football): *Bill Walsh Legacy Game*

Everybody knows that Stanford has an annual nonconference game with Notre Dame, but very few realize that the Cardinal have another rival outside the Pac-12. San Jose State, which is located about 20 miles down I-280, has been a fixture on Stanford's schedule since 1900, though the Cardinal have a commanding lead in the series thanks in part to hosting all but four match-ups between the two schools. Ironically enough, the most competitive stretch of this rivalry happened during the 1979–1982 seasons, when John Elway was quarterback at Stanford. Then again, considering Jack Elway was coaching the Spartans at the time, perhaps it should not have been too surprising that father got the better of son. The game is named in tribute of the legendary Bill Walsh, a San Jose State grad who had two stints as the Stanford football coach.

SMU/TCU (Football): *Iron Skillet*

In 1915, a mere four years after the university's founding in Dallas, SMU made their debut on the football field. Their very first opponent was none other than TCU, who welcomed the Mustangs to Fort Worth with a 43–0 beating. The two schools have been at each other's throats since, creating one of the Southwest Conference's legendary rivalries and keeping the game on the schedule even after the schools went their separate ways in conference affiliation. While this game no longer has the end of season prestige it held during the SWC's heyday, it is still one of college football's most intense September match-ups. The *Iron Skillet* was adopted as a trophy in 1946, when SMU fans were frying frog legs as a joke before the game began. TCU fans understandably took offense and wound up taking both the skillet and the legs, saying that the winner would get to keep them when the final horn rang. The Horned Frogs would go on to win, and the skillet has been a trophy since then.

Southern Miss/Tulane University (Football): *The Bell*

Separated by 115 miles, Southern Miss and Tulane became rivals in 1979 as a way of filling out their respective independent schedules. The series was played in each of the next twenty-eight seasons and became an important rivalry for both schools as they entered Conference USA. For a short period of time, it was the longest continuous series for either team. A reconfiguration of the league turned this game into a two-every-four-years' event, though the current instability in Conference USA could lead to that changing in the very near future.

St. John's University Minnesota/University of St. Thomas (Football): *The Holy Grail*

Arguably one of the best sports rivalries in Division III, the Tommies and the Johnnies have been battling for state supremacy since 1901 and are the reigning powerhouses in the Minnesota Intercollegiate Athletic Conference. St. John's and St. Thomas have played every season since 1952, which was one year before the legendary John Gagliardi took over the St. John's program and turned the Johnnies into a juggernaut. When Gagliardi first interviewed for the job, the final question he was asked was whether or not he could beat St. Thomas. After racking up a 43–17 record against the Tommies, on his way to an NCAA-record 489 victories in his 60-year career, it's safe to say that he was successful. The winner of this game receives the Holy Grail trophy.

Syracuse University/West Virginia University (Football): *Schwartzwalder Trophy*

Another longtime rivalry that was lost to expansion, Syracuse and West Virginia first met in 1945 and scheduled each other on a yearly basis from 1955 to 2011. This rivalry began as a way for these longtime independents to fill their football schedules, but continued when both teams joined the Big East for football in 1991. It was rare that both teams were good at the same time, meaning this rivalry is defined by long stretches of dominance by one or the other. The trophy, which is named after former Syracuse head coach and WVU alum Ben Schwartzwalder, was added in 1993 and was in the Mountaineer trophy case for eleven of its nineteen seasons of existence. Many thought that this rivalry would be gone for good when Syracuse announced it was jumping to the ACC and West Virginia responded by heading to the Big 12, however, it received an unexpected revival during the 2012 postseason, with the Orange handing the Mountaineers a 38–14 pasting in the Pinstripe Bowl.

University of Texas/Texas A&M (Football): *Lonestar Showdown*

One of the great travesties of conference realignment is that the *Lone Star Showdown*—the most famous of all rivalries in the state of Texas—is no longer an annual event. From 1894 to 2011, Texas and Texas A&M met on the gridiron 118 times, giving the two schools the third most frequent rivalry in all of FBS football. It was almost always the final regular season game for both teams, frequently falling on Thanksgiving Day. This game was also the de facto Southwest Conference Championship for many years, considering the Longhorns and Aggies won or shared forty-four SWC titles between them. Not much changed when the Southwest Conference merged with the Big 12, though Texas and Texas A&M found themselves facing tougher competition from the rest of the league than ever before.

But this was not always the most evenly matched rivalry, with Texas holding a two-to-one edge in the overall series and winning five or more in a row on multiple occasions. That gave many the impression that Texas A&M was the little brother school, which Aggies faithful long resented, and caused them to look elsewhere for conference membership. When the SEC (the Aggies' preferred choice even before the fall of the SWC) finally offered a way out, Texas A&M did not hesitate to leave this rivalry behind. It seemed only fitting that the Texas band played the song "Thanks for the Memories" at halftime of their final meeting, only to hand the Aggies one final heart-breaking loss to end the series.

University of Texas/Texas Tech (Football): *Chancellor's Spurs*

Because Texas Tech is a relatively young university, the rivalry between the Red Raiders and the state's flagship program is a fairly recent phenomenon. These two schools first met in 1928—a mere five years after Texas Tech was founded—and the two did not become regular opponents until a few years after the Red Raiders joined the well-established Southwest Conference in 1956. Texas has a commanding lead in the overall series, but the Texas Tech program had progressed so much that the Red Raiders (with an assist from the state legislature) were included as part of the SWC–Big 12 merger in 1996. It was in this year that the *Chancellor's Spurs* was created as a traveling trophy. Named in tribute of Texas Tech's first chancellor, the Spurs are made of gold and silver and engraved with the logos of each university. The rivalry has progressed since then, particularly with Texas Tech's last second 39–33 victory in the 2008 meeting, in which both schools were ranked in the top five of the national polls.

Texas A&M University-Commerce/Texas A&M University-Kingsville (Football): *Chennault Cup*

A match-up of two of the newest additions to the Texas A&M University System, Texas A&M-Commerce (formerly East Texas State) and Texas A&M-Kingsville (formerly Texas A&I) have a rivalry that dates back to 1930 and has withstood numerous name changes over the decades. To the winner goes the *Chennault Cup*, a trophy with an identity crisis of its own. Originally the prize for the East Texas State-Livingston (AL) game, it was nearly abandoned when the two schools could not agree to continue their series. But Texas A&M-Kingsville stepped up to the challenge, and the trophy was transferred to the new rivalry in 1992.

University of Utah/Utah State University (Football): *Battle of the Brothers*

The most played rivalry in the Beehive State, Utah and Utah State first played in 1892 and was a staple of both team's schedules throughout the twentieth century. The *Battle of the Brothers* was one of the first college football games to become a Thanksgiving Day staple, though the two schools elected to do away with that tradition in 1958. Utah and Utah State were conference rivals from 1914–1962, after which the Utes became a founding member of the WAC and began to focus on BYU as their biggest foe. But Utah State remained on the schedule, and the next two decades wound up being the most competitive stretch of football between the two schools. The Utes have since regained dominance and have built on their already commanding lead in the overall series. The two schools elected to take a short break after the Utes won twelve games in a row from 1998–2009, but once restarted, this game became a part of the greater competition for the *Beehive Boot*.

University of Virginia/Virginia Tech (Football): *Commonwealth Cup*

The two schools first met in 1895 and have played annually since 1970. *The Cup* is a relatively new tradition, having been created in 1996. For the first century of this rivalry, Virginia and Virginia Tech met only as nonconference opponents. The only time they were ever in the same conference during the twentieth century was from 1907–1921, when they were both members of the South Atlantic Intercollegiate Athletic Association, though they never actually played each other during that stretch. Virginia and Virginia Tech would not become league rivals until 2004, when the rise of the Hokies as a football power (and some pressure from the Virginia state legislature) convinced the ACC to extend an invite alongside Miami. Through the 2012 season, Virginia Tech has yet to lose to their state rivals in a league game.

University of Virginia/Virginia Tech (Rugby): *Commonwealth Shield Match*

The men's and women's rugby teams from the University of Virginia and Virginia Tech recently announced a new shield trophy match to commemorate their ancient intrastate rivalry. The creation of this annual event was inspired by the time-honored tradition of the two schools playing for the

Commonwealth Cup in football. The University of Virginia hosted the first of these matches on its home pitch in the *Mad Bowl* on October 29, 2011. Five matches are held on a single day—men's A and B teams, women's A and B teams and a special match that pits the men's alumni teams against each other. Separate shield trophies are awarded to the winners of the men's A team, women's A team, and the alumni team.

Virginia Tech/West Virginia University (Football): *Black Diamond Trophy*

Although this rivalry dates back to 1912, it was not until the 1950s that Virginia Tech and West Virginia became an annual rivalry. The two schools often used the game to fill their schedules as independents, before becoming conference foes once they joined the Big East in 1991. The *Black Diamond Trophy* was introduced in 1997 as a tribute to the rich coal heritage in the region. Virginia Tech won six of the nine games that featured the trophy, but West Virginia holds a 28–22–1 lead in the overall series. The 1999 game was probably the best in series history, as Michael Vick rallied Virginia Tech to a last minute field goal to preserve the Hokies' unbeaten regular season. Sadly, this rivalry came to an end when the Hokies left for the ACC and has not been played since the 2005 season.

University of Washington/Washington State University (Football): *Apple Cup*

This rivalry has been played almost continuously since 1900, with the *Apple Cup trophy* being adopted in 1962. Traditionally, it has been the final regular season game for both teams. While this is the most historically lopsided of the Pac-12's traditional rivalries, Washington and WSU have a long history of spoiling each other's championship hopes. UW's 23–10 victory in the 1981 game not only put the Huskies in the Rose Bowl but also denied WSU their first berth in fifty-one years. The Cougars returned the favor in 1982, stunning the Huskies 24–20 in the first match-up in Pullman since 1958. Sections of the goal posts that fans tore down following the upset remain in the Palouse River to this day. WSU would deny UW again in 1983 and 1992, while wins by the Huskies prevented the Cougars from a share of the conference crown in both 2001 and 2003. The winner of this game receives the Apple Cup, which replaced the *Governor's Trophy* in 1962, and is named for the state's bountiful apple crop.

University of Wisconsin–Eau Claire/University of Wisconsin–Stout (Football): *I-94 Trophy*

Less than thirty miles separates these longtime Division III rivals, both of which are part of the University of Wisconsin system. While the series dates back to 1917, it was not until 2008 that the Blugolds and Blue Devils decided to spice up the rivalry with a traveling trophy.

19

VENUES

There are places we'll remember all our lives, though some have changed. Some forever, not for better. Some have gone and some, thank God, remain. All these places had their moments, and nearly all will again . . . and again . . . and again. They're the great venues in college sports. Venues that have witnessed wonderful traditions.

The stadiums, arenas, and playing fields, are the scenes of so many keepsakes. They're places in the heart and in our collective memory banks.

Where to begin? Why, almost anywhere . . .

In Knoxville, in *Neyland Stadium* on a football Saturday: once the Volunteer Navy's docked on the Tennessee River and satisfied their tailgate appetites, UT fans walk on *Peyton Manning Pass* to watch their Vols play. Remember when a freshman tailback named Herschel (no last name needed) introduced himself to Bill Bates and the rest of the country one night? Remember how Steve Spurrier and his then Florida Gators tormented Phil Fulmer and his guys? We do. Always will.

In Athens, *between the hedges*: back when Herschel (again, surname unnecessary) returned Georgia to glory, glory in *Sanford Stadium*, the world's largest pet cemetery. Remember when he won the Heisman? We do. Always will. RIP, all you *Uga's entombed in Sanford's canine mausoleum.*

Especially you, Uga V, who famously, on the road in Auburn's *Jordan-Hare Stadium*, dawged-up in 1996. When Auburn receiver Robert Baker celebrated in the end zone after scoring the game's first touchdown, he ventured too close to *Uga's* turf.

From *Damn Good Dogs!*, a history of Georgia's line of English Bulldogs: "When it appeared they would collide, Uga went airborne, aiming for Baker's . . . midsection, to put it diplomatically. He might have made contact, but Baker put on the brakes and Charles Seiler pulled back on the leash—sparing Uga an unnecessary roughness penalty and Baker a trip to the hospital."

As *Sports Illustrated* noted in 1997, in declaring Uga V the number 1 mascot in the land and an SI coverboy: "If you can't appreciate the swaggering gait and Churchillian physiognomy of Uga V, the Bulldogs' bulldog, you must be a cat lover."

It's not just the games people play, but where they play them.

In downtown Lexington, Kentucky: In *Rupp Arena*, for its sheer size (capacity 23,500) and the, uh, . . . rabidity of Kentucky basketball fans, as well as their dogged devotion to the 'Cats. Any Ashley sightings yet? That would be Ashley Judd, a UK diehard and Kentucky's most celebrated celebrity fan.

Under coach Mike Martin, Florida State baseball at *Dick Howser Stadium* has become one of college baseball's best and toughest venues. Named for the late Kansas City Royals manager and FSU coach, and the Seminoles' first baseball All-American, the stadium is now home to *Mike Martin Field*. Martin coached nearly four decades in Tallahassee, where baseball's long been a happy happening. Unless, of course, you're playing against the 'Noles.

Farewell to the late Ron Fraser, the imaginative salesman and marketing showman who built Miami Hurricanes baseball into a dynasty. From 1963–1992, he coached the 'Canes, won 1,271 games and two College World Series, and turned *Mark Light Stadium* into a beacon of baseball light. Unless, of course, you were playing against Miami.

Or at Louisiana State, at least once Skip Bertman got there in 1984: Bertman, an assistant to Fraser at Miami and a protégé of his principles and promotional genius, told John Manuel of *Baseball America* about his arrival in Baton Rouge in 1984. "It seems," Manuel wrote, "the baseball IQ of Tigers fans was a little lacking."

"Hey Bertram, we're one point down!"

Bertman replied, "Sir, they're runs, and we're trying to get one."

"Ref, you suck!"

Bertman's response: "They're umps, sir, and they do suck."

He turned LSU into one of the very best and most daunting atmospheres in college baseball. Bertman, who became the school's athletic director following the 2001 season, won five College World Series titles, made 11 CWS trips to Omaha—RIP, dear old *Rosenblatt Stadium*—and annually led the nation in attendance.

In Baton Rouge, of course, stands one of two *Death Valleys* (Clemson has the other): *Tiger Stadium*. Nothing compares to a Saturday night game in Death Valley, except, perhaps, the *Big Ragoo's Pregame Tailgate*. That would be Marvin Dugas, a.k.a., the *Big Ragoo*, whose *Krewe of Ragoo Cajun Tailgate* is easily the greatest, tastiest, and most celebrated tailgate this side of *the Grove* at Ole Miss. "Cher, pinch the tail and suck the head off that crawfish, and wash it down with an Abita."

Of course, Joe Cahn, the self-proclaimed *Commissioner of Tailgating* who has written a book about that fine art sagely says, "The best place to tailgate is wherever you are that weekend."

Yet it's inside *Tiger Stadium* that the real magic happens. With *Mike the Tiger*, a real Bengal tiger, roaring in a cage just outside the tunnel leading from the visitors' locker room.

Here's CBSSports.com's Dennis Dillon in October 2009, on a night game atmosphere in Baton Rouge: "It has turned the knees of All-Americans to goo. It has caused coaches to lose their coaching minds. It only happens at a special place at a special time. LSU can be up, LSU can be down, but LSU's best weapon remains . . . sunset."

ESPN.com once proclaimed Death Valley "The scariest place to play in America." Later, Wright Thompson of ESPN.com wrote, "It was electric. When Death Valley is rocking, it seems as if it might actually take flight."

This, from the LSU archives regarding October 8, 1988: *The Night the Tigers Moved the Earth*: "When LSU quarterback Tommy Hodson passed to Eddie Fuller for the winning touchdown against Auburn, the explosion of the crowd was so thunderous that it caused an earth tremor that registered on a seismograph meter in LSU's geology department across campus."

And then there's Billy Cannon's *Halloween Night* run in 1959, when Cannon, who would win the Heisman Trophy, saved the unbeaten and top-ranked Tigers. With LSU trailing number 3 Ole Miss 3–0 in the fourth quarter, Cannon returned a punt eighty-nine yards for a touchdown and a 7–3 triumph. And Death Valley erupted like Vesuvius. From the archives: "The legend goes that families living near the campus lakes came running out of their homes, fearing the noise that was erupting all around them."

In Charlottesville, only select students live in the rooms on *The Lawn* at Mr. Jefferson's University. But at Virginia football and basketball games and other sporting events, or just at the drop of a hat, everyone can—and does—sing "The Good Old Song of Wahoowa" to the tune of "Auld Lang Syne" before the Wahoowa-ing cheers begin.

At NC State, that howlin' Wolf bays at the moon after another Wolfpack touchdown or big basket. It's hardly *the Swamp* in Gainesville, Florida, but then few places are. FSU, for one. Miami once was, when the 'Canes emerged from the tunnel and appeared out of the smoke in the old *Orange Bowl* and smoked the opposition. Not anymore.

The biggest stadium in the country? The *Big House*, or Michigan Stadium—capacity 109,901—is known and beloved by the Wolverine faithful. Penn State, Tennessee, Ohio State, Alabama, and Texas also exceed 100,00 in capacity. All rock 'n' roll, too. Especially these days in *Bryant-Denny Stadium* in Tuscaloosa, where Alabama's *Million Dollar Marching Band* has a lot to toot about these days. The Crimson Tide as of the 2012–2013 season, has won three of the last four BCS national championships. All that, and Katherine Webb, too, cheering for her guy A. J.

There's nothing parochial about *Notre Dame Stadium*, not in a pigskin sense. Lay critics and Irish haters aside, it's one of the quintessential college stadiums and campuses in the country. It's Rockne, Leahy, Ara, and Holtz. It's home to seven Heisman Trophy winners, none of whom has had his number retired. It's *Touchdown Jesus*. It's where Rudy finally got into a game, and where *Rudy* was filmed. It also inspired a T-shirt that I own: "Rudy Was Offsides."

In the Pacific Northwest, *Autzen Stadium* at Oregon became an electric atmosphere during the Ducks' offensive blitzkriegs under head coach Chip Kelly. Now that he's left Eugene for Philadelphia to coach the NFL Eagles, let's see how dynamic the Ducks remain.

In Washington, a $250 million remodeling of *Husky Stadium* is scheduled to debut in the 2013 opener against Boise State. The view from the shore of Lake Washington and Portage Bay has long been idyllic. Tailgating—or stern gating, as many Huskies fans have done for decades, arriving by boat and docking and noshing in one of the most picturesque settings in the nation—may even reach new heights.

Back in Eugene, Oregon's *Hayward Field* reigns as track and field's most cherished venue. It's the home of numerous NCAA and USTAF national championships, and several United States Olympic Trials. It's where running, as Steve Prefontaine knew, is a way of life. It's where the late, great Pre ran like the wind, and home to the most knowledgeable track and field fans.

Franklin Field at the University of Pennsylvania is renowned for the *Penn Relays*, the annual weekend-long track and field carnival held in the hallowed old stadium in Philadelphia. It's where, legend has it, a sportswriter once looked at all these meet officials with their stopwatches and cracked, "These are the souls that time men's tries."

At the *Drake Relays* in Des Moines, Iowans know and love their track and field.

Back to the West Coast, and down to Los Angeles, the home of UCLA, or rather, to Pasadena, where the Bruins play their home games in the *Rose Bowl*, whenever the sun is setting over the stadium's rim, it's one of the signature sights in college sports. That's especially true when the Rose Bowl itself is played in the old stadium, even in these BCS-reconfigured times, if it's TCU—and not UCLA or USC—playing Wisconsin.

Back in Madison, at *Camp Randall Stadium*, between the third and fourth quarters, Badgers fans do the *Jump Around*. It's done to the ballistic sound of that House of Pain tune. When nearly 80,000 fans jump up and down, it makes the stands shake.

At Texas A&M in College Station, when all those Aggies fans link arms and sway back and forth during games, the *Kyle Field* press box moves, too. Honest.

Even in the wake of the recent horrific scandal, Penn State's *whiteout* of 100,000 or so fans still turn *Beaver Stadium* just that: white.

One football fan's guilty pleasure: a big Georgia Tech game on a Thursday night. On the *Flats*, as the downtown campus is known, while the rest of the nation is watching on ESPN, when the Atlanta skyline's all aglow above the upper deck of the east stands, when a native New Yorker transplant can tell family and old friends back home, "I took the subway to *Bobby Dodd Stadium* and watched the Jackets beat Florida State. Had two chili dogs at the Varsity, too."

For those who prefer driving and tailgating, New York offers one of the absolute best venues: West Point. The United States Military Academy. Especially the tailgating at historic *Buffalo Soldier Field*.

There's the pomp and pageantry of an Army football Saturday. Never mind how far its football fortunes have fallen in the last couple of decades. This is still West Point, where the grounds are hallowed and historic, the pre-game parade of cadets still thrills and the view across the Hudson River—especially once the leaves have turned but not yet fallen—is stunning.

So is the atmosphere inside *Michie Stadium*. Every Army player passes this plaque as he enters the stadium: "I want an officer for a secret and dangerous mission. I want a West Point football player." . . . General George C. Marshall, chief of staff during WWII.

Every home football game begins with a special delivery: Four members of the famed *Black Knights Parachute Team* will leap out of a helicopter one at a time, all attempting to land on the Black Knights logo on the fifty-yard line in Michie. One will hand-deliver the game ball.

Before one game against South Florida, Wayne Drehs of ESPN.com hopped aboard for a ride in the chopper.

"It's a beautiful day and I'm about to jump out of an airplane into a football stadium," Cadet Brian Montgomery told Drehs before his jump from 3,500 feet. "Things couldn't be any better."

"Put it this way," Cadet Ryan Dennison said to Drehs. "Picture the wildest, craziest roller coaster you've ever been on. Picture that on steroids. That's what it's like."

Not to worry. All four parachutists—one after another—landed safely and precisely on the fifty, right on the logo. Even the pilot was impressed. So was Drehs.

"I'm still in a state of shock," Cadet Dennison told him. "I'm just totally numb. Every time I'm up there, it's absolutely surreal."

In Durham, North Carolina, *Cameron Indoor Stadium* has its own crazies. The Cameron Crazies, those privileged Dukies who've helped give coach Mike Krzyzewski and his Blue Devils one of the great home-court advantages. They camp outside in any weather/temperature, in their tent city *Krzyzewskiville*, waiting to get tickets and prime locations once inside Cameron.

Yes, they can be very amusing, even clever at times. No, not everybody buys their shtick. It played much better back in the eight-team heyday of the ACC. Especially when Lefty and his Terps came to town, or Norm Sloan and NC State. A sign poked fun at a new player on the Wolfpack one season. It read: "Mrs. Sloan Loves Norm's Tiny Pinder."

In Chapel Hill, first in *Carmichael Auditorium* and now in the cavernous *Dean Dome*, North Carolina basketball remains royalty under ol' Roy. Since returning to UNC, Roy Williams has won two national championships with the Heels (2005, 2009). Spontaneous celebrations still occasionally break out on Franklin Street after big wins. Under ol' Roy, the old bromide holds true: "If God is not a Tar Heel, then why is the sky Carolina blue?"

In lacrosse, there's no place like Homewood. *Homewood Field*, the home of Johns Hopkins lacrosse in Baltimore. The United States Lacrosse Museum and National Hall of Fame is housed there, too. The Blue Jays have won forty-four national championships, including nine Division I titles since the first NCAA tournament in 1971.

Whether at Homewood or away, in whatever football stadium the men's Final Four is now held, lacrosse is the fastest-growing sport in the nation. It's a three-day, family affair, and a Memorial Day weekend happening with NCAA Division I, II, and III titles at stake.

The sport's burgeoning popularity has long been a staple at Syracuse, which plays its home games in the *Carrier Dome*. The Orange holds the most NCAA titles in the Division I era with ten.

Syracuse also has a numbers' tradition. It awards jersey #22 to its best all-around player, The man with the most talent, most flair, most creativity. Back in the day, it would've been the football star who once wore number 44 in both football and lacrosse: Jim Brown, whose football #44 is now retired.

The best in women's lacrosse, which is also booming? Go to Evanston, Illinois. To Northwestern, which won the 2012 title for its seventh NCAA championship in eight years. Bring your stick, too. And don't forget to cradle (lacrosse term).

In January 2013, ESPN aired a Saturday full of great rivalries and venues in college basketball. It was a feast for aficionados, even for the occasional fan. You want venues? They had venues:

Seth Greenberg, who last coached at Virginia Tech and now works for ESPN, on all those banners hanging in Cameron with great names, champions, title and numbers: "I'd take my team in a day early and show them all that and say, 'Fellas, we're not playing against any of those guys.'"

Jay Bilas, who played on Mike Krzyzewski's first Final Four team and is now a lawyer/broadcaster, on *Butler's Hinkle Fieldhouse*: "The Fenway Park of College Basketball. All different angles and [quirks]."

Butler's Hinkle Fieldhouse. *Butler University*

340

CHAPTER 19

Brad Stevens, the Butler coach who took his Bulldogs to consecutive Final Fours and championship games, said, "A little bit of that *Hinkle magic* that everyone gets to see."

This, after Roosevelt Jones, who recently had a late, seemingly fatal turnover in the closing seconds that night, stole the inbounds pass and hit a floater at the buzzer to give number-8 Butler a stunning 64–63 win over number-13 Gonzaga.

Bilas again: "They [Butler] believe that they can win any one game."

Especially in *Hinkle*, the site of the cinematic Hoosiers of Hickory High, and where Bobby Plump starred for the Butler Bulldogs. It was Plump who hit the last second jumper for tiny Milan High (161 students) to upset mighty Muncie Central 32–30 in 1954. Milan was the last small school to win Indiana's all-comers state tournament. It was broken into classifications by enrollment after 1997.

"I'm not saying this one's going to last forever," Rece Davis, the host of *ESPN Game Day*, said after a long day and night, "but a lot of people are going to remember when Roosevelt Jones made a steal and went down and beat Gonzaga."

A lot of people need to make the pilgrimage to Butler, which reached consecutive NCCA championship games in 2010–2011. The Bulldogs lost 61–59 to Duke in 2012, when Gordon Hayward's last second, half-court shot hit the backboard and bounced off the rim. In 2011, Butler fell to Connecticut 53–41.

If you're a true hoops fan, you must go to Hinkle (capacity 10,000), where the baskets are still ten-feet high and the magic lives on.

The Carnegie Hall of college basketball: That's how Indiana's *Assembly Hall* has come to be known. It's the site of Chuck Crabb's public-address system greeting before each game: "Ladies and gentlemen, good evening. Indiana University welcomes you to the Assembly Hall."

It's where the Hoosiers take the floor in their classic red-and-white, candy-striped warm-up pants to the fight song played by the IU Pep Band. "Ladies and gentlemen," Crabb always says, "Your Indiana Hoosiers!"

It's where the best timeout in basketball, as the under 8:00-minute time-out in the second half has come to be known. With the band blaring the "William Tell Overture" and the cheerleaders cheering and flag-bearers waving flags all over the court. It concludes with more than 17,000 Hoosiers singing, "Indiana, Indiana, Indiana we're all for you! I-U!"

It's all that and more. "There are some people," said Dan Dakich, who played at IU, coached under Bob Knight and is now a TV analyst, "who come into this arena and they're done before the game's even started. They're intimidated."

Afterward, it's a stop at *Nick's English Hut*, since 1927, an institution and popular student hangout on Kirkwood Avenue the main college drag in Bloomington. It's also where a left-handed gym rat and noted NCAA bracketologist first dropped by for a beer on April 11, 2008: Barack Obama, on his first presidential campaign trail.

The *Cathedral of College Basketball*. That's how the *Palestra* is widely known, loved and revered. Any true college hoops fan must come to Philadelphia, where the late, great Dick Clark once hosted TV's *American Bandstand* and where the Palestra, the ancient arena on the University of Pennsylvania campus, has long been the American grandstand.

It's the ancestral home of the Big 5: Penn, St. Joseph's, Villanova, Temple, and LaSalle. Five Philly schools, all with rich basketball traditions and lots of homegrown hoopsters. The Palestra, which opened January 1, 1927, is the oldest operating college basketball arena in the country and the site of more college basketball games than any other arena. Capacity 8,722, all wooden bleachers. It's a holy place that long housed the *Holy War*, as St. Joe's-Villanova is known, and other showdowns between the Big 5. Four of them sometimes played doubleheaders. Nowadays add Drexel, a short walk from the Palestra, and it's an occasional six-team city series.

It's legendary coaches: Dr. Jack Ramsay and now Phil Martelli at St. Joe's. Temple's Harry Litwack, John Chaney and now Philly homeboy Fran Dunphy, who played at LaSalle, coached at Penn, then moved to Temple. It's Penn's Chuck Daly and Villanova's Jack Kraft and Rollie Massimino, whose Wildcats upset Georgetown 66–64 to win the 1985 NCAA title. And now, Jay Wright.

It's great players: LaSalle's Tom Gola, who led the Explorers to the 1954 NCAA title. Temple's Hal "King" Lear and Guy Rodgers. Penn's Corky Calhoun and Tony Price, star of the 1979 Quakers, the last Ivy League team to reach the Final Four. St. Joe's Cliff Anderson, and Jameer Nelson, who nearly led the Hawks to a perfect season and the 2004 Final Four. And 'Nova's legendary Paul Arizin and those 1985 Cats, who hit twenty-two of twenty-eight shots, nine of ten in the second half against Georgetown.

It's the Palestra concourse, now a veritable Big 5 museum. It's rollouts, the long, often hilarious and sometimes profane paper signs that are rolled out during Big 5 games and tweak the opposition.

This, from Penn students during a 2007 Ivy League showdown shortly after the sudden death of a celebrity: "Anna Nicole Smith Died of Boredom from Watching Princeton Offense."

It's Dan Harrell, once the Palestra's long-time custodian who earned a Penn degree in his spare time and, at 68, is still at Penn and a Palestra historian of sorts.

"It's a sacred place," Harrell told me in 2002. "I'm not trying to be funny. It's a cathedral, a special place. It's just the way it is. I don't think some of the young people understand. It's like our PA announcer John McAdams says before each game: 'Welcome to the Palestra, America's most storied gymnasium.' It's still the best place to sit in the stands and eat hot dogs and pretzels and enjoy the game."

It's why a plaque on the wall just inside the main entrance captures the essence of the Palestra, the Big 5, and this city's long-standing love affair with college basketball:

> To Win The Game Is Great . . .
> To Play The Game Is Greater . . .
> But To Love The Game Is The Greatest of All.

In women's basketball, UConn's a you-can't-miss. In Gampel Pavilion on campus in Storrs, or surely in the next Final Four. And the one after that. What Geno Auriemma hath wrought hath made the Huskies seven-time national champions and perennial NCAA contenders.

Just as Pat Summitt once built the Tennessee Lady Vols into a program that transformed the women's game. In cavernous *Thompson-Boling Arena* on campus, the court was renamed *The Summitt*. No embellishment needed. Not for the woman who coached UT from 1974–2012, compiled a 1098–208 record and won eight NCAA titles. I was in attendance at one of the last games Coach Summitt coached, and feel very fortunate for having seen her.

In April of 2012, Summitt was diagnosed with early-onset dementia, Alzheimer's type. She's now coach emeritus of the Lady Vols. Go see them play in Knoxville. Go see what Pat Summitt built, and the legacy she'll leave. It's no coincidence that the Women's Basketball Hall of Fame opened in Knoxville in 1999, with Summitt leading the inaugural class of inductees.

Women's hoops rocks at Notre Dame, where Skylar Diggins stars, and at Stanford, as usual. And especially now in Waco, Texas, since Baylor coach Kim Mulkey and 6-foot-8 Brittany Greiner went 40–0 as the Lady Bears won the 2012 NCAA title.

Farewell, Big East. At least the Big East tournament we knew and loved in *Madison Square Garden*, in those Saturday night finals that seemed more like heavyweight title fights:

John Thompson and Patrick Ewing's Georgetown Hoyas. Jim Boeheim's Syracuse Orange, whether Gerry McNamara shooting three after three after three, or the Orange going six overtimes to beat Connecticut 127–117 in 2009. Time of game: 3 hours, 46 minutes. "I've never been prouder of any team I've coached," said Boeheim, whose 2003 Orange was the NCAA champion.

Jim Calhoun's UConn Huskies, who won seven Big East championships for their coach; and Kemba Walker, the Bronx kid who willed the Huskies to the 2011 Big East title, then to Calhoun's third—and most unlikely—NCAA crown.

Looie, of course. Lou Carnesecca, whose St. John's Redmen won their first Big East title in 1983 on sacred ground: in the Garden. "Today," Looie began his post-game press conference, "my guys walked with kings." Especially Chris Mullin.

(We interrupt this college hoops reverie for two football venues: The old, original *Orange Bowl* in Miami, the home of the Hurricanes, especially when Jimmy Johnson coached the 'Canes and they entered out of a tunnel and through a cloud of smoke, then smoked the opposition. And the Cal-Stanford game, especially when it's played in Berkeley and viewed from *Tightwad Hill*. That spot high above the field and stadium, where Cal fans can sit and see most of the action for free. We return you now to Hoops Heaven).

The Pit in Albuquerque, and its mile-high altitude: It's the home of the New Mexico Lobos and the site of the 1983 NCAA Final, when Jim Valvano's NC State Wolfpack shocked Houston's Phi Slamma Jamma 54–52 on Lorenzo Charles' last second dunk of an air ball. It's also where a head coach from a prominent conference once told his team, "Don't worry about the altitude. We're playing the game indoors."

Pauley Pavilion no longer strikes fear into opponents' hearts. At least not like it did when John Wooden worked his basketball wizardry and his UCLA Bruins were the greatest dynasty in college sports history.

Between 1964 and 1975, Wooden's teams won ten NCAA championships in twelve years, seven consecutive from 1967 to 1973. UCLA won a record thirty-eight straight NCAA tournament games, and his Bruins compiled an NCAA-record eighty-eight-game winning streak from 1971–1974 before falling at Notre Dame 71–70.

He was, and shall ever remain, the *Wizard of Westwood*. The Los Angeles neighborhood where the UCLA campus sits and where Pauley Pavilion was the place to be on game day, unless, of course, you played for the opposition.

Wooden, an Indiana native and Purdue All-American from 1932–1934, and the first person to be inducted into the Naismith Memorial Basketball Hall of Fame as both a player and a coach, won with small trapping teams and tall strapping men. He won with guards Walt Hazzard and Gail Goodrich. He won with 7-foot-2 Ferdinand Lewis Alcindor, who later changed his name to Kareem Abdul-Jabbar after converting to Islam. He won with Bill Walton and sidekick Swen Nater, whose 1971–1972 team went 30–0 and outscored opponents by an average of 30.3 points, the NCAA Division I record.

Wooden won with his famous *Pyramid of Success*, the principles and foundation for his coaching success and how he lived his life. His maxims included "Be quick, but don't hurry"; "Failure to prepare is preparing to fail"; and "Never mistake activity for achievement." As each of Bill Walton's four sons became basketball players, Walton would write some of Wooden's maxims on their lunch bags each day.

Every UCLA fan knew the maxims by heart. Knew the fight song and cheers, too. The UCLA Song Girls were legendary, especially Julie Hayek at the 1980 Final Four in Indianapolis. By then, Wooden had retired in 1975 after beating his protégé, Louisville's Denny Crum, in the semifinals and Kentucky in Wooden's farewell.

UCLA has since won one national championship, in 1995.

In November, 2012, Pauley Pavilion reopened after a two-year, $136 million renovation. The previous two seasons, the Bruins played their home games in the *aging Los Angeles Sports Arena* or the *Honda Center* in Anaheim. Now, they play in a gorgeous arena where a statue of Wooden stands outside the north entrance where the corridor on the east side of Pauley is named *Wooden Way*, where three large cabinets are filled with mementoes of the Wooden era, and the wood surrounding those cabinets was taken from Pauley's old floor: the *Nell and John Wooden Court*, as it was named in 2003 for Wooden and his beloved Nellie, his wife of fifty-three years who died in 1985. Wooden mourned her daily until his death on June 4, 2010, at the age of ninety-nine.

Now, in the new-and-improved Pauley, Wooden's gold-upholstered seat—Seat 6, Row B, right behind the Bruins' bench—stands out among the blue seats.

Pauley's capacity has increased by 1,000 to 13,800. It's a beautiful place, but no longer instills real fear in opponents' hearts. As Jamaal Wilkes, one of Wooden's greatest players and a wing bank-shooter extraordinaire, said when asked for his favorite memory of old Pauley: "Winning."

On Saturday, February 2, 2013, Oklahoma State came to Lawrence, Kansas, to *Allen Fieldhouse*, where the Cowboys hadn't won since 1990.

Where second-ranked Kansas, on an eighteen-game winning streak, had won its last thirty-three home games on *James Naismith Court*. Where Bill Self's Jayhawks were an astonishing 102–1 in their previous 103 games in *the Phog*, as Allen Fieldhouse is known and beloved by KU fans, feared and dreaded by opponents.

Somehow, Oklahoma State won 85–80. You can look it up. The numbers don't lie. They do, however, reinforce this truth: Allen Fieldhouse is not only the best venue in college basketball, but the most daunting and toughest, too.

Says who? Says Scott Van Pelt for starters. "In my opinion, Phog Allen Fieldhouse is the best venue I've seen," said the ESPN reporter/talking shaved head. "Cameron's an unbelievable venue," Van Pelt said of Duke's famed indoor stadium. "Rupp's an unbelievable venue, too. But if you love college basketball, go to Allen Fieldhouse. Check it out and get back to me. They invented the game, let's start from there."

Dr. James Naismith, who invented the game of basketball in 1891 at the YMCA in Springfield, Massachusetts, came to Kansas in 1898 to teach and coach. The original Dr. J, who went 55–60, is the only Kansas coach with a losing record. His successor? "The Phog." Dr. Forrest "Phog" Allen, considered the father of basketball coaching. Two assistants who apprenticed under him were Dean Smith and Adolph Rupp.

Allen coached Kansas for thirty-nine seasons, in two stints, compiling a 590–219 record and winning the first of KU's three NCAA titles in his 1952 farewell season. He's the man behind the Phog. That's what all Kansas fans call Allen Fieldhouse. The enormous sign is up there, high above the stands behind the north basket, and serves as a warning to opponents, one and all:

> Pay Heed All Who Enter,
> Beware of The Phog.

It's how one of those classic pregame videos on the four-sided scoreboard above center court begins. This one from Paul Pierce, the great KU All-American and an NBA champion with the Boston Celtics.

"Beware of The Phog!" Pierce cries, eyes wide. Then the words appear on the screen, one after the other:

"The Nation's . . . Biggest . . . Home Court Advantage . . ."

There are thunderous dunks, primal screams, crazed KU fans. And you're thinking, *Gotta be a human sacrifice in there somewhere.*

More highlights, more shrieking. Then . . . "Over 100 Years . . . of History . . . And Glory . . . We Are Kansas!!!"

Then: "Get Ready . . . To Witness . . . The Nation's . . . Biggest . . . Home Court Advantage!"

And once again: "Over 100 Years . . . of Tradition! . . . We Are KANSAS!!!"

Larry Brown's 1988 Jayhawks, led by Danny Manning, entered the NCAA Tournament as a sixth seed. "If Kansas wins," Dick Vitale said, "I'll kiss the Jayhawk on the floor of Allen Fieldhouse." *Danny and the Miracles* upset Oklahoma 83–79 in the championship game. Eventually, Vitale kissed the floor in the Phog.

Hey, even Wilt Chamberlain played a season at Kansas. *The Dipper*, in the Phog.

Under Roy Williams, the class of 1998 seniors Raef LaFrentz, Billy Thomas, and C. B. McGrath were 58–0 at home in the Phog. LaFrentz also left part of a tooth embedded in the court after one particularly brutal practice.

Kansas fans aren't snide, they're prideful. They love their Jayhawks. They pack the Phog and root like crazy. When an opposing player fouls out, they stand and lift their arms overhead and sway them back and forth. *Waving-the-Wheat*, it's called. You know, like a field of Kansas wheat swaying in a prairie breeze.

Of course, they chant "Rock Chalk, Jayhawk, KU!" And they rejoiced over the 2008 NCAA final, when Mario Chalmers hit a last second three-pointer to force overtime and KU beat Memphis 75–68 for the national championship.

Kansas fans are proud and loud. Never more so than on February 25, 2012, in the final *Border War* game with Missouri before the Tigers' move to the Southeastern Conference. When Thomas Robinson blocked a last second shot in regulation and sent the game into overtime, the crowd set an Allen Fieldhouse noise record of 127 decibels. That's loud.

That's the Phog.

"It's Fenway," Kansas basketball operations director Barry Hinson told Vahe Gregorian of the *St. Louis Post-Dispatch*. "Wrigley. Old Yankee Stadium. It's the Coliseum. I mean, it is. And it's set down in a small town in Midwest America. On Naismith Drive."

VENUES BY SCHOOL

Cal (Football): *The Big C*

The *Big C* is located on Charter Hill above Memorial Stadium and was constructed in 1905 by the classes of 1907 and 1908. The road up to the

Big C was built in 1916 by the male members of the Cal student body in 3.5 hours using 2,000 picks and shovels that were donated by the Southern Pacific Railroad. The Rally Committee became the custodians and guardians of the Big C sometime after 1952. Since then, the Committee has been in charge of painting the Big C and protecting it from vandalism.

Clemson University (Football): *Death Valley*

Clemson's *Death Valley* is synonymous with *Clemson Memorial Stadium*. The Stadium was dubbed this affectionate title by the late Lonnie McMillian, a former coach at Presbyterian. He took his teams to play at Clemson, and they rarely scored, never mind gained a victory. Once he told the writers he was going to play Clemson up at Death Valley because his teams always got killed. It stuck somewhat, but when Frank Howard started calling it that in the 1950s, the term really caught on. Many people think the name is derived from the fact that there rests a cemetery outside the fence on the press box site of the stadium. But, although it would make sense, the name was actually first coined by Lonnie McMillian.

Duke University (Basketball): *Cameron Indoor Stadium*

Section 17 (for undergrads only) is the epicenter for the crazies.

East Stroudsburg University (Football): *Football Field*

East Stroudsburg's stadium stands now where a swamp was . . . Franklin Roosevelt's federal workers, both students and football players, filled the swamp.

Fordham University, Butler University, and the University of Pennsylvania (Basketball): *Oldest Basketball Arenas*

Fordham, Hinkle, and the Palestra arenas may be the oldest, continuously used basketball venues.

University of Georgia (Football): *Between the Hedges*

Between the Hedges is a reference to *Sanford Stadium* that dates back to the early 1930s. The famous Chinese privet hedges that surround Sanford's playing field were only one foot high when the stadium was dedicated in 1929 and were protected by a wooden fence. It was natural for a clever sports writer, referring to an upcoming home game, to observe "that the Bulldogs will have their opponent "between the hedges." At least one old-timer says the phrase was first coined by the legendary Atlanta sportswriter Grantland Rice.

Harvard (Football): *Oldest Stadium*

America's oldest football stadium was first used on April 14, 1903. It's still a magnificent structure as my family and I saw in 1992.

Lindenwood University (IL) (Football): *Striped-Colored Field*

Lindenwood recently began playing football, and wanted to start their pursuit with a unique tradition. So what better way than to rival Boise's State's blue turf? At Lindenwood, alternating five-yard increments are maroon-and-grey.

Lindenwood University's "Striped Field." *Lindenwood University*

Long Island University (Basketball): *Basketball in the Brooklyn Paramount Theatre*

From 1962 to 2005, the *Brooklyn Paramount Theatre* was used by Long Island University as their basketball venue. From its opening in 1928, the Brooklyn Paramount Theatre, hosted all performers of the era, including Dizzy Gillespie, Ella Fitzgerald, Miles Davis, Chuck Berry, Fats Domino, and Buddy Holly. The ceiling was painted with clouds, and a sixty-foot stage curtain was decorated with satin-embroidered pheasants. Huge chandeliers and fountains with goldfish were also present. The Wurlitzer organ in the Brooklyn Paramount was second in size only to the organ at Radio City Music Hall, with its 2,000 pipes and 257 stops. The organ was used at LIU sporting events for years.

University of Michigan: (Ice Hockey): *Yost Ice Arena*

Yost Ice Arena is often called the best place to see a hockey game. It's the Cameron Indoor Stadium of college hockey.

Long Island University's Brooklyn Paramount Theater. *Long Island University*

University of North Dakota (Ice Hockey): *Ralph Engelstad Arena*

Often called the *Versailles of the North*, it was named hockey's "Most Opulent" venue by the *Wall Street Journal*. It has chandeliers, marble floors, and framed gold mirrors.

Northeastern University (Ice Hockey): *Oldest Arena*

Northeastern plays in one of the oldest ice hockey arenas in the world (*Boston/Mathews Arena*). It opened in 1910.

Northern Arizona University (Various Sports): *Walkup Skydome*

Northern Arizona University's football team plays all its home games in one of the country's largest wooden structures, the *Walkup Dome*. It's a 97,000-square-foot, 15,000-seat marvel. Named for J. Lawrence Walkup, who was the university's president when it opened, the dome is among the biggest wooden domes in the world. Besides football, it's used for basketball, commencements, concerts, and other events. Its entrance is guarded by *Louie the Lumberjack*, a towering giant who once attracted diners to a restaurant along Route 66 at the other end of the campus.

Northwestern University (Football): *Dyche Stadium/Ryan Field*

Dyche Stadium from 1926–1996, and as *Ryan Field*, 1997 to the present, the little stadium by the lake simply oozes history and tradition. Often called the Wrigley Field of College Football.

University of Pittsburgh (Various Sports): *Varsity Walk*

On the University of Pittsburgh campus, between the Cathedral of Learning and Heinz Chapel, is a sidewalk known as the *Varsity Walk*. There, embedded in the stones, are the names of former Pitt athletes who have promoted the University through their athletic or academic achievements. The Varsity Walk was conceived in 1950 as a way to honor athletes, and new members are added each year, with distinctive hand-carved stones.

University of Southern California (Football): *The Coliseum*

The Coliseum has been USC's home since 1923. Very few venues in college sports also have an Olympic heritage.

Spring Hill College (Baseball): *Oldest Baseball Field*

Their baseball field (*Stan Galle Field*) has been in service since 1889 and is widely believed to be the oldest continually used collegiate field in the country. Due to its age and location, their fans have developed a rather unique tradition. The right field line runs right next to a brick wall that separates the field from a narrow walkway and the school's administration building. Since there's no room for bleachers on the home dugout side of the field, their fans and students sit on the wall and watch the game. It's quite a sight during Friday conference games to see the top of the wall lined with students and fans. Also, from 1889 to about 1990, when an outfield fence was constructed, SHC had an oak tree in left field that was in play.

University of Tennessee (Basketball): *Checkerboard Baseline*

Everyone knows about Tennessee's checkerboard end zones, but how many people know that they also have the checkerboard design on the baselines of their basketball court? How cool.

Trinity College (Squash): *Kellner Squash Center*

This 500-seat venue has seen Trinity College win all home matches for over fifteen years. The longest (home and away) winning streak in college sports was recently broken when Trinity lost at Yale, but a 252 match winning streak isn't too shabby.

Ursinus College (Football): *Sycamore Tree in End Zone*

Ursinus was well known for many years for its *Patterson Field* end zone, in which a large sycamore tree grew undisturbed. *Ripley's Believe it or Not* featured the famous tree for being the only one on an active field of athletic play, and the seclusion of the tree at night, for generations, afforded lovers a trysting place. Greek organizations initiated pledges into their mysteries under its branches. A new sycamore, growing since 1984 from a seedling taken from the old tree, now stands nearby.

Vanderbilt University (Basketball): *Unique Court Design*

Vandy's basketball court is higher than its surroundings, more in the nature of a stage. The areas out of bounds along the sidelines are very wide. As a result, player benches are at the end of the court versus along the sidelines, as is traditional.

20

WALKS

They walk *The Walk*.

So many do it now. It's become one of the most treasured traditions—and most copied—in college football. It's the pregame Walk. Whether from the athletic dormitory, through a parking lot near the Tate Center at the University of Georgia, down Yellow Jacket Alley on the Flats at Georgia Tech to Bobby Dodd Stadium, or straight from the football complex to the stadium and into the locker room.

They walk The Walk.

They do so as hundreds—usually thousands—of fans line the route, clear a path, clear their throats, and cheer their heroes.

The most copied tradition in all of college football, former Auburn athletic director David Housel once said of his school's traditional *Tiger Walk*, which had its genesis in the early 1960s.

Yet some walks go way, way back-back-back in time.

"You're just thinking about how many people have been walking down here," Sam Schwartzstein, the fifth-year senior starting center and a tri-captain on Stanford's 2012 Pac-12 and Rose Bowl champions told a school videographer on the day he took his final Walk. "It's been going on since the 1920s."

"I greatly value the Walk, a tradition I came to know and embrace as a young Stanford fan while my dad coached here," said Jim Harbaugh, whose father, Jack, was a Cardinals assistant coach in the early 1980s. Jim was

Stanford's head coach from 2007–2010 before becoming head coach of the San Francisco 49ers in 2011.

In the 1950s, Stanford players would dress in the old Encina Gym and walk the Walk from there to Stanford Stadium. Nowadays, they pass by countless tailgate parties, thousands of fans, see everyone from the infamous *Stanford Band* to the comical Tree mascot. It's a way for players to meet fans, kiss Mom, and get their game faces on.

"I always have to find my mother," said Schwartzstein, who eventually found her. "Something's wrong if I don't hug my mom on the Walk."

This is especially the case on that final Walk, when Stanford seniors wear "My Last Walk" T-shirts with the date printed beneath. It's their last home game. The last time, said Schwartzstein, "We'll play in the stadium we love." And play before the throngs who love them in return. So the Cardinal starts out from the Arrillaga Family Sports Center, down Sam McDonald Road, past the Chuck Taylor Grove, and to the Gate 1 entrance at Stanford Stadium. The Stanford Band assembles behind the team for the Walk, and Stanford fans go nuts. It's as if every one of them, by their presence, in their full-throated fervor is saying, "Walk this way."

There's nothing pedestrian about the Walk, wherever it takes place.

Especially in *the Grove*, a ten-acre patch of land on the Ole Miss campus and the most beautiful, bucolic, and best spot for tailgating in the country. It's in Oxford, within easy walking distance of Rowan Oak, William Faulkner's home. It's also about a football field away from Vaught-Hemingway Stadium, home of the Rebels.

In the shade of oaks, elms and magnolias, pretty coeds in sundresses, frat boys in blazers, and long-time Grove regulars savor their football Saturdays.

Sports Illustrated once deemed Ole Miss the number 1 tailgating school in the nation. The *Sporting News* anointed the Grove as the Holy Grail of tailgating sites.

The signature cheer—"Hotty Toddy!"—is liable to break out at any time.

> "Are you ready?"
> "Hell Yes! Damn Right!
> Hotty Toddy, Gosh Almighty!
> Who the Hell are we? Hey!
> Flim Flam Bim Bam,
> Ole Miss by Damn!"

In the Grove, as everywhere on campus, the speed limit is 18 miles per hour. This is in honor of Archie Manning, who wore number 18 while becoming the greatest quarterback and most beloved football player in

Ole Miss history. That was well before becoming a hard-luck New Orleans Saint, and now as the patriarch of the First Family of the NFL: sons Peyton and Eli, each Super Bowl champs, and their once-upon-a-time homecoming queen mother, Olivia.

The Mannings all love the Grove, too. Especially before kickoff, when it's time to Walk. When the Ole Miss players march into the Grove and then beneath an arch that bears these words: *Walk of Champions*. Win or lose, champions.

(A traffic advisory: on Manning Way, the road around Vaught-Hemingway Stadium, the posted speed limit is 10 MPH, not 18 MPH, in honor of Eli's uniform number 10).

The Mother of All Walks, however, took place in 1989, in the *Loveliest Village on the Plain* at Auburn University, on that long-awaited day when Alabama finally deigned to come to Auburn.

The Auburn-Alabama rivalry, the most bitter and fierce in the college game, is unlike any other. It was interrupted early in the twentieth century over a dispute between the two schools. Thus the Tigers and Crimson Tide did not play from 1907–1948.

When the *Iron Bowl* rivalry was finally renewed, it was played at Legion Field, the allegedly neutral stadium in Birmingham. It almost always had an air of Alabama arrogance.

In 1958, once Paul "Bear" Bryant left Texas A&M and returned to his alma mater, the Tide ruled the rivalry. Bryant, the greatest coach in college football history, belittled Auburn, dismissing it as "that little cow college across the state." Bryant refused to play at Auburn, and never did. He died in 1982, barely a month after coaching his last game.

But during the 1980s, once Pat Dye became the Auburn coach and built an SEC power, he and school officials began pressuring the SEC office and politicians to force Alabama to play Auburn on a home-and-home basis.

That day finally arrived on Saturday, December 2, 1989. The day the Tide came to Auburn.

Ivan Maisel, an Alabama native and long-time ESPN senior writer, on-air commentator and college football historian, was there that epic day.

"Only once have I genuinely feared for my safety," Maisel later wrote. "That was at Tiger Walk in 1989."

Alabama was 10–0 and ranked second in the nation. Auburn, 8–2, was number 11.

Some 20,000 fans lined both sides of Donahue Drive as the Auburn players walked the Walk from their football dorm down the hill to the south end of Jordan-Hare Stadium.

Maisel later wrote:

The Auburn fans roared, their eyes glazed with a mixture of fervor, pride, passion and perhaps a touch of the Jack Daniels. We [he and another sportswriter] were five or six deep and couldn't get any closer to the street. We were also hemmed in, and didn't have the zeal-fueled adrenaline to ward off the elbows and other parts of the bouncing, heaving, deafening masses. I no longer had any interest in taking notes, which was just as well, because the noise and the lack of space made it impossible. My own adrenaline kicked in, and I worked my way into an open space.

Later, after Auburn upset the Tide 30–20 before a delirious, then-record crowd of 85,319 in Jordan-Hare, Dye would say, "I'm sure that [scene] must have resembled what went on the night the wall came down in Berlin. I mean, it was like they [Auburn fans] had been freed and let out of bondage, just having this game at Auburn."

"You'll never see that commotion again," David Housel said. "The Children of Israel entered the Promised Land for the first time only once."

Yes, beating undefeated, number 2 Alabama was so satisfying. "But the victory on the field, while important, paled beside the victory off the field," Maisel wrote.

"Because when Alabama arrived on campus, Auburn had arrived, too."

WALKS BY SCHOOL

University of Alabama (Football): *Walk of Champions*

The *Walk of Champions* begins approximately two hours and fifteen minutes prior to kickoff. The team is dropped off by the team buses on the north side of the stadium at University Boulevard and proceeds through the Walk of Champions (a brick plaza which features sixteen granite monuments set into the walkway commemorating the Crimson Tide's SEC and national championship teams throughout the years) into the stadium.

University of Arizona (Football): *Wildcat Walk*

The *Wildcat Walk*, first done in 2010, is one of Arizona's newest traditions. Before every home game, the team's buses take them from their hotel and drop them off several blocks north of the stadium. The fans and the marching band line Cherry Avenue as the team walks to the stadium.

University of California (Football): *March to Victory*

Began in 2002, spirit groups form a human tunnel to cheer for the team as they walk from the buses to the locker room.

University of Maryland (Football): *Terp Alley*

Testudo (their mascot), the spirit squad, and the marching band walk the football team down *Terp Alley* to Byrd Stadium approximately two and a half hours before kickoff on every home game Saturday.

University of Memphis (Football): *Tiger Walk*

The team offloads from the bus at Liberty Bowl Memorial Stadium and walks through all the fans that are tailgating at *Tiger Lane*. They walk through Tiger Lane and then head to the locker room prior to pregame warm-ups.

University of Minnesota (Football): *Gopher Victory Walk*

Two hours before kickoff of home games, the entire team (players and coaches) walk down Oak Street, meeting thousands of fans who line the street and sing "The Minnesota Rouser."

University of Nebraska (Football): *Tunnel Walk*

After leaving the locker room, Nebraska players and coaches begin walking a winding path lined with red carpet. The pathway is packed with fans that help cheer the players on before they take the field, exiting through the tunnel. The first *Tunnel Walk* was in 1994 and is set to the song "Sirius" by Alan Parsons Project. Although it is one of the more modern traditions, the Tunnel Walk has garnered a huge amount of fan support.

University of North Texas (Football): *Mean Green March*

The *Mean Green March* is a parade featuring the marching band, the dancers, the cheerleaders, Talons (a spirit group) and the Mean Green football team. The march starts at Traditions Hall and proceeds through Mean Green Village, culminating at the football locker room. The Mean Green March takes place two hours before kickoff as the team makes its way to the locker room for final pregame preparations.

Northwestern University (Football): *Walk With Us*

Beginning in 2006, the Walk takes place two and a half hours before kick-off at home games, and fans are encouraged to line the area now known as *Walker Way* and cheer on the 'Cats.

University of Notre Dame (Football): *Walk After Team Mass*

Prior to the start of the game, the team attends mass in suits-and-ties at the Sacred Heart Basilica. At the conclusion of mass, fans form a line from the chapel to the stadium, which the team walks through.

University of Tennessee (Football): *Vol Walk*

Tradition began in 1990. The walk down Yale Ave was renamed to Peyton Manning Pass in December of 1997, to honor Peyton's achievements. The walk allows fans to get close to the team as they walk from Gibbs Hall to the stadium, two hours prior to the game.

West Virginia University (Football): *Mountaineer Mantrip*

Starting in 2011, the team is escorted by their mascot, cheerleading squad, and the band. Following the team's arrival at the stadium, the squad walks down to the field, where they stop for a team gathering on the fifty-yard line before proceeding into the locker room. *The Mantrip* is named after the shuttle that typically transports miners down into an underground mine at the start of their shift. Miners take the Mantrip into work every day, so the football team uses their Mantrip as an analogy of going to work while honoring the coal industry and their state's reputation as the hardest-working state in the country.

21

YELLS, CHEERS, AND CHANTS . . . OH, MY!

They say "Rock Chalk!" You say "Rockar!"

They say "Rammer Jammer!" You say "Stockar!"

They are mighty Kansas—"Rock Chalk, Jayhawk, KU!"

And almighty Alabama—"Rammer Jammer Yellowhammer!"

Two of the BCS behemoths in big-time collegiate sports. And you?

You're tiny Bethany College in Lindsborg, Kansas, a comparative Little House on the Prairie athletically. An NAIA school but, like the Jayhawks and Crimson Tide, one that takes its sports seriously.

You're fans of the Swedes, as Bethany's teams are known. And your traditional yells, cheers, and chants are as cherished as KU's and 'Bama's. One in particular.

Anyone for some Swedish smack?

"ROCKAR! STOCKAR! THOR OCH HANS BOCKAR!

KOR IGENOM! KOR IGENOM! TJU! TJU! TJU! BETHANIA!"

Rockar! Stockar! That legendary cheer, yelled in Swedish and based on Swedish mythology, began at the turn of the twentieth century. Back in the Bennie Owen era at Bethany, when the *Terrible Swedes*, as they were then known, were feared and respected by all. In December 1902, a group of students, dissatisfied with the old school yells, used their Swedish mythology studies to create a new one. An instant classic, if you will.

Several members of the class of 1904 memorized the words and, before a crucial football game, performed the first public rendition of Rockar! Stockar! It was a figurative home run. A tradition like no other.

The words refer to the big man on campus—Thor, the Nordic god. A rough translation:

The jarl wore a jacket (*rockar*) and was on a log raft (*stockar*) braving the perils of the Baltic Sea. Thor was going forward with lightning speed, driving his irresistible thunderbolts through all opposition (*Thor och hans bockar*) and he sought to drive through the line (*kor igenom*). Then, (*tju*) is a Swedish interjection that is chanted three times in a row, followed by Bethany (*Bethania*).

And you thought Georgia's *How 'Bout Them Dawgs?* was cool. Actually, it is. Way, way cool. This too, all 92,000 of you between the hedges in Sanford Stadium whenever—or wherever—Georgia kicks off: Goooooooooooo DAWGS! Sic 'em! WOOF-woof-woof-woof-woof!!!

Swedish translation: WOOF-woof-woof-woof-woof!

As for Bennie Owen, he was the quarterback for Fielding Yost's undefeated Kansas team of 1899. He later coached Bethany from 1902–1904, when the Terrible Swedes were terrific: 22–2–1 in that span, including a Thanksgiving Day beat-down of Oklahoma. No dummies, the Sooners lured Bennie away from Bethany.

He coached Oklahoma for two decades, turning it into a powerhouse, before becoming the athletic director. He's the Owen in *Owen Field*, where the Sooners play, and a member of the College Football Hall of Fame.

Meanwhile, back in Bethany, the Swedes kept playing football to roars of *Rockar! Stockar!* Playing it quite well, especially under Ted Kessinger. He coached the Swedes from 1976–2003, went 219–57–1 in NAIA play and never had a losing season. In twenty-eight seasons, Kessinger won at least a share of the Kansas Collegiate Athletic Conference sixteen times and led his teams to thirteen NAIA playoff appearances.

Give that man a rousing *rockar!* A standing-O *stockar* too. Somewhere, Thor's smiling.

So's the Alabama fan base, whenever the Tide rushes into the end zone and another Rammer Jammer Yellowhammer chant begins. Normally used before and after games in Bryant-Denny Stadium, the cheer's set to the cadence of the Ole Miss ditty: *Hotty Toddy*. The cheer—which has never been shouted in Swedish—is a hybrid of *The Rammer Jammer*, a student newspaper back in the roaring twenties, and the yellowhammer, the state bird of Alabama.

Originally, the cheer was performed by the 'Bama crowd before football games. Hence, the lyric, "We're gonna beat the hell outta you!" The *you* being Florida or LSU or, ideally, Auburn. Nowadays, it's chanted towards the end of regulation, when victory's certain and all's well in Bear Bryant's hound's tooth hat world. Let the screaming commence, with one lyrical change: "Hey Auburn! Hey Auburn! Hey Auburn! We JUST BEAT the hell out of you! Rammer Jammer, Yellowhammer, gave 'em hell, Alabama!"

At Arizona basketball games, during the first four minutes of each half or until the first media timeout of each period, the band and student sections ratchets up some chants. Each dribble by an opposing player begets a *Boing!* Every pass, a *Pass!* Every shot, a hopeful *Brick!* You get the idea.

In 1960, Baylor's yell leaders introduced a new hand signal. The *Bear Claw* is made by slightly curving all five fingers inward to form—ta-da!—a claw. It's accompanied by a "Sic 'em, Bears!" yell. Give 'em yell, Baylor.

Initially, the reaction to the Bear Claw and Sic 'em shout was mixed, by students and faculty alike. It became, believe it or not, a topic of heated debate on campus. The Claw and Shout were employed sporadically until 1972, when Grant Teaff became Baylor's new football coach and embraced both shticks. They became sporting staples, symbolizing Baylor athletic pride.

The Bear Claw is held aloft during the singing of "That Good Old Baylor Line." Before Robert Griffin III (or RG3) won the 2011 Heisman Trophy,

Baylor fans making a "Bear Claw" with their hands. *Baylor University*

RG3, who now kneels as a Washington Redskin after scoring a touchdown and makes the sign of the cross, also makes the sign of the Bear Claw.

UC-Irvine's mascot? An anteater. Not an actual anteater. *Peter the Anteater*. A student in anteater's clothing.

There is no one Peter the Anteater. Several students don the mascot costume for games and performances throughout the school year. Salary: $10 an hour. Nice work if you can get it, and you can get it if you try out.

The coolest part? *Zot*. What? The "Zot, Zot, Zot" chant at athletic events, very popular among UCI students. The Zot is the sound made by the tongue of an anteater in the comic strip *B.C.* as it flicks out to catch an ant. Zot's all, folks.

Air ball! Air ball!—a cheer said to have originated at Duke. And lots of other student . . . stuff you hear and see during Duke basketball games in Cameron Indoor Stadium. Where the *Cameron Crazies* go . . . well, crazy.

At Cornell, the operative hockey word isn't "eh?" but "boring!" That's what Big Red fans taunt when the visiting team is introduced. They also shake newspapers, then crumple and throw them on the ice. Those Ivy guys and gals are also fond of shouting "Safety school!" during games. It's another way of belittling opponents' universities.

Whatever the sport may be at Furman University, Palladin' fans invoke what's known as an *implication cheer*. It's brilliant in its simplicity: *FU all the time*!

"How 'bout them Dawgs?" How'd that come about? Grammar, be damned. Georgia fans in the mid-to-late 1970s began invoking the phrase regularly, especially during the 1978 season when the Bulldogs and their opportunistic *Junkyard Dogs* defense pulled off several unlikely, come-from-behind victories. It wasn't a question so much as a declaration, especially during the Dawgs' unforeseen run to the 1980 national championship, courtesy of freshman Herschel Walker's speed and power, a dynamic defense, Buck Belue's miraculous "Lindsay Scott! Lindsay Scott!" last-minute touchdown pass versus Florida, and Notre Dame's collective oops when neglecting to field a kickoff in the Sugar Bowl. Maybe Georgia fans screamed "WOOF-woof-woof-woof-woof!" so loud in the Superdome that the Irish return men couldn't communicate. Whatever. Herschel scored twice and Georgia won 17–10.

And in sports sections across the country, in newspaper game stories and headlines and on TV and radio, "How 'bout them Dawgs?" became part of our lexicon.

Even the little guys yell their lungs out. Even little Goldey-Beacom College in Wilmington, Delaware. In the early days, before it became Goldey-

Beacom in 1951, Goldey College specialized in business, bookkeeping, and, yes, penmanship. Logically, it would follow that they actually composed and published this as the *official Goldey College yell* for all sporting events:

> Debit, credit, petty cash;
> Half length, double length, curve and dash;
> Coalescents, F-V hook,
> Journal, ledger, entry book!

Good luck making a last second one-and-one free throw when Lightning fans yell that.

No less a sportsman than Teddy Roosevelt proclaimed *"Rock Chalk, Jayhawk, KU!"* as the best cheer he'd ever heard. Our rough-riding twenty-sixth president (1901–1909) was not alone in that regard.

The legendary Kansas chant was created back in 1886 by some science club students at KU. The original words began, "Rah, Rah, Jayhawk . . . KU!" repeatedly. The first two times slowly, then increasing in speed. But the "Rah Rahs" were replaced with "Rock Chalk," a reference to the chalk rock—or limestone—found at nearby Mount Oread in Lawrence, Kansas, but also common around the state. It was later certified as the university's official rally call.

In recent years, Kansas fans began adding a "whoo!" between verses of the chant. This generated national attention, with a Facebook Page dedicated to protecting the hundred-year-old tradition.

One KU student commented that the "whoo!" spoils the creepiness that "Rock Chalk, Jayhawk, KU!" so richly deserves. But it's undeniably true that when Kansas fans rock the Phog—as Allen Field House is known for

University of Kansas' "Rock Chalk, Jayhawk, KU!" *Photo courtesy of Kansas Athletics*

legendary coach Forrest "Phog" Allen (1919–1956)—with Rock Chalk, there's no other place like it. One wonders what Dr. James Naismith, who invented the game of basketball at the YMCA in Springfield, Massachusetts, in 1891 and later coached at Kansas from 1898–1907, would've thought of all this?

What might the original Dr. J have posted on Facebook? We think—what else?—Rock Chalk! Or Tweeted about Naismith's original *13 Rules of Basketball* being sold at auction by Sotheby's on December 10, 2011? The day Kansas alum David Booth paid $4.34 million for basketball's version of the Ten Commandments, which will be housed in a new museum at KU.

Can we get a "Rock Chalk, Jayhawk, KU!" for David Booth, local Lawrence High and KU alum made good? Mr. Booth, you can get anything you want in town. This Rock Chalk's for you.

At Louisiana-Lafayette, Ragin' Cajun fans do the funky *Hot Boudin* chant.

You can, too:

> Hot Boudin
> Cold Cush Cush
> Come on Cajuns
> Push! Push! Push!

And then you can wash it down with another Abita.

More than twenty years after his death, they still chant: "This is Hank's House! This is Hank's House!"

At Loyola Marymount University basketball games in Los Angeles, the crowds—so much smaller now than when Hank Gaithers played and scored, soared, and rebounded—keep Hank Gaithers' memory alive. He was a 6-foot-7, ferocious rebounder and scorer who in 1989 became the second player in NCAA Division I history to lead the nation in both scoring and rebounding.

But Gaithers also suffered from an irregular heartbeat. On March 4, 1990, he collapsed and died of a heart attack during a game against Portland University.

Somehow, Loyola—led by Bo Kimble, Gathers' closest friend—reached the Elite Eight in the NCAA Tournament before losing to eventual national champion University of Nevada–Las Vegas. Bo even shot a late-game free throw left handed to honor his friend, Hank.

Nowadays, Loyola Marymount is no longer a basketball power. But at times at home games, you can still hear it: "This is Hank's house."

Wisconsin hockey fans invented the Sieve! chant for when opposing goalies allow goals. Michigan crowds took that a taunting step further:

You're not a goalie, you're a sieve!
You're not a sieve, you're a funnel!
You're not a funnel, you're a vacuum!
You're not a vacuum, you're a black hole!
You're not a black hole, you just suck!

At Minnesota, the operative phrase is *"Ski-U-Mah!"* It's pronounced SKY-YOU-MAH. But then, you knew that. In 1884, two Minnesota rugby players, John W. Adams and Win Sargent, tried to come up with a team yell. They took the word *ski*, a Sioux battle cry meaning victory, and combined it with *U-Mah*—representing the University of Minnesota. You know, U-Mah rhymes with "rah-rah." Voila! A team cheer was born. The phrase was incorporated into both official school songs: "Hail Minnesota" and, more commonly used, in "The Minnesota Rouser," the Gophers' rousing fight song.

You say *Starkville*, we say *Cowbells*.

The most, uh, resounding symbol of tradition at Mississippi State is the cowbell. For decades, opposing teams and school authorities have tried to ban Bulldogs' cowbells from the fields of play. Keep tryin', folks. Mississippi State is still proclaiming victory and celebrating proudly with Starkville's version of "The Carol of the Bells."

Mississippi State cowbells.

One of us—not named Stan—composed this "Ode to a Cowbell":

Cowbells clang, are you listening?
In the stands, fans are whistling.
A beautiful noise keeps opponents annoyed,
Cowbells clanging in the SEC.

As best one can tell, cowbells apparently arrived on the Mississippi State sports scene in the late 1930s and early 1940s. That clank coincided with the golden age of Bulldog football pre-World War II.

Popular legend has it that during a home game in Starkville against arch rival Ole Miss, a Jersey cow wandered onto the field. State trounced the Rebels that Saturday and Mississippi State students promptly adopted the cow as a good luck charm. For quite some time, MSU students kept bringing a cow to football games. Eventually, the practice was discontinued in favor of bringing just the bell, not the cow. Or so the story goes.

By the late 1950s, cowbells were common at Bulldogs games. By the 1960s, the cowbell was established as the special symbol of Mississippi State. The great irony: the cowbell's popularity flourished during the long, lean years when MSU football was nothing to clang about.

According to the university, flaunting this anachronism from back in the Aggie days was a prideful response by students and alumni to outsiders who scorned the school's Cow College history.

Enter Earl and Ralph. No, not a Jersey or Holstein. Earl W. Terrell and Ralph L. Reeves, two university professors in the 1960s who helped take cowbell clanging to the next level. They obliged some students by welding handles on the bells, so they could be rung with much more convenience, authority and gusto. One might call Earl and Ralph . . . handles messiahs.

By 1963, the demand for their long-handed cowbells couldn't be met by home workshops alone. So at Ralph's suggestion, the student association bought bells in bulk and the Industrial Education Club agreed to weld on the handles. The following year, the university bookstore began marketing these newly-improved cowbells. A portion of the profits went to the student organizations.

Now many styles of cowbells are available on campus and around Starkville, although with Mississippi State's recent football resurgence cowbells are becoming harder to find. The top-of-the-line bell is a heavy chrome-plated model with a full Bulldog figurine handle.

Yet true cowbell connoisseurs insist the best—and loudest—results are produced by a classic long-handled, bicycle grip bell made of thinner and tightly welded shells.

Cowbells decorate offices and homes of MSU alumni. Many are passed down through generations of Bulldog fans, like heirlooms or Faberge Eggs. Or not.

In 1974, however, the Southeastern Conference cracked down on the clanging. It adopted a rule against artificial noisemakers, making it illegal to ring a cowbell during games. Opponents couldn't hear a thing. Quarterbacks couldn't call a play. Despite creative efforts by Mississippi State students to circumvent the dastardly ruling and continue the time-honored tradition of cow-belling, the ban lasted until 2010.

At last, at the SEC meetings that spring, all twelve schools in the conference agreed to a compromise on artificial noisemakers. All twelve acknowledged the unique and traditional role cowbells have played in the annals of Mississippi State University. The conference bylaw was amended. And in the fall of 2010, on a one-year trial basis with specified restrictions, cowbells were welcomed back and allowed in Davis Wade Stadium for the first time in thirty-six years.

Thanks to MSU fans' adherence to the rules outlined by the conference, cowbells returned in 2011 and again in 2012, with similar restrictions still in place, of course. No matter. In Starkville, you can still hear the sound of cowbells. It's got a beautiful ring to it.

Penn State: *"We are. . . Penn State!"* Still.

And Texas: Texas' world renowned *Hook 'em Horns* sign, created by head cheerleader Harley Clark in 1955, was voted the nation's top hand signal by Sports *Illustrated*.

Talk to the hand. Major props to the hand. It's the greatest hand in the land.

So, in the wise words of Will Ferrell: "More cowbell!"

OTHER YELLS BY SCHOOL

Arizona State University (Basketball): *Pom-Poms into Megaphones*

When an Arizona State player makes a free throw, the cheerleaders throw their pom-poms over their head (without looking) into megaphones being held by other cheerleaders.

University of Arkansas (Various Sports): *The Calling of the Hog*

In the 1920s, Arkansas added *"Woo pig sooie"* (with fans waving their hands over their heads). Did you know there is a proper way to call a hog? Razorback students have been perfecting the hog call at sporting events for years. Raise your arms over your head and say "Woo" for eight seconds, swing them down with clenched fists for the "pig," and shoot the right arm up and yell "sooie!"

BYU (Basketball): *Opposing Player Fouls-Out*

As an opposing team's player walks to his bench after fouling out, the BYU fans chant, "Left, Right," and so forth, for every step that he takes until he sits down.

UCLA (Basketball): *Frisbee Cheer*

In 1978, a UCLA student nicknamed *Frisbee* borrowed a cheer from Pepperdine and started busting it out at Bruins basketball games with his friends. One student calls out questions and the crowd answers him: Is this a basketball? Is that the court? Is that the lllllooooosing team? Is that the winning team?

UCLA (Basketball): *The Eight Clap*

Students often learn this catchy, rhythmic cheer by watching a YouTube demo.

UCF (Basketball): *Stomp-Stomp, Clap-Clap, Woosh*

One of the University of Central Florida's most unique basketball traditions is its free throw chant: *Stomp-Stomp, Clap-Clap, Woosh*. Started by the *Kirk's Jerks* in the 1990s, UCF fans started holding their right arms with clenched fists almost straight up when a UCF player shoots a free throw. When the basket is made, the fans would stomp their right foot twice, clap their hands twice, make a shooting motion with their right hand while chanting "Woosh." In the more recent years, after the appropriately named "Stomp-Stomp, Clap-Clap, Woosh" chant, fans will chant "U-C-F" afterwards, making a U, a C, and an F over their heads. During the 2010–2011 season, a group of students attempted to start a new tradition: if a UCF player makes all of his free throws, the chant is followed by "ballin'."

University of Connecticut (Basketball): *Lamb Shake*

The *Lamb Shake*, not to be confused with the Harlem Shake, is a dance that was done by player Jeremy Lamb that the students subsequently adopted. A viral video shows Jeremy teaching the university president how to do it.

University of Florida (Various Sports): *Gator Chomp*

Mimicking the chomping of a gator's mouth, the *Gator Chomp* is performed by fans during Florida sporting events by fully extending one's arm over the other and moving them together and back apart. It is said to have first been started on October 10, 1981, when the fans at Ben Hill Griffin Stadium performed the gesture in-time with the Gator's marching band during its rendition of the theme from *Jaws*.

Florida State University (Various Sports):
War-Chant Arm Motion

In the early 1980s, FSU's band, the Marching Chiefs, began the now-famous arm motion while singing the *War Chant*. Who knew that a few years later, the gesture would be picked up by other teams' fans and named the tomahawk chop? It's a term FSU did not choose and officially does not use. Florida State's War Chant appears to have begun with a random occurrence that took place during a 1984 game against Auburn, but in the 1960s, the Marching Chiefs band would chant the melody of a popular FSU cheer. In a sense that chant was the long version of FSU's current War Chant. During this thrilling game with Auburn in 1984, the Marching Chiefs began to perform the dormant melody. Some students behind the band joined in and continued the War Chant portion after the band had ceased. Most agree the chant came from the fraternity section, but many spirited Seminole fans added the hand motion to symbolize the brandishing of a tomahawk. The chant continued among the student body during the 1985 season, and by the 1986 season, it was a stadium-wide phenomenon. Of course, the Marching Chiefs refined the chant, plus put their own special brand of accompaniment to the War Chant, for the sound we hear today. Atlanta Braves fans took up their version of the song and chant when former FSU star Deion Sanders came to the plate as an outfielder. The Kansas City Chiefs first heard it when the Northwest Missouri State band, directed by 1969 FSU graduate Al Sergel, performed the chant while the players were warming up for a game against San Diego.

University of Kansas (Football/Basketball): *Wave-the-Wheat*

Kansas fans *wave-the-wheat* after each scoring drive in football, waving their arms like wheat in a breeze. They also do this when an opposing player fouls-out of a basketball game.

University of New Hampshire (Ice Hockey): *Hey, John*

At UNH, during the hockey games (both men's and women's hockey games) when there is 1:00 left to play in the period, the crowd yells out, "Hey, John! How much time is left?" The reason they call out, "*Hey, John*"

University of Kansas' fans "Waving the Wheat."
Photo courtesy of Kansas Athletics

is because the crowd is quite aware that the public address announcer's name is John DeVoe (longtime voice of UNH hockey). In response to their call, John announces (at the 1:00 mark), "One minute left to play in the period, one minute." To which the crowd responds, "Thank You!" The funny thing is, John (due to NCAA regulations . . . or so we've been told) is unable to respond to the fans. However, on senior day/during senior games, whenever the crowd calls out, "Thank You!" John always sighs (pretending it's a huge to-do) and says "You're welcome" which elicits a massive ovation from the crowd!

University of North Texas (Various Sports): *Eagle Claw*

The eagle hand sign is their universal sign of pride and unity. To display their pride, they hold up their fist; make a *"V" for victory* using their pointer and middle fingers, and extend their thumb and curl their fingers slightly toward their palm.

Oakland University (Basketball): *Traveling Call*

Oakland fans, at every basketball game, on the first traveling call (against the visitor), their PA announcer says, "That's traveling," and the crowd responds, "And you can't do that!"

Occidental College: *Latin Cheer*

Several yells have been used at athletic events in Occidental's history, but the most popular one to continue to the present is *Io Triumphe*, introduced to Occidental in 1905 by Frank P. Beal, class of 1907, of Albion, Michigan, where the yell was used by Albion College. According to Albion College history, the words "Io Triumphe" were probably borrowed from the Latin poems of the Roman writer, Horace. Both Roman troops and citizens used the phrase to mean literally, "Hail, triumphal procession," or less formally, "Hurrah, O triumph." At Albion College it was believed that parts of the yell were inspired by Euripides' play, *Iphigenia in Tauris*. Through the years Io Triumphe has moved beyond being used solely at athletic events to formal occasions, particularly those initiated by the alumni. By itself, Io Triumphe is used as a salutation or cheer by alumni:

> IO TRIUMPHE!
> Io Triumphe! Io Triumphe!
> Haben, swaben, Rebecca le animor,
> Whoop-te, whoop-te, sheller-de-vere-de,
> Boom-de, ral-de, I-de, pa
> Honeka, heneka, wack-a, wack-a
> Hob, dob, bolde, bara, bolde, bara
> Con, slomade, hob-dab-rahi.
> O! C! RAH

Oregon State University (Football): *First Down*

When the team makes a first down, the PA announcer says, "It is an O-S-U," and then the crowd finishes by saying, "First down," and then moves their arms (much like a tomahawk chop) in the direction the team is going.

University of South Alabama (Various Sports): *U-S-A*

The University of South Alabama has a chant of U-S-A! U-S-A!

University of South Florida (Various Sports): *Go Bulls Hand Signal*

The bullhorns created from the fingers on their students' hands create a powerful symbol that silently screams: *Go Bulls!* The signal, which first started as good luck for basketball free-throw shooters is now a symbol used during all athletic events.

Southern Miss (Various Sports): *Southern Miss to the Top*

"Southern Miss to the Top!" is the university's motto, and is used to celebrate or recognize Southern Miss accomplishments, and as a response cheer at athletic events.

Stephen F. Austin State University (Various Sports): *Ax-'em-Jacks*

The Lumberjacks have a cheer of *"Ax 'em, Jacks!"*

Texas A&M (Football): *Midnight Yell Practice*

A&M students take their role as the *12th Man* very seriously—so much so that the night before home games, roughly 20,000 students gather at *Kyle Field* for a de facto pep rally.

Texas A&M (Various Sports): *Yell Leaders*

Texas A&M does not have cheerleaders, they have *yell leaders*. Yell leaders use hand signals to indicate which yell will come next. Students on the front row pick up the signal and pass it along (upward) until the *12th Man* knows what yell is next. Each year the student body elects five students to serve as the yell leaders. While cheerleaders are a tradition at most college football games, Texas A&M dares to not only step away from the crowd, but to do so with style. On the eve of games, A&M's yell leaders direct a rehearsal of traditional Aggie yells. The sessions often draw more than 20,000 fans for practice at Kyle Field or at a designated site for road games, such as the steps of the Texas State Capitol in Austin during road games that were held against the University of Texas. Some yells seem perplexing with phrases such as, "Hulabaloo Caneck Caneck!" and "Chig-gar-roo-gar-rem, Rough! Tough! Real Stuff! Texas A&M!"

Texas Tech (Various Sports): *Guns-Up*

The *Guns Up* sign is the widely recognized greeting of one Red Raider to another. It is also the sign of victory displayed by the crowd at every athletic event. The sign is made by extending the index finger outward while extending the thumb upward and tucking in the middle, little, and fourth fingers to form a gun. The sign can be traced back to L. Glenn Dippel, a 1961 alumnus of Texas Tech. He and his wife Roxie were living in Austin and faced the daily presence of the *Hook 'em Horns* hand sign used by University of Texas fans. So, the Dippels decided to retaliate. They looked to mascot Raider Red and his raised guns for their inspiration and in 1971 developed the Guns Up hand symbol. The *Saddle Tramps* and Texas Tech cheerleaders immediately adopted Guns Up and a new tradition was born.

University of Virginia (Various Sports): *Wah-Hoo-Wah Cheer*

The origin of the *Wah-Hoo-Wah cheer* is uncertain, but the cheer was used to root on Virginia teams as early as 1890 and may have been borrowed from Dartmouth College, whose athletics teams were once known as the Indians. Legend attributes the yell to Natalie Floyd Otey, who sang the ballad, "Wherever You Are, There Shall My Love Be," at Charlottesville's Levy Opera House in 1893. The predominantly student audience noticed that Otey warbled the first three words of the song between each of the stanzas and decided to join-in the refrain. By evening's end, goes the legend, the crowd had corrupted "Wherever You Are" to "Wah-Hoo-Wah."

22

MY COLLEGE DID *WHAT*, FIRST?

First things first:

It's good to start first. Better still to be in first. Best of all, to finish in first place. Isn't that the American way of thinking? Especially when it comes to sports?

To go from worst-to-first, does it get any better than that?

Actually, yes. To be the first to do something first.

We're talking milestone moments. We're talking extraordinary, transformational athletic accomplishments or innovations. Not just first in war, first in peace, but my college did *what* first?

That would be, for instance, the first wedgie. No, not *that* kind of wedgie, silly. Football's first wedgie. The *Straight Wedge*, which debuted on October 25, 1884, in Philadelphia. It was conceived and employed by Princeton versus Pennsylvania, and was also known as the *V-Trick*. No, not Dickie V. Not then, not now, not ever.

The ball carrier was in the middle of the V, which was formed by his ten teammates. There were no rules requiring a certain number of players on the line of scrimmage. So all players other than the center—the point, or apex, of the V—could line up any distance behind the line. With the V formed, the ball carrier would run inside the V.

A tradition was born. The first wedgie. It gained forty-five yards.

One popular method of defending the wedge? Hit the apex man in the jaw.

The first flying wedgie? That came in 1892, on the second-half kickoff of the Harvard-Yale game. Harvard unveiled the *Flying Wedge*, which legendary football coach Amos Alonzo Stagg later called "the most spectacular single formation ever opened as a surprise play."

"It was," Stagg said, "a great play when perfectly executed but, demanding the exact coordination of eleven men, extremely difficult to execute properly."

"A sort of gridiron kamikaze weapon forged of human bodies," historian John Sayle Watterson wrote of the human V aimed at one undersized target.

The Flying Wedge would injure many players. The Flying Wedge did *what?* It would also nearly kill or destroy football itself.

The Flying Wedge was used on the kickoff because the rules then called for a team to begin each half by kicking the ball to itself, as is still done in soccer. So Lorin Deland, a military tactician, chess aficionado, and Harvard supporter, divided the eleven players into two groups of five stationed at opposite sidelines. When Captain Bernie Trafford gave the signal, each group sprinted diagonally toward the center of the field. As the groups reached full speed, Trafford tapped—gently kicked—the ball to his running back, Charlie Brewer.

Quickly, one of the groups of five executed a quarter of a turn so that the wedge would be focused at Yale's weakest defenders. The play gained thirty yards before the pursuit stacked it up by grabbing the legs of both the blockers and the ball carriers.

"What a grand play!" the *New York Times* declared the next day. "A half ton of bone and muscle coming into collision with a man weighing 160 or 170 pounds."

There are other pioneers, other claimants to other firsts. Did Harvard unveil *the first scoreboard* on Thanksgiving Day, 1893, as it claimed? Or was it Penn, two years later in brand-new Franklin Field in Penn's season opening 40–0 shutout of Swarthmore? In neither game do the *New York Times'* accounts mention a scoreboard.

The *first televised college football game*: September 30, 1939, when Waynesburg College of Pittsburgh played then-mighty Fordham University at Triboro Stadium on Randall's Island in New York City. NBC televised the game on its experimental station W2XBS based in the Empire State Building. The broadcast range, approximately 50 miles, to a potential audience of some 100 TV sets. Even those few Waynesburg-area fans who had TV sets couldn't receive the telecast.

Many people in New York watched the game on TV monitors while visiting the RCA Pavilion at the World's Fair. NBC used one camera, stationed on the sideline. Renowned radio sportscaster Bill Stern called the play-by-play action.

The *first college touchdown ever scored on television*? Waynesburg's Bobby Brooks, who broke loose on a sixty-three-yard touchdown run. Alas, Fordham won, 34–7.

Army–Navy? They played football for the first time in 1890. Baylor? It lays claim (as do Missouri and others) to *starting the tradition of homecoming* in 1909, and as every college football fan knows, there's no place like homecoming on a college football fall Saturday.

Colgate? Its swim team made its first trip to Fort Lauderdale, Florida, in 1936 for spring break training at the Casino Pool. This begat the *College Spring Break*. Now that's a first-rate first. And remember, tan, don't burn, get a Coppertone tan.

The significance of August 3, 1852? Harvard (who else?) and Yale (ditto) engage in *America's first collegiate sporting event*: a two-mile crew race on Lake Winnipesaukee in Center Harbor, New Hampshire. Harvard wins.

November 13, 1875 was the first Harvard-Yale football game.

Christmas Day, 1907, LSU becomes the *first college football team to play in a foreign country*—Cuba. LSU shuts out the University of Havana, 56–0. There are no Honey Badgers in sight. *Feliz Navidad*, Bengal Tigers.

In 1936, Rollins College crew triumphs over Manhattan College on the Harlem River in New York City. This, with Sally Stearns as coxswain. She was the first-ever woman coxswain in a men's boat in the sport of rowing. The Rollins' men's varsity eight disguised Sally as a boy.

And then there's Radcliffe Crew. No, not Harvard Women's Crew. Radcliffe Crew. Clad in black and white and well-read all over. Not—repeat, not—clad in crimson.

From the GoHarvard.com athletics website:

"Why Are We Called Radcliffe Crew?

The question is common and understandable—if we apply to, take classes and graduate from Harvard, why are we called "Radcliffe Crew?" To best answer the question, it is important to understand the unique and deep history of Radcliffe and Harvard Colleges, and the beginning of Radcliffe Crew.

Radcliffe College, founded in 1879, was the female counterpart to the all-male Harvard College. A series of steps toward merging into one coed institution began in the 1960s, when Radcliffe students were first allowed to take classes at Harvard. This process was finally completed in 1999 with the transformation of Radcliffe from an undergraduate college to the Radcliffe Institute for Advanced Study, a graduate center for interdisciplinary scholarship; meaning that all current undergraduate students apply to, take classes at, and graduate from, Harvard.

Radcliffe Crew, the oldest women's rowing program in the Ivy League, was organized in the fall of 1971 by a group of enterprising Radcliffe athletes. The progress of the newly formed team was phenomenal, and in 1973 Radcliffe won the national championship and represented the United States in the Eastern European Championships in Moscow. In 1974, the Eastern Sprints League (EAWRC) was formed, and in 1974 and 1975 Radcliffe won consecutive sprints titles.

In 1976, two years after Harvard's Department of Athletics took over administration of Radcliffe athletics, the captains of the women's teams took a vote on whether they should remain Radcliffe in name and continue to compete in black and white or be called Harvard and compete in crimson. When the voting was done, only women's rowing had chosen to remain Radcliffe. The respect gained for women's athletics at Harvard by the early Radcliffe crews carried over to the 1976 vote and is maintained today by the Harvard women who race for Radcliffe in black and white. "Our team is proud of the determined women who began our program and proud of the women who continue to race and win, as we always have, under the name Radcliffe Crew."

"The rowers said no, that's how we started and we're going to hang onto that," said Radcliffe Varsity Heavyweight coach Liz O'Leary, who started her coaching career at Radcliffe—not Harvard—in 1986. In 2003, O'Leary won the Varsity Eight and NCAA team national titles.

"Black and white are our colors, not crimson," O'Leary said. "So yes, tradition is an important part of rowing here."

And thus they remain Radcliffe Crew. Totally Rad. First, still and always.

A chronological listing of college firsts follows.

COLLEGE FIRSTS BY SCHOOL

Harvard: Circa 1780: *Athletic competition among Harvard students begins* when a group of sophomores issue a challenge to members of the freshman class for a wrestling match. Afterward, the winners are treated to dinner by the vanquished.

On August 3, 1852, Harvard and Yale University meet in *America's first intercollegiate athletic event*: A Crew Race on Lake Winnipesaukee in

Center Harbor, New Hampshire, Harvard wins the two-mile contest and sets into motion a rivalry that thrives to this day. The Harvard and Yale heavyweight crews now hold an annual four mile contest on the Thames River in New London, Connecticut, the longest race of its kind in the country.

June 19, 1858, Harvard distinguishes itself from its competition as their crew team wore red Chinese silk bandanas during a regatta: It is believed to be the *first time a sports team features an identifying mark*.

Amherst College played Williams College in the *first intercollegiate baseball* game in 1859.

Princeton University and Rutgers were the *first two schools to play football* (in 1869).

Rutgers pioneered the *use of a school color* (school adopted one in 1869).

July 1874: *Track gets its intercollegiate start* at Harvard.

Statue, at Rutgers University, commemorating the "First College Football Game"—between Rutgers and Princeton. *Rutgers University*

June 4, 1875: Harvard plays Tufts University and Harvard is outfitted in *formal uniforms*, believed to be the first time a team has been so. The squad is adorned in the newly chosen school colors, with a uniform of white shirts and pants, with crimson trimming and crimson hose.

November 13, 1875: The *first Harvard versus Yale University football game* is played.

March 14, 1889: Harvard holds what is believed to be the *first spring football practice*.

Yale University is said to have had the *first live mascot*—Handsome Dan, a bulldog—in 1889.

Mansfield University played the *first night football game* on Sept 28, 1892.

Johnson C. Smith University played Livingstone College in the *first game between traditionally black colleges* (Dec 27, 1892).

November 30, 1893: Harvard versus the University of Pennsylvania; the *first football scoreboard* is used in the game.

Smith College is considered to be the *birthplace of women's college basketball*. They began in 1893, just two years after James Naismith invented the game.

The *football huddle* was invented at Gallaudet University in 1894, by the team's star quarterback, Paul Hubbard. Hubbard worried that other teams—deaf and hearing teams—were stealing his hand signals at the line of scrimmage. So he gathered his players in a huddle to keep his sign language private. Other teams liked the idea. Now, the huddle is as much a part of football as helmets and shoulder pads.

July 1895: A combined Harvard–Yale track team meets one from Oxford-Cambridge at the Queens Club in London. The meet, now held every two years, stands as the *world's oldest continuing international inter-collegiate competition*.

January 19, 1898: Harvard plays Brown University in ice hockey. The rivalry is the *oldest continuing hockey series* in the country.

Spring 1900: Harvard's Dwight Davis funds an international tennis competition that subsequently becomes known as the *Davis Cup*.

August 1901: *Field hockey is first introduced* to America at Radcliffe College.

Stetson University was the *first football team in Florida* (1901).

October 31, 1903: Glenn S. "Pop" Warner, coach of the famed Carlisle Indians, *introduces the hidden ball trick* in a game against Harvard.

April 1, 1905: Harvard plays in the *first intercollegiate soccer match* against Haverford College.

December 1905: U.S. President Theodore Roosevelt calls for a conference at the White House to discuss violence in football after 18 college
players are killed and 159 seriously injured during the season. As a
result of these meetings, the *Intercollegiate Athletic Association of the
United States (IAAUS)*—the forerunner of the NCAA—*is formed* with
sixty-two member institutions.

Fall, 1908: The *first cross-country collegiate championships* are held.

The University of Pittsburgh was the *first school to wear numbers on
football jerseys* (1908).

Around 1911, Indiana, University of Michigan, and Northern Illinois
University all held homecoming-like events prior to Baylor University,
the University of Illinois, and the University of Missouri—each of
which claims to have *invented homecoming*. Indiana, Michigan, and
Northern Illinois early-events were without the traditional football
game, bonfires, parades, and other hallmarks.

April 9, 1912: Harvard plays in the *first baseball game held at Fenway
Park*. The Crimson took-on the Boston Red Sox in an exhibition contest.

Duquesne University was the *first college to use home and away jerseys*.

West Virginia University, in 1921, was a participant in the *first game
broadcast on radio*.

Duquesne University and their coach Elmer Layden (one of the Four
Horsemen), devised the *hand signals used by officials to explain pen-
alties*.

March 3, 1923: Harvard changed ice hockey forever with their *innovation of substituting entire forward lines* instead of individuals (in a
game versus Yale University).

Winter 1923: Radcliffe College meets Sargent College in the *first wom-
en's intercollegiate swim meet*.

University of Hawaii, in 1923, made their *first trip to the mainland for a
game* (by ocean liner).

The *first baseball catcher's mask* is used when inventor Fred Thayer of
Harvard takes the concept of a fencing mask and adapts it. Harvard's
starting catcher made only two errors in his first game with the mask,
an exceptionally low number for even a professional in that era.

Northwestern University *started Dad's Day* in 1923: One of the longest-
running annual named days, Dad's Day was eventually phased out to
make way for the more politically correct *Family Weekend*.

University of North Carolina, and Washburn University, are each credited (in 1928) with the *first forward pass in a game*.

Northwestern University's 1928 team sported a peculiar purple set of
stripes on each sleeve: a narrow stripe, over a wide stripe, over a narrow stripe. While NU wasn't the first athletic team to wear the pattern
(some basketball teams had worn it), the 'Cats were possibly the first
football team to use it. The look was the *first modern uniform* in football history.

University of Nebraska-Omaha was the *first football team to travel by
plane to a game* (in the 1930s).

Hope College claims perhaps the *first domed stadium* was their Holland's Riverview Park where the Flying Dutchmen played their football games from 1932 through 1978. Fans on the home side of the field
were protected by a covered grandstand that had been moved to the
site from the Holland fair grounds.

University of Maryland versus University of Pennsylvania was *one of the
first games televised* on Oct 5, 1940; televised to 200 homes by WPTZ
in Philadelphia. Fordham University versus University of Pennsylvania
and NYU versus Georgetown University were also broadcast on TV in
1940.

Youngstown State University's first football coach is credited with *starting the use of penalty flags* by officials in 1941. His wife sewed the flags
and was known as the Betsy Ross of football.

October 11, 1947: Chester "Chet" Pierce, a standout tackle for the Harvard football team, becomes the *first African American to play against
a white college in the South* when the Crimson meets the University of
Virginia in Charlottesville.

The University of Minnesota is said to have *invented cheerleading*.

Princeton University *started the concept of downs in football*.

Princeton University *began the idea of fixing players into a line and
backfield*.

The 1952 Rose Bowl was the *first nationally televised college football
game*.

Seton Hall University's Bob Davies is credited with *inventing the behind-
the-back dribble*.

The September 18, 1965, Texas Tech game against the University of
Kansas—a 26-7 Tech win—was the *first intercollegiate football contest to use instant video replay* (Ampex). Robert "Daddy Warbucks"
Walker, a Texas Tech grad, pioneered the equipment used by coach JT
King to review plays immediately. However, the new twist was eliminated by the NCAA in 1967 because the technology was too costly for
some schools.

The University of Houston played the *first collegiate game on artificial turf* (Sept 23, 1966) vs. Washington State University.

West Virginia University's Georgeann Wells was the *first woman to dunk in a college game* (in 1984).

Fans at many schools *wave towels* (of their school colors) in support of their teams. Western Kentucky University claims to have begun this tradition in honor of one of their legendary coaches that clutched a Red Towel for 1,062 games.

BIBLIOGRAPHY

Bartosek, Nancy. "Hhwaaaaaaaaaah!" *TCU Magazine*, http://www.magazine.tcu
.edu/Magazine/Article.aspx?ArticleId=386 (5 May, 2013).

Belmont Student Affairs, "100-Year-Old Pembroke Hall Built on Strong Traditions," *Belmont University / Student FYI*, http://blogs.belmont.edu/
studentfyi/2012/10/26/100-year-old-pembroke-hall-built-on-strong-traditions/ (5
May, 2013).

"The Best Post-Game Tradition in America," *SI Vault*, 31 August 1992, http://sports
illustrated.cnn.com/vault/cover/featured/9344/index.htm (5 May 2013).

"Best Traditions," *SI Vault*, 22 Aug 2011, http://sportsillustrated.cnn.com/vault/
article/magazine/MAG1189369/ (2 May 2013).

Brettman, Allan. "Nike Special-Edition Shoes Will Cheer University of Oregon's
'Pit Crew'," The *Oregonian*, 12 Oct 2011, http://www.oregonlive.com/business/
index.ssf/2011/10/nike_special-edition_shoes_wil.html (4 May 2013).

Caple, Jim. "Road Warrior: Best College Tailgating," *ESPN.com*, http://espn.
go.com/espn/thelife/news/story?id=3037293 (5 May 2013).

Casagrande, Michael. "Larranaga Doesn't Sleep After 'Canes Crushed Duke',"
Sun Sentinel, 24 Jan 2013, http://articles.sun-sentinel.com/2013-01-24/sports/
fl-miami-duke-aftermath-0125-20130124_1_coach-jim-larranaga-durand-scott
-duke (2 May 2013).

———. "Pulling out the Stops," *SI Vault*, 02 Sep 1996, http://sportsillustrated.cnn
.com/vault/article/magazine/MAG1008655/index.htm (3 May 2013).

Conroy, Pat. *The Lords of Discipline*, (New York: Random House Publishing
Group, 2002), 547.

Copeland, Todd. *The Immortal Ten: The Definitive Account of the 1927 Tragedy
and Its Legacy at Baylor University* (Waco, Tex.: Baylor University Press, 2001).

Davis, Seth. "Utah State Receives Much-Deserved Notoriety from Legend of 'Wild Bill,'" *SI.com*, 2011, http://sportsillustrated.cnn.com/2011/writers/seth_davis/02/10/utah.state/index.html (5 May 2013).

Dodd, Dennis. "Night in Death Valley Summons Noise, Humidity, Even Ghosts," *CBSSports.com*, 2009, http://www.cbssports.com/collegefootball/story/12331973 (5 May 2013).

Dooley, Vince. *Dooley: My 40 Years at Georgia* (Chicago: Triumph Books, 2005).

Drehs, Wayne. "The View from Above, Game Day at West Point," *ESPN.com*, http://espn.go.com/page2/s/drehs/030925army.html (5 May, 2013).

"Duke Mascot's Head Found on Top of UNC Bookstore," *Winston-Salem Journal*, 13 Feb 2013, http://www.journalnow.com/sports/colleges/basketball/article_e2124604-765c-11e2-853f-0019bb30f31a.html (2 May 2013).

Dwyer, Olivia. "M. Lacrosse Follows 'Hard Hat' Tradition," *The Cornell Daily Sun*, 20 Apr 2007.

Editorial Board, "A&M-Kingsville Is Right to Ban Tortilla Tossing," *Caller.com*, 2010, http://www.caller.com/news/2010/sep/02/am-kingsville-is-right-to-ban-tortilla-tossing/ (5 May 2013). "ESPN Host Tabs Silent Night as Best College Hoops Tradition," *Taylor University*, 11 Dec 2011, http://athletics.taylor.edu/news/2011/12/11/MBK_silent-night-national.aspx (5 May 2013).

Enderson, James. *Peregrine Falcon: Stories of the Blue Meanie,* (Austin, Tex.: University of Texas Press, 2005), 224-226.

"Every Jersey Tells Another Cancer Story," *The Chautauqua Star*, 26 Jan 2012, http://www.starnewsdaily.com/viewby/tag/story/Every-jersey-tells-another-cancer-story-2012-01-26 (4 May 2013).

Falla, Jack. "NCAA: The Voice of College Sports," *National Collegiate Athletic Association*, 1981, http://books.google.com/books/about/NCAA_the_voice_of_college_sports.html?id=sQ2CAAAAMAAJ (3 May 2013).

Finkel, Michael. "The Mother of All Tugs-of-War Is Held Each Fall at Hope College in Michigan," *SI Vault*, 2 Sep 1996, http://sportsillustrated.cnn.com/vault/article/magazine/MAG1008655/index.htm (5 May 2013).

Finley, Patrick. "UA Softball: Best Tradition on UA campus Is Found at Hillenbrand Stadium," *Arizona Daily Star*, 01 Mar 2012, http://azstarnet.com/sports/softball/college/wildcats/ua-softball-best-tradition-on-ua-campus-is-found-at/article_cf8c3c6c-14a2-58d3-8db8-533ff16b71a8.html (4 May 2013).

Fitzgerald, Tom. "Cancer Takes Jill Costello, Cal Coxswain," *SFGate.com*, 2010, http://www.sfgate.com/collegesports/article/Cancer-takes-Jill-Costello-Cal-coxswain-3183997.php (5 May 13).

"Floyd of Rosedale," *MyGopherSports.com*, https://www.mygophersports.com/online/default.asp?doWork::WScontent::loadArticle=Load&BOparam::WScontent::loadArticle::article_id=BCE6C6B7-3BC2-4B63-AF8C-27A392719139 (5 May, 2013).

Fowler, Chris. "Game Day Goes Off the Beaten Path to Find the Biggest Little Rivalry," *ESPN.com*, 8 Nov 2007, http://sports.espn.go.com/ncf/columns/story?columnist=fowler_chris&id=3099894 (5 May 2013).

Franks, Ray. "What's in a Nickname? Exploring the Jungle of College Athletic Mascots," *R. Franks Publishing Ranch*, 1982, http://books.google.com/books/about/What_s_in_a_Nickname.html?id=G4gYAAAAIAAJ (5 May 2013).

Glier, Ray. *How the SEC Became Goliath: The Making of College Football's Most Dominant Conference* (New York: Howard Books, 2012).

Gluskin, Michael. "Cutting Down the Nets Part of Winning Fabric," *USA Today*, 23 March 2005, http://usatoday30.usatoday.com/sports/college/mensbasketball/tourney05/2005-03-23-trimming-nets_x.htm (5 May 2013).

Gregorian, Vahe. "Beware of the Phog," *St. Louis Post-Dispatch*, 24 February 2012, http://www.stltoday.com/sports/college/mizzou/beware-of-the-phog/article_2659347e-23d3-5413-9dd6-0b83b4522bcc.html (5 May 2013).

Guadagnoli, Tony. "Toasting One of Football's Oldest Friends: Penn," *The Seattle Times*, 20 Oct 2011, http://seattletimes.com/html/take2/2016552501_taketwo20.html (5 May 2013).

Heistand, Michael. "'Game Day' Flag Relay Is Worth a Salute," *USA Today*, 10 Oct 2008.

Hemphill, Paul. *A Tiger Walk Through History: The Complete Story of Auburn Football from 1892 to the Tuberville Era* (Tuscaloosa, Ala.: University of Alabama Press, 2008).

"Hope College Celebrates Its Students as Part of NCAA Division III Initiative," *Hope College Athletics*, 2013, http://www.hope.edu/athletics/d3identity1011.html (5 May 2013).

Hyland, Tim. "Howard's Rock at Clemson University: How a Rock Became the Enduring Symbol of Clemson Football," *About.com College Football*, http://collegefootball.about.com/od/traditions/a/Tradition-Clem.htm (4 May 2013).

Hyland, Tim. "Texas vs. Oklahoma: The Red River Rivalry," *About.com College Football*, http://collegefootball.about.com/od/rivalries/a/rivalry-red.htm (5 May, 2015).

"Instant Classic! Syracuse Defeats UConn 127-117 in 6 OTs," *SUathletic.com*, http://www.suathletics.com/BE/summer09/pdf/page-10.swf (5 May, 2013).

Jenkins, Sally. "Tickled Pink by Iowa's Locker Room," *Washington Post*, 1 Oct 2005.

Johnson, Jeremiah. "Another Buzzer-Beater! Roosevelt Jones Leads Butler to 64-63 Victory Over Gonzaga," *Fox59.com*, http://fox59.com/2013/01/19/butler-beats-gonzaga-64-63-on-buzzer-beater/#axzz2SRVQQo4G (19 Jan 2013).

Jones, Beren. "There Will Be Mud," *Mansfield Storrs Patch*, 2013, http://mansfield.patch.com/groups/schools/p/there-will-be-mud-annual-oozeball-tournament-at-uconn (5 May 2013).

Judd, Ashley. "Essay on UK Basketball," *AshleyJudd.com*, 2004, http://ashleyjudd.com/writings/essay-on-uk-basketball/ (4 May 2013).

Keith, Braden. "TSC Traditions: Harvard's Iron Man Meet," *Swim Swam*, 22 Dec 2010, http://swimswam.com/tsc-traditions-harvards-iron-man-meet/ (4 May 2013).

Kentsches,Tom. *Cracked Sidewalks and French Pastry: The Wit and Wisdom of Al McGuire*, (Madison, Wis.: University of Wisconsin Press, 1 Nov 2002), 107.

King, Jason. "King's Court: Home Sweet Home," *ESPN.com*, http://espn.go.com/ mens-college-basketball/story/_/id/8848242/nation-best-homecourt-advantages -college-basketball (16 Jan 2013).

Layden, Tim. "The Forgotten Hero," *SI Vault*, 2011, http://sportsillustrated.cnn .com/vault/article/magazine/MAG1191803/ (5 May 2013).

"Little 500," *Working Bikes Cooperative*, Mar 2012, http://workingbikescoop .blogspot.com/2012/03/little-500.html (2 May 2013).

Lovinger, Jay. *The Gospel According to ESPN: The Saints, Saviors, & Sinners of Sports* (New York: Hyperion, 2002), 212.

Maisel, Ivan. "The Best Walk in America," *ESPN.com*, 1989, http://espn.go.com/ page2/s/maisel/031120auburn.html (5 May 2013).

Manuel, John. "Amateur Executive/Coach," *Baseball America*, http://www.baseball america.com/today/features/bertman0125.html (5 May, 2013).

"The Most Exciting 25 Seconds in College Football," *SI Vault*, 22 Aug 2011, http:// sportsillustrated.cnn.com/vault/article/magazine/MAG1189369/2/ (5 May 2013).

"Navy Tops Army for 11th Consecutive Win in Series," *USA Today*, 8 Dec 2012, http://www.usatoday.com/story/sports/ncaaf/2012/12/08/navy-tops-army-17-13 -11th-straight-win-in-series/1756049/ (5 May 2013).

Neff, Craig. "No. 1 Mascot Uga V," *SI Vault*, 1997, http://www.ebay.com/itm/ Sports-Illustrated-1997-Georgias-No-1-Mascot-UGA-V-1-/160310626644 (5 May 2013).

Nissenson, Herschel "Tales from College Football's Sidelines," *Sports Publishing LLC*, 2001, http://books.google.com/books?id=skFXK5hFvhkC&pg=PA107&lpg =PA107&dq=What+kinda+sport+is+that,+where+you+sit+on+yo%E2%80% 99+ass+and+go+backwards?!%E2%80%9D&source=bl&ots=m-E51gj6PP&sig= CSzvhJ1k9Nx8_KoAWZD6PPE6p0g&hl=en&sa=X&ei=xjSFUYCLJoXw8QSQ8 oGADQ&ved=0CDMQ6AEwAA#v=onepage&q=What%20kinda%20sport%20 is%20that%2C%20where%20you%20sit%20on%20yo%E2%80%99%20ass%20 and%20go%20backwards%3F!%E2%80%9D&f=false (3 May 2013).

"NYU Women Play Their Own 'Subway Series'," *D3Hoops*, http://www.d3hoops.com/ seasons/women/2011-12/contrib/2011112352e0ma (2 May 2013).

O'Toole, Thomas. "Zombie Nation Takes Over at Crunch Time in College Are-nas," *USA Today*, 20 Feb 2009, http://usatoday30.usatoday.com/sports/college/ mensbasketball/2009-02-19-zombie-nation-arena-music_N.htm (4 May 2013).

Page 2 Staff, "Worst College Football Teams of All Time," *ESPN.com*, http://espn .go.com/page2/s/list/colfootball/teams/worst.html (5 May, 2013).

Reilly, Jerry. "Every Jersey Tells Another Cancer Story," *SUNY Fredonia State*, 2012, http://www.fredoniabluedevils.com/news/2012/1/25/MHOCKEY_0125123137. aspx (5 May 2013).

Reilly, Rick. "Extra Credit," *SI.com*, 5 March 2003, http://sportsillustrated.cnn .com/inside_game/rick_reilly/news/2003/03/04/life_of_reilly0310/ (5 May 2013).

Rhea, Timothy. "The Sudler Trophy," *The John Philip Sousa Foundation*, http:// www.sousafoundation.net/Default.aspx?ID=39 (4 May 2013).

Rice, Grantland. "The Four Horsemen," New *York Herald Tribune*, 18 Oct 1924, http://archives.nd.edu/research/texts/rice.htm (4 May 2013).

Roberson, Doug. "GSU Rallies to Beat William and Mary," *Atlanta Journal Constitution*, 17 Jan 2013, http://www.ajc.com/news/sports/college/gsu-rallies-beat-william-and-mary/nTynn/ (3 May 2013).

Rovell, Darren. "Lefty's Midnight Run Started All the Madness," *ESPN.com*, 2000, http://static.espn.go.com/ncb/s/2000/1011/812806.html (5 May 2013).

Schlabach, Mark. "Gift from Death Valley Became 'Death Valley' Tradition," *ESPN. com*, 2007, http://sports.espn.go.com/ncf/columns/story?columnist=schlabach_mark&id=3017840 (5 May 2013).

Seiler, Sonny, and Kent Hannon, *Damn Good Dogs: The Real Story of Uga, the University of Georgia's Bulldog Mascots* (Athens, Ga.: University of Georgia Press, 2011), 108.

Severson, Kim, and Robbie Brown, "Clemson Fans Hold Fast to a Tradition Worth More Than the Paper It's Printed On," *New York Times*, 3 January 2012, http://www.nytimes.com/2012/01/04/sports/ncaafootball/clemson-fans-hold-fast-to-a-tradition-worth-more-than-the-paper-its-printed-on.html?_r=0 (5 May 2013).

Sidel, Robin. "PNC Learns Banking Southern Style," *The Wall Street Journal*, 2 Jan 2013, C1.

Slyter, Chad. "Valley City State and Jamestown Meet for the 100th Time," *Victory Sports Network*, http://staging.victorysportsnetwork.com/Clip/news/page992.htm (5 May, 2013).

Smebak, Leslie. "First Points Scored in Bremner Cup," *The Cornelian*, 9 Oct 2012.

"Spirit of Aggieland," *Aggie Athletics, Texas A&M University Traditions*, http://www.aggieathletics.com/ViewArticle.dbml?DB_OEM_ID=27300&ATCLID=205414581 (2 May 2013).

"Springfield College Set to Host 101st Gymnastics Exhibition Home Show," Springfield *College Pride Athletics*, 13 Oct 2010, http://www3.spfldcol.edu/homepage/athletics.nsf/0/6F8EF20FF69E8B83852577BB00682710 (4 May 2013).

Staff Writer, "Slug Gymnasts Make Their Debut," *University of California Santa Cruz Newscenter*, 7 Nov 2007, http://news.ucsc.edu/2007/11/1724.html (2 May 2013).

Steinberg, Dan. "Coach K Says Maryland Will be 'Outsiders' in the Big Ten," *Washington Post, DC Sports Blog*, http://www.washingtonpost.com/blogs/dc-sports-bog/wp/2013/01/15/coach-k-says-maryland-will-be-outsiders-in-the-big-ten/ (2 May 2013).

Stewart, Bruce. "American Football," *American History*, Nov 1995, http://wesclark.com/rrr/yank_fb.html (5 May 2013).

Stewart, Pearl. "Jackson, Mississippi.to Lose Capital City Classic in 2012," *Diverse*, 13 Jul 2012.

Thamel, Pete. "Have You Seen Me Lately (on the sideline)? Part III", New *York Times, The Quad*, 2007, http://thequad.blogs.nytimes.com/2007/09/01/have-you-seen-me-lately-on-the-sideline-part-iii/ (2 May 2013).

Thompson, Wright. "10 Reasons Why LSU's Home Field Is the Best in All of Sports," *ESPN.com*, 2008, http://sports.espn.go.com/espnmag/story?id=3693406 (5 May 2013).

"Throwing out the Fish," *University of New Hampshire Athletics*, http://www.unh wildcats.com/fanZone/Traditions (2 May 2013).

"Tiger Stadium," *Football.Ballparks.com*, http://football.ballparks.com/NCAA/ SEC/LSU/ (5 May, 2013).

"Top 100 Things You Gotta Do before You Graduate," *SI Vault*, 2003, http://sports illustrated.cnn.com/2003/sioncampus/09/24/100_things0930/ (5 May 2013).

"Traditions: The Sod Cemetery," *Official Athletic Site of Florida State University*, http://www.seminoles.com/trads/fsu-trads-cemetery.html (2 May 2013).

Twain, Mark. *The Adventures of Tom Sawyer*, (New York: P.F. Collier & Son Company, 1920) 45.

"The University of Kansas Wins Naismith Student Section of the Year Award," *PR Newswire, The Collegiate Licensing Company*, 14 Mar 2012, http://www .prnewswire.com/news-releases-test/the-university-of-kansas-wins-naismith -student-section-of-the-year-award-142620486.html (4 May 2013).

Veatch, Diana. "Putting College Traditions to Good Use by Supporting Cancer Research," *Today@Colorado State*, 17 Nov 2010, http://www.today.colostate.edu/ story.aspx?id=4916 (2 May 2013).

Walters, John. "Best Intramural Use of Dirt," *SI Vault*, 28 Apr 1997, http://sports illustrated.cnn.com/vault/article/magazine/MAG1009978/2/index.htm (5 May 2013).

———. "The Biggest Little Game in the Nation," *SI Vault*, 26 Aug 1991, http:// sportsillustrated.cnn.com/vault/article/magazine/MAG1140752/index.htm (5 May 2013).

Watterson, John Sayle. *College Football: History, Spectacle, Controversy*, (Baltimore: Johns Hopkins University Press, 2000), 13.

Weber, Jim. "Super Fans in All Shapes and Sizes," *ESPN.com*, 16 Aug 2010, http:// sports.espn.go.com/ncf/preview10/news/story?id=5461666 (4 May 2013).

Weinberg, Rick. "The Moment," *ESPN, the ESPY Awards*, 04 Mar 1993, http:// sports.espn.go.com/espn/espn25/story?page=moments/50 (4 May 2013).

"Why Are We Called Radcliffe Crew?" *Harvard University*, 2010, http://www .gocrimson.com/sports/wcrew-lw/tradition/whyradcliffe (4 May 2013).

Wilkinson, Jack "100th Meeting Ends in Midshipmen Victory," *Atlanta Journal-Constitution*, 5 December 1999, E-6.

———. "Feet First . . . The Ron Hunter Story," *GSU Magazine*, Jul 2011, http://www.georgiastatesports.com/ViewArticle.dbml?DB_OEM_ID= 12700&ATCLID=205157218 (4 May 2013).

———. "Picking up Butch (and vice-versa)," *Atlanta Journal-Constitution*, 8 February 2004, D-1.

———. "The Big Five Shrine," *Atlanta Journal-Constitution*, 24 February 2002, E1, E18.

———. "Unchanging Wooden," *Atlanta Journal-Constitution*, 20 January 2002, D1, D6-7.

———. *The Georgia Tech Football Vault: The History of the Yellow Jackets* (Atlanta: Whitman Publishing, 2008).

Wojciechowski, Gene. "Last Call," *ESPN the Magazine*, 29 Jan 2001, http://espn.go.com/magazine/geno_20010129.html (3 May 2013).

Woodley, Kayci. "A Tone of Tradition," *National Collegiate Athletic Association*, http://www.ncaa.org/wps/wcm/connect/public/ncaa/champion+features/a+tone+of+tradition#sthash.IVnXeOTz.dpbs (2 May 2013).

Woods, Tim. "Immortalizing 'The Immortal Ten' at Baylor," *Waco Tribune-Herald*, 11 Feb 2007, http://www.chron.com/news/houston-texas/article/Immortalizing-The-Immortal-Ten-at-Baylor-1546555.php (4 May 2013).

Yang, and Samira Puskar, "'Dead Fred,' a.k.a. ex-Justice Fred Vinson, Resurrected for Debate," *First Read on NBCNews.com*, http://firstread.nbcnews.com/_news/2012/10/11/14370671-dead-fred-aka-ex-justice-fred-vinson-resurrected-for-debate?chromedomain=dailynightly&lite, (5 May, 2013).

INDEX

ABOUT THE AUTHORS

Stan Beck has built a unique reputation as the preeminent expert on college sports traditions, and has been interviewed on the subject by numerous publications and radio broadcasts, including ESPN Radio.

Jack Wilkinson is the author or coauthor of eight books, the most recent of which include *Of Mikes and Men: A Lifetime of Braves Baseball* (2010) and *100 Things Braves Fans Should Know and Do Before They Die* (2011). A three-time Georgia Sportswriter of the Year, Wilkinson has written for such publications as *Newsday*, the *Miami News*, the *Chicago Daily News*, the *New York Daily News*, the *Atlanta Journal-Constitution* and the *Associated Press*.